Philosophic Thoughts

AMERICAN UNIVERSITY STUDIES

SERIES V
PHILOSOPHY

Vol. 214

PETER LANG
New York · Washington, D.C./Baltimore · Bern
Frankfurt am Main · Berlin · Brussels · Vienna · Oxford

GARY JAMES JASON

Philosophic Thoughts

Essays on Logic and Philosophy

PETER LANG
New York · Washington, D.C./Baltimore · Bern
Frankfurt am Main · Berlin · Brussels · Vienna · Oxford

Library of Congress Cataloging-in-Publication Data

Jason, Gary James.
[Works. Selections]
Philosophic thoughts: essays on logic and philosophy / Gary James Jason.
pages cm. — (American University studies. V, Philosophy; v. 214)
Includes bibliographical references and index.
1. Philosophy, American. I. Title.
B945.J371 191—dc23 2013032447
ISBN 978-1-4331-2382-5 (hardcover)
ISBN 978-1-4539-1222-5 (e-book)
ISSN 0739-6392

Bibliographic information published by **Die Deutsche Nationalbibliothek**.
Die Deutsche Nationalbibliothek lists this publication in the "Deutsche Nationalbibliografie"; detailed bibliographic data is available on the Internet at http://dnb.d-nb.de/.

I wish to thank Mr. Scott Partridge for allowing the use of his artwork for the cover of this book.

The paper in this book meets the guidelines for permanence and durability of the Committee on Production Guidelines for Book Longevity of the Council of Library Resources.

29 Broadway, 18th floor, New York, NY 10006
www.peterlang.com

Printed in Germany

For my brother, John—fine father, audacious aviator

Contents

Introduction ix

PART I Essays on Logic, Argumentation Theory, and Computer Science 1

1. "Notes towards a Formal Conversation Theory" 3
2. "Is there a Case for *Ad Hominem* Arguments?" 23
3. "Are Fallacies Common? A Look at Two Debates" 29
4. My review of: *Logical Dialogue-Games and Fallacies* 47
5. "The Nature of the Argumentum *Ad Baculum*" 51
6. My review of: *Logic: A Computer Approach* 61
7. "Erotetic Logic as a Specification Language for Database Queries" 65
8. "Dialog as an Abstract Data Type" 93
9. My review of: *Expert Systems: Artificial Intelligence in Business* 101
10. "Hedging as a Fallacy of Language" 103
11. "Fallacies are Common" 115
12. My review of *Logics for Artificial Intelligence* 125
13. "Does Virtue Epistemology Provide a Better Account of the *Ad Hominem* Argument? A Reply to Christopher Johnson" 129

PART II	Epistemology, Philosophy of Science, and Philosophy of Psychology/Cognitive Science	153
14.	"The Concept of a Discovery"	155
15.	My review of: *The Foundations of Psychoanalysis*	165
16.	"Science and Common Sense"	171
17.	"Two Problems of Induction"	177
18.	"Epistemologies and Apologies"	201
19.	My review of: *The Myth of Neurosis: Overcoming the Illness Excuse*	219
20.	My review of: *The Mind's New Science: A History of the Cognitive Revolution*	223
21.	"The Role of Error in Computer Science"	231
22.	My review of: *A Skeptic's Dictionary*	245
23.	My review of: *Unauthorized Freud*	249
24.	My review of: *Remembering Trauma*	255
PART III	Ethical Theory, Applied Ethics, and Social/Political Philosophy	263
25.	"Deontologism and Dialectic"	265
26.	"Dialectic and Desiderata"	281
27.	"On the Nonexistence of Computer Ethics"	289
28.	My review of: *Libertarianism: For and Against*	297
29.	"The Market for Body Parts"	311
30.	"The Ethics of Tort Reform"	319
31.	"The Ethics of Closed Shops"	331
32.	"The Ethical Case for Boycotting Chrysler and GM"	339
33.	"The Case for Free Trade"	343
34.	My review of: *Happiness, Economics, and Public Policy*	363
35.	My review of: *A Rat is a Pig is a Dog is a Boy*	367
PART IV	Miscellany	371
36.	"Is the Soul-Making Defense Sound?"	373
37.	"Roadblocks to Research" One Part-Timer's View"	377
38.	My review of: *Can Modern War be Just?*	381
39.	"Using Philosophical Dilemmas to Teach Composition"	385
40.	My review of: *Abusing Science: The Case against Creationism*	393
41.	My review of: *Profiles, Probabilities, and Stereotypes*	397
42.	My review of: *Explaining Postmodernism*	403
	Index	411

Introduction

In this volume I have collected together many of my essays on philosophy, published in a wide range of venues from 1979 to 2011.

Part I, the first group of essays, consists of my writings on logic, argumentation theory and some applications in computer science. These essays fall broadly into two areas.

One recurring area of my interest is informal fallacies. In "Is there a Case for *Ad Hominem* Arguments," I argued that the number of cases in which it is logically legitimate to attack a person's character or background is more limited than some commentators had been suggesting, and I more recently expanded on this theme in "Does Virtue Epistemology Provide a Better Account of the *Ad Hominem* Argument?" In another pair of articles, I take up the issue of just how useful the standard and traditional analysis of informal fallacies really is. I argue in "Are Fallacies Common? A Look at Two Debates" that it is very useful, because informal fallacies as standardly defined are indeed prevalent in ordinary discourse, and continue the defense of that view in a rejoinder to one of my critics in "Fallacies *are* Common."

Additionally, I have tried to amplify the standard treatment of informal fallacies in several of my writings. In "The Nature of the *Argumentum ad Baculum,*" I suggest that appeals to fear more often involve scare tactics than actual threats, a view that was included in my treatment of informal logic in my introductory logic text, *Introduction to Logic.*[1] In "Hedging as a Fallacy of Language" I urge that the category of fallacies of language be expanded beyond the usual focus on fallacies of ambiguity to include the use of understatement. I eventually expanded the category of fallacies of language even further in Chapter 6 of my later critical thinking text, *Critical Thinking: Developing an Effective Worldview.*[2]

The second broad area of my interest has been non-standard or "deviant" logics, especially non-assertion logics—specifically, the logic of questions (erotetic logic) and dialog logic (formal dialectic). This interest grew out of both my teaching of informal fallacies and my research into philosophy of science, research that culminated in my book *The Logic of Scientific Discovery.*[3] In "Notes towards a Formal Conversation Theory" I sketch out some ideas on formal dialectic, and I review some ideas on the subject by some other writers in my review of *Logical Dialogue-Games and Fallacies.* And the use of non-standard logics in computer science I explore in my articles "Erotetic Logic as a Specification Language for Database Queries" and "Dialog as an Abstract Data Type," as well as in my review of *Logics for Artificial Intelligence.* I also include in this section my reviews of *Logic: a Computer Approach* and *Expert Systems.*

The essays in Part II consist of my essays on epistemology and philosophy of science, including psychology and cognitive science.

One area of my interest has been in the logic of scientific discovery and what Peirce termed abductive inference. In "The Concept of Discovery," I explore some of the meanings of the term "discovery," and in "Science and Common Sense," I consider whether the processes we use for scientific research differ from common sense. In "Two Problems of Induction," I argue that inductive logic is dialectical in nature, and in "Epistemologies and Apologies," I argue that while the sort of pragmatism that Peirce espoused may not face the traditional problem of induction, it faces its own functional analog (the problem of convergence). In "The Role of Error in Computer Science," I explore the constructive role that searching for (and eliminating) error plays in computer software design.

Another broad area of interest to me is cognitive science and what it has to say about traditional views of the unconscious. In my reviews of *The Foundations of Psychoanalysis* and *The Myth of Neurosis*, I summarized some of the traditional critiques of Freudian psychoanalytic theory. In my more recent reviews of *Unauthorized Freud* and *Remembering Trauma*, I review more recent critiques. I also include a review of a useful book on pseudoscience, *The Skeptic's Dictionary.*

Part III of this anthology consists of my essays on ethics and (some of my essays on) social and political philosophy.

One area of work is on a sketch of my ethical theory, something of a variant on that of W.D. Ross. In "Deontologism and Dialectic," I infuse multiple rule deontologism with dialog logic and pragmaticism, suggesting that the deliberation process in ethical reasoning is dialogical in structure, and truth in such deliberative matters lies in convergence over the long term. In "Dialectic and Desiderata," I extend the sketch to outline a mental-state theory of happiness in which happiness is conceived of as a balance among various desirable feelings (including, but certainly not limited to, pleasure), a balance that is achieved by dialogical reasoning.

Another broad area of my interest has been trying to craft a satisfactory classically liberal social and political philosophy. In my review essay on the book *Libertarianism: For and Against*, I sift through in detail the major arguments for the philosophy of minimalist government, trying to separate the stronger from the weaker.

Overlapping this is my work in applied ethics. In "The Market for Body Parts," I argue on convergent ethical theoretical grounds that society ought to allow competent adults the right to sell their own body parts (within reasonable regulation). In "The Ethics of Tort Reform," I again use different ethical theoretical arguments to suggest that the United States ought to move to the "British rule" (or the "loser pay") system of tort law.

Several of my more recent articles have been on topics in business ethics. In "The Ethics of Closed Shops," I argue that contracts requiring workers to support a union are not ethical and ought not to be allowed. In "The Ethical Case for Boycotting GM and Chrysler," I argue that the recent nationalization of most of the American auto industry raised serious ethical issues. And in my review essay "The Case for Free Trade," I argue that while the ethical case for free trade is clearly compelling, the opposition to it is based in evolutionary psychology so not easy for most people to recognize.

I also include in this section my article "On the Nonexistence of Computer Ethics" (in which I question whether we need a separate category in applied ethics for issues that arise in computing), my review of *Happiness, Economics, and Public Policy* (a book on recent empirical economics research on what causes happiness), and of *A Rat is a Pig is a Dog* (a book on the animal rights movement).

Finally, in Part IV I include in a group of pieces on miscellaneous topics. In my article "Is the Soul-Making Defense Sound?"—my earliest philosophy article—I argued that the problem of evil is not solved by the "soul-making" theodicy. In "Roadblocks to Research," I review the difficulties faced by adjunct faculty in conducting research, and in "Using Philosophical Dilemmas to Teach Composition" I discuss a technique I have used for many years to teach introductory philosophy students how to craft argumentative essays.

I also include some book reviews, including of *Can Modern Wars be Just?* (on whether classical just-war doctrine applies to modern conflicts), of *Abused Science: The Case against Creationism*, of *Profiles, Probabilities, and Stereotypes*, and a review essay on *Explaining Postmodernism.*

I have generally kept the language of the original publications without change, except in the articles on formal logic. In these, given the difficulty of printing subscripted subscripts, I use a slash convention: '$\alpha_{i/j}$' means a with α subscript 'i' itself subscripted with a 'j'. I have also brought the spelling of certain words into line with American usage: "dialogue" is now "dialog" and "analogue" now analog."

Notes

1. Boston, MA: Jones and Bartlett Publishers,1994.
2. Belmont, CA: Wadsworth Publishing Company, 2001.
3. New York: Peter Lang Publishing, 1989.

Part One

Essays on Logic, Argumentation Theory, and Computer Science

1

"Notes towards a Formal Conversation Theory"

first appeared in Grazer Philosophische Studien Vol. 10 (1980), pp. 119–139

Introduction: Conversation Theory versus Dialectic

My purpose in writing this article is to define a study, which I will call **Formal Conversation Theory,** which is intended to do for certain sorts of conversation what formal deductive logic does for deductively valid arguments, and what inductive logic allegedly does for inductively strong arguments.

I choose the awkward term "conversation theory" to mark a key ambiguity in the term "argument." The term "argument" can mean something I give (a claim and my evidence for it): but it can also mean something you and I have (a conversation of a special sort). Logic is most often conceived of as the analysis of arguments in the first sense; the analysis of arguments in the second sense is generally treated (if at all) under the rubric of "fallacies" or (worse yet) "informal logic." The distinction between logic as the analysis of implication-relations and logic as the analysis of conversation-structure is precisely the difference between logic strictly so-called and what I propose to call **conversation theory**. To reiterate, my purpose is to define the subject (in both the real and the nominal sense).

Now, some readers may be tempted to respond to my remarks by saying that such a study is really nothing new, having been practiced for centuries under the rubric "dialectic." Indeed, dialectic, as a philosophic discipline, has a long history. But the work has been totally non-analytic; that is, it has been carried out by philosophers who do not analyze the concepts they employ in dealing with the philosophic problems addressed. Thus I seek to differentiate the analytic study of conversations from the non-analytic study of conversations (whether by the Marxist, Ramean or other approaches). I reserve the term "dialectic" for the latter and Conversation Theory (hereafter abbreviated CT") for the former.

If I will be contrasting CT with ordinary logic, I ought to briefly state what I mean by "ordinary logic." (I speak of "ordinary" logic to indicate I do not have in mind deviant logics like erotetic, deontic, temporal or other such studies). Let me begin with the term "argument."

I mean by an **argument** a set of declarative sentences (or if you prefer, statements—the difference will not be important for us), some of which are its premises, and one of which is its conclusion.[1] By **logic**, then, I mean the study, involving both explication and evaluation, of evidential relations between premises and conclusions of arguments. **Formal logic** (inadequately characterized as "symbolic logic") is the explication of the evidential relations between premises and conclusions of arguments by means of symbolic models.

An argument is **deductively valid** if and only if it is impossible for the premises to be true and the conclusion false. An argument is **inductively strong** if and only if it is not valid, but if it is highly improbable that the conclusion is false given that the premises are true. **Deductive logic,** then, is essentially the study of deductively valid arguments; **formal deductive logic** involves the creation of partially interpreted symbolic languages with context-free transformation rules. **Inductive logic** is essentially the study of inductively strong arguments; formal inductive logic has no agreed upon method.

The most important thing—for our purposes—to note about an argument is that it is a pair, consisting of a set of declarative sentences (premises) and another declarative sentence (the conclusion). Moreover, this set is ordered; after all, the notion of "being evidence for" involves order. The premises are evidence for the conclusion, and not vice versa.

Let us now briefly define **CT** as the study, involving both explication and evaluation, of conversations, and turn now to a more precise definition of the concept of a conversation.

To begin with, we must make the traditional distinction between a process and a product of that process. An argument (in the sense defined above) is the result, the summation, of the process of reasoning. Similarly, a conversation (in the sense I will be using it) is the result of conversing, somewhat like a court transcript is a result or—more precisely—a summation of the actual proceeding. We will be constructing a definition of conversation (as product) by looking at aspects of (the process of) conversing, but the reader should keep the process/product distinction in mind.[2]

The first aspect of a conversation to note is that it is conducted by a number of participants for a certain length of time. We somehow must capture the notion of length and number of participants in the final definition of conversation. Well, does length of a conversation mean the number of sentences in it? No, this wouldn't be accurate, for one of the participants may keep talking after the other participants have left. Rather, by "length" of a conversation we have in mind the number of rounds, the number of sentence-plus-responses-to-it sets. If there are n participants, a round consists of a sentence and (n-l) responses to it. Hence, the length m of a conversation is the number of n-tuples of sentences in it, where n is the number of participants.

The reader should recall the difference between an ordered set and an unordered one. The very notion of a "response" involves order: if sentence y is a response to sentence x, then the set of x and y must be ordered. Again, the very notion of a "round" involves order: the first round is followed by the second round, the second in turn by the third, etc. So the rounds are likewise ordered: $<R_1, \ldots, R_m>$, where m is the length of the conversation, and $R_i = <S_1, \ldots, S_n>$ with n the number of participants.

Summing up, while an argument is an ordered pair consisting of a set of premises (or a conjunction thereof) and a conclusion, a conversation is an ordered set of m ordered n-tuples of sentences. Thus we can visualize a conversation as an m by n (m rows, n columns) matrix, with $S_{i,j}$ denoting the jth response in the ith round:

$$
\begin{array}{l}
S_{1,1}, S_{1,2}, \ldots S_{1,n} \ldots \text{first round} \\
S_{2,1}, S_{2,2}, \ldots S_{2,n} \\
\ldots\ldots\ldots\ldots\ldots\ldots \\
\ldots\ldots\ldots\ldots\ldots\ldots \\
S_{m,1}, S_{m,2}, \ldots S_{m,n} \ldots\ldots \text{last round}
\end{array}
$$

But there remains much more to be said.

People converse for various reasons. People chatting to pass the time, lawyers arguing in court, scientists debating a scientific point, parishioners participating in a mass, children playing games, old men engaged in heated political argument—all have different goals in mind, different reasons for conversing.[3] More to the point, if we remember to distinguish between the purpose of the conversation and the purposes of the participants, the *conversations* have different purposes. The lawyers may want to win the case and collect fat fees, but the purpose of the *trial* is to assess guilt; the scientists may want to gratify their egos, but the purpose of their *debate* is to arrive at the truth about physical reality; the parishioners may be trying to impress their neighbors with their piety, but the *mass* is intended to commune with God.

The purpose of the conversation shows up (in the process), among other ways, in the kind of speech acts involved. For instance, idle chit-chat involves questions, promises, exhortations, statements, exclamations and every other kind of speech act I can think of. On the other hand, legal conversations (trials) essentially involve (need only involve) questions, statements and oaths (akin, I suppose, to promises). Yet again, scientific debates (carried out, say, in journals) essentially involve questions and statements.[4] And what sort of speech acts characterize masses, group prayer, "razzing" (the mutual exchange of insults by opposing athletic teams), I leave to the reader to figure out. The point is this, though: the kind of speech acts countenanced in the process is represented in the sort of sentences (interrogative, declarative, exclamatory) in the product conversation.[5]

Thus, another key difference between an *argument* (as defined earlier) and a *conversation* (as defined above) is that an argument consists of statements, whereas a conversation includes questions, proposals, exclamations, and so on.[6]

On the other hand, the purpose of a conversation also shows up in the sort of moves allowed, i.e., in the rules governing how people should converse to that purpose. When speaking in terms of conversations as products, "rules governing how we should converse" amount to rules of acceptability of dialogs, in a sense that will be investigated in section three of this paper.

Let us restrict our field of vision at this point. I have been speaking of developing a theory of conversations; however, we are basically interested in conversations whose purpose is to acquire information about the world. Such conversations essentially involve only questions and statements, so we should lay down the following stipulative definition. By a **dialog** I mean an ordered set of m ordered n-tuples of sentences, each of which is either an interrogative or a declarative. From this point on, I will mean by **CT** the study, involving both explication and evaluation, of dialogs.

But immediately two questions arise, centering around the relation of CT to logic. First, how do we "evaluate" dialogs? (Are some dialogs "good" and some "bad"? Why and in what way? In the way an argument is valid or invalid?) Second, how does the evaluation of a dialog differ from the evaluation of the moves in that dialogue? (Can't we use ordinary logic, perhaps augmented by a deviant logic?) Both these questions will be addressed in section three; however, further preliminary remarks are in order.

CT versus Gricean Analysis

To give further insight into CT as I conceive it, let me contrast it with something it is not. I do not have in mind as being CT the sort work done by H.P. Grice in his delightful article "Logic and Conversation."[7]

In this article, Grice is concerned to refute the doctrine that there are "divergences in meaning" between the logical symbols "(∃x)", "(∀x)", "&", "~", "v", "→" and "↔" (given the usual semantic interpretation) and their analogs in ordinary language. Grice is further concerned to show that this mistaken (in his view) doctrine arises from the neglect of the conditions governing conversation. In trying to establish these claims, Grice attempts to delineate the general conditions which govern or apply to any conversation "irrespective of its subject matter."[8]

Grice points out that rational conversations do not merely consist of random comments by the participants, but rather are cooperative efforts. There is a common purpose, which may change as the conversation goes along, but which rules out some possible conversational moves as unsuitable. Grice formulates a sort of overarching condition on participants, called the "Cooperative Principle": "Make your conversational contribution such as is required, at the stage at which it occurs, by the accepted purpose or direction of the talk exchange in which you are engaged."[9]

As subsidiary groups of more specific rules of conversing, Grice lists these:[10]

I. Rules of quantity:
 1) Make your contribution as informative as required;
 2) Do not make it more informative than required.

II. Rules of quality.
 1) Do not say what you believe false;
 2) Do not say that for which you lack adequate evidence.

III. Rules of relation:
 1) Be relevant (Grice admits the lack of clarity of this rule).

IV. Rules of manner:
 1) Avoid obscurity of expression;
 2) Avoid ambiguity;
 3) Be brief;
 4) Be orderly.

Grice feels that not only do these rules describe how people actually converse, but also how they ought to converse. How to show that latter claim he is apparently unsure, but he thinks that it would involve showing that anyone interested in the central goals of communication (exchange of information and influencing others) would have to participate in conversations governed by those rules.

Now, I heartily recommend Grice's work for its subtle analysis of conversation in general, and conversational (as opposed to logical) implication in particular. Yet I do not view this work as contributing to CT as I view the subject. There are two key differences between what he is doing and what I call CT.

First, Grice's approach is, to use a distinction similar to that made by Hamblin,[11] descriptive, whereas CT is meant to be a formal study. By a **descriptive study** of conversation I mean a non-symbolic analysis focusing upon how people actually converse. By a **formal study** of conversation I mean a symbolic analysis of how (ideally) people ought to converse. In keeping with the narrowed scope mentioned at the end of section one, this means a symbolic analysis of how people ought to converse if they are to increase their information about the world.

Now, the reader might object that Grice already has this in mind –he feels his rules govern not only how people do, but how they ought to converse. Although this is true, he begins by concentrating on realistic conversations, I propose to look at highly idealized models, which I will call **conversation games** ("**c-games**" for short), and develop CT piecemeal from the analysis of these simplified models. Compare this approach with perhaps the paradigm of a formal study, classical mechanics, which gives a mathematical description of how particles would behave were they perfectly elastic spheres (the "billiard-ball model"). In a formal study of the behavior of entities of a given kind one seeks to find particular models (or one comprehensive model) which exhibit how entities of that sort would behave were they to have certain ideal properties. In CT, one seeks to develop models which exhibit how ideally rational participants in a conversation (whose purpose is to acquire information about the world) would converse. Thus it is of the essence of CT that we look at model dialogs in trying to develop a method of evaluating dialogs.

The second central difference between Gricean analysis of conversations and CT is that the former is a pragmatic undertaking, while the latter is intended to be a semantic/syntactic one. This is best brought out by considering Grice's rules. Granted "pragmatic" is an ambiguous word, meaning to some "involving explicit reference to context", to others "involving explicit reference to the speakers", and to others "involving explicit reference to the community of language users"; still, Grice's rules of conversation are pragmatic by anybody's definition. I will only say at this point that CT is "pragmatic" only in the sense that the semantic context of dialogs must be taken into account. We will return to this matter in the next section.

Rules in CT

I said in the first section of this paper that CT is the analysis, involving both explication and evaluation, of dialogs; moreover, in the second section I indicated that the analysis is a semantic task best approached piecemeal, by examining model dialogs (c-games). In section four I will begin (only begin) that analysis; but first I want to examine more closely what it is to "explicate and evaluate" dialogues.

The key insight required to see why conversations are evaluable, have a structure which can meaningfully be called "good" or "bad", is the recognition that there can be both rational and irrational paths to the same logically defensible conclusion. This insight is analogous to the recognition that there can be both moral and immoral paths to (means of achieving) a given laudable end.[12] Even if two different dialogs arrive at the same conclusion, even though that conclusion is quite true, one of those dialogs may have an acceptable structure while the other has a completely unacceptable structure. The same situation obtains in ordinary logic, and in CT we must address it in the same way: concentrate on finding rules which allow us to demonstrate when a given dialog has an acceptable form.

Thus, to "explicate" a dialog is to reveal its form; to "evaluate" a dialog is to evaluate its form, which requires us to adduce a set of rules of justification of dialogs (akin to the rules of natural deduction in deductive logic). But what sort of rules governs the evolution of a "good" or "acceptable" dialog?

First, there are rules governing the structure of any given round, that is, governing the responses to any given move. I will call these rules the narrow rules of response. To delineate the narrow rules of response, we must study the form of acceptable responses to any given type of move. Since a dialog consists only of statements and questions, to study the epistemic relations between any move and the responses to it is just to study the epistemic relations between statements and other statements and the epistemic relations between statements and questions. Hence the task of delineating the narrow rules of response is not a study unique to CT; it is simply the study of ordinary (inductive and deductive) logic plus deviant (specifically, erotetic) logic. Hence, part of doing CT is investigating the logic of statements and the logic of questions.

An example may help make this clear. Consider this one - round dialog:

A. All men are evil, and Jason is a man.
B. Therefore, it follows that Jason is evil.

Here, B is responding to A by drawing out a logical consequence of his statements. But the rules governing B's inference (and hence the adequacy of his response) are simply the rules of deductive inference. Usually, I draw conclusions from statements I have made. But (as reflected in our definition of "argument"), it is a matter of indifference whether you state the premises or if five people do so: in either case, the product is the same.

Thus, the narrow rules of response evaluate the relation of deductive implication, and (as a similar dialog would show) the relation of inductive "implication" (if one there be), and the relations between various types of questions and answers. They do so because these are the ways participants in a dialog (as opposed to other types of conversation) can respond to a given initial move in a round.

Besides the narrow rules of response, however, there are other rules governing the evolution of (acceptability of) dialogs. If we view dialogs as information-games (take c-games as our models of dialogs), we see that there are "rules of strategy" governing the playing of the game. Compare, if you will, the game of poker. In poker, there are rules (listed, for example in Hoyle) that define how the game is played and state what moves are legitimate. But there are also rules of strategy, such as "never draw to an inside straight", which any player is free to break, but which he would do well to follow. Indeed, the analogy extends to deductive logic: any good logic textbook[13] will contrast the rules for justifying steps in a proof (inference rules) with rules of strategy for devising those proofs.

There is yet a third type of rule governing the evolution/acceptability of dialogs. In contrast to the rules of strategy, these rules are part of the essence of the game. But in contrast to the narrow rules of response, these rules govern the evolution of the rounds, the relation between responses to a given move and prior moves, and between any given move and prior moves. Let me call such rules the **broad rules of response**. Some examples: never ask the same question twice; never ask a question which presupposes the negation of a previous answer; never ask a question with a false presupposition; etc.

This is where the analogy with poker breaks down. These are nothing like broad rules of response in poker, because the legitimacy of a move in any given hand is never dependent upon prior hands. Hands in a poker game are not like rounds in a conversation. Put another way, poker would not be a good model of dialogs, not a good choice as a c-game.

Of the rules of strategy for dialogs I will have nothing more to say. Any consideration of such rules falls under what C.S. Peirce called the "economics of research," and is beyond the scope of this paper. Basically, then, the heart of doing CT is delineating the narrow rules of response (really, as I said earlier, a task for logicians) and the broad rules of response (a task unique to CT). This task is to be done by looking at progressively more complex models; moreover, these rules must be (ultimately) semantic in their formulation. Clearly the narrow rules of response are semantic—indeed, they are context-free. But what about the broad rules of response, which are context-sensitive? Recall that I include as semantic context-sensitive rules of a special sort. I can now elaborate on this.

Let's look at the process of conversing from a grossly pragmatic point of view. Each of the participants in a given dialog is a member of a large welter of communities—social, political, ethnic, economic, religious, linguistic, cultural, etc. And certainly the disparate backgrounds of (say) a Canadian Catholic lawyer and an American Protestant businessman determine in great part the shape of their discussion. But since dialogs (as I defined the term) are discussions concerned with acquiring information, and since we are interested in reasons for belief rather than psychological causes of it, we are interested only in what I call the epistemic community of each participants. By **epistemic community** $\{S_1, \ldots, S_n\}$ (abbreviated "**EC** $\{S_1, \ldots, S_n\}$") I mean the set of people who believe statements $S_1, \ldots, S_n$. This will be an important concept in what follows.

There is some distortion involved in focusing in on epistemic communities; after all, a religion is more than a set of tenets, a political orientation more than the mere espousal of a set of doctrines. But even though the communities to which a participant in a dialogue belongs are not each equivalent to a set of statements held by the members of that community, we can represent to any desired degree of precision each community as an EC.

Clearly, then, any given person is simultaneously a member of a large number of epistemic communities: he may at once be a member of those who hold 1979 American middle-class "common sense" beliefs, of those who accept the Copenhagen interpretation of quantum theory, of those who accept the tenets of the Republican Party, etc. Further, if you accept Whorf's thesis, then all members of a linguistic community are *ipso facto* joint members of at least one EC.

On the other hand, it is plausible to suggest that no two people have precisely the same belief system, so there are probable many ECs which have only one member. Indeed, we can represent the entire epistemic background—or any portion we consider relevant—of any dialogue participant as a set of statements taken as defining an EC. We will return to this point in section four.

Let me digress to look at a seeming difficulty with the concept of an EC. Basically, we identify an EC by the set of beliefs $\{S_1, \ldots, S_n\}$ shared by the people in the community. But $S_1, \ldots, S_n$ are all presumably sentences in *our* language (the meta-language), Standard American English. And there is an abstract problem of translation, i.e., of telling whether someone who speaks a different language believes what is said using a given sentence from one's own language. Actually, this problem is more than abstract, for if T.S. Kuhn's views (as expressed in *The Structure of Scientific Revolutions*) are correct, every alteration in scientific thought, every scientific revolution, changes the language, and thus people in different paradigms (holding different theories) speak different languages. Thus, e.g., Standard American English as spoken by a proponent of the General Theory of Relativity would differ from the Standard American English of a Newtonian. How could we, using the former as our meta-language, tell if our ascription of sentence S to a speaker of the latter is correct? We can't ask him, since our language and his are incommensurable!

How, indeed? My guess is that Kuhn's "incommensurability thesis" is false; but more to the point, even if his thesis is true, the question whether to ascribe a belief stated in one language to a person of a different language is simply an empirical question, answerable by linguistic and historical research carried out in our meta-language. But whether the reader agrees with my assessment of this problem or not, the whole issue will be irrelevant to what follows. In the cases we will consider, the language of the dialog participants (the object language) and the language in which we carry out the analysis (the meta-language) will be precisely the same.

Having introduced the concept of an EC, let's now employ it to return from the domain of pragmatics to the realm of semantics. Clearly, many of the statements and questions in the dialog will involve presuppositions. Some of these presuppositions will be the results (answers or inferred conclusions) from previous rounds. But some will be background assumptions, part of the EC to which all of the participants belong. (It is clear why there must be an E.C. to which they all belong: if the participants in a dialog did not share some beliefs, the dialogue could never "get off the ground"). Thus the EC "shapes" the dialog, as it were. And the broad rules of response must, in part, address the epistemic (background) context of the dialog, for the acceptability of questions and statements depends in great measure on that epistemic context.

But by representing epistemic communities as sets of statements, we can then state the context-sensitive rules without reference to communities of speakers, cultural or ethnic groupings, or other undeniably pragmatic types of context. The context with which CT is concerned is merely a set of statements, and the (context-sensitive) broad rules of response simply state what transformations of sentences are allowed in given forms of context. How this works in practice will be examined in the next section.

At the end of section one I framed two questions about CT. First, I asked what sort rules of justification characterize CT. We can now answer that: the broad rules of response, unique to CT, are context-sensitive in the semantic sense outlined above. We discover these rules by looking at model dialogs, and noting how later moves depend upon prior ones, and the first move depends upon the EC the participants belong to. And we can enunciate such rules without referring to the speakers. To the second question about whether CT is a subject over and above logic, we now turn.

To see the force of the second question, consider how a hypethetico-deductivist views scientific method.[14] Under this view, a scientist investigating a problem conceives an hypothesis (in a manner not susceptible of logical analysis), call it "H_1" and then deduces a test from it. If this observational consequence is false, the hypothesis H_1 is refuted, and the scientist conceives another, H_2. Again, a consequence (observational test) is deduced and checked. If it turns out true, then the hypothesis H_2 is confirmed, and another consequence is deduced and tried. We can thus represent this dialectical trial-and error process as a chain of arguments:

Argument #1:
$$\begin{array}{l} H_1 \rightarrow O_1 \\ \sim O_1 \\ \hline \therefore -H_1 \end{array}$$

Argument #2:
$$\begin{array}{l} H_2 \rightarrow O_2 \\ \sim O_2 \\ \hline \therefore \sim H_2 \end{array}$$

.
.
.

Argument #n: $H_n \rightarrow O_n$
$\sim O_n$
___
$\therefore \sim H_n$

Argument #(n+1): $H_{n+1} \rightarrow O_{n+1}$
O_{n+1}
___
$\therefore$ H_{n+1} is confirmed.

.
.
.

Argument #(n+k): $H_{n+k} \rightarrow O_{n+k}$
O_{n+k}
___
$\therefore$ H_{n+k} is established

Here, the first n arguments are all deductive, while the last k arguments are all inductive.

Thus, since we can view a scientist's research as a dialog between himself and nature, if we generalize upon the hypethetico-deductivist account, we might say that any process of conversation is representable as simply a chain of arguments. Thus CT as such would not exist; only ordinary (and perhaps deviant) logic would be needed to explicate and evaluate dialogs.

This seems to me to be a powerful objection, and indeed kept me from recognizing the existence of CT for a considerable length of time. However, I think there are several reasons why one cannot even in such simple cases as trial and error dialogs (much less dialogs in general), represent dialogs as chains of arguments.

First, a dialog consists of questions and statements, not just statements alone. Consider the hypethetico-deductivist account again. Note that it is singularly weak on explaining where the initial hypothesis H_i (or any of the other hypotheses) comes from. The hypethetico-deductivist ignores the fact that an hypothesis is a conjectured answer to a problem (a question).

Much of the concern about the role of "background theories," "paradigms", and "presuppositions" reflects the fact that even the simplest dialogs involve questions, and moreover, that the initial question especially involves presuppositions assumed by the EC to which the dialog participants belong. Also, the Duhemian point that when we say (e.g.) "O_1" was seen to be false" we are in fact saying something hypothetical (because we assume in testing an hypothesis many auxiliary hypotheses dealing with experimental design, etc.), is a recognition of the fact that at all points in the dialog, statements and questions presuppose beliefs held by the EC of the participants.

The second reason we cannot represent even simple dialogs as chains of arguments is that the broad rules of response are completely overlooked. Consider our example of the hypethetico-deductivist (trial-and-error) model of scientific research: it clearly overlooks the fact that there are rules governing the introduction of new hypotheses. For example, H_j cannot be the same as (the previously rejected) H_i. And the set of beliefs that characterizes the EC of the researchers acts as a set of constraints upon the introduction of new hypotheses.

Such considerations are the main force behind the demand for a "logic of discovery," and simply reflect the fact that besides narrow rules of response governing the interior structure of each round in a conversation, there are broad rules of response which govern the evolution of the rounds, in the context of the EC and the results of prior rounds. To say a dialog is more than a string of arguments—and thus CT more than just logic—is in part to indicate that the broad rules of response exist over and above the narrow rules of response.

However I will concede this to my critic. CT is not some new vast uncharted continent—it is more like a hitherto uncharted island. The narrow rules of response far outnumber the broad. Moreover a complete CT must await the development of both inductive and erotetic logic. In sense, especially, CT may be said to depend upon logic.

I trust by now the reader has a general idea of what CT is supposed to be. Let me try to impart a more concrete vision of the subject by looking at a few c-games, sketching out an analysis of them, and then concluding with a discussion of what my future research focus on.

Some Simple C-games

Recall that we can represent a conversation as being a matrix

$$\begin{array}{l} S_{1,1}, \ldots, S_{1,n} \\ S_{2,1}, \ldots, S_{2,n} \\ \cdot \\ \cdot \\ \cdot \\ S_{m,1}, \ldots, S_{m,n} \end{array}$$

Each $S_{i,j}$ of which is either a statement $p_{i,j}$, a question ? $p_{i,j}$, or else ∅ (the null response). We can represent any null response by the tautology "p v ~p". In what follows, however, this cumbersome notation will be unimportant.

What will be important, is this simplification: in the games we will consider, there are two participants, an active partner A, and a "dummy" partner D. As the name indicates, A is the one who plays the game, while D simply answers questions put to him by A. Thus we need only consider the EC to which A belongs. Note that winning any of these c-games amounts to discovering the desired information.

C-game #1: Let's begin with a very simple game, called "the proof game." In this game, A is given several statements by D, and is told to take them as premises. D then feeds A proposition after proposition, requiring A to prove each given proposition from the original given premises.

Clearly, in this game, the EC to which A belongs is EC = {the given premises}. The narrow rules of response are the rules which govern deductive inference, the rules of natural deduction. But what are the rules of response? Well, does any round depend upon prior rounds? No—after proving any given proposition from the premises given initially, A is given another. But the order in which the propositions to be deduced are given is irrelevant. Thus there are no rules governing the evolution of the rounds, since the rounds are independent of one another, hence there are no broad rules of response.

However, it is easy to imagine a variant game which does have broad rules of response. Imagine D giving the first proposition P_1 to A, requiring him to check whether it follows from the given premises (by truth tables, say; let's assume we are dealing with sentential arguments only), if it does having A prove it follows, and if it doesn't, having A add P_1 to the group of premises. D then gives another proposition P_2, and A does the same as in round one except the EC set of premises now includes P_1. Here, the broad rule of response is: in any round, prove the proposition given (if it is deducible) using the initial information plus all the propositions given previously not entailed by that set.

C-game #2: In the proof game, the narrow rules of response are deductive. A more interesting game is "the evidence game". In this game, D sets forth a set of propositions—the initial set of information. D then gives A a proposition, and A must select from the EC set (the initial information) those statements which most support it, but without entailing it.

I cannot state explicitly the narrow rules of response for this c-game, since there is no inductive logic analogous to deductive logic, with inference rules and the like. Also, in c-game #2, there are no broad rules of response, but (as with c-game #1) we can devise variants of the game which do have broad rules of response.

C-game #3: In this game, called "the one-card game", D draws a card from a regular deck of playing cards, and A must determine what card D drew without seeing it. A can only ask whether-questions ("yes-or-no" questions). Thus, unlike the first two c-games, this c-game involves interrogative as well as declarative sentences. Clearly, A is a member of EC = {the card drawn is one of the following: ace of spades, two of spades, …, king of spades, ace of hearts, two of hearts, …, king of hearts, ace of clubs, two of clubs, …, king of clubs, ace of diamonds, …, king of diamonds}. We can imagine several ways the game might proceed, i.e., there arc several equally acceptable such dialogues. For instance:

Round 1:	A: Is the card a spade?
	D: No.
Round 2:	A: Is it a club?
	D: Yes.
Round 3:	A: Is it a club higher than eight?
	D: No.
Round 4:	A: Thus it is either an eight or less than an eight.
	D: ∅ (Null response).
Round 5:	A: It is a club higher than five?
	D: Yes.
Round 6:	A: Then it is the six, the seven, or the eight.
	D: Null response.
Round 7:	A: Is it the six of clubs?
	D: Yes.
Round 8:	A: The card is then six of clubs.
	D: ∅ (End game).

But A could equally well (from the *logical* point of view, though not from a *strategic* point of view) have simply worked through the deck, card by card, asking D whether the unknown card is the ace of spades, the king of spades, and so on. Again, figuring out what the best *strategy* is in any c-game is a study in the economics of research, and beyond the scope of this paper.

Any acceptable c-game #3, however, is governed by the rules of deductive inference plus the rule that when D is faced with a whether-question, he must select one of the two alternatives (i.e., D must answer yes or no, not maybe). These are the narrow rules of response. The single broad rule of response is that the whether-question in any round (r+1) may not presuppose the falsity of any answer given in rounds 1 through r.

C-game #4: called "the hide-and-seek game", is in part similar to c-game #3. In hide-and-seek D hides an object o, and A must find it. A can only ask whether-questions. We can suppose without loss of generality that the game is played in a 20' by 20' room, that A has a ruler, and that o is a ball-bearing hidden in the carpeting. So the EC to which A belongs is identified by the set {o is a ball bearing hidden in the carpeting in a 20' by 20' room}. Further, A can look at the rug.

In this game, the narrow rules of response are simply (as in c-game #3) the rules of deductive logic plus the restrictions on how whether-questions can be answered. And the broad rule of response is (as before) that the whether-question in any round must incorporate in its formulation (must not presuppose the negation of) the answers (the information discovered) in the previous rounds, or the initial information.

Note something very different about c-game #4, however. While A could simply ask questions like "Is o closer to the north wall than the south?" "Is o within ten inches of the west wall?" etc., and within a finite time get arbitrarily close to the location of o, this would obviously be a bad strategy. A is, after all, permitted to look at the rug. Thus a could, if he wished, simply get down on his hands and knees and begin checking the rug visually. Again, this would be bad strategy, but still rational or "logically" acceptable. A's best strategy would be to ask several questions to narrow down the area where o can possible be, and then visually check that area. The question is, then, how do we represent this observational input?

Let me introduce the concept of channels of information: a **channel of information** for a given participant in a dialog (and we usually focus on one participant, the active partner) is any mode by which he can acquire information not already in the set of propositions defining the EC to which he belongs. Thus, besides the other participants (especially dummy partners) in the dialog, observation, perusal of relevant literature, and such like, are all channels of information, and can be represented by (but not equated with) other dialog participants.

Thus, we can profitably represent a c-game #4 where A does use observation like this:

Round 1: A: Is o within two inches of the west wall?
O: (observation): ∅
D: Yes.

Round 2: A: Then o is either in the two inch strip which runs from the from the north wall to the half-way line dividing north and south, or else in the two inch strip which runs from the dividing line to the south wall.

O: o is not in the two inch strip which runs from the north wall to the dividing line.
D: ∅

Round 3: A: Then o is in the strip which runs from the dividing line to the south wall, (and so on).

Concluding Remarks

I regret that the foregoing section was so brief: however, I merely wished to give the reader a concrete illustration of CT to complement the abstract characterization sections of this paper. To illustrate just how much work remains to be done in CT, let me mention just a few of the simplifications inherent in the four c-games I considered.

First, the dialogs had only two participants. In reality, however, most conversations have several participants, even several active participants. Think of modern scientific research: gone are the days of one scientist engaging in solitary work (the lone scientist being the active partner, nature the observation channel). Now, science is a cooperative effort of groups of researchers, or better, *teams* of researchers.

Second, the dialogs I considered had either no questions, or only whether-questions, allowed. But there are many other types of questions to consider, chief among them being why-questions. And the most interesting sorts of dialogs (conversations devoted to acquiring information) involve seeking explanations for phenomena of interest, involve asking why-questions. (My current work in CT is focusing in on just this area).

Third, we have viewed the EC to which the participants belong as remaining static over the course of the conversation. But "background information" rarely remains an inert lump, merely acting as a set of constraints, during the process of discovering information. The constraints themselves are modified by the information acquired, in a very subtle and complex way.

Thus, CT as I conceive it, has much ground to cover. Still, the sooner we start, the sooner we will finish.

Bibliographical Appendix

Needless to say, there has been much philosophical work done on many of the areas upon which my paper touches. For instance, the literature devoted to Dialectics is vast, beginning (if not with Plato himself) at least in the Middle Ages, and is continued to this day by Marxist and non-Marxist scholars alike. To single out books from this vast literature for special recommendation is perhaps an exercise in hubris, but I make the following recommendations:

- *Logic and Reality. An Investigation into the Idea of a Dialectical System*, by Leslie Armour, 1972, Van Gorcum & Co., Assen.
- *Dialectics*, by Nicholas Rescher, 1977, State University of New York Press, Albany, N.Y. However, my approach is rather different from Dialectics, and my focus much narrower. I am primarily interested in the analysis and assessment of model dialogues, conversations, analogous to (but not equivalent to) "proofs." A roughly similar task is addressed in:
- *Elemente der Sprachkritik*, by Kuno Lorenz, 1970, Suhrkamp Verlag, Frankfurt am Main, esp. pp. 147–242.
- *Fallacies*, by C.L. Hamblin (cited earlier in footnotes). However, their approach is pragmatic, mine syntactic/semantic. In my paper, I did not take up the topic of erotetic logic, although erotetics (the logical study of questions) clearly figures in to conversation theory as I conceive it. I highly recommend to the reader:
- *The Logic of Questions*, by Nuel Belnap and Thomas Steele, 1976, Yale University Press, New Haven, Conn. not only for its clear presentation of erotetic logic, but also for its very complete and excellent bibliography of articles and books on the logical structure of questions and answers. Finally, it should be noted that many of the issues I have raised are approached from a linguistic perspective in "text linguistics" or "text grammar". See especially:
- *Studies in Text Grammar*, ed. by J.S. Petofi and H. Rieser, 1973, D. Reidel. Dordrecht.

Notes

1. The definition I give of "argument," "deductive logic," and "inductive logic" are from the introduction to Sidney Luckenbach's *Probabilities, Problems, and Paradoxes* Encino, CA: Dickinson Publishing Company, 1972.
2. Actually, I would prefer to state the distinction this way: we must distinguish between an *activity* and a *representation*, or idealized description, of that activity. Reasoning, researching, and conversing are all rational activities. We represent these activities in various ways, and logic (and CT) assesses those *representations.* Naturally, in representing an activity, we focus on some aspects of that activity and ignore other aspects

of that activity. One may view CT as focusing on a different aspect of reasoning from the one that logic focuses on.

3. I do not mean to equate masses, trials, and such like, as conversations: I merely intend to represent them as such for the purposes of this paper.
4. This claim may seem implausible, at first. But scientists distinguish quite strongly between polemical writing, which includes exhortations and promises (of future achievements), and scientific discussion. In respected journals polemical articles rarely appear. Note that the difference between a polemical and a scientific article appears, not only in the speech acts countenanced, but also in the rules of procedure as well. For instance, in the former special pleading is acceptable, whereas it is strictly verboten in the latter.
5. Naturally, one can use declarative sentences to ask questions, interrogative sentences to make statements, and so on. When I say "Do you really believe Sue is innocent?", I am really stating that Sue is not innocent. (We call such pseudo-questions "rhetorical questions"). But we can require the participants to use an interrogative when and only when they want to ask a question, use a declarative when and only when they want to make a statement, etc.
6. Again, the difference between a question and an interrogative sentence, a proposition and a statement and a declarative sentence, etc. will be unimportant for our purposes.
7. H.P. Grice, "Logic and Conversation," in *The Logic of Grammar*, edited by Donald Davidson, Encino, CA: Dickinson Publishing Co. 1975. Reprinted in *Understanding Argument* by Robert Fogelin, NY: Harcourt, Brace, Jovanovich 1978, pp. 329–343.
8. *Ibid.*, p. 331.
9. *Ibid.*, p. 333.
10. *Ibid.*, p. 335.
11. C.I. Hamblin, Fallacies, London: Methuen 1970, p. 256.
12. This useful analogy was suggested to me by Professor Tom Nickles of the University of Nevada, Reno.
13. For instance, see Donald Kalish and Richard Montague, *Logic: The Techniques of Formal Reasoning*, NY: Harcourt, Brace, Jovanovich, 1964.
14. There is a deep connection between the study of dialogues and the study of scientific method. One can view the research of a scientist in any given domain as a dialogue between the researcher (and other researchers working in that domain) and nature. Indeed, I believe that the dispute over whether there is a "logic" of discovery is as sterile as it is because "logic" is taken in too narrow a sense. CT is meant to remedy that.

I wish to thank *Grazer Philosophische Studien.*

2

"Is there a Case for *Ad Hominem* Arguments?"

first appeared in the Australasian Journal of Philosophy, Vol. 62, No. 2, June 1984, pp. 182–185

Lawrence Hinman has argued (*Australasian Journal of Philosophy,* December 1982) that a case can be made for *ad hominem* arguments, at least in certain situations for certain classes of arguments. However, I think that the classes of arguments he indicates do not suffice to make any case for allowing *ad hominem* reasoning even in those contexts.

By an *ad hominem* argument we usually have in mind something of the form:

1. The advocates of (proposition, claim, proposal) C have traits x, y, z, … .
2. x, y, z, … are all bad.

∴ C is (probably) false.

Hinman allows that such reasoning is often clearly fallacious. Indeed, this is hard to deny in any country where elections are held. He also notes that in cases where C is some kind of testimony, the argument form is not fallacious (and most textbooks—even "bad old logic textbooks"—clearly state this).

So when may we accept arguments of this form if C is *not* a statement of testimony? Hinman cites four classes of cases.

Class 1: Cases in which the advocates back up C by some premises (i.e. *argue* for C) and where one does not have sufficient independent evidence about those premises. In that case, "one must make some judgment about the reliability of the one who is claiming that those premises ought to be accepted."

This seems dubious. Suppose an anti-nuclear-power spokesperson says "We should not build any more nuclear power plants". Clearly to reject this claim on the basis of the (real or imagined) bias of that spokesperson is unwarranted. Unless you have reasons for or against the claim, you can conclude nothing about its truth. The bias of the spokesperson is not a reason for or against the claim (since it is not personal testimony).

Now suppose the anti-nuclear spokesperson says (i.e. *argues*), "The Fitch study has shown that nuclear power plants are more dangerous than coal-fired plants. The Stewart study has shown that our energy needs can be satisfied by coal plants alone. So we should not build any more nuclear power plants." Despite what Hinman seems to hold, the case is again clear. We are just moving back a step from the conclusion to the premises. My knowing that the spokesperson is biased tells me nothing about whether the Fitch and Stewart studies have shown what the spokesperson alleges. If I have no "independent" (i.e. real) evidence about the Fitch and Stewart studies, I can draw no conclusion about the premises. Hence I can say nothing about the soundness of the spokesperson's argument. As a practical matter, I ought to read those studies myself.

Of course, this assumes the spokesperson is not making his claim as testimony on the basis of his/her expertise. That, all hands agree, is a quite different matter.

Class 2: Hinman next considers cases in which I and the other person are both considering some inductive evidence for a claim which interests us. (We are now talking not about a person making a claim, nor even about a person arguing, i.e., making a claim and offering reasons for it, but about someone evaluating an argument.) Hinman argues that I am within my logical rights to "raise questions about one's opponent's background and motives insofar as such questions are focused on the issue of whether the person's background and motives have led to setting the demand for certainty too high or too low." (p. 340)

I am puzzled by this scenario. Suppose my opponent pegs the degree of inductive support the premises offer to the conclusion at 95%, and I agree with his assessment and with the premises. (If I disagree with his assessment of the degree of support, we must both turn to inductive logic—not his background—for information to decide the matter. If I disagree with the premises, we are back to the case discussed above.) If he judges that the conclusion ought to be accepted, that is a claim on his part. Logically, if I want to assess his claim, my only recourse is to look into the topic (not his background) and decide for myself whether 95% certainty is enough in this case. Again, unless my opponent is saying that I should accept his claim that 95% is enough on his say so as some kind of expert (in which case we are back to testimony), his background is not logically relevant.

Class 3: Hinman points out that Marxists, sociologists of knowledge and existentialists often accept *ad hominem* (more exactly, genetic) reasoning. (So as to not offend readers, let us be clear that we mean "some people who are generally taken to be Marxists," and so on.)

To this the reply is "so what?" Are philosophers and sociologists necessarily good at logical reasoning? But Hinman has more to say: "…in the case of beliefs which include an account of their own origins (e.g. religious beliefs) or an account of the role that they play in contemporary society, an approach (whether based on Marxism, sociology of knowledge, or existentialism) which challenges the account of either the origins or the present function of those beliefs is clearly relevant to the assessment of those beliefs," (p. 394)

This is again unclear. Which beliefs are we talking about? If the members M of a religion believe that God exists and He talked to prophet J, the leader of an ancient people P, I haven't proved *all* their beliefs wrong if I prove that in fact J never existed, and that P acquired those beliefs from a neighboring people. I have proved *only* that their belief in the origin of their belief system is mistaken. The other beliefs in that system still stand. And I haven't done it by looking at the background of the current group M, which would be *ad hominem.* I have presumably done it by looking at the ancient people P—which is *not ad hominem,* since the group P stands to the present-day group M in the role of witnesses giving testimony. No exception here.

Class 4: Hinman takes his start now from the Lockean version of *ad hominem* argument. This version involves pressing a man with the consequences of his own principles. I shall talk about this different version in a moment; for now, let us look at Hinman's class of counterexamples.

These involve transcendental arguments (including, I suppose, private language arguments). I waive the discussion as to whether these arguments are sound (i.e. whether the premises involve the verifiability principle, and whether it is defensible). The question is whether such arguments are *ad hominem* and, if so, whether they are therefore fallacious. Hinman believes they are *ad hominem* in nature, but are not fallacious:

Here we have the most forceful version of a Lockean *ad hominem* argument which may be sound. Considered as a parasitism argument, a transcendental argument typically proceeds in the following way. If a person asserts a proposition *p* (often a skeptical claim), one that attempts to show that *p* implies *q*, i.e. the truth of *q* is a necessary condition of asserting that *p* is either true or false; one then tries to show that *q* entails non-*p* … . And as such it is *ad hominem* in a very specific sense: given an original assertion, it attempts to show that this assertion is inconsistent with another proposition whose truth is presupposed necessarily by the one making the original assertion. (p. 343)

Whether transcendental arguments (and private language arguments and transcendental deductions) are sound or not again is a matter of dispute, but in contrast to Hinman, I don't see any *ad hominem* character to them. One's suspicions are aroused when one reads (p. 344), "They are indeed arguments directed toward the man, but what distinguishes them from other types of *ad hominem* arguments is that they claim to be equally valid no matter *which* man they are directed against." This is a curious kind of *ad hominem* attack, indeed.

It seems clear that what we really have in transcendental arguments are arguments of the form:

1. If experience (language, assertion) is possible at all, *p* must be true *(a priori,* necessary).
2. Experience (language, assertion) is possible.

∴ *p* must be true.

which is clearly not *ad hominem,* and the proof of premise 2 involves either asking the skeptic to verify it by examining his own behavior (testimony again), or else pointing out the skeptic's own behavior. This last is not *ad hominem,* since you are proving that something is possible by pointing to at least one case where it happens. The only reason you pick the skeptic and not someone else is that the skeptic may have doubts about the existence of other minds. But (as Hinman himself notes) it doesn't matter who you pick, but only that you prove something is possible by indicating an occurrence of it.

What can be said in general about the Lockean version of pressing someone with the consequences of his/her own beliefs? We must be careful here. If I try to convince you of C by citing P where you believe P, but I don't, I am being illogical. I am persuading you, not by sound argument, but by what I believe to be unsound argument. If, however, I try to persuade you of C by citing P, where you and I both believe P, yet I cannot prove P, then that is different. For, while the best argument is one in which C follows from true premises, in reality the best we can hope for are arguments whose premises are "starting points" for our epistemic community—beliefs that are in our mutual commitment-store (to use Hamblin's phrase). So far as Locke may have had the second situation in mind, it seems to me not *ad hominem* at all.

I wish to thank *The Australasian Journal of Philosophy.*

3

"Are Fallacies Common? A Look at Two Debates"

first appeared in Informal Logic, Vol. VIII, No. 2, Spring 1987, pp. 81–92

The last decade has seen a healthy debate regarding the nature of fallacies. The "standard textbook account" has been criticized extensively, and new theoretical approaches have been tried, centering around the formal theory of dialogues. The debate has taken on new importance since the recent widespread adoption of "critical thinking" requirements at many colleges.

One aspect of the standard textbook account that has drawn considerable criticism is the claim that fallacies are "commonly made" errors in reasoning. Such a claim has struck some scholars as an exaggeration or as perhaps merely a motivational remark to induce the student to study harder. Finocchiaro has put this criticism with special sharpness:

> What is wrong with such accounts of fallacies? One problem concerns the paucity of actual examples, just mentioned. It is in fact puzzling that logic textbooks shouldn't be able to come up with more examples of fallacies actually committed given that fallacies are supposed to be common errors in reasoning. One gets the suspicion that logically incorrect arguments are not that common in practice, that their existence may be largely restricted to logic textbook examples and exercises.[1]

He concludes:

> The conclusion I wish to draw from such "consultations" is not that errors in reasoning are probably not common in real life, but that there probably are no

> common errors in reasoning. That is, logically incorrect arguments may be common, but common types of logically incorrect arguments probably are not.[2]

In this article I wish to give empirical evidence that fallacies are indeed common—where by the term "fallacy" I mean the sort of errors in argumentation labeled in standard logic texts. Whether the standard definitions should be altered or clarified by means of formal dialectic is a question I won't address here.

It would be wise to get clear on what the claim "fallacies are common" really involves. Clearly, nobody means to suggest that fallacies occur commonly in all aspects of our daily lives. Most of the waking hours of most people are spent on entertainment, transportation, recreation and so on. Fallacies aren't common in such activities, for the trivial reason that no argumentation—bad or good—takes place in those activities. If we are to fairly test the claim that fallacies are common, we must focus on contexts of argumentative persuasion.

In the realm of literature, focusing upon contexts of argumentative persuasion generally rules out fiction and a good deal of non-fiction as well. After all, most mainstream newspapers tend to simply describe events, except in the Op/Ed pages. Quite a bit of nonfiction is devoted to simply explaining current developments in, say, science or art.

What then are clear contexts of argumentative persuasion? The reader's list may differ from mine, but I would include: advertisements, editorials, position papers, essays, letters to editor, debates, as well as books and articles that advocate some position. It is those sorts of contexts to which the claim that fallacies are common is meant to apply.

It is easy to get the impression that fallacies are uncommon if one reads scientific or philosophic journals or books. Such literature is by its very nature closely reasoned. Even if fallacies are not commonly present in such writings, that doesn't mean that fallacies are not common; rather, it only shows that careful thinkers can avoid what are otherwise errors in reasoning. Indeed, those of us who teach the standard material hope that eventually those fallacies will become uncommon precisely because people will become more careful thinkers.

But it is equally easy to get the impression that not only are fallacies common, but *non-fallacious* reasoning is *uncommon,* if one reads the tabloids. *The National Enquirer* is the best selling newspaper in the U.S.A., and its numerous clones also sell well. The typical issue of such a tabloid is loaded with fallacies of the traditional sort: ads which appeal to popular sentiment or contain fallacious appeals to authority ("this diet is doctor-tested!"); editorials filled with invective, personal attacks and loaded language; ambiguous headlines intended to make uninteresting stories interesting ("NUN WALKS HUNDREDS OF MILES –TO LOSE WEIGHT!" screams the headline, while the story describes a perfectly banal case of a nun who walks several blocks every evening for exercise, and over the years it adds up to hundreds of miles); ads with key clauses put in fine print ("accent"); and so on.

However, if the claim that fallacies are common is to be fairly tested, we ought to avoid extremes— contexts either especially "clean" or especially "dirty." If the claim that fallacies are common is taken fairly, it clearly is meant to apply to ordinary contexts of argumentative persuasion: opinion editorials in good quality newspapers and newsmagazines; letters to the editor of good quality newspapers, newsmagazines, political opinion journals (such as *National Review, New Republic, Atlantic,* and so on), and other nonfiction magazines (such as *Byte, Car and Driver,* and so on); political debates; position papers; and so on.

I propose to empirically investigate the claim that fallacies as commonly defined are common by selecting a fair context of argumentative persuasion, one that is clearly of influence on the opinions of millions of Americans: political debates. Political debates are quite common in American political life. One thinks immediately of classical debates such as the ones between Lincoln and Douglas, but of course such debates have had even wider impact since being televised (starting with the Nixon/Kennedy debates, then moving on to the Carter/Ford, then Carter/Reagan, then Reagan/Mondale debates). To make this investigation more useful, we will look at two debates, separated widely in time but similar in importance: the third Kennedy/Nixon debate (held on October 13, 1960) and the second Reagan/Mondale debate (held on October 21, 1984). Both debates were very important in the respective elections; indeed, both resulted in turnarounds in the polls for the candidates who eventually won their respective races. In what follows, I will select fallacies failing in certain recurring categories for commentary, rather than reproducing the whole debates. While each debate has between forty and fifty readily identifiable standard fallacies, I have tried to select the most instructive for analysis. If the reader suspects me of having been biased in my selection, I am willing to send him transcripts of both debates with the numerous fallacies indicated.

Fallacies of Ignoring the Issue

In examining the texts of the two debates, one is immediately struck by the large number of times in which the candidates ignore the issue. Some examples:

> **Mr. Nixon**: Now, looking to the U-2 flights, I would like to point out that I have been supporting the President's position throughout. I think the President was

correct in ordering these flights. I think the President was correct, certainly, in his decision to continue the flights while the conference was going on. I noted, for example, in reading a particular discussion that Senator Kennedy had with Dave Garroway shortly after the uh - his statements about regrets, that uh-he made the statement that he felt that these particular flights were ones that shouldn't have occurred right at that time, and the indication was how would Mr. Khrushchev had felt if we had had a flight over the United States while he was visiting here. And the answer, of course, is that Communist espionage goes on all the time. The answer is that the United States can't afford to have an espionage lack—or should I say an intelligence lag—any more than we can afford to have a missile lag.

It is clear from the passage that Kennedy had raised the issue of whether U-2 flights should have been conducted while Khrushchev was visiting here, and Nixon addressed the different issue of whether the US should engage in espionage. I don't think I am being uncharitable in interpreting Nixon's remarks as having evaded the issue; indeed, Kennedy rebutted him shortly after Nixon made his comment:

Mr. Kennedy: Number two, on the question of the U-2 flights. I thought the U-2 flights in May just before the conference was a mistake in timing because of the hazards involved, if the summit conference had any hope for success. I never criticized the U-2 flights in general, however. I never suggested espionage should stop. It still goes on, I would assume, on both sides.

In the example above, the candidate ignored the issue by "setting up a strawman"—that is, distorting his opponent's position. Also common in the debates are cases in which candidates did not answer the questions put to them, but instead raised irrelevant issues or reverted to earlier issues.

Example:

Mr. McGee: Mr. Vice President, some of your early campaign literature said you were making a study to see if new laws were needed to protect the public against excessive use of power by labor unions. Have you decided whether such new laws are needed, and, if so, what would they do?

Mr. Nixon: Mr. McGee, I am planning a speech on that subject next week. Also, so that we can get the opportunity for the questioners to question me, it will be before the next television debate. I will say simply, in advance of it, that I believe that in this area, the laws which should be passed, as far as the big national emergency strikes are concerned, are ones that will give the president more weapons with which to deal with those strikes.

Now, I have a basic disagreement with Senator Kennedy, though, on this point. He has taken the position, when he first indicated in October of last year, that he would even favor compulsory arbitration as one of the weapons the president might have to stop a national emergency strike. I understand in his last speech before the Steelworkers Union, that he changed that position and indicated that he felt that government seizure might be the best way to stop a strike which could not be settled by collective bargaining. I do not believe we should have either compulsory arbitration or seizure. I think the moment that you give to the union, on the one side, and to management, on the other side, the escape hatch of eventually going to government to get it settled, that most of these great strikes will end up being settled by government, and that will be in the end, in my opinion, wage control; it would mean price control—all the things that we do not want. I do believe, however, that we can give to the president of the United States powers, in addition to what he presently has in the fact- finding area, which would enable him to be more effective than we have been in handling these strikes.

Nixon does not answer the question whether he would propose new laws restricting the power of unions, and if so, which ones. He says he will give a speech the next week on the subject, he criticizes Kennedy's position on compulsory arbitration, but aside from saying that the President needs greater powers to deal with "national emergency strikes," he says nothing. Speaking in generalities is one way candidates ignore the specific issue raised by a questioner.

Another example:

Mr. McGee: Senator Kennedy, a moment ago you mentioned tax loopholes. Now your running mate, Senator Lyndon Johnson, is from Texas, an oil-producing state and one that many political leaders feel is in doubt in this election year. And reports from there say that oil men in Texas are seeking assurance from Senator Johnson that the oil depletion allowance will not be cut. The Democratic platform pledges to plug loopholes in the tax laws and refers to inequitable depletion allowance as being conspicuous loopholes. My question is, do you consider the twenty seven and a half percent depletion allowance inequitable, and would you ask that it be cut?

Mr. Kennedy: Mr. McGee, there are about a hundred and four commodities that have some kind of depletion allowance—different kinds of minerals, including oil. I believe all of those should be gone over in detail to make sure that no one is getting a tax break; to make sure that no one is getting away from paying the taxes he ought to pay. That includes oil; it includes all kinds of minerals; it includes everything within the range of taxation. We want to be sure it's fair and equitable. It includes oil abroad. Perhaps that oil abroad should be treated differently than the oil here at home. Now the oil industry

> recently has had hard times. Particularly some of the smaller producers. They're moving about eight or nine days in Texas. But I can assure you that if I'm elected president, the whole spectrum of taxes *will* be gone through carefully, and if there is any inequities in oil or any other commodity, then I would vote to close that loophole. I have voted in the past to reduce the depletion allowance for the largest producers; for those from five million dollars down, to maintain it at twenty-seven and a half percent. I believe we should study this and other allowances; tax expense, dividend expenses and all the rest, and make a determination of how we can stimulate growth; how we can provide the revenues needed to move our country forward.

Note that Kennedy never specifically answered the questions whether the present 27½% depletion allowance is inequitable and whether he would cut it. In many of their other answers, Kennedy and Nixon ascended to generalities.

Ignoring the issue was also a prominent feature of the Reagan/Mondale debate— occurring fifteen times or more. Again, some examples:

> **Question**: Mr. Mondale, two related questions on the crucial issue of Central America. You and the Democratic Party have said that the only policy toward the horrendous civil wars in Central America should be on the economic developments and negotiations with, perhaps, quarantine of Marxist Nicaragua. Do you believe that these answers would in any way solve the bitter conflicts there? Do you really believe that there is no need to resort to force at *all?* Are not these solutions to Central America's gnawing problems simply again too weak and too late?
>
> **Mondale:** I believe that the question oversimplifies the difficulties of what we must do in Central America. Our objectives ought to be to strengthen the democracy, to stop Communist and other extremist influences and stabilize the community in that area.
>
> To do that, we need a three-pronged attack. One is military assistance to our friends who are being pressured. Secondly, a strong and sophisticated economic aid program and human rights program that offers a better life and a sharper alternative to the alternative offered by the totalitarians who oppose us. And finally, a strong diplomatic effort that pursues the possibilities of peace in the area.

The crucial question about whether military force is needed was never specifically addressed. Instead, Mondale spoke in generalities.

> **Question**: Mr. Mondale, if I could broaden the question just a little bit. Since World War II, every conflict that we as Americans have been involved with has

> been in nonconventional or irregular terms and yet we keep fighting in conventional or traditional military terms. The Central American wars are very much in the same pattern as China, as Lebanon, as Iran, as Cuba in the early days. Do you see any possibility that we are going to realize the change in warfare in our time or react to it in those terms?
>
> **Mondale:** We absolutely must, which is why I responded to your first question the way I did. It's much more complex. You must understand the region, you must understand the politics in the area, you must provide a strong alternative, and you must show strength and all at the same time. That's why I object to the covert action in Nicaragua. That's a classic example of a strategy that's embarrassed us, strengthened our opposition and undermined the moral authority of our people and our country in the region.

Again, Mondale ignores the central question (which was how the U.S. should handle unconventional wars) by speaking in glittering generalities.

Example:

> **Question**: Mr. President, I want to ask you about negotiating with friends. You severely criticized President Carter for helping to undermine two friendly dictators who got into trouble with their own people, the Shah of Iran and President Somoza of Nicaragua. Now there are other such leaders heading for trouble, including President Pinochet of Chile and President Marcos of the Philippines. What should you do and what can you do to prevent the Philippines from becoming another Nicaragua?
>
> **Reagan**: Morton, I did criticize the President because of our undercutting of what was a stalwart ally, the Shah of Iran. And I am not at all convinced that he was that far out of line with his people or that they wanted that to happen. The Shah had done our bidding and carried our load in the Middle East for quite some time and I did think that it was a blot on our record that we let him down. Had things gotten better, the Shah, whatever he might have done, was building low-cost housing, had taken land away from the mullahs and was distributing it to the peasants so they could be land-owners, things of that kind. But we turned it over to a maniacal fanatic who has slaughtered thousands and thousands of people calling it executions.
>
> The matter of Somoza, no, I never defended Somoza. And as a matter of fact, the previous Administration stood by and so did I—not that I could have done anything in my position at that time. But for this revolution to take place and the promise of the revolution was democracy, human rights, free labor unions, free press. And then just as Castro had done in Cuba, the Sandinistas ousted the other parties to the revolution. Many of them are now the Contras.

> They exiled some, they jailed some, they murdered some. And they installed a Marxist-Leninist totalitarian Government. And what I have to say about this is, many times— and this has to do with the Philippines also— I know there are things there in the Philippines that do not look good to us from the standpoint right now of democratic rights. But what is the alternative? It is a large Communist movement to take over the Philippines.
>
> They have been our friend for— since their inception as a nation. And I think that we've had enough of a record of letting, under the guise of revolution, someone that we thought was a little more right than we would be, letting that person go and then winding up with totalitarianism pure and simple as the alternative and I think that we're better off, for example, with the Philippines of trying to retain our friendship and help them right the wrongs we see rather than throwing them to the wolves and then facing a Communist power in the Pacific.

Note that Reagan ignores the issue of what he would do to prevent the Philippines from becoming another Nicaragua.

Why do candidates so often ignore the issues raised by the interviewers and the opposing candidates? Here we must remind ourselves that attributing a fallacy to someone is not necessarily to accuse that person of dishonest argumentation. A fallacy is an error in argumentation but not necessarily a dishonest or deliberate one. In a sense, political candidates in a televised debate are prisoners of the format. They cannot say "I don't know, I'll have to think about it" to a new and difficult issue. Nor can they tell an interviewer that his question is hopelessly naive, impertinent, asinine, unfairly specific, or ridiculously broad, for fear of appearing churlish. The fault for such logical lapses may lie not in our politicians but in us, for making up our minds about for whom to vote on the basis of one or two short debate performances.

However, one might argue that political candidates are not completely compelled to ignore the issue when asked a question whose fully detailed answer would take much more than the time allotted. For instance, perhaps the candidates could sketch out a general answer, and then indicate which of the position papers he has issued amplify upon his views. But there are difficulties with such a suggestion. It is hard for candidates to anticipate in advance all the issues upon which questions will be asked, and so it would be hard for them to issue position papers in advance. And any candidate who promises to issue a paper only after the debate is over is likely to appear foolish. But perhaps some other means can be devised to allow candidates to really grapple with complicated issues.

False Cause

In reading the transcripts of the debates, one is struck also by the number of times one candidate A will argue that since bad things happened when the other candidate B (or his party) was in office, B was the cause of those bad things, or that since good things happened while A (or his party) was in office, A was the cause of those good things. Such arguments are fallacies of false cause (specifically *post hoc ergo propter hoc).* Examples:

> **Mr. Nixon**: Yes. As a matter of fact, the statement that Senator Kennedy made was that—to the effect that there were trigger-happy Republicans, that my stand on Quemoy and Matsu was an indication of trigger-happy Republicans.
>
> I resent that comment. I resent it because it's an implication that Republicans have been trigger-happy and, therefore, would lead this nation into war. I would remind Senator Kennedy of the past fifty years. I would ask him to name one Republican president who led this nation into war. There were three Democratic presidents who led us into war. I do not mean by that that one party is a war party and the other party is a peace party. But I do say that any statement to the effect that the Republican party is trigger-happy is belied by the record.

We might interpret this passage charitably by taking Nixon's statement "I do not mean by that that one party is a war party ..." at face value; however, since Republicans such as Ford, Dole, and Bush have made the same point in later debates (that all wars in this century were started under Democratic presidents), I think we may fairly suspect that Nixon was attempting to paint the Democrats as being responsible for wars.

Example:

> **Mr. Nixon**: One last point I should make. The record in handling strikes has been very good during this Administration. We have had less man-hours lost by strikes in these last seven years than we had in the previous seven years, by a great deal. And I only want to say that however good the record is, it's got to be better. Because in this critical period of the sixties we've got to move forward, all Americans must move forward together, and we have to get the greatest cooperation possible between labor and management. We cannot afford stoppages of massive effect on the economy when we're in the terrible competition we're in with the Soviets.

A fair construal of Nixon's remarks is that since fewer man-hours were lost by strikes during the Republican administration, it (and by some further inference, *he)* therefore should be given credit. But any number of other factors may be the cause of reduced strike activity (besides the administration's policies). Indeed, under the American economic system, the President and his administration have little to do with union activities and corporate wage decisions.

Example:

> **Mr. Kennedy**: On the question of the cost of our budget, I have stated that it's my best judgment that our agricultural program will cost a billion and a half, possibly two billion dollars less than the present agricultural program. My judgment is that the program the Vice President put forward, which is an extension of Mr. Benson's program, will cost a billion dollars more than the present program, which costs about six billion dollars a year, the most expensive in history. We've spent more money on agriculture in the last eight years than the hundred years of the Agricultural Department before that.

A fair construal of Kennedy's remarks is that because more money has been spent on Agriculture during the years while the Republicans were in the White House, they must be responsible for that increased spending. But again, other factors (such as Congressional actions) may have been the actual cause of the increase. Indeed, at the federal level, the President does not have the line-item veto: he must either veto the budget as a whole (which can lead to great economic disruptions), or approve it. That limits a President's power to control spending considerably. Moreover (again, in the American system), it is not unusual for one political party to control the White House and the other party the Congress (where spending bills originate). That also dramatically limits a President's power to control spending. So merely pointing out that spending increased under x's administration does not come anywhere near showing that x is responsible for it.

Another case:

> **Mr. Nixon**: I am never satisfied with the economic growth of this country. I'm not satisfied with it even if there were no Communism in the world, but particularly when we're in the kind of a race we're in, we have got to see that America grows just as fast as we can, provided we grow soundly. Because even though we have maintained, as I pointed out in our first debate, the absolute gap over the Soviet Union; even though the growth in this Administration has been twice as much as it was in the Truman Administration; that isn't good enough. Because America must be able to grow enough not only to take care of our needs at home for better education and housing and health —all these things we want.

Nixon asserts that he won't be content with the growth rate achieved under the current Republican administration, even though it is double the rate in the previous (Democratic) administration. It is reasonable to view this passage as containing the enthymeme that because under the Republican administration the growth rate was double what it was under the Democratic one, that the Republicans are responsible for the higher rate. Later in the debate, Nixon reiterated the argument:

> **Mr. Nixon**: American has not been standing still. Let's get that straight. Anybody who says American's been standing still for the last seven and a half years hasn't been traveling around America. He's been traveling in some other country. We have been moving. We have been moving much faster than we did in the Truman years. But we can and must move faster, and that's why I stand so strongly for programs that will move America forward in the sixties, move her forward so that we can stay ahead of the Soviet Union and win the battle for freedom and peace.

Consider next an example from the Reagan/Mondale debate:

> **Mr. Mondale**: Where I part with the President Is that despite all of those differences, we must, as past Presidents before this one have done, meet on the common ground of survival. And that's where the President has opposed practically every arms control agreement, by every President of both political parties, since the bomb went off. And he now completes this term with no progress toward arms control at all, but with a very dangerous arms race underway instead. There are now over 2,000 more warheads pointed at us today than there were when he was sworn in, and that does not strengthen us.

Mondale seems to be arguing that since there had been no arms control agreements under Reagan, Reagan must be the cause. But other causes are possible; for instance, the instability in the Soviet government (several Soviet Premiers died during Reagan's first term). Perhaps we should be very charitable and say that Reagan's hawkish statements and affiliations are well-known, and that Mondale is rightly appealing to background knowledge. But even granting that that is truly uncontested background knowledge (which I suspect Reagan and his supporters would vigorously deny), it still does not come near proving that Reagan is responsible for the lack of agreements on arms. Some Republicans have signed arms agreements (e.g., Nixon), and some Democrats have failed (e.g., Kennedy, who got a partial test ban but no arms limitations treaty).

At the very least, Mondale needed to point to specific proposals made in good faith by the Soviets which Reagan refused to consider, or specific occasions where the Soviets were willing to negotiate and Reagan wasn't. Perhaps Mondale could have done so, but what he said did not constitute proof, but only a false cause fallacy.

In the following exchange, several instances of false cause were committed.

> **Mondale**: One of the biggest problems today is that the countries to our south are so desperately poor that these people who will almost lose their lives if they don't come north, come north despite all the risks. And if we're going to find a permanent, fundamental answer to this, it goes to American economic and trade policies that permit these nations to have a chance to get on their own two feet and to get prosperity so that they can have jobs for themselves and their people.
>
> And that's why this enormous national debt, engineered by this Administration, is harming these countries and fueling this immigration. These high interest rates, real rates that have doubled under the Administration, have had the same effect on Mexico and so on, and the cost of repaying those debts is so enormous that it results in massive unemployment, hardship and heartache. And that drives our friends to the north--to the south—up into our region, and the need to end those deficits as well.
>
> **Moderator**: Mr. President, your rebuttal.
>
> **Reagan**: Well, my rebuttal is I've heard the national debt blamed for a lot of things, but not for illegal immigration across our border, and it has nothing to do with it. But with regard to these high interest rates, too, at least give us the recognition of the fact that when you left office, Mr. Mondale, they were 22%, the prime rate; it's now 12%, and I predict it'll be coming down a little more shortly. So we're trying to undo some of the things that your Administration did.

The national debt grew under Reagan, so Reagan caused it (and that, curiously, caused the illegal immigration from Mexico!), to which Reagan responds by saying that the interest rates were high under Carter, so Carter caused that problem (and so, curiously, that Mondale is to blame).

Again, we must be fair and realize that giving a candidate one minute to explain what causes (say) high interest rates is not a way to encourage in-depth causal analysis.

Ad populum

Quite unsurprising is the large number of appeals to patriotism, "us-versus-them" emotions and so on. These sorts of appeals are apparent in many of the sample passages cited earlier (especially in the passages appealing to our collective fear of the Soviets). Some additional examples:

> **Mr. Nixon**: Now what do the Chinese Communists want? They don't want just Quemoy and Matsu; they don't want just Formosa; they want the world. And the

> question is if you surrender or indicate in advance that you're not going to defend any part of the free world, and you figure that's going to satisfy them, it doesn't satisfy them. It only whets their appetite; and then the question comes, when do you stop them? I've often heard President Eisenhower in discussing this question, make the statement that if we once start the process of indicating that this point or that point is not the place to stop those who threaten the peace and freedom of the world, where do we stop them? And I say that those of us who stand against surrender of territory this or any others – in the face of blackmail, in the face of force by the Communists are standing for the course that will lead to peace.

In this passage, Nixon associates himself with the popular President Eisenhower, and places himself in the class of those who oppose Communistic blackmail, who favor peace – in short, places himself on the side of the angels (and Ike!). There is also arguably a slippery-slope fallacy lurking in the passage: if we do not defend Quemoy and Matsu, we don't know where they will stop.

Example:

> **Mr. Nixon**: Beyond that, as far as the gold supply is concerned, and as far as the movement of gold is concerned, we have to bear in mind that we must get more help from our allies abroad in this great venture in which all free men are involved of winning the battle for freedom.

Again, grandiose appeals to freedom used to (somehow) buttress a position.

Example:

> **Mr. Nixon**: Of course, both Senator Kennedy and I have felt Mr. Truman's ire; and consequently, I think he can speak with some feeling on this subject. I just do want to say one thing, however. We all have tempers; I have one; I'm sure Senator Kennedy has one. But when a man's president of the United States, or a former president, he has an obligation not to lose his temper in public. One thing I've noted as I've traveled around the country are the tremendous number of children who come out to see the presidential candidates. I see mothers holding their babies up, so that they can see a man who might be president of the United States. I know Senator Kennedy sees them, too. It makes you realize that whoever is president is going to be a man that all the children of America will either look up to, or will look down to. And I can only say that I'm very proud that President Eisenhower restored dignity and decency and, frankly, good language to the conduct of the presidency of the United States. And I only hope that, should I win this election, that I could approach President Eisenhower in maintaining the dignity of the office; in seeing to it that whenever any mother or father talks to his child, he can look at the man in the White House and, whatever he may think of his policies, he will say: "Well, there is a man who maintains the kind of standards personally that I would want my child to follow."

Nixon paints a picture of mothers holding babies looking up to a clean role-model, the immensely popular Eisenhower, and clearly hopes the audience will transfer those warm respectful feelings to him.

The closing statements in the Reagan/Mondale debate also brought out some appeal to the crowd. Two short examples:

> **Mr. Mondale**: I want this nation to protect its air, its water, its land and its public health. America is not temporary. We're forever. And as Americans, our generation should protect this wonderful land for our children. I want a nation of fairness, where no one is denied the fullness of life or discriminated against, and we deal compassionately with those in our midst who are in trouble. And above all, I want a nation that's strong. Since we debated two weeks ago, the United States and the Soviet Union have built 100 more warheads, enough to kill millions of Americans and millions of Soviet citizens.

> **Mr. Reagan**: We shouldn't be dwelling on the past or even the present. The meaning of this election is the future, and whether we're going to grow and provide the jobs and the opportunities for all Americans and that they need. Several years ago I was given an assignment to write a letter. It was to go into a time capsule and would be read in 100 years when that time capsule was opened. I remember driving down the California coast one day. My mind was full of what I was going to put in that letter about the problems and the issues that confront us in our time and what we did about them, but I couldn't completely neglect the beauty around me – the Pacific out there on one side of the highway shining in the sunlight, the mountains of the coast range rising on the other side, and I found myself wondering what it would be like for someone, wondering if someone 100 years from now would be driving down that highway and if they would see the same thing.

The reader should not interpret my remarks as saying that only deceitful politicians would stoop to *ad populum* appeals. No, even very decent politicians engage in such rhetoric. But *ad populum* appeals should be recognized as such, even if we understand their usage in contexts such as the one under consideration.

Ad hominem Attacks

Less frequent in the two debates are overt *ad hominem* attacks. I found this surprising, given how frequently personal attacks occur in ordinary arguments and letters to the editor of magazines and newspapers. Perhaps candidates in a nationally televised debate are reluctant to attack the other too blatantly, lest the debate turn into a mudslinging contest. But sly digs are managed:

> **Mr. Kennedy**: Mr. Griffin, I believe, who is the head of the Klan, who lives in Tampa, Florida, indicated in a statement, I think, two or three weeks ago that he was not going to vote for me, and that he was going to vote for Mr. Nixon. I do not suggest in any way, nor have I ever, that that indicates that Mr. Nixon has the slightest sympathy, involvement, or in any way imply any inference in regard to the Ku Klux Klan. That's absurd. I don't suggest that. I don't support it. I would disagree with it.

Kennedy protests too much – he himself brings up the fact that the head of the KKK came out in support of Nixon, and it is not uncharitable, I think, to believe that Kennedy was suggesting that since the KKK supported Nixon, Nixon was suspect (guilt by association).

Another case:

> **Mr. Nixon**: [responding to Kennedy's point that the U.S. had slipped in prestige, as evidenced by Gallup polls taken in other countries, and U.N. votes]: Well, I would say first of all that Senator Kennedy's statement that he's just made is not going to help our Gallup Polls abroad and it isn't going to help our prestige either. Let's look at the other side of the coin. Let's look at the vote on the Congo, the vote was seventy to nothing against the Soviet Union. Let's look at the situation with regard to economic growth as it really is. We find that the Soviet Union is a very primitive economy. Its growth rate is not what counts; it's whether it is catching up with us and it is catching up with us. We're well ahead and we can stay ahead, provided we have confidence in America and don't run her down in order to build her up. We could look also at other items which Senator Kennedy has named, but I will only conclude by saying this: in this whole matter of prestige, in the final analysis, it's whether you stand for what's right. And getting back to this matter that we discussed at the outset, the matter of Quemoy and Matsu. I can think of nothing that will be a greater blow to the prestige of the United States among the free nations in Asia than for us to take Senator Kennedy's advice to go against what a majority of the members of the Senate, both Democrat and Republican, did— said in 1955, and to say in advance we will surrender an area to the Communists.

Nixon insinuates that Kennedy's point is suspect because it hurts our reputation, and that those who want America held in high regard should avoid such comments.

Other standard fallacies are discernible in the two debates, including loaded questions (by the questioners), appeals to authority, false analogies, slippery slope arguments, and hedging. I found no cases of composition or division, and only one rather unclear case of begging the question. Some of the candidates—

Kennedy and Reagan, in particular —deflected questions by humorous diversion. It is plausible to suggest that those candidates who are by nature witty will utilize their wit to out of answering questions they don't wish to answer (for whatever reasons).

Example:

> **Mr. Von Fremd**: Senator Kennedy, I'd like to shift the conversation, if I may, to a domestic political argument. The chairman of the Republican National Committee, Senator Thurston Morton, declared earlier this week that you owed Vice President Nixon and the Republican Party a public apology for some strong charges made by former President Harry Truman, who bluntly suggested where the Vice President and the Republican party could go. Do you feel that you owe the Vice President any apology?
>
> **Mr. Kennedy**: Well, I must say that Mr. Truman has his methods of expressing things; he's been in politics for fifty years; he's been President of the United States. They are not my style. But I really don't think there's anything that I could say to President Truman that's going to cause him, at the age of seventy-six, to change his particular speaking manner. Perhaps Mrs. Truman can, but I don't think I can. I'll just have to tell Mr. Morton that. If you'd pass that message on to him.

Another example:

> **Moderator**: Mr. Trewhitt, your question to President Reagan?
>
> **Question**: Mr. President, I want to raise an issue that I think has been lurking out there for two or three weeks, and cast it specifically in national security terms. You already are the oldest President in history, and some of your staff says you were tired after your most recent encounter with Mr. Mondale. I recall, yes, that President Kennedy, who had to go for days on end with very little sleep during the Cuba missile crisis. Is there any doubt in your mind that you would be able to function in such circumstances?
>
> **Reagan**: Not at all, Mr. Trewhitt – and I want you to know that also I will not make age an issue of this campaign. I am not going to exploit for political purposes my opponent's youth and inexperience. If I still have time, I might add, Mr. Trewhitt, I might add that it was Seneca or it was Cicero, I don't know which, that said if it was not for the elders correcting the mistakes of the young, there would be no state.
>
> **Question**: Mr. President, I'd like to head for the fence and try to catch that one before it goes over but – without going to another question.

This was perhaps the most famous moment in the Reagan/Mondale debate. The President turned aside Trewhitt's question with a quip which made everyone including Mondale laugh, and did much to defuse the "age issue." (The questioner, Mr. Trewhitt, realized that the President had scored a home run on *that* pitch!)

In both the debates examined, roughly forty to fifty standard fallacies are discernible, without, it must be admitted, being overly charitable. The numbers are reduced if we bend over backwards to be charitable, but the clear fallacies are still sufficiently numerous to justify the claim that the standard fallacies discussed in "old time" logic texts are indeed common. A student who read Whately's *Elements of Logic* would have no trouble applying the definitions of fallacies contained therein to the debates we have been examining.

Not only do fallacies as defined in standard texts seem common, but it seems likely that we can empirically correlate type of fallacy with type of argumentative context. Political debates seem to call forth ignoring the issue and *ad populum* arguments. Sales pitches seem to involve *ad populum* and special pleading. However, much more *empirical* work needs to be done to say for sure.

It is hard enough to teach standard introductory logic well when one has confidence that what he or she teaches truly edifies the student. Let us not lose confidence by supposing that traditional categories of logical error, seemingly discerned by scholars of many different cultures over millennia, are in fact an illusion.

Notes

1. Maurice Finocchiaro "Fallacies and the Evaluation of Reasoning," *American Philosophical Quarterly*, Vol. 18, No.1, Jan. 1981, p. 14.
2. *Ibid.* p. 15.

Permission to reprint courtesy of *Informal Logic*.
I wish to thank the journal.

4

My review of *Logical Dialogue-Games and Fallacies*

(by Douglas Walton, Lanham, MD: University Press of America, 1984) first appeared in Philosophia, Vol. 17, No. 1, January 1987, pp. 97–99

Since the appearance of Hamblin's Fallacies in 1970, considerable work has been done in the area of formal dialectic (or logical dialog games). Generally, research into the formal theory of dialogs has been motivated by the desire to develop a better tool than standard FOL (first order logic) for explicating informal fallacies. Douglas Walton has written a considerable amount on both fallacies and dialog games, and thus one would expect his recent book, *Logical Dialogue-Games and Fallacies* to shed new light upon these issues. The result, however, is not fully satisfactory.

Walton begins by reviewing, the standard informal fallacies (*ad hominem*, begging the question, *ad ignorantiam*, irrelevant conclusion, complex question, emotional appeals and straw man arguments). He indicates some of the problems with the use of traditional symbolic logic to explicate these informal fallacies. For instance, what sort of failure of argument (as usually defined in FOL texts) is involved in an *ad baculum* argument? If a mugger says:

(1) If you don't give me your wallet, I'll shoot you.
(2) You don't want to be shot.

∴ You ought to give me your wallet.

is he giving a good argument (if not valid in the deductive sense, then perhaps in the sense of a practical syllogism)? If not, then what makes it logically bad? The sorts of difficulties Walton discusses will be familiar to any instructor who has tried to unify FOL and informal fallacies in the same course.

Walton then reviews the dialog models most prevalent in the literature. He discusses models of dialogs put forward by Hamblin, Mackenzie, Hintikka and Rescher. I found this to be the most valuable section of the book, because Walton lays out the models clearly, and contrasts them by looking at sample dialogs. He gives good explanations of dialog strategy and the use of graph theory to represent dialogs. The book also has a good bibliography which focuses on research on formal dialectic done over the last fifteen years.

Walton then moves on to apply dialog games to the explication of informal fallacies. This of course is what the reader is waiting for, but the results are disappointing. For instance, arguments from expert testimony are covered. These methods involve assigning probability weights to the experts, and selecting from their statements that maximally consistent subset which maximizes probability. This method, while interesting, was explored years ago by Rescher (in his *Plausible Reasoning*), and doesn't seem to have much to do with formal dialectic.

Even where the dialog games are brought to bear on informal fallacies, we don't see to get much out of the exercise. For example, consider Walton's treatment of the *tu quoque* form of the *ad hominem* argument. Most traditional textbooks would regard a son who dismissed his father's advice to quit smoking on the basis of the fact that his father still smokes as having committed a fallacy. But Walton suggests we view the son as accusing the father of "positional inconsistency," and such *ad hominem* refutations can be a correct mode of argument if one's opponent does have a positional inconsistency. (The son would be committing a fallacy only if his accusation of positional inconsistency is false or if he draws the wrong conclusion from it.) And different dialog games have different things to say about how positional inconsistencies are handled: some models view inconsistency as entailing the immediate loss of the dialog game, others as merely requiring the player to resolve the inconsistency in his position.

But the formal dialectic/dialog games tell us little of substance about *ad hominem* arguments, especially regarding the crucial issue in *tu quoque*: is it inconsistent for a man to say smoking is wrong and yet himself smoke? Not in the sense of logical inconsistency: the statements "I smoke" and "I believe smoking is bad" can certainly be both true at the same time. And even if a person's belief system is shown by the attacker to be inconsistent, does that make the *tu quoque* argument acceptable? If the son proves that the father's belief system is inconsistent, would it not be shifting the burden of proof to require the father to embark on the task of straightening out his belief system?

Similarly, when we apply dialog game theory to the fallacy of arguing in a circle, we don't get a particularly enlightening explanation:

> Begging the question is similarly harmless, and seems equally silly as a strategic sequence of play in dialogue. If my thesis to be proved is T, then since the game is a disputation, you will not be strategically inclined to accept T, or any statement that directly implies T. Therefore if I ask you to accept T by a rule of the game, you are hardly likely to acquiesce. Assuming you are even moderately experienced or knowledgeable in playing the game, my moves will almost certainly be wasted in such an obtuse ploy.
>
> We concluded then, somewhat paradoxically … that neither arguing in a circle nor begging the question are fallacies. (p. 287)

But people do in fact succeed in getting others to accept propositions by circular arguments or even simple repetition—as Goebbels showed only too well. When the ploy succeeds, we still want to say that a fallacy was committed (by the arguer, not the listener).

So far formal dialectic has not lived up to its promise as a tool for explicating the traditional informal fallacies. Why that is, I cannot say. But we ought not to conclude that formal dialectic is useless. Besides being interesting from the purely mathematical point of view, formal dialectic is potentially useful in analyzing the logic of scientific discovery, and also in artificial intelligence, specifically in the development of expert systems for scientific research.

Permission to reprint courtesy of Springer. I wish to thank the journal *Philosophia* as well.

5

"The Nature of the Argumentum *Ad Baculum*"

first appeared in Philosophia, Vol. 17, No. 4, December 1987, pp. 491–499

Introductory logic students are rightly puzzled by the explanations of the *argumentum ad baculum* they meet in many logic texts. They are told "The *argumentum ad baculum* is the fallacy committed when one appeals to force or the threat of force to cause acceptance of a conclusion", and that "the use or threat of 'strong-arm' methods to coerce political opponents provide contemporary examples of this fallacy."[1] The student is often given examples of this sort:

> I have exhausted my patience with you, Mr. Findley. I have done all I can to persuade you that selling the plans for the bombsight to my government would be the right thing for you to do. I'm afraid you now leave me no choice. Let me tell you this, if you do not give us the plans, your crippled wife, you blind daughter, and your poor bedridden mother will be—shall we say—sent to happier place. Now what do you say, American pig?[2]

But such explanations (and examples) are puzzling. How can physical force or the threat thereof be an argument? What are the premises? And if an argument, why a fallacy? If someone "argues" that I should turn over the plans to a bombsight or else he will kill my family, why would it be illogical for me to do so?

In this paper I will defend the view that there is indeed a fallacy *argumentum ad baculum*, but that its nature has been misunderstood. It has been misunderstood because people have focused upon what I shall call direct threats rather than indirect scare tactics. I want to clarify the nature of this fallacy, as I believe it is more prevalent and more insidious than most logicians suspect.

I will begin by reviewing a few basic concepts. None of the definitions I give are very novel or controversial; they are all straight out of mundane logic texts.

An **argument** is a set of premises together with a conclusion. A **fallacy** is just a logically flawed argument. Any argument is either logically good or else it is fallacious. (By "logically good" I mean either deductively valid or inductively strong. If the reader wishes to add a third type of evidential relation, such as "retroductive-plausibility" he is free to do so.)

Arguments are used to do various things. The paradigm use of an argument is to persuade the listener that the conclusion is true. But one can use an argument to explain why a certain conclusion is true (where the listeners are antecedently convinced that the conclusion is true). One can use an argument to joke, as Lewis Carroll was wont to do. And one can use an argument to cause the listener to act.

Of special importance for our discussion is the so-called practical syllogism, which can be roughly formulated as follows:

(1) Act A would accomplish X's goal better than the alternatives open to X.
(2) X wants to accomplish his goal.

∴X ought to do A.

There is some controversy about the logical status of the practical syllogism. In order to avoid begging some important questions, I will assume that the practical syllogism is logically good. But I will insist that we recognize how uninformative this argument is. The "ought" in the conclusion is simply the prudential "ought," not "ought" in any moral sense. (You morally ought not to murder people even if it benefits you.) With practical syllogism, one should pay close attention to detect any equivocation in the use of the word "ought".

Quite often, life is logically sweet: we attempt to cause action by persuading with a logically good argument. But also quite often, we use non-arguments to cause action. By "non-argument" I mean anything from pushes and shoves to shouts to statements. For example, I may stop my child from reaching for an electric cord by pulling her away from it, or by shouting "No!" at the top of my lungs, or by making the statement that electrical current can hurt her.

Using a non-argument to cause (or stop) action is good or bad depending upon motives and circumstances. I don't want to spend more time on ethical issues than is necessary; however, clarity about these matters will prove useful in what follows.

Using a non-argument is morally justified only if certain obvious conditions are met. First, the harm done must be commensurate with the good which results from the action. Thus, a slap may be justified to stop my child from swallowing a tack, but striking her with a stick wouldn't be. Second, my motive must be to help her, not hurt her. Third, there must be no less harmful device which can be employed to equal effect. Slapping my child to get her to not swallow the tack would be unjustified if I could stop her action by simply shouting.

That third condition has an important consequence. In most cases, if a logically good argument can be used instead of a non-argument to cause an action, then the argument should be used instead. When logic is as effective as non-logical devices such as physical coercion, logic should be employed. This seems clear, at least if we assume that other people are rational agents, whose actions should grow out of their own free deliberations as opposed to external compulsion or manipulation. Such an assumption seems part of the whole idea of treating others as ends rather than means. Of course, the key clause in the claim "if logic is as effective as non-logical devices in a given situation, then logic should be employed" is the antecedent. If danger is imminent, we may not have time to argue, so arguing may not be as effective as (say) physical intervention. For example, it would be rather silly to try to argue the merits of stepping out of the roadway to a man who is two seconds away from being run over by a truck. And, of course, on many occasions the agent involved is not fully rational, and argument may not be very effective. This, I take it, is why children are ordered about so much. But the general point still holds: if logical persuasion is as efficacious as anything else in a given situation, if should be used.

Having thus become clear on the use of non-arguments to cause action, we can be equally clear about using fallacies to cause action. There are occasions when the use of fallacies is justified, but those are occasions when the harm is commensurate with the goodness of the action caused, when the arguer is trying to help rather than hurt the listener, and where there is no other logical way to get the job done.

Let us make one last preliminary point. A fallacy is just an illogical argument. But as a matter of pragmatics, we usually add the condition that there be something persuasive or plausible about the fallacy. Since some precision will be required in what follows, however, I will mean by "fallacy" only an illogical argument, a fallacy is persuasive to X if it gets X to believe the conclusion. By my definition, very likely most fallacies are unpersuasive.

Let us now turn to the topic at hand. The usual definition of the *argumentum ad baculum* is that it is committed when the arguer uses threats to get his point accepted. Let's consider some candidates for this fallacy.

(a) Give me your money or I will blow your head off.
(b) I'm sure that you'll agree that our bill deserves your support, Senator Jason. Don't forget that our organization has over one million members, all of whom vote the way we tell them to.
(c) Do you want to die a horribly painful death? There is no more painful death than Beriberi, where your gums rot and your bones crumble, which you can only scream and scream again in desperate pain. This disease is caused by vitamin deficiency. Protect yourself. Buy these vitamin supplements.

In example (a), it isn't clear that there is even an argument given at all. Probably the most accurate way to represent the situation is as a non-argument (the gun, to which the mugger's statement draws your attention) is used—quite effectively—to cause an action.

Still, we might say the mugger has an argument, something like:

(1) If you don't give me your money, I will blow your head off.
(2) You don't want your head to be perforated by a bullet.

∴ You ought to give me your money.

This argument is logically acceptable, if we avoid equivocation and view the "ought" as purely prudential. The mugger is not arguing that your act of surrendering your wallet would be somehow morally correct, only that it would be prudent.

In the case of a direct threat like (a), either there is no argument involved or else the argument is logically good. Either way, no fallacy is committed. So no *argumentum ad baculum* is committed.

Now look at (b). One way to view this passage is to view the lobbyist as merely a polite mugger, and accordingly either view him as using a non-argument or else a straightforward practical syllogism. But a second way to view the passage is to view it as expressing the argument:

(1) Our members number a million.
(2) They vote as we tell them to.
(3) We support this bill.

∴ This bill is meritorious.

The difference here is that instead of the conclusion being (as in the practical syllogism) "You ought to vote for this bill", the conclusion is a statement to the effect that the bill is a good one. What is odd about that second construal of the argument? Simple: it is such an obvious *non-sequitur*, such a howler, that nobody could be persuaded by it. The support of a lobby is simply no evidence at all that the bill supported is a good one.

The upshot of our examination of (a) and (b) is that direct threats may not be fallacies at all (since they are often either non-arguments or practical syllogisms about how the listener should act), and to the extent they can be viewed as fallacies, they are utterly unpersuasive.

But the writers of logic texts only deal with fallacies which are persuasive—so should we not just drop *argumentum ad baculum* entirely?

Let us hold off drawing such a conclusion until we examine example (c). The argument here is curious. There seems to be a practical syllogism involved:

(1) You are in danger of acute vitamin deficiency.
(2) Taking vitamins is the best way to prevent acute vitamin deficiency.
(3) Acute vitamin deficiency causes a horrible death.
(4) You don't want to die horribly.

∴ You ought to buy vitamins.

This argument is quite different from (a) and (b). Those other arguments involve direct threats, whereas (c) involves only an indirect threat. A **direct threat** is one in which the person articulating the threat would be involved in carrying it out if it is indeed carried out. An **indirect threat** is one in which the person who articulates the threat would not be involved in carrying it out if it is indeed carried out.

The logic of the above argument is acceptable, and premises (3) and (4) are clearly true. But where do premises (1) and (2) come from? Why accept them? The threat here is indirect, i.e., the listener's refusal to buy the vitamins will not cause the seller to cause him (the listener) to have such a deficiency. And in reality, very few Americans are in danger of acute vitamin shortage, because whatever else is wrong with the American diet, vitamin shortage is not a problem. Here is where the fallacy comes in: scare tactics (the loaded language) are used to incline the listener to accept the dubious premises (1) and (2).

That the scare tactics are essential can be seen by comparing (c) with this example:

(d) Studies have shown that 90% of all Americans have acute vitamin deficiency, in spite of an adequate diet. Acute vitamin deficiency can lead to terrible diseases, and vitamin supplements can cure that deficiency. So you ought to buy some supplements.

In (d), actual, genuine evidence (which is, of course, factually false) is presented to show that the threat of vitamin deficiency really is a threat to the listener. In (c), only scare tactics are used.

These examples suggest a better definition of *argumentum ad baculum*. All the examples involve threats. But in (a) and (b), the threats are direct—the arguer directly causes the threat to apply to the listener. And in (d), evidence is presented which shows that the threat does indeed threaten the listener. In (c), which alone seems clearly a persuasive fallacy of *ad baculum* reasoning, the threat is based solely on scare tactics. Thus we might try this definition: an *argumentum ad baculum* is an argument in which the arguer attempts to get his point accepted on the basis of scare tactics. Scare tactics are statements or other devices (such as verbal imagery, sounds or pictures) which make the listener feel threatened, but which don't actually constitute evidence that he (the listener) is in fact threatened to any great degree.

Let's consider an actual case, and see if our analysis helps clarify things. There is a movie (produced in England) which is intended to convince people to not smoke cigarettes. Perhaps you have seen this movie—it is remarkably powerful. It has pictures of and interviews with people dying of lung cancer, mainly cowboys, in an ironic counterpoint to those Marlboro ads which pictured handsome cowboys smoking. So, for instance, you see one poor fellow riding the range with oxygen bottles strapped inside his saddlebags and the tube up his nose.

I take this case as significant, and so does the American tobacco industry, which has protested vociferously against attempts to get this movie shown on the major American networks. What are we to make of this case? I will consider two questions: first, does it involve a fallacy; and second, if so, is it justified in doing so?

As regards the first question, the answer is clear on my principles. The argument presented in opposition to smoking is:

(1) If you smoke, you run a dangerously high risk of lung cancer.
(2) Lung cancer is a horrible way to die.
(3) You don't want to die horribly.

∴ You ought not to smoke.

But insofar as most of the scenes are of the misery of lung cancer, either we view the thrust of the movie as ignoring the issue (arguing the unquestioned premises (2) and (3)), or else—more likely—trying to prove the key premise (1) by scare tactics.

Sound arguments against smoking can be formulated, of course, but their formulation requires rather subtle decision theoretic analyses.[3] The bare statistical facts alone are not compelling:

Percentage of American Men Aged 35 expected to Die Before Age 65	
Nonsmokers	23%
Cigar/pipe Smokers	25%
Cigarette Smokers	
Less than 1/2 pack per day	27%
1/2 to 1 pack per day	34%
1 to 2 packs per day	38%
2 or more packs per day	41%

From these facts alone, the average person might well conclude that cutting down on his cigarette usage or maybe switching to cigars is the appropriate action to take.

Indeed, the failure of the "dry facts" to persuade most smokers to quit is what inclines some groups to favor the use of scare tactics. Is the use of *ad baculum* argumentation to get people to "kick the habit" justified?

There is no question that those who use *ad baculum* arguments to persuade smokers to quit intend to help rather than harm the smokers of the world, but it is still an open question whether or not the rational case against smoking can be made more effectively than it has heretofore. Unless we are prepared to assert that smokers are such hopeless nicotine addicts that they are not rational agents, it seems that continued attempts at rational *persuasion* are to be preferred over scare tactics.

Moreover, it is also unclear whether—even granting that rational argumentation has been shown not to work against smoking—the harm caused by *ad baculum* tactics is proportionate to the good produced. Clearly, deaths due to lung cancer and other smoking-related ailments are a tremendous evil. But there are several evils attendant upon the use of scare tactics in lieu of facts. First, of course, is the fear produced in the people subjected to such tactics. This is not inconsiderable. We are daily bombarded by warnings against salt, cholesterol, sugar, alcohol, and low fiber in the diet. People are now quite worried that what they eat is killing them and that fear is quite inordinate. Also to be figured in is the loss of confidence in the government and/or the news media experienced by people subjected to such scare campaign. When emotional appeals are substituted for rational arguments—even in a worthy cause—the level of public dialog is lowered.

Even more troublesome is the possibility that those who employ scare tactics in a good cause may get used to such tactics, and may later use them in less worthy or even bad causes. This is a danger especially to modern democracies, in which the daily lives of citizens are affected as much or more by bureaucratic decisions as by the decisions of elected representatives. To use scare tactics is to manipulate rather than persuade is a common tactic of bureaucrats, and when bureaucrats get used to manipulation, they may well keep it up in those situations in which the reason they can't logically persuade the public is not because the public is less than rational (say, because nicotine addiction has dulled the senses), but rather because the evidence is not compelling.

Examples are depressingly common. Foreign policy decisions are made behind close doors, and then "justified" by scare tactics ("if we don't send arms to Nicaragua, the communists will soon be at our border!" cry the conservative policy makers; "if we send arms to Nicaragua, we will be in another Vietnam!" cry the liberal policy makers.) Domestic policy is also set bureaucratically and justified by scare tactics. For example, in the U.S. today, there is a governmental campaign to get people to obey the 55 MPH speed limit. The 55 MPH law was passed a decade ago as a measure to lower gasoline usage during the energy crisis. The public, through their representatives, voted the law in. However, long after the energy crisis ended, the Department of Transportation has pushed to keep the law enforced, and has put messages in all the media to the effect that the 55 MPH limit saves lives. Their messages invariably show horrible automobile accidents and other such frightening scenes. Yet the statistical evidence for the claim that the lower speed limit does indeed save lives is absolutely insufficient. The scare tactics are used precisely because the evidence is lacking for a policy the bureaucrats wish to keep in place for antique reasons (i.e., simple entrenchment of a policy).

I have argued that the real nature of *ad baculum* arguments lies not in the realty of direct threat, but rather indirect scare tactics. The possibility (by no means a fact) that there may be situations in which scare tactics are morally justifiable does not make those tactics less fallacious.

Notes

1. Copi, Irving *Introduction to Logic* (7th Ed.) NY: MacMillan 1986, p. 91.
2. Munson, Ronald *The Way of Words: An Informal Logic* Boston: Houghton Mifflin Company, 1976, p. 270.
3. See for example, Richard Jeffrey, *The Logic of Decision (2nd Ed.)* Chicago: University of Chicago Press, 1983, pp. 11–12, 21–22, 42–44. The facts cited are taken from page 11.

Permission to reprint courtesy of Springer. I wish to thank the journal *Philosophia* as well.

6

My review of: *Logic: A Computer Approach*

(by Morton Schagrin, Randall Dipert, and William Rapaport, NY: McGraw-Hill 1985) appeared in Philosophia Vol. 17, No. 4 December 1987, pp. 557–558

It is amazing that virtually all logic texts ignore computer applications of FOL (first order logic). It is amazing, given the historic linkage between FOL and computer science, and given the continuing importance of mathematical logic in AI and other areas of Computer Science. Of course, there is BERTIE (and its descendants), a large CAI (computer assisted instruction) logic-proof construction software package that some universities have installed on their mainframes. But as yet the computer revolution has not greatly affected the teaching of logic, nor is it in evidence in most logic texts.

Messrs. Schagrin, Dipert and Rapaport have sought to correct things with their recent book *Logic: A Computer Approach*. They attempt to teach the basics of symbolic logic (i.e., sentential and quantificational calculus) by discussing algorithms to carry out various logical tasks (checking well-formedness, generating truth tables, checking natural deduction derivations, etc.). Most of those algorithms are standard in the literature, but it is very nice to see them drawn together in one text.

The authors have given us a text with a number of merits. The book is succinct, with good discussions of the history of attempts to mechanize reasoning, of Wang's algorithm, and sub-proof construction (pp. 168ff.). The exercises are numerous and good, as are the suggestions for implementing the various algorithms. Moreover, the appendices (one on switching theory, the other on Turing machines) are very appropriate.

However, the drawbacks of this text are numerous, at least from the perspective of the person who teaches FOL with a natural language orientation. For one thing, fully parenthesized notation is used throughout the book, whereas some informal rules regarding dropping parentheses could easily have been discussed and adopted. Also, some of the book's stylistic conventions are pedagogically cumbersome. For example, boldface letters are used as variables, which are difficult to write on the blackboard and too easily confused with constants. Again, the numerals '0' and '1' are used as truth values, which are mathematically nice but is too far divorced from natural language.

More troublesome is the short shrift given to topics so important in a first course in logic. As much time is spent on flowcharts as is spent on models. Worse yet, only 50 of the 340 pages are devoted to quantificational logic!

Even from the point of view of computer science this text under review has drawbacks. The algorithms are in many cases very sketchily put (see, for example, p. 139), making implementation rather difficult for the average student. The algorithms given are almost all unstructured, with GOTO's and multiple halts everywhere. Amazingly, none of the algorithms are recursive—very unfortunate, given the role of recursion in modern programming. Thus, many of the algorithms are far more complicated than they need to be. (Compare in this regard, for example, the authors' algorithm for truth value calculation with the one found in Tannenbaum and Augenstein's *Data Structures Using Pascal* (Prentice-Hall)). Flowcharts are used alongside PDL ("pseudo-code"), resulting in considerable wasted space. And the algorithms do not exploit the Boolean functions present in virtually all higher-level languages. Finally, in the discussion of Wang's algorithm, the concept of a stack is invoked with little discussion of what a stack is and what the stack functions (push, pop, top, etc.) are.

As a matter of emphasis, I would suggest that topics such as normal forms, Polish notation and the connectives NAND, NOR, XOR be relegated to the appendices.

I suspect that the reason the book under review has the flaws mentioned above is that it attempts to do what is impossible. One simply cannot cover in one book that which is normally covered in a symbolic logic course (FOL including identity/definite description with a natural language focus) and what is normally covered in an introductory programming course. I would suggest that anyone attempting to design a computer-oriented logic text simply give up the hope of teaching computer program design, and instead focus on teaching logic, but have starred sections (which can be omitted by the computer illiterate) which would outline the relevant procedures. That way, those who want to learn just logic can do so; those (mathematics, engineering, and computer science students) who want to look at some sophisticated programs may do so. A CAI package could then be provided whose design is based upon the programs discussed in the book, and be made accessible to all students (whether or not they are accomplished programmers). Speculating further, such a CAI tutorial package would be designed best for microcomputers, since at most colleges it is easier for humanities students to have access to Apples than to mainframes.

We still have not seen a truly computer-oriented symbolic logic text.

Permission to reprint courtesy of Springer. I wish to thank the journal *Philosophia* as well.

7

"Erotetic Logic as a Specification Language for Database Queries,"

was published as the thesis in support of my Master's degree in Computer Science at Kansas State University in 1987, and was delivered as a talk before the Naval Research Laboratory (Washington, DC) later that year

Introduction: An Overview of Fourth-Generation Logics

In fairly recent times, logicians have developed a profusion of non-classical logics: many-valued, modal, temporal, fuzzy and so on. Some of these logics, which I shall call "fourth-generation logics," have already been developed and exploited by computer scientists. Temporal logic has been used in AI and for the formal specification and verification of concurrent programs. Many-valued logic has been used in circuit design and fuzzy logic in AI. In this paper I would like to discuss an area of fourth generation logic, erotetic logic, which may be of use to computer scientists working AI and database theory.

I have coined the term "fourth generation logics" for two reasons. First, while the more customary term[1] for these logics is "deviant logics," that phrase makes it sound as if people who do research on such logics are somehow strange or weird. Second, the phrase "fourth-generation" is at least roughly historically accurate.

We can distinguish generations of logic, in part on the basis of time of origin. Following Bartley (1977) and Jorgensen (1931), we can view the first generation of logic as beginning with Aristotle in the fourth century B.C. First-generation logic (also called "traditional," "Aristotelian," or "syllogistic") logic, focused upon reasoning in natural language. Logicians were concerned to formulate rules for casting propositions into categorical forms and for assessing arguments ("syllogisms") built up out of those categorical propositions.

The second generation of logic, Boolean or algebraic logic, dates from the work of George Boole (1847) and the work of Auguste DeMorgan, John Venn, Lewis Carroll, and others later in the nineteenth century. Second-generation logicians kept the earlier concern with natural language argumentation, but extended logic to cover a wider class of arguments (ones involving relational propositions). More importantly, the algebraic logicians subtly shifted the focus of research to the application of mathematics to logic. Graphical methods (Venn diagrams, Euler diagrams, Carroll diagrams, and so on) for assessing syllogisms were developed, and methods for expressing propositions algebraically were devised.

Thus the second-generation logicians greatly expanded on the scope of analysis beyond traditional syllogistic, and greatly increased the formalization of logic. They also were concerned with devising techniques for *drawing* relevant inferences from premises, i.e., with *solving* problems or *discovering* solutions, as opposed to merely verifying the correctness of already formulated proofs. This concern shows up in the exercises found in second generation logic texts (such as Lewis Carroll's *Game of Logic*): puzzles that call upon the student to determine what conclusion about some situation can be derived from the given information. (Vestiges of the second-generation concern over logical puzzles are still found in some elementary logic texts, and several modern logicians—most notably E.R. Emmet and Raymond Smullyan—have written books of such logic puzzles.)

Third-generation logic is classical First Order Logic ("FOL"). While we might date the birth of FOL with the publication of Frege's *Begriffschrift* in 1879, it is more accurate to date the third generation in logic to the first decade of this century, when Russell brought Frege's work to public notice. Eminent logicians such as Peirce, Whitehead, Russell, Godel, Church, Gentzen and many others rapidly developed FOL, with many major results in place by the 1930's. Third-generation logic is concerned much less with argumentation in natural language than with the foundations of mathematics and proof theory. Hence the focus of research was on consistency proofs, axiomatizations, decision procedures, and so on. Indeed, many third generation logicians were avowed **logicists**, i.e., they wanted to reduce all of mathematics to logic and set theory.

Fourth-generation logic is harder to date. We might date it lat in the nineteenth century, with Peirce's work on many-valued logic. It would be more accurate, however, to fix the date in the 1920's and 1930's with the work of Lukasiewitz on three-valued logic and the work of C.I. Lewis on strict entailment (modal logic). But in terms of purpose, the difference between third and fourth generation is clear. Fourth-generation logicians are much less concerned with the foundations of mathematics, and are once again concerned with reasoning and knowledge expressed in natural language. Typically, the fourth-generation logician feels that FOL is inadequate to explicate some interesting feature of rational discourse, and he seeks to find some modification of or replacement for FOL. The fourth-generation logician has the same goal of the first- and second-generation logicians, but wants to use *some* formal apparatus in addition to (or in lieu of) FOL.

Most logicians would concede that FOL does not sufficiently explicate all natural language reasoning. (Indeed, some logicians have even argued that FOL should *not* be taught as "logic" at all—see, for example Shoenfield (1967) pp. 447–456.) This is perhaps not surprising: FOL explicates mathematical reasoning well, but in mathematics there is no cause and effect, before and after, or questioner and respondent.

In any event, in the last forty years there has been a proliferation of fourth generation logics. Even classifying them is controversial. Some, such as Turner (1985) and Haack (1978), have divided fourth-generation logics into those which seek to *extend* FOL and those which seek to *replace* it. For example, standard modal logic extends FOL by adding modal operators, but the theorems of FOL remain valid. On the other hand, many-valued and intuitionist logics replace FOL in the sense that various theorems of FOL (e.g., the Law of Excluded Middle) fail in those logics.

I find that distinction unhelpful. To begin with, modal logics *are* many-valued in that they add a third truth value (necessary truth) to the classical values (true and false). More generally, *logics* don't seek to do anything: *logicians* do. And most fourth generation logicians don't seek to replace FOL; like scientists in other fields, they view conservativeness as a virtue in a theory. That is, faced with two new proposed theories that aim to succeed where an established theory failed, scientists will naturally choose the one that least conflicts with the established theory (all this being equal). A fourth-generation logician doesn't seek to replace FOL—he may be driven to it, but he doesn't seek it.

It may be suggested that I have misconstrued the proposed division. The point is (it might be urged) that some alternate logics accept as theorems the theorems of FOL, and some do not. But this seems to be an unhelpful point. Many of those logics in which some classical theorems fail have analogues that replace the failed theorems – for example, while the Law of Excluded Middle fails in a three-valued logic, the Law of Excluded Fourth may still hold.

I suggest that a more interesting division of fourth-generation logic is between **assertion** (or "assertoric") logics (those that concern logical connections between statements) and **non-assertion** logics (those concerned with questions and answers, commands, dialogic structure and such like). Some of the major types of fourth-generation logics as listed below.

FOURTH GENERATION LOGICS

- Non-classical Assertion Logics
  - many-valued (including Quantum logics and intuitionist logic)
  - modal, temporal and causal logics
  - entailment logics
  - fuzzy and probabilistic logics
  - other (epistemic logics, free logic, etc.)
- Non-assertoric Logics
  - question logics
  - imperative logics
  - dialog logics

Several references are worth noting. Haack (1978) has a good survey of fourth generation logics and the issues surrounding them from the philosopher's point of view, while Turner (1985) has a survey of temporal, many-valued and fuzzy logic from the AI point of view. The classic survey of modal logic is Hughes and Cresswell (1968)—updated by Hughes and Cresswell (1984). A fine survey of many-valued logic is Rescher (1969) and of temporal logic is Rescher and Urquhart (1971). AI researchers are currently exploring the potential of relevance logic, and the Bible of such logics is Anderson and Belnap (1975).[2]

A fourth-generation logic that is unfamiliar to many computer scientists is erotetic logic.

Roughly put, **erotetic logic** is the logic of questions. More precisely, if standard logic (assertion logic) involves explicating statements and the relations between statements, erotetic logic is the extension of assertion logic to explicate questions and the relations between questions and answers. By "explicate questions" I mean reveal the structure of questions in a way analogous to the way assertion logic explicates the structure of statements. For example, in standard FOL the two relational sentences "John loves Mary" and "Mary is loved by John" are symbolized the same way ("Loves (John, Mary)") because while the surface structures of the English declaratives differ, the semantic structures of the statements are the same. Similarly, any adequate erotetic logic should symbolize

(1a) What are the good restaurants in Topeka?
(1b) Which Topeka restaurants are good?

identically, because while the surface structures of the English interrogatives differ, the semantic structures of the questions are the same.

Again, just as any assertion logic categorizes statements (as being conditionals, negations, existentially quantified or whatever), any adequate erotetic logic should be able to categorize questions, and reveal the differences between:

(1) Which restaurants in Topeka are good?
(2) What are some good restaurants in Topeka?
(3) What is a good restaurant in Topeka?
(4) Why are there no good restaurants in Topeka?
(5) Why do you say that there are no good restaurants in Topeka?
(6) Is "The Loft" a good Topeka restaurant?
(7) Where is "The Loft" located?

By "explicate the relation between questions and answers" I mean the formulation of rules governing the acceptability of a given answer to a given question. For example, question (1) admits the answer

The Loft and the Amarillo Grill are the only good restaurants in Topeka.

while none of the others do. Crucial here is the notion of a **direct** answer, an answer that supplies the requested information, but no more. That is why "The Loft and the Amarillo Grill are the only good restaurants in Topeka" is not an acceptable answer to (3), because (3) only requests one example of a good restaurant in Topeka, not a complete list.

Thus to construct an adequate erotetic logic we must do three things. First, we must decide upon a typology of questions. Second, we must develop a formal system—presumably an extension of some formal assertion logic—that will allow us to symbolize questions. Third, we must formulate a set of admission rules, i.e. rules that specify the syntactic form of an acceptable answer to a given type of question.

Developing a typology of question requires considerable work, mainly of a philosophic and linguistic nature. There is a large body of literature on this topic (see the bibliography to Belnap and Steele (1976)). To simplify the issues treated in this paper, we will adopt the following typology:

```
QUESTIONS
     |____Simple
     |        |____whether
     |        |____which
     |        |____why
     |        |____how
     |____Compound
```

Whether-questions: These questions present their subjects (their range of alternatives) explicitly and request the respondent to select from among them.Example:

(8) Is Fred Rich?
(9) Which should Fred take: FORTRAN, COBOL, C++ or BASIC?

(8) presents the alternatives "Fred is rich" and "Fred is not rich," while (9) presents the alternatives "Fred should take FORTRAN," "Fred should take COBOL," "Fred should take C++," and "Fred should take BASIC."

Which-questions: These questions present their subjects by means of statement functions, and request the respondent to select the data satisfying those functions. Examples:

(10) Which cars are expensive?
(11) Who will come to the party?
(12) What are Fred's office hours?

(10) presents the subject by means of the proposition function "x is a car and x is expensive," (11) by "x is a person and x will come to the party," and (12) by "x is an office hour of Fred."

Why-questions: These questions are of two sorts. The first sort of why-question is a request of the respondent to explain an acknowledged fact. Examples:

(13) What is the cause of the oversupply of Ph.D.'s?
(14) Why do dogs bark?

The second sort of why-question is a request of the respondent to prove a point that the questioner doubts. Examples:

(15) Why do you say that Fred is unhappy?
(16) What are his reasons for buying that stock?

The topic of why-questions is important in philosophy of science and will probably become important in AI; however, it is not relevant to this paper.

How-questions: These questions also are of two types. The first type of how-question requests from the respondent a set of instructions. Examples:

(17) How do I get to Oklahoma City?
(18) How can we buy a new car?

The second sort of how-question is a request for the respondent to impart a skill. Examples:

(19) Can you show me the fox-trot?
(20) Do you know how to get this bottle-cap off?

Again, while the topic of how-questions is interesting and potentially relevant to AI, it is not relevant here.

Compound questions: Questions, like statements, can be compound. Examples:

(21) Who is that masked man, and what does he want?
(22) Where and when shall we get together?

Questions can be compounded with statements:

(23) If Fred wants to buy a car, where will he get the money?

In this paper we will not pursue the topic of compound questions.[3] Questions that are truth-functionally compounded together we can handle in an obvious way. For example, an acceptable answer to (22) would simply be a conjunction of acceptable answers to "Where will we get together?" and "When will we get together?" Moreover, most cases in which statements are compounded with questions seem to be cases in which the statement is a guard against presupposition failure. For example, we would ask (23) rather than the simple question

(24) Where will Fred get the money to buy the care he wants?

because (24) presupposes that Fred wants to buy a car, and we may not be sure that he does. But presupposition failure will be accounted for in our treatment (below) of simple questions.

In short, the formal apparatus we develop will be geared toward which-and whether-questions, since they seem to be the most crucial for database theory (as opposed to AI or philosophy of science).

A Formal Erotetic System

Having picked out the types of questions in which we are interested, we now construct a formal system for putting those questions.[4] Since a formal erotetic language is an extension of an assertoric language, we need first to lay out the grammar of that underlying logic. The language we will take to be FOL. The vocabulary (or "alphabet") consists of:[4]

- Infinitely many individual variables: x, y, z, x_1, y_1, z_1, …
- Individual constants: a, b, c, …
- Predicates of any arity: A, B, C, ... (The number of places of the predicate is indicated by the number of individual variables and constants that follows it).
- Punctuation symbols: (,), [,], {,}
- Logical constants: → (if then), & (and), v (or), ~ (not), ↔ (if and only if), ∀ (universal quantifier), ∃ (existential quantifier)

In philosophic literature, predicates and constants are kept to one letter. In computer science literature, predicates are often whole words (e.g. "Restaurant (x)"). The difference is purely one of style, but for readability we prefer the computer science style.

The well-formed formulas are characterized as follows. (Here I will use boldface font to indicate meta-linguistic variables). We say that variables and constants are **terms**. We say that an n-ary predicate followed by n terms is an **atomic formula** $\mathbf{P(t_1,\ldots,t_n)}$. If all the t_i's are constants (i.e., individual names), then $\mathbf{P(t_1,\ldots,t_n)}$ is a **ground** atomic formula (a "particular statement"). Then the set of well-formed formulas (wffs) is the set defined by the rules:

- Any atomic formula '**P**' is a wff
- If **P** is a wff, then so is '~**P**'
- If **P** and **Q** are wffs, then so are '**P** v **Q**', '**P** → **Q**', '**P** ↔ **Q**' and '**P** & **Q**'
- If **x** is a variable and **P** a wff, the so are '(∀**x**)**P**' and '(∃**x**)**P**' No other expressions are wffs.

We don't need a full-blown first-order language to formulate a database. We say that a first-order language is a **relational language** if and only if it has at least one but most finitely many constants, it has only finitely many predicates, has equality (denoted by 'x = y') as a predicate, and has a set of "types." A **type** is a unary predicate **T** (a **simple** type) or Boolean combinations of simple types. (Types allow us to capture the notion of the "domain" of a given relation).[6]

When types are defined we allow ourselves the luxury of type-restricted quantifiers. We will use

$$(\forall \mathbf{x}/\mathbf{Tx})\ \mathbf{Px}$$

to mean

$$(\forall \mathbf{x})(\mathbf{Tx} \rightarrow \mathbf{Px})$$

and

$$(\exists \mathbf{x}/\mathbf{Tx})\ \mathbf{Px}$$

to mean

$$(\exists \mathbf{x})(\mathbf{Tx}\ \&\ \mathbf{Px})$$

In a standard way we can interpret the language **L**. An **interpretation M** consists of a domain **D** of individuals over which the variables range, a mapping **F** of the constants of the language onto individuals of **D**, and a mapping **E** of the predicates of the language onto sets of tuples of individuals of the domain. We can then characterize truth or satisifiablity under **M** (written $|=_M$) as follows. For a given mapping **V** of variables of **L** into **D**, define another mapping **R** as follows:

R(**c**) = **F**(**c**) for every constant **c** of **L**
R(**x**) = **V**(**x**) for every variable **x** of **L**

Then define $|=_{R,M}$ as follows:

1) $|=_{R,M}$ $\mathbf{P(t_1,...,t_n)}$ iff $\mathbf{(R(t_1),...,R(t_n))} \in \mathbf{E(P)}$ for every atomic formula of **L**.
2) $|=_{R,M}$ $(\mathbf{A_1}\ \&\ \mathbf{A_2})$ iff $|=_{R,M}\mathbf{A_1}$ and $|=_{R,M}\mathbf{A_2}$.
3) $|=_{R,M}$ $(\mathbf{A_1}\ \mathrm{v}\ \mathbf{A_2})$ iff $|=_{R,M}\mathbf{A_1}$ or $|=_{R,M}\mathbf{A_2}$.
4) $|=_{R,M}$ ~**A** iff not $|=_{R,M}$**A**.

5) $|=_{R,M} (\mathbf{A}_1 \rightarrow \mathbf{A}_2)$ iff $|=_{R,M} (\sim\mathbf{A}_1 \lor \mathbf{A}_2)$.
6) $|=_{R,M} (\mathbf{A}_1 \leftrightarrow \mathbf{A}_2$ iff $|=_{R,M} [(\mathbf{A} \rightarrow \mathbf{A}_2) \;\&\; (\mathbf{A}_2 \rightarrow \mathbf{A}_1)]$.
7) $|=_{R,M} (\forall \mathbf{x})\mathbf{A}$ iff for all $\mathbf{d} \in \mathbf{D}$, $|=_{R^*M} \mathbf{A}$ where $\mathbf{R}^*$ is identical to **R** except for mapping **x** to **d**.
8) $|=_{R,M} (\exists\, \mathbf{x})\mathbf{A}$ iff $|=_{R,M} \sim(\forall \mathbf{x}) \sim\mathbf{A}$

Then we can define $|=_M \mathbf{A}$ as: $|=_M \mathbf{A}$ (read "**A** is true in interpretation **M**") iff $|=_{R,M} \mathbf{A}$ for all **R**. **M** is said to be a model for **A** if $|=_M \mathbf{A}$.

In interpreting a relational language, we stipulate that equality hold of every individual in the domain, and we also stipulate a set of integrity constraints. An **integrity constraint** for a predicate **P** has the form (where $\mathbf{T}_1,\ldots,\mathbf{T}_n$ are the types):

$$(\forall \mathbf{x}_1)\ldots(\forall \mathbf{x}_n)\ [\mathbf{P}\ (\mathbf{x}_1,\ldots\mathbf{x}_n) \rightarrow (\mathbf{T}_1\mathbf{x}_1 \;\&\; \ldots \;\&\; \mathbf{T}_n\mathbf{x}_n]$$

For example, we might lay down a constraint upon

Spouse (x,y)

that x be a person and y be a person (we don't allow people to marry animals, and we don't apply the concept of marriage to pairs of animals):

$$(\forall x)\ (\forall y)\ [\text{Spouse}\ (x,y) \rightarrow (\text{Person}\ (x)\ \&\ \text{Person}\ (y))]$$

Now that we have the assertoric logic set forth, we turn to the erotetic extension. Our goal is to develop a formalism that will allow us to specify what it is for a given statement to correctly answer a given question. We will do this in two stages: first, we will devise a set of rules that govern the *acceptability* of answers, and then (in the next section) we will state a criterion for *truth* of answers.

Following Belnap (1963) and Belnap and Steele (1976), whose term system we will adopt, we view a question as having the form '?**RS**,' where **R** is the **request** and **S** the **subject**. Roughly defined, the request specifies the amount of information desired, while the subject specifies the sort of information to be examined. The question mark we view as an operator that takes request-subject pairs onto questions. A **query** is just a question applied to (or "raised within") a database. In this section we will focus on representing questions without concern for databases; we will look at queries later.

We discuss the subject S first. The subject of a whether-question presents it range of alternatives explicitly. That is, the subject has the form of a set of statements {$\mathbf{A}_1$, $\mathbf{A}_2$,..., $\mathbf{A}_n$} where none of the Ai's are repetitions or conjunctions solely of the others of the set. For example, the subject of the question

Is John married?

is the pair

{John is married, John is not married}

Symbolically

{Married (John), ~Married (John)}

Again, the subject of

Has John stopped abusing drugs?

is

{Has_abused (drugs, John) and Now_abuses (drugs, John), Has_abused (drugs, John) & ~Now_abuses (drugs, John)}

A more elaborate example:

Which are on sale today: ham, turkey, or steak?

has the subject

{On_sale (ham, today); On_sale (turkey, today); On_sale (steak, today)}

The subject of a which-question presents a potentially infinite set of alternatives, by means of statement functions, some of which are type constraints and the others the matrix. For example, the question

Which Topeka restaurants take credit cards?

has as subject matrix

Accepts (x, credit_cards) & Located (x, Topeka)

and as type constraint

Restaurant (x).

We will separate the subject types from the matrix by a double slash:

{Restaurant (x)//Accepts (x, credit_cards) & Located (x, Topeka)}

In general we can symbolize the subject of a which-question as

$$\{T_1x,\ldots,T_rx_r\ //\ A(x_1,\ldots x_n)\}$$

where $0 \leq r \leq n$.

Note two things. First, we can push the type constraints over into the matrix if we choose, although there is no good reason for doing so. For example, the subject

{Woman (x), Man (y)//Wife (x,y)}

can be put equivalently

{Woman (x)//Man (y) & Wife (x,y)

or even

{∅ // Woman (x) & Man (y) & Wife (x,y)}

where '∅' is the null symbol.[7]

Second, we should note that the subject of a whether-question is a special case of the subject of a which-question (and so whether-questions are a subset of which-questions). Consider the examples of whether-questions given earlier. The subject of

Is John married?

is

{Married (John), ~Married (John)}

But this can be put instead as the subject of a which-question (using the identity operator, present in any relational language)

{∅ // (x = John) & Married (x)}

Again, the subject of

Has John stopped beating his wife?

can be put

{∅ // (x = John) & Stopped_beating_wife (x) & Now_beats_wife (x)}

We will take the view, then, that whether-questions are but a special case of which-questions, and state our rules (governing the acceptability of answers) in terms of which-questions only.[8]

The **request** of a question is a four-tuple <**Rrange**, **Rcomplete**, **Rdistinct**, **Rdefault**>. The **selection-size specification Rrange** is a specification about the lower and upper limits of the size of the selection. The lower bound 'l' is some integer greater than or equal to one (any question requests at least an alternative be selected). The upper bound 'u' can be any finite positive integer greater than or equal to the lower bound, or may be omitted entirely (which we indicate by using the null symbol '∅'). Thus Rrange takes the form

$l \ldots u \ (1 \leq l \leq u)$

or

$l \ldots \varnothing \ (1 \leq l)$.

The selection-size specification allows us to express the difference between

What is the only Indian restaurant in Topeka?

and

What are some Indian restaurants in Topeka?

The first question involves a request for a single alternative, so Rrange = 1...1, while the second question involves a request for at least one alternative but sets no upper limit on the answer, so Rrange = 1...∅.

The second element of the request is the **completeness-claim specification Rcomplete**. Some questions, like

Which Chinese restaurants in Topeka take credit cards?

implicitly require the respondent to make a claim that the list given is complete, while other questions, like

What are some Chinese restaurants in Topeka that take credit cards?

do not. The completeness-claim is always a comparison of the number of alternatives selected with the total number of true alternatives. The completeness-claim could be that all the true alternatives have been given, or all but one, or most, or 10%, but in practice only one completeness-claim is important, namely, the claim that all true alternatives have been given. This is an especially important claim if the database is incomplete. Accordingly, we will stipulate that Rcomplete take the form of either '∀' or '∅' depending upon whether the maximum completeness-claim (that all true instances have been selected), or else that no such claim is specified.

The **distinctness-claim specification Rdistinct** is a specification regarding whether or not the selection given contains any redundancies. For example, the statement

> The Greenhouse and the Holiday Inn South restaurant are restaurants in Topeka.

would in most situations not be an acceptable answer to the question

> What are two different restaurants in Topeka?

if it turns out that "The Greenhouse" is in fact just the name given to the restaurant in the Holiday Inn South.

As with completeness-claims, various sorts of distinctness-claims are theoretically possible (that some of the alternatives are distinct, that all but one are, and so on) but in practice only two are important. We will say Rdistinct has the form '≠' or '∅', depending upon whether the answer is to include a claim that all the alternatives are distinct or whether no such claim is to be made. In most cases in ordinary contexts and with most databases, questions and queries assume that the selection given in response consists of entirely distinct individuals.

The final element of the request is the **default specification** Rdefault. Rdefault specifies what is to be done in the face of presupposition failure. A **presupposition** of a question is any statement that must be true if that question is to have any true direct answer. For example,

> Has John stopped abusing drugs?

takes as direct answers

> John has stopped abusing drugs.

and

> John has not stopped abusing drugs.

But for one of those alternatives to be true, it has to be true that he has beaten his wife.[9] Of course, this example is the classic example of a loaded question: whether John answers yes or no, he commits himself to the proposition that he has beaten his wife in the past. Questions that presuppose something false are called **loaded** and are best answered by a direct answer but a **corrective** answer (one that corrects false presupposition). Examples:

(question) Has John stopped beating his wife?
(direct answer) Yes.
(corrective answer) He has never beaten his wife.

(question) What is an Indian restaurant in Topeka?
(direct answer) The New Dehli Deli.
(corrective answer) There are no Indian restaurants in Topeka.

We will take the position that a person may well desire a corrective answer to his question if he cannot be given a direct answer—indeed, this seems to be the rule rather than the exception. We can allow the request for a correction in case of presupposition failure by indicating a **default** question **D**. (The guard question cannot, of course, be identical to the original question.) For example, the question

What is an Indian restaurant in Topeka?

can be guarded by the default question

Is there an Indian restaurant in Topeka?

The null symbol indicates that no default question is specified—we may suppose that an error message is printed in case of presupposition failure.

Here then are a few examples of questions and their formal expression.

(1) Is Hunam a restaurant?

is formalized as:

?(1..1, ∅, ∅ ,∅){ // (x = Hunam) & Restaurant (x)}

or

?(1..1, ∅, ∅, ∅) {Restaurant (x)//x = Hunam}

if "Restaurant" is a type.

(2) Which of these are (different) Chinese restaurants: Hunam, The Peking Duck, and Solley's?

?(1..∅, ∀, ≠, ∅) {Restaurant (x)//Chinese (x) & [(x = Hunam) v (x = The_Peking_Duck) v (x = Solley's)]}

(3) Which if any of these are (different) Chinese restaurants: Hunam, The Peking Duck, and Solley's?

?(1…∅, ∀, ≠, ∅) {Restaurant (x)//Chinese (x) & ((x =Hunam) v (x = The Peking_Duck) v (x = Solley's))}

where

D = ? (1..1, ∅, ∅, ∅) {(Restaurant (Hunam) & Chinese (Hunam)) v (Restaurant (The_Peking_Duck) & Chinese (The_Peking_Duck)) v (Restaurant (Solley's) & Chinese (Solley's))}

(4) What are two (different) Greek restaurants in Topeka?

?(2…2, ∅, ≠, ∅) {Restaurant (x)//Greek (x) & Located (x, Topeka)}

By making the exact form of the request and the subject explicit, we can formulate rules governing the form any acceptable answer to a given question must have. We will state these rules recursively. The first set of rules applies to questions without default questions specified. We then state a general rule that applies to any questions with a default question specified. In what follows, κ will represent the question and α the answer.

First, consider a which-question that specifies a size range but specifies neither a completeness claim nor a distinctness claim. Then the constraint on any answer is that it be a conjunction of instances of the type constraints and matrix. Formally, where '**Q**' is the question and '**A**' the answer:

Rule 1: if **Q** is

$$?(1\ldots u, \varnothing, \varnothing, \varnothing)\ \{(T_1x_1\ ,,,\quad T_rx_{r)}\ //\ Ax_1\ldots x_n\}$$

then **A** must be

$$(T_1a_{1/1}\ \&\ldots\&\ T_ra_{1/r}\ \&\ Aa_{1/1}\ldots a_{1/n})\ \&\ldots\&\ (T_1a_{s/1}\ \&\ldots\&\ T_ra_{s/r}\ \&\ Aa_{s/1}\ldots a_{s/n}),$$
$$1 \leq s \leq u$$

Example:

What is an example of a friendly bear?

Rule 1 allows

Yogi is a bear and Yogi is friendly.

but does not allow

Yogi is not a bear and Yogi is friendly.

nor does it allow

Yogi is a bear and Yogi is not friendly.

Next, consider a which-question that specifies a selection size range and a completeness-claim. Then any acceptable answer must involve a conjunction where each conjunct satisfies the type and matrix conditions and where the number of conjuncts falls in the range where the number of conjuncts falls in the range indicated, and a claim that if any individuals satisfy the type and matrix conditions they are identical to the ones cited. Formally:

Rule 2: If **Q** is of the form

$$?(1\ldots u, \forall, \varnothing, \varnothing)\ \{T_1x_1, \ldots, T_rx_r\ //\ Ax_1 \ldots x_n\}$$

then **A** must be

$$\{[T_1a_{1/1}\ \&\ldots\&\ T_ra_{1/r}\ \&\ Aa_{1/1}\ldots a_{1/n}\ \&\ldots\&\ T_1a_{s/1}\ \&\ldots.\&\ T_1a_{s/r}\ \&\ Aa_{s/1}\ldots a_{s/n}]\ \&\ \forall x_1\ldots\forall x_n\ [(T_1x_1\ \&\ldots\&\ T_rx_r) \rightarrow (Ax_1\ \ldots x_n \rightarrow ((x_{1,n} = a_{n/1,\,n})\ \text{v}\ldots\text{v}\ (x_1,n = a_{s/1},_n))))]\}$$

where $(x_{1,n} = a_{k/1},n)$ is the conjunction $(x_1 = a_{k/1})$ &...& $(x_n = a_{k/n})$ and $l \leq s \leq n$. We could also state the completeness-claim using type-restricted quantifiers:

$$(\forall x_1/T_1)\ldots(\forall x_r/T_r)\ (\forall x_{r+1})\ldots(\forall x_n)[Ax_1\ldots x_n \rightarrow (x_{1,n} = a_{1/1,n})\ \text{v}\ldots\text{v}\ (x_{1,n} = a_{s/1,n}))]$$

Example:

Which bears are friendly?

Rule 2 allows

> Yogi is a bear and Yogi is friendly and for any x, if x is a bear then if x is friendly then x is identical to Yogi.

but does not allow

> Yogi is a bear and Yogi is friendly.

Next, consider a which-question that specifies a selection-size range and a distinctness-claim, but no completeness-claim. Then an acceptable answer will assert a conjunction where each conjunct satisfies the type and matrix conditions and where the number of conjuncts falls in the specified range and where an assertion is made that no two individuals cited are the same.
Formally:

Rule 3: If **Q** has the form

$$?(l...u, \varnothing, \neq, \varnothing)\ \{T_1x_1,...T_rx_r // Ax_1...x_n\}$$

then **A** must have the form

$$\{[T_1a_{1/1}\ \&...\&\ T_ra_{1/r}\ \&\ Aa_{1/1}...a_{1/n}\ \&\ T_1a_{s/1}\ \&...\&\ T_1a_{s/r}\ \&\ Aa_{s/1}...a_{s/n}]\ \&\ [\mathbf{\&}(1 \le i \le j \le p)\ \mathbf{V}(1 \le \kappa \le n)\ (a_{i/\kappa} \neq a_{k/k})]\}$$

where $l \le s \le u$ and where

$$\mathbf{V}(1 \le k \le n)\ (a_{i/k} \neq a_{j/k})$$

abbreviates

$$(a_{i/1} \neq a_{j/1})\ v...v\ (a_{i/n} \neq a_{j/n})$$

i.e. the statement that the ith and j^{th} conjuncts are distinct, and so the full claim that all conjuncts are distinct will look like

$$\mathbf{\&}\ (1 \le i \le j \le p)\ \mathbf{V}\ (1 \le k \le n)\ (a_{i/k} \neq a_{j/k}).$$

So, for example, to say that the list

(11, 13, 17)

is not redundant is to say

$$(11 \neq 13) \text{ and } (11 \neq 17) \text{ and } (13 \neq 17).$$

Also, to say that the list of pairs

$$((1,2), (1,3), (3,4))$$

is not redundant is just to say

$$\{[(1 \neq 1) \vee (2 \neq 3)] \ \& \ [(1 \neq 3) \vee (2 \neq 4)] \ \& \ [(1 \neq 3) \vee (3 \neq 4)]\}.$$

Example:

> Which different bears are friendly?

Rule 3 accepts

> Yogi is a bear and Yogi is friendly and Winnie is a bear and Winnie is friendly and Yogi is not identical to Winnie.

but does not accept

> Yogi is a bear and Yogi is friendly and Winnie is a bear and Winnie is friendly.

Finally, consider a which-question that specifies a size range, completeness-claim, and distinctness-claim. Then the form of the answer is just the fusion of the two rules above.

Rule 4: If **Q** has the form

$$?(l...u, \forall, \neq, \varnothing)\ T_1x_1,...T_rx_r \ // \ Ax_1...x_n$$

then **A** must be of the form

$$\{[T_1a_{11} \ \&...\& \ T_ra_{1/r} \ \& \ Aa_{1/1}...a_{1/n} \ \&...\& \ T_1a_{s/1} \ \&...\& \ T_ra_{s/r} \ \& \ Aa_{s/1}...Aa_{s/n}] \ \&$$
$$(\forall x_1)...(\forall x_n) \ [(T_1x_1 \ \&...\& \ T_rx_r) \rightarrow (Ax_1...x_n \rightarrow ((x_{1,n} = A_{j/1,n}) \text{ v...v } (x_{1,n} =$$
$$a_{s,n}))))] \ \&$$
$$[\boldsymbol{\&}(1 \leq i \leq j \leq r) \ \mathbf{V} \ (1 \leq k \leq n) \ (a_{i/k} \neq a_{j/k})]\}, \ l \leq s \leq u.$$

Example:

> Which different bears are friendly?

Rule 4 sanctions:

> Yogi is a bear and Yogi is friendly and Winnie is a bear and Winnie is friendly; and for any x, if x is a bear then if x is friendly then either x is identical to Yogi or is identical to Winnie; and Yogi is not identical to Winnie.

In this manner we can explicate questions that do not involve a default specification. Questions that do not specify a default question can be handled easily.

Rule 5: Let $\mathbf{Q}_D$ be a question involving a specified default question **D** and let **Qø** be the same question without a default specification. Then any acceptable answer **A** to $\mathbf{Q}_D$ will have the form $\mathbf{A}_1$ or $\mathbf{A}_2$, where $\mathbf{A}_1$ is an acceptable answer to **Qø** and $\mathbf{A}_2$ is an acceptable answer to **D**.

Example:

> What (if any) is an Indian restaurant in Topeka?

Rule 5 allows

> The New Delhi Deli

And

> There are no Indian restaurants in Topeka

but not

> <error>.

The grammar of elementary question, then, consists of FOL plus a new operator '?,' a few obvious additional rules of construction (for the various particular forms of '?<Rrange, Rcomplete, Rdistinct, Rdefault> S') and five rules governing the acceptability of answers. These latter rules are the heart of the subject, of course; they are perhaps reminiscent of rules of inference or transformation in FOL itself, but, of course, are not to be considered as such. They are better called "rules of response," rules which govern, not how information is to be transformed, but how (in what form) it is to be conveyed.

Formal queries

We now have an apparatus for specifying questions exactly. This apparatus allows us to get a start on the formal specification of the correctness of answers. An answer to a given question is **correct** if and only if: (a) it has acceptable form and (b) it is true. And we can now specify (by rules 1–5) what it is for an answer to have an acceptable form. We now want to specify formally what it is for an answer to be true.

Here databases enter the picture. We take the view that answers are true or false only against the backdrop of some body of information, i.e., some database. And so if we are to develop a formal account of truth relative to a database, we need to develop some formal model of databases.

Reiter (1984) contrasts two ways to formally represent databases. The first he calls the "model theoretic" view, the dominant view since the work of Codd and others in the early 70's. The second way of formally representing databases he calls the "proof theoretic" view. Reiter argues that the proof theoretic view is better in that it naturally allows for the representation of disjunctive information, null values, general facts, events, property inheritance (IS-A) hierarchies, and other "world knowledge." I find his arguments persuasive, but will not rehearse them here. Rather, I will work with the proof theoretical model because it very nicely compliments the erotetic apparatus outlined earlier.

Under the proof theoretic view, a database is taken to be a first order theory (in an underlying first order relational language). A **first order theory T** of language **L** is just a subset of the well-formed formulas of **L**. For example, with FOL as defined earlier, we might have a first order theory with ground atomic formulas:

> **T** = {Restaurant (Hunam); Restaurant (The_Peking_Duck); Restaurant (The_New_Dehli_Deli); Chinese (Hunan); Chinese (The_Peking_Duck); Indian (The_New_Dehli); Located (Hunan, Topeka); Located (The_New_Dehli_Deli, Topeka); Hunam=Hunam; The_New_Dehli_Deli=The_New_Dehli_Deli; The_Peking_Duck=The_Peking Duck; Topeka = Topeka}

We can then express truth with respect to the database in terms of derivability:

> **T** |-- **A**

means that **A** is derivable from **T** taken as a set of premises. In our example above, clearly

> Restaurant (Hunam)

i.e., the fact that Hunam is a restaurant is derivable from the database—trivially, since it is an explicit member of the set. Less trivially,

(∃x) [Chinese (x) & Restaurant (x) & Located (x, Topeka)]

i.e., we can derive from the theory that there is at least one Chinese restaurant in Topeka. We can now try a plausible approach to defining what it is for an answer **A** to a query **Q** applied to a database **T** to be true: **A** is true with respect to **Q** if and only if **T**|-- **A**. More generally, a given question **Q** applied to a database **T is correctly answered** by **A** if and only if (a) **A** is of acceptable form as answer to **Q** (i.e., meets rules 1–5), and (b) **T** |-- **A**.

Let's follow this suggestion to see where it leads. Suppose we ask (of our sample database)

Which restaurants in Topeka are Indian restaurants?

The correct answer should be

[Restaurant (The_New_Dehli_Deli) & Indian (The_New_Dehli_Deli) & Located (The_New_Dehli_Deli, Topeka)] & (∀x) [Restaurant (x) & Indian (x) & Located (x, Topeka)) → (x = The_New_Dehli_Deli)]

But while

τ |-- [Restaurant (The_New_Dehli_Deli) & Indian (The_New_Dehli_Deli & Located (The_New_Dehli_Deli, Topeka)]

we cannot derive the completeness claim

(∀x)[(Restaurant (x) & Indian (x) & Located (x, Topeka)) → (x = The_New_Dehli_Deli)]

Since universal claims cannot be derived from a theory consisting solely of ground atomic formulas, Reiter suggests first adding to τ a **domain closure axiom** to the effect that all individuals in the interpretation are named (present in) in the database. In the example above, this axiom has the form:

(∀x) [(x = Hunam) v (x = The_Peking_Duck) v (x = The_New_Dehli_Deli v (x = Topeka)]

More generally, if the domain of the interpretation is $(d_1,\ldots,d_n)$ the domain closure axiom is:

$(\forall x)\ [(x = d_1) \text{ v} \ldots \text{v } (x = d_n)]$

Also, we must add to τ completion-axioms for each predicate (to allow the derivability of negations such as

~Restaurant (Topeka).

In our small example, the completion-axioms would be:

(∀x) [Restaurant (x) → ((x = Hunam) v (x = The_Peking_Duck) v (x = The_New_Dehli_Deli)]
(∀x) [Indian (x) → (x = The_New_Dehli_Deli)]
(∀x) [Chinese (x) → ((x = Hunam) v (x = The_Peking_Duck))]
(∀x) (∀y) [Located (x,y) → (((x = Hunam) v (x = The_New_Dehli_Deli) v (x = The_Peking_Duck)) & (y = Topeka)))]

Happily, this all accords with our intuitions: to correctly answer a question that demands a completeness-claim, we have to know that the database to which the question is addressed is complete.

Again, suppose that we ask of our sample database.

What are two different Chinese restaurants in Topeka?

The correct answer should be

[Chinese (Hunam) & Resaturant (Hunam) & Located (Hunam, Topeka)] & [Chinese (The_Peking_Duck) & Restaurant (The_Peking_Duck & Located (The_Peking_Duck, Topeka)] & ~(Hunam = The_Peking_Duck)

But from τ, even including the closure and completion axioms, we cannot derive the distinctness-claim

~(Hunam = The_Peking_Duck)

We need to add more axioms to τ, namely, **unique name axioms**

$\sim(C_1 = C_j)$

for all (C_i, C_j), $i \neq j$, in the set of constants of our relational language. When those axioms *are* added, the distinctness claim is derivable.

Again, happily this accords well with our intuitions. To answer correctly a question that demands a distinctness claim, we have to know that our database contains no duplicate names. This is standardly assumed about databases in practice, and it s a very nice result that our formal specification mechanism *forces us to make that assumption explicit.*

When τ consists of the ground atomic formulas, a domain closure axiom, unique name axioms, completion axioms (and equality axioms specifying the reflexibility, transitivity and symmetry of the equality predicate), the only model for τ is the original interpretation, and thus truth in the interpretation amounts to provability in the theory. This completes our definition of correctness of answers to queries.

Conclusion

I have argued above that a relatively unnoticed area of fourth-generation logic, erotetic logic, devised by philosophical logicians over the last thirty years or so, can be use to complement database theory. In particular, erotetic logic complements very nicely the approach to representing databases taken by Reiter and other workers in the area of the domain calculus, enabling us to formally represent questions and the correctness of answers.

Of course, I suspect that there are other benefits to employing erotetic logic in database theory. One area of possible interest is the verification of relational database queries. That is, given a question posed in natural language, we may be able to verify that a query posed in one of the relational database query languages (domain algebra, domain calculus, transform languages such as SEQUEL/SQL, or graphic systems such as Query-By-Example) will correctly answer the question. For example, to verify that

> Which Chinese restaurants in Topeka take credit cards?

will be correctly answered by the SEQUEL query

```
SELECT NAME
FROM RESTAURANT
WHERE TYPE = 'CHINESE'
    AND CREDIT = 'YES'
    AND LOCATION = 'TOPEKA'
```

applied to a database containing the relation

```
RESTAURANT (NAME, LOCATION, TYPE, CREDIT)
```

we need to verify that

?(1...∅, ∀, ∅, ∅) {Restaurant (x) // [Chinese (x) & Located (x, Topeka) & takes_ credit cards (x)]}

will be correctly answered by the query commands. Assuming that the *implementation* of the select command has been verified (it is presumably just a linear search routine, which can be verified in the standard way), we can show that the query will produce a complete list of names that fit the matrix and type constraints. However, we still need to conjoin the completeness-claim explicitly since it is not present as a datum in the relational database. The point here is that Reiter's view of a database as a first order theory is not something we can immediately implement in a standard relational database. A suggestion worth pursuing is that Reiter's view be implemented in PROLOG. After all, PROLOG does allow the inclusion of general rules as well as particular facts in the database.

In addition, AI researchers may find erotetic logic useful. Generally, erotetic logic gives us a handle on an important aspect of natural language, viz., the asking and answering of questions. More specifically, a number of philosophers of science have pointed out the central role why-questions play in scientific research (see especially Bromberger (1966)). Besides "capturing" (i.e., representing) world knowledge, we need to understand the various and intricate ways people interrogate that knowledge. Erotetic logic can help us in that quest.

Notes

1. The phrase "deviant logic" appears, for example, in W. V. O. Quine's book *Philosophy of Logic* (Englewood Cliffs, NJ: Prentice-Hall 1970).
2. Logicians vary in their enthusiasm for fourth generation logic, from unbridled enthusiasm to skepticism (even outright hostility). Typical of the enthusiasts is Routley:

   On the whole there has been far too much effort expended on trying to accommodate philosophical clarifications to going logical systems and strait-jackets... rather than trying to develop logical systems to handle the evident data and to deal with going philosophical problems. Classical logical (i.e., FOL), although once and briefly an instrument of liberation and clarification in philosophy and mathematics, has, in becoming entrenched, become rigid, resistant to change and highly conservative, and so has become an oppressive and stultifying influence....Classical logic is, as now enforced, a reactionary doctrine.

   Routley quoted in Brodie, et. al. (1984), p. 143

Routley touches upon one of the main arguments employed by many fourth generation logicians: that logic ought to be "empirical," that is, should square with the facts of cognitive life. And fourth generation logicians argue that FOL is not empirically adequate. Many logicians are skeptical, however. Quine (1970) is only one of many who resist the move to go beyond FOL:

> ...let us not underestimate the price of a deviant logic. There is a serious loss of simplicity... And there is a loss, still more serious, on the score of familiarity...The price is perhaps not quite prohibitive, but the returns had better be good. (p. 86)

Those who are reluctant to embrace fourth generation logic seem to me to have two basic objections: first, that the newer logics are not extensional (hence lack many nice features present in FOL, which *is* extensionalist); second, that the newer logics are proliferating, yet don't fit together well (hence lack the elegance and simplicity of FOL). Let me elaborate.

We say that a logical expression is **extensional** if and only if co-referential expressions can be substituted for each other without changing the truth value. That means replacing singular terms with terms of the same denotation (e.g., 'Mark Twain' and 'Sam Clemens'), predicates with predicates of the same extension (e.g., 'man' and 'featherless biped'), or component sentences with sentences of the same truth value, does not change truth-value of the whole proposition. While FOL is extensional, fourth generation assertoric logics are typically intensional (i.e., non-extensional). Thus they often lack the simple decision procedures found in classical propositional logic.

And again, fourth generation logics are bewildering in their variety. Some seem to be more extensions of FOL than replacements, others seem to be wholesale replacements. It is quite unclear whether they all can be fitted together, and if so, just how.

3. The reader may wish to see Belnap and Steele's discussion of compound questions (Belnap/Steele (1976), pp. 87–107.
4. This system is similar to that of Belnap and Steele (1976) which grew out of Belnap's earlier work (Belnap (1963) with a number of simplifications and modifications. In particular, I view whether-questions as special cases of which-questions and I build default questions (guards) into the specification of simple questions. I do this to bring the symbolism closer to actual database queries. (The reader may wish read the alternate system devised by Aqvist (Aqvist (1965). For an elegant and highly formal account, see Kubinski (1980).
5. For a review of FOL, see Mendelson (1979) or Schoenfield (1967). In particular, the notion of interpreting a first language is discussed in Chapter Two of Schoenfield (1967).

6. Types are discussed in Schoenfield (1967), pp. 88–92; and also in Reiter(1984). Note that instead of using types, one can use a many-sorted logic to the same effect. For an explanation of the role of category or type conditions in erotetic logic, see Belnap (1963), pp. 72–73.
7. We can do the converse, i.e., push matrix conjuncts over into the type constraints, only if those conjuncts are types or if we are willing to allow new types to be created at will—not a very practical approach.
8. This formal reduction can have a cost in simplicity. For example, the subject of the whether-question

   Which of the following are on sale: ham, chicken, steak, lobster and turkey?

   is

   {(On_sale (ham, today), On_sale (chicken, today), On_sale(steak, today), On_sale (lobster, today), On_sale (turkey, today))}

   but turned into the subject of whether -question is

   {Ø // On_sale (x, today) & ((x = ham) v (x = chicken) v (x = steak) v (x = lobster) v (x = turkey))}

   which is rather more awkward.

   Even more awkward are questions involving quantified statements, e.g. the subject of

   Are all swans white? is

   {(∀x)[Swan (x) → White (x)] , ~(∀x) [Swan (x) → White (x)]}

   That can only be represented as the subject of a which-question if we use a universal type Ux true of all individuals (or if dealing with a language with no types, the function Ax v ~Ax will serve as well). Then the equivalent subject is

   {Ø // Ux & (∀x) (Swan (x) → White (x))}
9. This point is more subtle if we interpret the question as a whether-question:

   {Ø // (x = John) & Has_beaten_wife (John) & Now_beats_wife (John)}

   Posing the question with that subject gets as direct answers

   Has_beaten_wife (John) & Now_beats_wife (John)

   and

   [Has_beaten_wife (John) & ~Now_beats_wife (John)]

   That latter alternative does not logically imply that John did beat his wife. However, it is still true under this construal that to answer "Has John stopped beating his wife?"

by "no, it is not the case that he has stopped beating his wife" does not correct the presupposition of the question.

Bibliography

1. Anderson, Alan Ross and Nuel Belnap *Entailment: The Relevance and Necessity (Vol. I)* Princeton: Princeton University Press (1975).
2. Aquist, Lennart *A New Approach to the Logical Theory of Interrogatives* Uppsala: Filosofiska Studier (1965).
3. Bartley, W.W. *Lewis Carroll's Symbolic Logic* NY: Clarkson Potter, Inc. (1977).
4. Belnap, Nuel D. *An Analysis of Questions: Preliminary Report* Technical Memorandum issued by System Development Corporation (1963).
5. Belnap, Nuel and Thomas Steel *The Logic of Questions and Answers* New Haven: Yale University Press (1976).
6. Bridge, Jane *Beginning Model Theory* Oxford: Oxford University Press (1977).
7. Bromberger, Sylvain "Why-Questions," in *Mind and Cosmos* ed. by Robert Colodny Pittsburgh: University of Pittsburgh Press (1966).
8. Haack, Susan *Philosophy of Logics* Cambridge: Cambridge University Press (1978).
9. Hughes, G. E. and M. J. Cresseell *An Introduction to Modal Logic* London: Methuen (1968).
10. Hughes, G. E. and M. J. Cresswell *A Companion to Modal Logic* London: Methuen (1984).
11. Jorgenson, Jorgen *A Treatise of Formal Logic* London: Oxford University Press (1931).
12. Kubinski, Tadeus *An Outline of the Logical Theory of Questions* Berlin: Akademie-Verlag (1980).
13. Mendelson, Elliot *Introduction to Mathematical Logic (2*nd *Ed.)* NY: Van Nostrand (1979).
14. Quine, W. V. *Philosophy of Logic* Englewood Cliffs, N.J.: Prentice-Hall (1970).
15. Reiter, Raymond "Towards a Logical Reconstruction of Relational Database Theory" in Michael Brodie et. al. (eds) *On Conceptual Modeling* NY: Springer-Verlag (1984).
16. Rescher, N. *Many-Valued Logic* NY: McGraw-Hill (1969).
17. Rescher, Nicholas and Urquhart, A. *Temporal Logic* NY: Springer Verlag (1971).
18. Shoenfield, Joseph *Mathematical Logic Reading* Mass: Addison-Wesley (1967).
19. Thomas, Stephen *Practical Reasoning in Natural Language (3rd Ed.)* Englewood Cliffs, N.J.: Prentice-Hall (1986).
20. Turner, Raymond *Logics for Artificial Intelligence* Chichester: Ellis Horwood Ltd (1985).

I wish to thank the Department of Computer Science of the Kansas State University.

8

"Dialog as an Abstract Data Type"

was delivered in an AI seminar class at University of California, Irvine in 1987

Since the 1930s at least, a number of scholars have investigated non-classical (sometimes termed "deviant" or "philosophical") logics. Such logics typically seek to modify or extend standard first order logic to handle types of argumentation or explicate forms of reasoning besides that found in mathematical (or more exactly, extensional) discourse. We may divide these logics into *non-classical assertion* logics (sometimes called "assertoric" logics), which deal with the relations between statements (entailment, consistency or proof relations). These include many-valued, modal, causal, temporal and fuzzy logics. *Non-assertion* logics are those which deal with relations between statements and other linguistic objects. These include erotetic (i.e., question), imperative and dialog logics.

Non-classical assertion logics have proven useful beyond the realm of philosophy. Specifically, computer scientists have found uses for several philosophic logics. Temporal logic has proven useful in the specification and verification of concurrent programs. Many-valued logics have proven useful in circuit design and (more recently) in AI. (Indeed, the IEEE has held annual symposia on many-valued logics for many years). And of course AI researchers have explored fuzzy and temporal logics.

Less familiar to computer scientists are non-assertion logics. Of particular philosophic interest over the last couple of decades have been dialog logics, i.e., logics that aim to explicate the structure of information-oriented (or information-seeking) conversations. (The phrase "information-oriented" is employed to distinguish dialogs from other conversations). Dialog logics have been of interest to logicians and epistemologists, especially with the appearance of C. L. Hamblin's seminal work, *Fallacies* (Hamblin 1970). He was the first scholar to attempt to devise formal models of dialogs, and he did so as a tool to analyze informal fallacies. Many other philosophers have continued to use dialog logic in that manner. Other philosophers have used dialog logic as a tool to explicate scientific discovery (Jason 1988) and inductive reasoning (Jason 1985). Some use dialog logic to provide an alternate semantics for first-order logic (Kambartel & Schneider 1981, and Hintikka & Kulas 1983). In this paper I will focus on the use of dialog logic in AI, to enable better modeling of human argumentation and informal fallacies.

A dialog takes place among a number of **participants** ($P_1, \ldots, P_n$) over a number of **rounds** ($r_1, \ldots, r_m$). Associated with each participant is a **commitment-store**, which is a record of the statements to which he/she is committed at any point in a dialog. We can represent a dialog at least partially as a matrix of locutions:

$$
\begin{array}{l}
l_{11} \; . \; . \; . \; l_{1n} \; \text{....first round} \\
. \quad . \; . \; . \; . \\
. \quad . \; . \; . \; . \\
. \quad . \; . \; . \; . \\
l_{m1} \; . \; . \; . \; l_{mn} \; \text{....last round}
\end{array}
$$

where m is the number of rounds and n the number of participants, and each l_{ij} is either a question, a statement or a command, made by the jth participant in the ith round. For example, consider the following small 2-participant dialog:

A: I don't think President Smith will win re-election.
B: Why?
A: He doesn't have the support of labor, and has not achieved any foreign policy successes.

This dialog can be set out as:

	Participant A	Participant B
Round 1	I don't think that Smith will win.	Why?
Round 2	Smith doesn't have the support of labor and he has not achieved any foreign policy successes.	∅

The null symbol "∅" indicates no response.

For simplicity, we may view questions as being either requests for proof ("Why p?") or inquiries ("Is p true?"). Again, for simplicity, we may view commands as being either commands to withdraw a locution ("Withdraw p!) or to store a locution (Store p!").

To keep track of what each participant is committed to, we associate with each participant j a set C_{ij} which contains the statements to which he/she is committed at round i. We can do this recursively. We begin by setting all commitment stores to empty. If any participant wants a statement to be withdrawn, it is withdrawn from his store. If a statement is challenged (by any participant asking, "Why p?"), it is removed from the questioner's store but added to any other participant's store who doesn't challenge it. If a participant challenges a statement and someone else proves it for him (i.e., demonstrates it to him), both the statement and the conditional linking the proof to it are added to everyone's commitment store.

One goal of dialog logic is to delineate rules for acceptable or "legal" dialogs, just as it is a goal of standard assertion logic to delineate rules for valid arguments. Different dialog logics propose different rules, and I don't want to explore in detail various sets of alternatives, but it easy to see what such rules look like. Examples: no legal dialog can contain an ill-formed locution; if a given round contains a question for a given participant, the dialog is not legal unless the following round contains that participant's answer; and so on.

We consider a more fleshed out dialog logic below. But first we need to define more precisely what sort of abstract data type a dialog is, and how the rules governing dialogs may be stated formally.

An **abstract data type** consists of mathematical objects together with operations defined on those objects. For example, the abstract data type "array" is a function (with domain the set of index values and range the set of component values), and the operations which characterize it are fetch and store.

Identifying plausible objects as dialogs is not easy. Clearly, sets won't work—there is too much order in a dialog (rounds succeed rounds, and within rounds, responses succeed responses). We might look to sequences, i.e., ordered sets. (In what follows, all sets are taken to be finite). We can indeed capture the order inherent within a round as a sequence:

$$< l_1, l_2, \ldots, l_n >$$

where $l_1, \ldots, l_n$ are locutions (questions, statements or commands) by the participants (1 through n). But how can we capture the ordering of the rounds?

One approach would be to view a dialog as a sequence of sequences, each sequence representing a round (as above):

$$D = <<l_{11}, \ldots, l_{1n}>, <l_{21}, \ldots, l_{2n}>, \ldots, <l_{m1}, \ldots, l_{mn}>>.$$

But we can also represent the dialog as a set of sequences where each round sequence is numbered

$$D = \{<1, l_{11}, \ldots, l_{1n}>, <2, l_{21}, \ldots, l_{2n}>, \ldots, <m, l_{m1}, \ldots, l_{mn}>\}.$$

We will take the former approach, and view dialogs in part as sequences of sequences.

Yet there is more to the story: we need to keep track of the commitment stores. Again, there are several ways we might do this. We might list the commitment stores as either sequences of sequences:

$$C = <<c_{11}, \ldots, c_{1n}>, \ldots, <c_{m1}, \ldots, c_{mn}>>$$

or else as a set of numbered sequences

$$C = \{<1, c_{11}, \ldots, c_{1n}>, \ldots, <m, c_{m1}, \ldots, c_{mn}>\}.$$

Again, we shall take the former course.

In sum, our view is that the object of the abstract data type "dialog" is a tuplet <R, C> where R is a sequence of rounds

$$R = <r_1, \ldots, r_m>$$

each round r_i being in turn a sequence of locutions (statements, questions or commands), and where C is a sequence of snapshots of the participants' commitment stores at each round

$$C = <s_1, \ldots, s_m>$$

Each snapshot s_i is a sequence of commitment stores, where each commitment store is a set of locutions.

Having defined the objects of the abstract data type, we turn next to defining the operations. To begin with, we need an operation that initially sets the commitment stores to empty:

$$\text{Initstore}(P_i): c_{0i} \leftarrow \varnothing.$$

We also need to be able to add and delete items from any commitment store:

Addtostore(l, c_{ij}): $c_{ij} \leftarrow c_{ij} \varnothing \{l\}$

Deletefromstore(l, c_{ij}): $c_{ij} \leftarrow c_{ij} - \{l\}$.

The above operations will allow us to express the rules governing changes in the commitment stores. But we need to express rules governing responses to give locutions, rules such as: if somebody asks for proof of proposition q, the answer must be of the form "p & (p→q)" where p is an element of the asker's commitment store. We thus need to have an operator which detects the presence or absence of a given string at a given round, and one that detects the presence or absence of a given string in a given commitment store:

Inround(l, i, j) (boolean): inround(l, i, j) ← true if l = j^{th} element of round i;
inround(l, i, j) ← false otherwise.

Instore(l, c_{ij}) (boolean): instore(l, c_{ij}) ← true if $l \in c_{ij}$;
instore(l, c_{ij}) ← false if $l \notin c_{ij}$.

With these operators we can formally express the rules governing the structure of legal dialogs. For simplicity, let us consider the case of 2-party dialogs. (Generalization to n-party dialogs presents no particular problems). And we will keep the rules simple. The participants are P_1 and P_2. First, we can recursively define the commitment function that assigns locutions to commitment stores as axioms on the abstract data type:

Base step: initialize all commitment stores to nil:

A_1: initstore(P_1);

A_2: initstore(P_2).

Inductive step: for any participant, if he/she asserts something, then that statement gets added to everybody's commitment store. If any participant doesn't accept that commitment, he/she must delete it explicitly:

A_3: [inround(store p, i, P_1) v inround(store p, i, P_2)] → [addtostore (p, $c_{i+1,1}$) & addtostore(p, $c_{i+1,2}$)].

For any participant, if he/she withdraws a statement explicitly, it is deleted from his commitment store:

A_4: inround(withdraw p, i, P_1) → deletefromstore(p, $c_{i+1, 1}$);

A_5: inround(withdraw p, i, P_2) → deletefromstore(p, $c_{i+1, 2}$).

If any participant asks for proof of p, then all participants must delete p from their commitment stores, and the asker must add "why p?" to his/hers:

A_6: inround(why p?, i, P_1) → [deletefromstore(p, i+1, P_1) & deletefromstore (p, i+1, P_2) & addtostore(why p?, i+1, P_1)];

A_7: inround(why p?, I, P_2) → [deletefromstore(p, i+1, P_1) & deletefromstore (p, i+2, P_2) & addtostore(why p?, i+1, P_2)].

Representing the rules of legality of dialogs as axioms is also possible in terms of the defined operations.

If any participant is committed to "Why q?" at any round, then in some succeeding round there must appear "p & (p→q)" where p and p→q are elements of his commitment store.

A_8: instore(why q?, i, P_1) → (∃j)[j>i & instore(p, j, P_1) & instore(p→q, j, P_1) & inround(p&(p→q), j, P_1)];

A_9: instore(why q?, i, P_2) → (∃j)[j>i & instore(p, j, P_2) & instore(p→q, j, P_2) & inround(p&(p→q), j, P_2)].

By using similar axioms, any other such rules of dialog logic (like those found in Mackenzie (1985) or Walton (1984)) can be expressed in a natural fashion.

In the foregoing section, we defined the mathematical objects and operations of the abstract data type dialog, and were able to express the rules of dialog logic as axioms about the data type. We want now to consider how this new abstract data type can be implemented by lower level data types.

Several possible implementations come to mind. First, we might implement a dialog as a coordinated pair of m by n matrices, one to hold the locutions, the other to hold the commitment stores. But in actuality, such arrays would almost always be very sparse. Consider the simple 3-party dialog below:

A: I doubt that Smith will be given tenure.
B: Why?
A: He hasn't published much, and is not popular with the students, and the department only tenures in those who publish and are popular.

C: I disagree—Smith has published a lot.
A: Okay, but he is still not popular with the students.

Looking at just the locutions, we see:

A	B	C
~T	Why ~T?	∅
~P & ~S & [T→(P&S)]	∅	P
~S & [T→(P&S)]	∅	∅

Notice that the matrix has almost half its entries null. As the number of participants and the number of rounds increase, the matrices which represent the locutions become increasingly sparse. As such, alternate data structures besides two dimensional arrays become attractive for representing dialogs.

One approach would be to represent a dialog as a set of triplets <i, j, l>, where i is the round number, j the participant, and l the locution. The triplets could then be stored in some search structure that would allow for fast access, such as a hash table or a binary search tree. A second method for storing (sparse) dialogs would be linked allocation, in which the primary list has nodes which hold the round numbers (of nonempty rounds), one link field holding the address of the first node of the secondary list (which in turn would hold the participant numbers and locutions in that round), and link to the next node. Alternatively, we could use a one-dimensional array indexed by the round numbers to hold the addresses of the secondary lists.

In the foregoing sections I have argued that we can define an abstract data type with axioms that captures the central elements of dialog logic, and implement that abstract data type in various ways. I would like to conclude by sketching some reasons why this logic may be of interest to computer scientists.

Logics—any logics—can be utilized in different ways by different scholars. The philosopher views logic as a tool to analyze arguments. The artificial intelligence designer views logic as a tool in knowledge representation and in inference engine design. The software engineer is interested in logic as a tool in the specification and verification of programs.

Dialog logic, as I suggested earlier, is potentially useful in AI because it holds promise for helping model argumentation more broadly, especially explicating informal fallacies. And dialog logic holds the promise of explicating the process of scientific discovery. Essentially, the process of scientific discovery can be modeled as an extended dialog between scientific researchers and nature, and dialog logic has a use in representing that process. (See Jason (1988) for an extended discussion of that thesis).

Dialog logic is potentially useful in the specification and verification of parallel programs. This is because the rules of dialog logic allow the natural expression of constraints upon the way individual processors work together in the solution of a problem.

Bibliography

1. Hamblin, C. L. (1970) *Fallacies*, London: Methuen & Co.
2. Hintikka, Jaakko & Kulas, Jack (1983) *The Game of Language: Studies in Game-theoretical Semantics and its Applications,* Reidel: Dordrecht.
3. Jason, Gary (1985) "Two Problems of Induction," *Dialectica*, Vol. 39, no. 1, pp. 53–74.
4. Jason, Gary (1988) *The Logic of Scientific Discovery,* N.Y.: Peter Lang.
5. Kambartel, Friedrick and Schneider, Hans Julius (1981) "Constructing a Pragmatic Foundation for Semantics," G. Floistad (Hg.), *Contemporary Philosophy: A New Survey,* Vol. 1, Den Haag 1981, pp. 155–178.
6. Mackenzie, Jim (1985) "No Logic Before Friday," *Synthese* 63 pp. 329–331.
7. Walton, D. (1984) *Fallacies and Logical Dialogue Games,* N.Y.: University Press of America.

I wish to thank the Department of Computer Science of the University of California, Irvine.

9

My review of: *Expert Systems: Artificial Intelligence in Business*

(by Paul Harmon and David King. New York: John Wiley & Sons) first appeared in Technology and Culture, January, 1988, pp. 894–895

The dream (or nightmare) of intelligent machines has been a recurrent one since the days of La Mettrie. In the 1950s and 1960s, artificial intelligence (AI) was touted as being the fulfillment of that dream. AI was oversold, however, and by the 1970s a reaction set in; it was no longer as highly publicized or funded. Yet by the early 1980s, it was back in fashion, and over the last few years it has proved increasingly commercially viable. Paul Harmon and David King have written an excellent book that explains why this change occurred and gives a good survey of the recent history and present status of the field.

The key reason for the resurrection of AI was a paradigm shift. The early paradigm in AI research was the grand synthesis, the high-level reasoning program that would mimic the human mind's ability to reason and learn across a broad spectrum of domains. The work by Newell and Simon on the General Problem Solver is a case in point. But the recent paradigm is the lower-level program which mimics how an expert in a small domain reaches judgments. Such programs, called, appropriately enough, "expert systems," have proved more successful in achieving the goals of AI.

Harmon and King give the reader a solid introduction to the most successful of the expert systems developed in the mid 1970s. They devote two chapters to the most influential early expert system, MYCIN, which is a program that helps physicians diagnose and treat bacteremia and meningitis. They survey other early expert systems, such as DENDRAL, MACSYMA, HEARSAY, PROSPECTOR, and PUFF, and they discuss recent expert systems such as XCON, GENESIS, DRILLING, ADVISOR, STEAMER, and DELTA.

Besides giving the reader an overview of specific expert systems, Harmon and King give more general surveys as well. They devote several chapters to the techniques AI researchers use to represent knowledge and mimic human patterns of inference and problem solving. Techniques of knowledge representation, such as symbolic logic, frames, semantic networks, and object/attribute/value triplets are explained clearly and succinctly.

Moreover, they survey the existing AI languages (such as **lisp** and **prolog**) and existing "environments" or "tools"—that is, meta-programs that allow the programmer to rapidly develop an expert system. Also useful is the survey of the present commercial market for expert systems and the prospects for the next five years.

In sum, this is an excellently written book that focuses on a crucial decade in software technology and covers a very important domain of that technology. It deserves to be on the shelf of any student of the history of computing.

10

"Hedging as a Fallacy of Language"

first appeared in Informal Logic X.3, Fall 1988, pp. 169–175

While there has been considerable progress in the study of fallacies over the twenty years since the publication of Hamblin's excellent monograph on the subject, the treatment of the fallacies of language still remains much as it has always been. The usual suspects—equivocation, amphiboly, accent, composition, and division—are rounded up, and covered in an abbreviated fashion. In this paper I would like to discuss another fallacy of language, hedging, with an eye to broadening our view of fallacies of language. Specifically, I want to accomplish three things.

First, I want to convince the reader that hedging is indeed common (and so should be added to the admittedly burgeoning list of standard fallacies). Second, I want to give an adequate theoretical (i.e., linguistic) treatment of the fallacy. Third, I want to show how the standard treatment of fallacies of language can be modified to include not only hedging, but other fallacies as well.

The fallacy of which I speak is exemplified by the following paradigm dialog:

A: Henry is a totally selfish man.
B: I don't find him so – indeed, he once helped me find a job.
A: Well, about things that affect his wallet, he is totally selfish.
B: Yet he has on many occasions loaned money to his friends.
A: Well, about matters that affect his wallet he can be very selfish.

In this simple dialog, A puts forward a claim, and then systematically evades B's counter-evidence by weakening the initial claim (rather than, say, retracting it). This is the first paradigm for the fallacy of hedging: a claim which is reasonably qualified at the beginning of the dialog gets systematically weakened as the dialog proceeds to avoid the thrust of counter-evidence. In our paradigm, A simply will not come to grips with the substantial evidence B has offered that Henry is not selfish. A's final weak claim is totally uninformative: anybody "can be" selfish, but is Henry selfish in fact? Contrast this with honest and non-fallacious backing down (i.e., retraction of an initial claim): A ought simply to have said, "I can't at the moment recall the incidents which lead me to think that Henry is selfish. Let me think about it. Maybe I'm wrong."

Consider next this sample dialog:

A: I believe that a Christian is going to be less likely to commit crimes than a Moslem in the same circumstances.

B: That seems ridiculous to me. Look at the high crime rate in the U.S.A., which is a predominantly Christian country, and compare it to any Moslem country.

A: Ah, but the U.S.A. is different from Moslem countries in that those countries have harsh laws.

B: Well, okay then, let's just look only at the U.S.A. Moslems in the U.S.A. have a lower crime rate than the general Christian population.

A: Yes, but the so-called Christian population includes many people who are not true Christians.

In this paradigm case, A puts forward a provocative claim, but in the face of counter-argument, winds up hedging it round with the weasel words "true", and "so-called," which allow A to make it completely unclear to whom the term' 'Christian" applies. (The phrase "weasel word" is a colloquial expression denoting qualifying phrases and detensifiers. Those are defined below.) Thus B's legitimate attempts to test A's claim with relevant evidence are frustrated. One wants to shout at A, "Look, do you genuinely believe that Christians are less criminally inclined than Moslems? Then allow us to bring some facts to bear on the issue. Otherwise, shut up and don't insult the Moslems."

Again, contrast A's hedging with honest and non-fallacious backing down (i.e., retraction). A could simply have said "Well, maybe I'm wrong. Let me check into some statistics and we'll talk later." Temporarily retracting one's claim until he or she has better evidence for it is a logically acceptable way to save face; hedging is not.

Looking at the paradigms given above, then, we can define roughly the fallacy of *hedging* as the systematic weakening of a claim, or the putting forward of an unreasonably restricted initial claim, so as to avoid refutation. We will tighten this definition later.

It might fairly be asked whether the fallacy of hedging, defined as above, is so frequently committed in ordinary argumentation as to merit placing it on the list of "standard fallacies." The lexicon of fallacies is already large, and so the burden of proof is on the proposer of an addition to that lexicon to give some reason for further expansion.

In defense of adding hedging to the rogue's gallery of fallacies, I would point out how common it is for politicians to hedge in debates and news conferences to avoid taking positions which will cost them votes. Consider these examples from the second Reagan/Mondale presidential debate:[1]

Example 1:

> **Question:** Mr. President, in the last few months it has seemed more and more that your policies in Central America were beginning to work. Yet just at this moment we are confronted with the extraordinary story of the C. I. A. guerrilla manual for the anti-Sandinista Contras, whom we are backing, which advocates not only assassinations of Sandinistas but the hiring of criminals to assassinate the guerrillas we are supporting in order to create martyrs. Is this not in effect our own state-supported terrorism?
>
> **Reagan:** No, but I'm glad you asked that question because I know it's on many people's minds. I have ordered an investigation; I know that the C.I.A. is already going forward with one. We have a gentleman down in Nicaragua who is on military tactics, the Contras. And he drew up this manual. It was turned over to the agency head of the C.I.A. in Nicaragua to be printed, and a number of pages were excised by that agency head there, the man in charge, and he sent it on up here to the C.I.A., where more pages were excised before it was printed. But some way or other, there were 12 of the original copies that got out down there and were not submitted for this printing process by the C.I.A. Now those are the details as we have them, and as soon as we have an investigation and find out where any blame lies for the few that did not get excised or changed, we certainly are going to do something about that. We'll take the proper action at the proper time.
>
> **Question:** Well, Mr. President, you are implying then that the C.I.A. in Nicaragua is directing the Contras there. I'd also like to ask whether having the C.I.A.

investigate its own manual in such a sensitive area is not sort of like sending the fox into the chicken coop a second time.

Reagan: I'm afraid I misspoke when I said there is a C.I.A. head in Nicaragua. There's not someone there directing all of this activity. There are, as you know, C.I.A. men stationed in other countries in the world, and certainly in Central America, and so it was a man down there in that area that this was delivered to. And he recognized that what was in that manual was a direct contravention of my own executive order in December of 1981, that we would have nothing to do with regard to political assassinations.

In the first question, Reagan was asked about a provocative pamphlet allegedly produced by the C.I.A. His answer inadvertently revealed that the C.I.A. had a man in charge of the military tactics of the Contras. When pressed, he hedged by saying there are C.I.A. men all over, and "it was a man down there in that area it was delivered to."

Example 2:

Question: You've been quoted as saying that you might quarantine Nicaragua. I'd like to know what that means. Would you stop Soviet ships as President Kennedy did in 1962 and wouldn't that be more dangerous than President Reagan's covert war?

Mondale: What I'm referring to there is the mutual self-defense provisions that exist in the inter-American treaty, the so-called Rio Pact, that permits the nations, our friends in that region, to combine to take some steps, diplomatic and otherwise, to prevent Nicaragua when she acts irresponsibly in asserting power in other parts outside of her border, to take those steps, whatever they might be, to stop it.

In the question, Mondale is pressed on his position that he would possibly quarantine Nicaragua. In reply he hedges by talking about "our friends" combining with us to "take some steps," "diplomatic or otherwise," to prevent Nicaragua from acting "irresponsibly," "in asserting power." Some sort of action by the U.S. is being indicated, but the statement is so heavily qualified that the audience cannot tell what that action would be (thus how dangerous it would be), and what acts by Nicaragua would bring it on.

Another area in which hedging is common is in the statement of conditions in contracts, especially statements of guarantees which accompany various products. Such guarantees are often so heavily qualified as to be virtually useless. For example, one manufacturer of color photographic film guaranteed for quality puts the guarantee as follows:

> This product, if defective in manufacture, labeling, packaging or shipping, or if damaged by us, will be replaced with like fresh film or purchase price refunded, at our option. This is your exclusive remedy and the limit of all contract or tort liability. Since color dyes may change in time, no warranty against any color change is expressed or implied. This film will not be replaced or purchase price refunded for any change in color.

A guarantee for color film which is hedged to be optional at the will of the manufacturer and to not apply to changes in color is a pretty worthless guarantee. Contrast this with a completely un-hedged guarantee by Gillette Corporation for its razors:

> Complete shaving satisfaction guaranteed or Gillette will replace free of charge or refund full purchase price.

No qualifications are put forth, and the option for return lies solely with the customer.

If hedging is reasonably common, then why is it so commonly overlooked in accounts of fallacies of language? I suspect it is because fallacies of language are often equated with, or at least limited to, fallacies of ambiguity.[2] To see why such an equation is wrong, reconsider fallacies of ambiguity for a moment. Is ambiguity *per* se bad? Surely not. Very likely most English words are ambiguous, and unavoidably so. As one semanticist has noted:

> A moment's reflection will show that, far from being a defect of language, polysemy [i.e., ambiguity] is an essential condition of its efficiency. If it were not possible to attach several senses to one word, this would mean a crushing burden on our memory: we would have to possess separate terms for every conceivable subject we might wish to talk about. Polysemy is an invaluable factor of economy and flexibility in language: what is astonishing is not that the machine occasionally breaks down. but that it breaks down so rarely.[3]

Yet ambiguity is not normally a problem, because context usually makes the intended meaning clear. A word can be ambiguous without being used ambiguously in a given conversational context, as a number of logic texts have noted.[4] What gives rise to a fallacy of ambiguity, i.e., a fallacious *use* of ambiguity, is the use of an ambiguous phrase one way in one premise of an argument and a different way in another premise (or the conclusion).

The vision that emerges here is that of a pervasive feature of language which is not normally bad, but which can be used to commit fallacies. Viewing fallacies in this way naturally leads us to ask what other pervasive features of language might be liable to misuse in argumentation.

One such feature that comes to mind is vagueness. Many words are vague, but context usually clarifies the meaning precisely enough for conversation to proceed. Vagueness is often useful, as when in law it allows room for the application of a term to new cases undreamt of when the original law was passed. But vagueness can be used to commit slippery slope fallacy, as when a person exploits the vagueness of a term to change the issue by degrees. Also, again as noted by several authors, vagueness can be used to equivocate, as when a person interprets a vague term loosely in one premise and strictly in another.[5]

Another feature of language liable to misuse is ladenness, by which I mean theoretical or emotional connotation. Terms can be theory-laden without being emotion-laden ("electron," "ionic bond"), or emotion-laden without being theory-laden ("dirty rat," "punk"), or both theory- and emotion-laden ("IQ," "nation"). Again, very likely most words are laden to some degree. Ladenness is not bad *per se*; it is how the ladenness is used that makes all the difference. It is not fallacious to use a theory-laden term in a context in which the theory at hand is not under question. It is not fallacious to use an emotion-laden term in a context in which the expression of emotion is the central purpose of the discourse. What *is* fallacious is to use laden language to presuppose that which is in dispute, or to persuade by emotion rather than reason.

Thus ladenness can be used to commit fallacies, but those fallacies usually are not presented as fallacies of language. Instead, ladenness which is used to presuppose that which is under dispute is usually termed "question-begging epithets" and lumped in as a form of *petitio.* Ladenness which is used to bias the description of evidence is characterized, if at all, as a kind of special pleading.[6] I am suggesting that fallacies of ladenness can be viewed as fallacies of language in their own right.

When we view fallacies of language more broadly as including fallacies of vagueness and ladenness as well as the traditional fallacies of ambiguity, the way is clear to include hedging. The feature of language that is misused in hedging is understatement. Let us turn our attention to that feature, so as to achieve a better theoretical understanding of hedging.

To understate a claim is to use words which diminish the force or content of the claim. Understatement can be achieved in a number of different ways.[7] To begin with, the predicate of the claim can be diminished by any of a large group of adverbs of degree linguists call "detensifiers." A partial list of common English detensifiers is given below.

Common English Detensifiers

sort of	rather	relatively
more or less	quite	kind of
to some extent	a bit	moderately
technically	basically	barely
slightly	somewhat	in most respects
a fair amount	a little	in many respects
mainly	in part	in some respects
almost	scarcely	partially
practically	virtually	mildly

For example, the claim "dogs are friendly" can be understated by detensification: "dogs are rather friendly," "dogs are somewhat friendly" and so on.

Detensification is only one method of understatement. Qualification is another. A *qualifier* is a phrase which limits the scope or range of application of a predicate. Consider the following sequence of claims.

a) I will tell the truth.
b) I will tell you the truth.
c) I will tell you the truth about this matter.
d) I will tell you the truth about this matter today.

Notice that the claims get steadily weaker, because the area of application grows smaller (from telling everyone the truth about everything all the time, to telling one person the truth about one thing one time).

A third sort of understatement involves substituting contradictories for contraries. For instance, one can understate the claim

"Kelly is bad"

by saying

"Kelly is not good."

The contradictory of "good" ("not good") has been substituted for the contrary ("bad"). Calling a person "not good" weakens the claim, since it leaves open the possibility that the person is neither good nor bad.

So far we have been dealing with unmodalized assertions, that is, statements not containing modalities. But modalities are commonly used in statements. Words such as "surely," "obviously," "evidently," "certainly," "clearly," "must," "has to" and so on indicate that the speaker has complete confidence in the claim. Words such as "think," "suppose," "believe," "probably," "presumably," "supposedly," "should" and so on indicate confidence but some doubt. Words such as "guess," "seem," "can," "may/maybe/might," "possibly," "perhaps," "conceivably" and so on indicate less confidence and more doubt. Modalized assertions thus are open to a fourth sort of understatement, viz., the substitution of a weaker modality for a stronger one. The sequences below illustrate this sort of understatement.

1a) The rabbit must have gone down this hole.
1b) The rabbit should have gone down this hole.
1c) The rabbit may have gone down this hole.

2a) It is obviously a plane.
2b) It is presumably a plane.
2c) It is conceivably a plane.

As a special case of the above, unmodalized statements can be understated by adding modalities – often parenthetically – as in the examples below.

1a) The President is honest.
1b) The President is, I believe, honest.

2a) Pigs cannot dance.
2b) Pigs, to the best of my admittedly limited knowledge, cannot dance.

The point here is that when a speaker makes an assertion without a modality, the listeners assume that the speaker has no particular doubts about his statement. To parenthetically add a modality is a way to signal doubt, hence to understate.

These four devices for understatement (i. e., the use of detensifiers, the use of qualifiers, the substitution of contradictories for contraries, and the substitution of a weaker for a stronger modality) are of course not mutually exclusive. They can be used together, as in the cases below.

1a) The President is honest.
1b) The President is probably honest about this matter.

2a) Hitler was evil.
2b) Hitler was, in my opinion, not good.

3a) Fred is dead.
3b) Fred, I rather suspect, is sort of dead.

(In 1b, a detensifier and a qualifier are used. In 2b, a parenthetical modality and contradictory are inserted. In 3b, a parenthetical and a detensifier are used.)[8]

I said earlier that understatement, like ambiguity, vagueness and ladenness, is a pervasive feature of language that has many logically unexceptionable uses. Quite often we understate to make a joke, as for instance when the humorists Bob and Ray claim they are heard "approximately Coast to Coast." The British are famous – not to say notorious – for using understatement as a humorous device. And quite often we use understatement to be courteous. Thus for example "I am not quite convinced that you are entirely right in this matter" is a very polite way of disagreeing with someone.

Hedging, then, is not the use of understatement, it is the *fallacious use* of understatement. To be precise, hedging takes place in two basic ways.

Hedging of the first sort occurs when a proponent offers a thesis T, and them presented with evidence E which refutes T, substitutes T^w, where T^w is a weakened version of T which is consistent with E. By "weakened version" we mean that T^w results from T by the addition of a detensifier, or a qualifier, or substituting the contradictory of a predicate for its contrary, or substituting a weaker modality for a stronger one. (In contrast, non-fallacious backing down involves simply retracting T, where the retraction is explicit. If the arguer wishes to argue separately for T^w, that is another matter). Hedging of the first sort, like arguing to an irrelevant conclusion, tends to work when the illicitly substituted claim is deceptively similar to the original.

Hedging of the second sort occurs when a claim is put forward which has so many qualifiers or detensifiers that it does not truly apply to the things that it appears to, or cannot be tested by counterevidence. Hedging of the second sort, like amphibolous predictions by fortune-tellers, tends to work when the emptiness of the claim is not immediately obvious to the audience.

Even adding understatement to ambiguity, vagueness and ladenness does not exhaust the list of the features of language that are misused to commit fallacies. For example, overstatement (hyperbole) is another common feature of language, often used to joke (as when Texans tell "tall tales" about their State). But we can overstate to commit a fallacy, namely, a type of straw man.

Generally speaking, the straw man fallacy is committed when a person inaccurately represents another person's position.[9] Very often, perhaps usually, this misrepresentation takes the form of overstating the opponent's position in order to make it harder to defend. That is, one common technique of straw man involves either eliminating detensifiers, or ignoring key qualifications, or replacing contradictory predicates by contraries, or by substituting a stronger modality for a weaker one, in the opponent's position. (This form of straw man thus works in an opposite fashion from hedging, because in hedging an arguer attempts to understate his own position in order to make it easier to defend).

Still other examples of features of language which can be misused to commit fallacies can be given. We could include hypostatization (or reification), which is used to commit the fallacy of misplaced concreteness.[10] And we might also consider the feature of synonymy, which can be put to good use (such as the elimination of repetition[11]), but which can also be used to commit the fallacy of begging the question.

The foregoing considerations suggest that the way to bring hedging into the informal logic curriculum, and possibly some other neglected fallacies as well, is to broaden of view of the fallacies of language, and what is involved in a fallacy of language.[12]

*My thanks to Perry Weddle, J. Anthony Blair, and Hans Hansen for their valuable criticisms of earlier drafts. Any errors that remain are my own.

Notes

1. The debate took place on October 21, 1984. All quotes from the debate are from *The New York Times* transcript of the debate, published October 22, 1989.
2. See for examples:
   a) Copi, Irving, *Introduction to Logic* (7th ed.) N.Y.: Macmillan Pub. Co. (1986) pp. 113–122;
   b) Thomas, Stephen Naylor, *Practical Reasoning in Natural Language* (3rd ed.) Englewood Cliffs, N.J.: PrenticeHall (1986) pp. 365–367;
   c) Engel, S. Morris, *With Good Reason,* N.Y., St. Martin's Press (1986) pp. 89–116;
   d) Toulmin, Stephen *et al., An Introduction to Reasoning,* N. Y .: Macmillan Pub. Co. (1979).
3. Ullmann, Stephen, *Semantics,* N.Y.: Barnes and Noble (1979) pp. 167–8.
4. See, for examples, Toulmin *op. cit.* p. 185 and Walton, Douglas, *Informal Fallacies,* Philadelphia: John Benjamins Pub. Co. (1987), p. 242.
5. See, for examples, Walton *op. cit.* p. 246, and Cederblom & Paulsen, *Critical Reasoning,* Belmont, CA: Wadsworth Pub. Co. (1982), p. 59. The point that vagueness is not necessarily fallacious is made by Trudy Govier in her *A Practical Study* of *Argument* Belmont, CA: Wadsworth Pub. *Co.* (1985), p. 356.

6. In particular, Govier *(op. cit.* p. 280) has noted that emotionally loaded language can vitiate the results of opinion polls.
7. For an extensive linguistic analysis of these and other techniques of understatement, see Huebler, Axel, *Understatements and Hedges in English,* Amsterdam: John Benjamines Pub. Co. (1983*)*.
8. A pedagogic aside: I usually assign my students exercises designed to strengthen their ability to spot understatement. I give them ten or so modalized assertions and have them understate each all four ways. Example: original claim: I am sure that Sam hates Jazz. Detensifier added: I am sure that Sam hates Jazz somewhat. Qualifier added: I am sure that Sam hates Jazz of this sort. Contradictory substituted: I am sure that Sam does not like Jazz. Weaker modality substituted: I believe that Sam hates Jazz.
9. This definition is close to that of Walton *(op. cit.* p. 10). Govier *(op. cit.* p. 109) has a more careful statement of straw man: "The straw man fallacy is committed when a person misrepresents an argument, theory, or claim, and then on the basis of that misrepresentation, claims to have refuted the position that he has misrepresented."
10. Engels *(op. cit.* pp. 98–106) has a nice discussion of this fallacy.
11. See Ullmann, *op. cit.,* p. 152 for a discussion of the use of synonymy to reduce repetition in prose.
12. One might even take the extreme position that there are no separate "fallacies of language." *per* se but rather that fallacious reasoning can occur because of misuse of language. For this extreme view to be made plausible, a case would have to be made for including the fallacies of ambiguity in some other category – say, as types of ignoring the issue. But whether or not such a case can be made is beyond our present topic.

Permission to reprint courtesy of *Informal Logic.*
I wish to thank the journal.

11

"Fallacies are Common"

first appeared in Informal Logic, XI.2, Spring 1989, pp. 101–106

Professor Secor recently has replied to an article of mine in which I argued that fallacies are common in ordinary discourse.[1]

Given what I believe is the importance of the specific issue (whether fallacies are common) as well as the more general issue (how relevant logic is as a discipline for assessing ordinary discourse), I feel that a reply is in order. Since I believe that many of her specific criticisms involve some general confusion about what I was doing, I will begin by making four general points, and then turn to the specifics of her reply.

To begin with, let me remind the reader that to show that fallacies are common in structured political discourse (debates, news conferences, position papers and other campaign literature, interviews and so on) is of course not to show conclusively that fallacies are common in all ordinary discourse. It is merely to give some evidence to that effect. The examination of structured political discourse should be viewed as only the first step in a small but not uninteresting research program of examining large areas of ordinary discourse to see whether fallacies are common. Other steps in the program (if I may be permitted to foreshadow) might be to examine sales pitches, product guarantees, letters to the editor, newspaper editorials, and such like.

Second, we ought to be clear on what the claim that such-and-such is "common" means. When I claim that (say) ravens are common in my part of the country, I am not claiming that all other species of birds are uncommon, i.e., that only ravens are common. Much less am I claiming that the majority of birds are ravens, i.e., that ravens predominate. I am merely claiming that in my area of the country, one often sees ravens. Similarly, when I claim that fallacies are common in structured political discourse, I am not claiming that most things politicians say are fallacious, only that in such discourse one often hears fallacies.

Third, we ought to distinguish two principals of charity, the interpretive and the motivational. Roughly put, the interpretive principal of charity is that, before assessing someone's argument, we ought to state it in its strongest form. Under this principle of charity, we should try to fill in omitted premises that would make the argument strong, spell out key terms so as to make the argument clear, and so on. (Specifying exactly what interpretive charity amounts to is, however, not a trivial matter). Again, roughly put, the motivational principle of charity is that we ought to assume that the person putting forward an argument is doing so in good faith, i.e., is motivated by a sincere desire to communicate with his audience by logically decent rhetorical standards.

It seems to me that the interpretive principal of charity, for all the unclarity about its application in particular instances, should be adopted by the logician. But the motivational principle of charity should not be adopted by the logician, for two reasons. First, it is dubious. People are quite often motivated by the desire to mislead their audiences, and use any rhetorical technique fair or foul to achieve their goals (sell a product, win an election, gain converts to a cult, or whatever). Second, it is irrelevant to the task of the logician. The logician is interested in the logical correctness of an argument, not the motives of the arguer who puts it forward. The fact that the arguer may be sincere, or under pressure, or that his audience may be satisfied with what he says, is irrelevant to the logical merits of what he says.

The last general point regards the definition of a fallacy, and the difference between the disciplines of rhetoric and logic. A fallacy is a logically incorrect (invalid or weak) argument. Whether a given type of fallacy is persuasive to a given group of people is an interesting rhetorical question, but is not strictly speaking a logical one. Very roughly, logic is the study of correct argumentation, while rhetoric is the study of persuasive communication. The two disciplines traditionally have had and continue to have different foci. It should be kept in mind that my focus is that of the logician.

Now, Secor's argument against my view seems to have three parts. First, the cases of ignoring the issue I cited are not in fact such. Second, the cases of false cause I cited are fallacious only by unreasonably high scholarly standards. Third, the cases of *ad populum* or *ad hominem* I cited are not fallacies at all, but are instead legitimate rhetoric. More globally, she argues that my occasional charitableness towards the participants undermines my concept of a fallacy, and that I have attempted to apply culturally universal ideals to public argumentation where no such ideals truly apply.

Let me begin with ignoring the issue. Let's be clear first on what counts as answering a question (i.e., addressing an issue), and what counts as evading it. Consider an example:

> Have you stopped beating your wife?

This admits of a number of responsive answers: "I don't know" (direct declaration of ignorance on the issue); "I've never beaten my wife" (a correction of a false presupposition); "Yes, I have," or "No, I haven't" (both direct answers). But the following are non-responsive answers: "You know, I think violence is a real problem in today's world" (a general discussion of a topic, not a specific answer to a question); "Well, look at Fred—he's a bigamist, and he beats both his wives!" (the introduction of an irrelevant specific issue); "ask me some other time" or "Oh, get lost" (simply deferring or dismissing the issue).

One can ignore a question/issue by talking in generalities, raising "red herrings" (irrelevant issues), or simply pooh-poohing it (deferring or dismissing it). My contention is that, in debates, news conferences, interviews and such like, it is common for politicians to ignore by those various means many of the questions put to them.

My examples reflected that contention. For example, I cited the case where Nixon was asked whether new laws were needed to protect the public against excessive use of power by the labor unions (which he had indicated he favored earlier in his campaign), and what those laws would be. What would have been a logically responsive answer from Nixon? On analogy with our earlier simple case, here are a few examples:

a) I have not yet thought of any specific laws.
b) Your question is based on a false presupposition – I have never suggested in my campaign that we need any new laws.
c) I have issued a position paper outlining my proposals in detail. Let me just mention one such law: in any strike shutting down a plant vital to national security, give the President power to order a 30 day "cooling-off" period.

Nixon did not answer in any of those ways.

Instead, he said:

> **Mr. Nixon:** Mr. McGee, I am planning a speech on that subject next week. Also, so that we can get the opportunity for the questioners to question me, it will be before the next television debate. I will say simply, in advance of it, that I believe that in this area, the laws which should be passed, as far as the big national emergency strikes are concerned, are ones that will give the President more weapons with which to deal with those strikes.
>
> Now I have a big disagreement with Senator Kennedy, though, on this point. He has taken the position, when he first indicated on October of last year, that he would even favor compulsory arbitration as one of the weapons a president might have to stop a national emergency strike. I understand in his last speech before the Steelworkers Union, that he changed that position and indicated that he felt that government seizure might be the best way to stop a strike which could not be settled by collective bargaining. I do not believe we should have either collective bargaining or seizure. I think the moment that you give to the union, on one side, and to management, on the other side, the escape hatch of eventually going to the government to get it settled, that most of these great strikes will end up being settled by the government, and that will be in the end, in my opinion, wage control; it would mean price control—all the things that we do not want. I do believe, however, that we can give to the President of the United States powers, in addition to what he presently has in the fact-finding area, which would enable him to be more effective than we have been in handling these strikes.

Nixon in effect answers the question by saying a) ask me again later, b) here are a couple of laws I don't like, and c) generally I really do think we need those laws! Nixon, it is clear, ignored the question. Indeed, even Secor seems to see that something is inadequate about the reply. She avers:

> In referring to his forthcoming speech Nixon might be criticized for being unspecific but not, I think, for being irrelevant. If the public can be protected from excessive union power either by directly restricting the unions or by increasing presidential power to intervene, Nixon clearly advocates the latter course of action. It may, of course, be in his political interest to withhold details until a future speech, but he is not really guilty of ignoring the issue. (p. 43)

But answering the question about which new laws the President should have to deal with strikes by saying he should have more laws to deal with strikes is a hopelessly general answer.

Let me digress a moment to talk about Nixon's motivation – not a logical matter, as I indicated earlier. But since the motivationally charitable remarks I made in my first article were used against me (as I shall explain shortly), let me make some uncharitable remarks now. I suspect that Nixon did not want to admit that after urging new laws against labor activity, he hadn't thought of any. This would have made him look ignorant to the voters. Moreover, he did not support the most obvious candidates for such laws (vis., laws that would allow the President to seize plants or at least force the parties into arbitration) because that would cost him votes in organized labor. So he talked around the question. But whether we are motivationally charitable and assume he was not clear on the question he was asked, or motivationally uncharitable, and assume that he was being evasive to avoid looking stupid or alienating labor, is irrelevant to the assessment of his response.

Let's re-examine another example. Consider next the example I cited in which Kennedy was asked whether he considered the oil depletion allowance of twenty-seven and a half percent inequitable and whether he would lower it. He replied,

> **Mr. Kennedy:** Mr. McGee, there are about a hundred and four commodities that have some kind of depletion allowance-different kinds of minerals, including oil. I believe all of those should be gone over in detail to make sure that no one is getting a tax break; to make sure that no one is getting away from paying the taxes he ought to pay. That includes oil; it includes all kinds of minerals; it includes everything within the range of taxation. We want to be sure it's fair and equitable. It includes oil abroad. Perhaps that oil abroad should be treated differently than the oil here at home. Now the oil industry recently has had hard times. Particularly some of the smaller producers. They're moving about eight or nine days in Texas.
>
> But I can assure you that if I'm elected president, the whole spectrum of taxes will be gone through carefully, and if there is any inequities in oil or any other commodity, then I would vote to close that loophole. I have voted in the past to reduce the depletion allowance for the largest producers; for those from five million dollars down, to maintain it at twenty-seven and a half percent. I believe we should study this and other allowances; tax expense, dividend expenses and all the rest, and make a determination of how we can stimulate growth; how we can provide the revenues needed to move our country forward.

Secor finds his reply perfectly fine:

> Jason comments that Kennedy "never specifically answered the questions." I would argue that although he says a great deal besides answering the questions, he does answer them. Kennedy says that in the past he voted to maintain the

> twenty-seven and a half percent allowance for smaller producers; we must therefore assume that he thought the allowance fair and reasonable at the time. Political wisdom being subject to change and development, he says that we "should continue to study this and other allowances." That is, he makes no guarantee that he would continue to support this specific tax provision in the future. The answer may not be equivocal, but it is not an ascent to generality that ignores the issue at hand. The questions, in this case and many others, are complex and often loaded, and the candidates need to answer them carefully. It would be misleading as well as politically imprudent for Kennedy to call the allowance unfair, especially when he voted for it, or fair, if he might withdraw his approval in the future. (p. 43)

But I stick by my original assertion that Kennedy's reply was evasive. To the conjunctive question "is the depletion allowance unfair, and will you lower it from its current twenty-seven and a half percent?" the following replies are responsive:

a) It is not unfair, and I will not lower it.
b) It is unfair, and I will lower it.
c) It is not unfair, but I will lower it.
d) It is unfair, but I will not lower it.
e) I honestly don't know.
f) You falsely presuppose that the allowance is twenty-seven and a half percent; actually it is only ten percent.

Kennedy could have given one of these basic responsive replies, embellished with all the rhetorical bells and whistles Secor could desire. But he chose not to. He instead ignored the issue by saying a series of nonresponsive things: there are a lot of things that also have depletion allowances (So what? maybe all depletion allowances are unfair); all depletion allowances should be examined to see whether they are fair (fine, pal, but is the oil depletion allowance—supported by your own Vice Presidential nominee—unfair?); perhaps oil abroad should be treated differently from oil here at home (irrelevant); the oil industry is going through tough times (yeah, so what—does this mean the allowance is fair?); ask me again later after I'm President because, hey, I'll look into it (sure—trust you, right?); I voted to lower it to its present level (yes, *but is that present level unfair and will you lower it?).*

I will again digress into motivational inquiry. Is Secor right to view Kennedy here as sincerely trying to answer a question which is "complex and loaded"? Of course she is not. First of all, the question, while being compound, was not at all loaded, since its presuppositions—that the allowance existed and was twenty-seven and a half percent—were true. Second, it is clear that Kennedy was deliberately evasive because it was politically expedient to do so: if he said he would lower the allowance, he would win support among many taxpayers but lose support in the oil-producing states; if he said he would not lower the allowance, he would lose taxpayer support (and lose the issue of unfair taxation with which he was tarring Nixon and the Republicans) although he would gain support in the oil-producing states. He chose the easy way out, and did "the old *ignoratio* shuffle." But whether Secor or I am right about Kennedy's motivations, clearly he ignored the issue.

I won't rehash the other examples I cited. Time and again, the politicians did not address the given issue squarely by either conceding ignorance, showing the question to have a false presupposition, or answering it directly and specifically. Instead, either they raised irrelevant issues, talked in generalities, or deferred/dismissed the question.

I turn next to the fallacies of false cause. I cited a number of cases in which a politician attempted to show that his opponent was responsible for some bad situation that occurred while his opponent was in office merely on the basis that it occurred while that opponent was in office.

Secor doesn't even try to show my examples fail to fit the traditional *post hoc ergo propter hoc* mold. Instead, she replies

> But once again, we might ask "false" or "inadequate" from what point of view? We all know that military strategists, economists, and historians make very elaborate causal arguments, constructing intricate models that take whole books to explain, work out, and verify. But the voter's perspective is not the same as the scholar's.
>
> It is reasonable to expect that there be some difference between arguing for causes in the forums of scholarly disciplines, where one's causal model must be very precise and anticipate the efforts of other scholars to refute it, and arguing for causes in the public forums of presidential debate, where notions of responsibility are much more diffuse. As Aristotle says, we can only ask of a subject the degree of precision that is appropriate to it. Politicians are not economists, and voters act on causal assumptions different from those of scholars. Thus fallacies of false cause may be obvious from the vantage of the academic critic, whose standard of evidence for causality may be very high, but such analysis tells us very little about the way voters make or even should make decisions. Perhaps that is just another way of saying that the rhetorical context of political discourse differs from that of scholarly discourse. (pp. 46–7)

Her reply is very weak, for several reasons. First, it is simply not true that even the politicians involved accept *post hoc* reasoning as logical even in "the rhetorical context of political discourse," much less that the hapless voters do. This is obvious from the fact that the politicians do *not* accept responsibility for every bad thing which occurs when *they* are in office. And certainly the voters do not accept responsibility for every bad thing which happens in the country while *they* reside in it! As C.S. Peirce noted, the ethics of belief requires that any argument form I apply to others I should equally be willing to accept applied to me. No principle of charity should stop us from calling a spade a spade: if a politician applies a form of argument to his opponent but rejects it for himself, then it is clear that *even he* does not think it a logically strong argument technique.

Second, there *are* ways a politician can establish a better logical case for social, political, or economic causal claims. One obvious way is to cite from scholarly works that truly establish such claims—something that politicians often do, please note. (Remember, my point is that politicians *often* commit false cause fallacies, not that they *always* or even *typically* commit them.) Another way is to sketch out the premises of a full argument for a causal claim, and tell the audience how they may obtain a position paper in which the full details are spelled out. Again, politicians often do this.

The upshot is that to demand that our would-be leaders do more to establish their causal claims than merely cite temporal connections (especially in a highly selective and self-serving way!) is not to impose impractical elitist standards, but rather to request something which politicians can and often do provide. We just need to see more of it.

Secor's third point is not clear to me. I had pointed out that the politicians in the debates engaged in a number of *ad populum* and *ad hominem* appeals. I charitably added that in some cases *ad populum* appeals could be condoned, though not so with *ad hominem* appeals. Secor seems to think that this undercuts my view that those appeals are fallacies:

> ...If we condone rather than condemn the use of such tactics, what is the use of talking about the *ad populum* as a fallacy? If fallacies are not the product of deceitful intent, as we saw earlier, and if they are used by quite decent politicians, and if we can condone their usage in the context of debate, there seems to be little reason to consider them errors. They are errors only if we hold political discourse to a purely rational ideal according to which candidates are asked perfectly straight-forward questions which they are expected to answer without any tint of emotion or bias toward their own candidacy. (p. 47)

But her line of argument here is muddled.

To condone is to forgive, not approve. We can condone an act of petty jealousy without approving petty jealousy as a general lifestyle. My point is a simple one: a fallacy is a logically bad argument. A person may commit a fallacy (i.e., put forward a logically bad argument) out of sincere ignorance, or deliberate and unpardonable deceit, or even deliberate yet pardonable deceit, but a fallacy is still committed. Whether we condemn the person is quite a different question from whether we condemn the argument form. One is a question of motivational *(not* interpretive) charity, the other of logic.

Let me conclude with a note on the question whether those of us who teach logic with the belief that we can at least to a small degree improve the level of intellectual taste if not the reasoning ability of our students are merely elitists with an "unrealistically superior and judgmental attitude toward ordinary discourse." Really, the amount of illogic which pervades our public and private lives is considerable. This would not be so bad, I suppose, if all public and private decisions concerning our lives were made by governmental or other institutions, and the leaders of those institutions reasoned well—i.e., if we were totally ruled by philosopher-kings. But true philosopher-kings are not as plentiful as blackberries, and, in any case, the global trend seems to be toward increasing democratization. It seems imperative, then, that all students need their reasoning skills improved. We teachers cannot improve those skills unless we point to rigorous standards of argumentation, and demand that our students adhere to those standards, and create in our students an expectation that those who seek to govern also adhere to these standards.

Notes

1. See my "Are Fallacies Common? A Look at Two Debates," *Informal Logic,* vol. 8 (1986), pp. 81–92, and Marie J. Secor "How Common are Fallacies?" *Informal Logic,* vol. 9, (1987) pp. 41–48. All page references in the present reply are to Secor's paper.

Permission to reprint courtesy of *Informal Logic.*
I wish to thank the journal.

12

My review of *Logics for Artificial Intelligence*

(Chichester: Ellis Horwood 1985) first appeared in Philosophia Vol. 19, No. 1, 1989, pp. 81–83.

One of the most exciting recent trends in computer science is the application of philosophical work in logic and epistemology to problems in AI (artificial intelligence). AI research is nothing if not eclectic in inspiration, and much use has been made in AI work of academic philosophy. The book under review is a case in point, for it surveys non-standard logic with an eye to its use in two key areas of AI: the representation of knowledge and the design of "inference engines".

Turner's book begins with a brief discussion of what "non-standard" logics are. (The term "non-standard" is preferable to the term "deviant", which is still used by many philosophers). Non-standard logics include: modal, temporal, many-valued, epistemic, intuitionistic, and other recent systems. As Turner notes, while non-standard logics have been investigated by philosophers and logicians since the 1930's at least, it was only in the late 1960's that McCarthy and others began to exploit those resources in AI.

In the second chapter, Turner takes up the topic of modal logic, and its descendant temporal logic. He describes how the syntax of modal logic, interpreted in terms of possible worlds, can be re-interpreted in a way more useful to computer scientists, viz., as states of an underlying machine. He then explains how the basic concepts of dynamic logic can be defined. He finishes the chapter by briefly discussing Moore's recent modal logic of knowledge and action, which may be of use in AI.

In chapter 3, many-valued logic is reviewed. Turner focuses on the three-valued logics of Kleene, Lukasiewicz, and Bochvar. (Kleene's logic was developed to accomodate undecided mathematical statements, so has a third truth value "u" for "undecided". Lukasiewicz's logic was developed to accommodate future contingents, so has a third truth value "i" for "indeterminate". Bochvar's logic was developed to accommodate semantic paradoxes, so has a third truth-value "m" for "meaningless".) The chapter finishes by tying in the three-valued systems of Bochvar and Kleene with non-monotonic reasoning.

In chapter 4, Turner discusses Martin-Lof's intuitionist logic. He rightly notes the importance of Bishop's work in the mid-1960's, which showed that many of the results of classical mathematics can be obtained intuitionistically. He devotes some detail to an exposition of Martin-Lofs theory of types, and shows how to reinterpret it as a kind of programming language. Roughly, he reinterprets an intuitionistic judgment $a \in A$, i.e., that a is a construction which proves A, as meaning that a is a program which achieves task specification A. He reviews an example (due to Nordstrom and Smith) of an intuitionist programming language. The result is quite attractive: at once, you have a specification language, a (purely functional) programming language, and a formal device for deriving programs from their specifications (thus verifying the adequacy of the programs).

Chapter 5 covers non-monotonic logics, i.e., logical systems in which the addition of new information (axioms) can invalidate old information (theorems). Non-monotonic logic is of great interest in AI. Turner reviews the non-monotonic system of McDermott and Doyle, which is a type of modal logic. He also reviews the markedly different approach to non-monotonic inference of Gabbay, which bases non-monotonic logic on intuitionism. The chapter ends with a brief discussion of Moore's auto-epistemic logic.

Chapter 6 is devoted to yet another variant of modal logic, viz., temporal logic. Turner reviews the temporal semantics of modal operations, and reviews various axiom systems. He then focuses on two particular temporal logics, McDermott's system (which has an event-based ontology) and Allen's (which has an interval-based ontology). Turner gives some very useful criticisms of both systems. He concludes the chapter by discussing the work by Manna, Pnueli, and others applying temporal logic to the specification and verification of concurrent programs.

In chapter 7, fuzzy logic and its application to expert systems is discussed. His discussion, of course, focuses on the work of Zadeh, who virtually created the subject. Chapter 8 briefly discusses many-sorted logic, and prospects for the future use of non-standard logic in AI.

Turner's book has a number of good features. It is clearly written at a level accessible to undergraduate math and Computer Science students. It has a good bibliography at the end of each chapter. Most importantly, it fills a large need for an up-to-date survey of a rapidly expanding field.

However, Turner's book also has some drawbacks. It overlooks some very promising recent areas of nonstandard logic, such as relevance logics and non-assertion logics (i.e., question logics, logics of imperatives, and dialogue logics). Worse yet, it is too much an overview: it is so sketchy in many places that it only informs the reader of the existence—but not the real nature—of a particular sub-domain. This is a book that leaves one hungry.

Permission to reprint courtesy of Springer . I wish to thank the journal *Philosophia* as well.

13

"Does Virtue Epistemology Provide a Better Account of the *Ad Hominem* Argument? A Reply to Christopher Johnson"

first appeared in Philosophy 84 (2009), pp. 251–266

Abstract: Christopher Johnson has put forward in this journal the view that *ad hominem* reasoning may be more generally reasonable than is allowed by writers such as myself, basing his view on virtue epistemology. I review his account, as well as the standard account, of *ad hominem* reasoning, and show how the standard account would handle the cases he sketches in defence of his own view. I then give four criticisms of his view generally: the problems of virtue conflict, vagueness, conflation of speech acts, and self-defeating counsel. I then discuss four reasons why the standard account is superior: it better fits legal reality, the account of other fallacies, psychological science, and political reality.

In a recent article in this journal, Christopher Johnson has argued that from the perspective of virtue epistemology, *ad hominem* attacks may not be fallacious, as is commonly held in logic texts today (as it has been for centuries).[1] In this paper, I will argue that his account of *ad hominem* reasoning is inadequate, and that the traditional account remains more satisfying.

Let me begin by briefly reviewing his thesis. Johnson's account of how to treat *ad hominem* reasoning is based upon virtue epistemology. Since there are a variety of versions of virtue epistemology, let's call his account 'the Johnson virtue ethics theory of *ad hominem* reasoning', or the 'JVET' for short. His view is that,

> …intellectual virtues, moral virtues and non-moral virtues can all be legitimate factors in deciding contentious issues that are otherwise irresolvable. When there is a dearth of information or capacity to make decisions, we can rely on these virtues and traits to help choose between courses of action to the extent that they compose coherent character portraits of the individuals who make arguments as to which course we should follow. This is most easily seen with intellectual virtues, but as moral virtues and non-moral character traits suggest intellectual virtues, and as all three mutually support, they all become considerable.[2]

After discussing an article by Lawrence Hinman[3] and my article in reply,[4] Johnson elaborates this view by saying,

> Taking as a starting point the idea that we have limited rational capacities, there will always be times when we just cannot do what Jason suggests we do in always engaging in further investigation or looking into the topic ourselves. We may either not have sufficient time to do this – or even if we do we may not have the necessary intellectual skills or abilities to understand the issues concerned. It may well be in such cases that the reply is made that judgment should thus be suspended; but often decisions are required of us even when we are unable to determine the issue fully factually to our satisfaction. In such cases it seems we have to appeal to criteria other than the facts of the case since those facts are underdetermining. Turning at this point to judging the people who consider the facts can now be a logical progression.[5]

So when I feel my time is better spent elsewhere, or I am otherwise too busy, I am justified in critiquing the character of the person offering me evidence for a claim, instead of evaluating that evidence, deferring my judgment, or seeking new evidence.

Further, in examining a person's character and background, not only is it reasonable to look at his or her intellectual virtue, but also traits as well:

> Furthermore, since moral virtues may be suggestive of intellectual virtues, these too may be considerable in deciding between arguments, and so also non-moral character traits.[6]

Johnson elaborates these views by discussing a number of cases, which I shall review after sketching the more traditional account, found in a variety of textbooks, which I shall call the 'Standard Account' (or 'SA' for short).

Under the Standard Account (a version of which I put forward in detail in my own critical thinking text[7]), criticizing a person is reasonable (logical) if it is relevant in the context, and unreasonable to do so when it is irrelevant in the context. Most logic texts take this view, although spelling out the notion of 'relevance' is usually left undone. In my view (elaborated in detail in my text[8]) is that relevance is an erotetic notion, that is, one that relates to the logic of questions and answers. Briefly, a statement S is **directly relevant** to a question Q if and only if S is either a direct answer to Q, a corrective answer to Q, an admission of ignorance, or an explanation why Q is impertinent in the context. (A direct answer to a question provides the information the question requested. A corrective answer to a question is a denial of one or more of the question's presuppositions. An admission of ignorance is a statement that the respondent doesn't know the answer. And an explanation of impertinence provides evidence that shows the question is not legitimate in the context.)

A statement S is **indirectly relevant** to Q if and only if it is logically good evidence for a directly relevant response. A statement S is **relevant** to Q if and only if it is either directly or indirectly relevant.

Note that the focus under the SA is put on the manner in which someone is responding to an issue, not the person him- or herself. So if the discussion is, say, whether the recession is over, the relevant answers would be the same no matter who was speaking. The responses would include directly relevant ones, such as: 'Yes, it is'; 'No, it isn't'; 'The economy hasn't been in recession'; 'I don't know'; and 'That question is impertinent, because we are here at the hospital to discuss how to treat out daughter's cancer.' The responses would include indirectly relevant ones, such as 'The stock market and employment rates are going up'.

Now, under the SA, there are certainly occasions when the character or background of the respondent is clearly relevant. One class of these occasions—which Johnson concedes is already widely recognized in logic texts[9]—is cases in which someone is giving testimony. Cases of testimony are cases in which the person *is* the evidence, that is, cases in which the person makes a claim and wants the listener to accept it on his or her say-so. So in the courtroom, juries typically have to reach a decision on an *overarching* question ('Did the accused commit the crime?') in part by listening to witnesses. When the jury is listening to the testimony of any witness, the *immediate* question at hand is, 'Is this witness telling the truth about this matter?' In eye-witness testimony, the witness asks the jury to believe something because the witness observed it personally. In expert testimony, the witness asks the jury to believe something because the witness has judged it or determined it to be so, on the basis of some presumed expertise and study of some presumed objective evidence. In both cases, the SA no less than the JVET would allow—in fact, encourage—examining the character and background of the witness (though the SA would be more focused in so doing, as I will explain below).

In bringing up testimony, Johnson only mentions legal contexts, but of course testimony is by no means limited to the courtroom. People very often testify informally in discussions and disputes, and when they do, then again examining the character and background of the witness is relevant, hence reasonable; to the extent it bears on whether the witness is speaking the truth.

Now, most basic logic and critical thinking texts talk in some detail about the criteria for evaluating expert testimony. The person evaluating such testimony is advised by the SA to look at eight criteria. How current is the expert cited? Is the expert clearly identified? How well qualified is the expert (by usual measures, such as degrees held, publication record, experience, and so on)? Is the expert unbiased? Is the expert basing his or her testimony on evidence that is open to the inspection of other experts? Is the expert testifying in his or her field of expertise? If quoted, is the expert quoted accurately? And is the expert basing his or her testimony on theories and practices widely accepted in the field?

Regarding eye-witness testimony, fewer logic and critical thinking texts talk about the criteria for judging such testimony. In my treatment,[10] the criteria are fairly obvious. How well positioned was the witness to observe the situation? Was or is the witness impaired (for example, under the influence of alcohol, or near sighted)? Is the witness biased? Is the witness's testimony consistent? Is there corroborating evidence? Do other eye-witnesses agree? And how plausible is the testimony?

Note that under the SA the criteria for judging testimony tend to be observational features, rather than general character traits (intellectual, moral or other). This is understandable, for one is usually not in a position to judge broad character traits – how would I know whether my doctor is generally just, or the eye-witness on the stand is generally honest? And even if one could ascertain general traits, the SA would focus only on the ones tied directly to the testimony itself. Yes, it would be relevant to accepting Sue's eyewitness testimony that she saw Fred rob the liquor store if I could ascertain that she is generally honest, but her lack of compassion (for instance) would be irrelevant.

Not mentioned by Johnson is a second broad area where the SA would suggest that examining the character or background of a person is relevant (hence reasonable). Those are cases in which the person *is* the legitimate question, namely, employment situations, where the question at hand is whether a given candidate should get the job. If Jones is applying for a job as a school bus driver, looking at his or her driving record is as clearly relevant (hence reasonable) under the SA as it is under the JVET.

Again, we need not simply limit this to formal job applications. In a presidential debate between candidates Jones and Smith, if Jones attacks Smith for being a big spender or a war monger, this would be would be relevant (if true)—after all, most voters clearly do not want a president to be fiscally profligate or militarily reckless. When you are running for office, saying why your opponent is unworthy is as legitimate as saying why you are worthy. (Of course, you may commit other fallacies while making your case, or tell falsehoods, but that is beside the point). This also applies to many personal or business situations – choosing a friend or a business partner of course will involve looking at the character and background of the other person.

It is important to note that in both the areas mentioned above in which critiquing a person's character or background are relevant (so reasonable) under the SA, there are clear limitations to that critique, dictated by the immediate question at hand. In probing a witness's testimony, a defense attorney might ask the witness about possible biases, say, or whether the witness had consumed alcohol on the day he or she claims to have witnessed the crime, for those bear on whether the witness is lying about or was not able to see clearly the incidents witnessed. But the attorney would not be right (and usually would not be allowed) to probe the witness on aspect of his or her background that did not bear on the immediate question, for example, the witness's sexual orientation.

The same holds for job interviews. The hiring committee can (from the SA point of view) ask questions about a candidate's character or background in so far as it bears on the immediate question, such as whether the candidate has ever been convicted of a felony, what the candidate's scholarly track record is, and so on. But it would not generally sanction questions about the candidate's sexual orientation, political views, or ethnicity.

A note about terminology is appropriate here. When talking about cases in which criticizing someone's character is clearly relevant, we have our choice. We could say they are cases in which the *ad hominem* argument is reasonable. Under this meaning, we would say that *ad hominem* reasoning is sometimes logically acceptable, sometimes not. This seems to be Johnson's usage.[11] Alternatively, we could say that cases in which criticizing someone's character or background is clearly relevant are not cases in which *ad hominem* argument occurs at all, taking '*ad hominem* argument' to refer solely to cases in which criticizing someone's character or background is irrelevant, hence unreasonable. Under this meaning, we would say that *ad hominem* reasoning is always logically unacceptable, i.e. always a fallacy. I favor the second usage.

To flesh out his account, Johnson gives us a number of imaginary cases. In each case, I will argue that the JVET seems plausible at first, but only because it is so vaguely put, and that when spelled out in more detail, the SA gives us a better account.

In the first case,[12] he asks us to imagine a case in which you are faced with two arguments from two scientists. You are not a scientist, and have only 'superficial' knowledge about the issue at hand. You are in a 'position of authority' and have to make a policy decision 'between the two arguments'. Both arguments seem equally 'coherent', and each scientist has impeccable credentials. 'Further investigation may reveal more evidence,' 'but it is doubtful that this new evidence will make either side more compelling'. So, Johnson says, it seems reasonable to look at the character of the two scientists. One scientist is very 'conservative' in his approach to research, generally respecting prior 'traditions' and feeling that it is best to 'gradually amend previous work'. The other scientist is more 'radical' and 'creative' in her approach, and believing that all previous approaches have failed, she advocates a 'shift in thinking'. Johnson concludes by saying we can reasonably decide between the two arguments by looking at 'the general approach that each person takes—as determined by their intellectual virtues…' (Johnson doesn't explicitly say which scientist is more virtuous in this case, but from his manner of presentation, I think that he means that you should choose the argument given by the creative scientist).

This example is so vague that it is unclear what Johnson is getting at. How 'superficial' is your knowledge—are you completely untrained in the field? Or slightly trained in the field (a few undergrad courses)? Or perhaps you have a Bachelor's degree but no grad training? Or you have a graduate degree, but not conversant with the research topic at hand? Are you deciding between the two *arguments* (recommendations/conclusions together with the evidence/premises offered), or merely between the two recommendations? If one scientist is creative and the other is merely a drudge, how is it that they have the same credentials? And does 'credentials' include their respective records of success in solving problems of this exact sort, or just their degrees, publications, and memberships in scholarly organizations? Does 'coherent argument' mean 'good argument'? If you are ignorant of the science, how could you possibly know that both arguments are equally good (factually and logically), much less that no further evidence would make either case compelling? And if you are ignorant of the science, how would you know (other than the pejorative connotation of the term 'conservative' and the positive connotation of 'creative') whether being conservative in scientific work was better or worse than being creative?

To elaborate that last point, note that creativity in science isn't always good. Thomas Kuhn, for example, made the point that scientific revolutions involve paradigm shifts, i.e. radical breaks with prior theories – presumably requiring creativity. But he also emphasized that normal science – which characterizes much of a mature, established science – involves working within an acceptable paradigm (and I am not aware that he thought it was therefore always 'uncreative'). Moreover, while we might hold that all scientific revolutions require creative breaks with tradition, it would scarcely follow that all creative breaks with tradition result in successful scientific revolutions. Many—arguably most—result in failure or even pseudoscience. Einstein was creative and successful; the men who claimed to have discovered 'cold fusion' were creative and unsuccessful. So even if I could judge one scientist more creative than the other, that wouldn't tell me which one to believe.

Now, let's try sketching a realistic case that fits the general parameters of the Johnson case, but spelled out in sufficient detail to see what the SA would say about it. Say you are a U.S. Senator. You majored in political science in college, taking only one general introductory physical science class along the way. You went to law school, and from there you went into politics. You are ignorant of all science, but now you have to vote on a bill on global warming, say, a 'cap and trade' tax on carbon dioxide emissions. You've listened to two scientists (both climatologists) who testified before our committee. What does the SA suggest?

First, don't both trying to evaluate their arguments — you're incompetent to do so. All the more you shouldn't bother trying to discover who is 'conservative' or 'creative'— you're incompetent to tell which approach is appropriate, or even what those terms mean, much less who of these two scientists is creative and who is not. The SA views this as an ordinary case of relying on expert testimony, and you would be better off taking the advice of psychologist Ilan Yaniv, and call more experts to testify. Yaniv makes the point that both statistical theory and psychological research indicate that when more experts agree, the likelihood that the common opinion is correct increases dramatically. As he notes,

> In the case of quantitative estimates, it can be outlined in simple terms why improvement is to be expected from combining estimates. A subjective estimate about an objective event can be viewed as the sum of three components: the 'truth', random error (random fluctuations in a judge's performance), and constant bias (a consistent tendency to over- or underestimate the event).

> Statistical principles guarantee that judgments formed by averaging several sources have lower random error than the individual sources on which the averages are based.[13]

How many experts to call is a matter of how confident you want to be in the matter. In this regard, Yaniv adds:

> As already noted, as few as three to six judgments might suffice to achieve most of what can be gained from averaging a larger number of opinions. This puzzling result that adding opinions does not contribute much to accuracy is related to my previous comments. Some level of dependence among experts is present in almost any realistic situation (their opinions tend to have some degree of correlation for a variety of reasons – they may rely on similar education sources, or simply consult one another…). Therefore, the benefits accrued from polling more experts diminish rapidly, with each additional one amounting to 'more of the same'.[14]

It is clear that two experts would be too few, six would be better, and given the gravity of the matter (if global warming is real, the results can be ecologically and economically devastating, but if it isn't, and you vote in an onerous tax on carbon, the results will be economically devastating and unnecessary), you might even call a dozen. Also, it is clear that you would want to call experts from a variety of places (universities and research institutes from all over the world), so as to better rule out sources of 'local biases.' But is all a question of expert testimony and it is hard to see how the creativity of the witnesses enters in, as opposed to more observable criteria emphasized by the SA.

The second case Johnson gives[15] asks you to suppose you are involved in 'determining public policy' and are presented with proposals from two 'analysts' who have 'examined the same data'. One analyst who is 'known to be more charitable' meaning she is likely to interpret 'inexact or somewhat vague data' as what 'she believes it implies rather than distinctly states'. The other analyst rejects the vague data as 'contaminated'. Here, Johnson concludes, 'there is no real truth to the matter as to which analyst is right or wrong, but the matter is decided based upon what sort of methodology one thinks is most appropriate'. If you are more concerned with exact results for a smaller sample, you choose the proposal from the first analyst; if you are more concerned with less exact results from a broader sample, you choose the proposal from the second.

Again, this is quite vague. Does 'analyst' mean scientist or medical doctor? If you are not knowledgeable enough to decide which analyst's data analysis is more reliable, how would you know which one of the more analysts is in fact more charitable in data analysis generally, or whether choosing a more charitable data analysis is appropriate in decision-making in this specific case, much less generally?

So if the case here is one in which you are ignorant about which methodology is right to use here, the SA would counsel that you not try to evaluate it, but call more witnesses to see what the preponderance of their opinion is *on this proposal.* Their general methodological inclinations would be irrelevant, because knowing which expert had which methodological inclination, and which inclination was generally more reliable, would be beyond your ken.

On the other hand, let's imagine a case where you do have a degree of knowledge about the data analysis. You are the CEO of a major manufacturer of widgets. You have an undergrad degree in Economics and an MBA. You are wondering whether to expand production. You hire two professional economists to look at the prospects of growth in the demand for widgets. Both examine the same data on past demand for widgets, but the cautious economist throws out two months of the data as 'outliers' (suspiciously low or high data points), and recommends you not expand. The charitable economist bases his projection on all the data points, and recommends that you expand. On what basis would you decide?

You certainly wouldn't rely on either economist's reputation for being charitable or cautious in data analysis. No, you would seek further information, more evidence. Specifically, you would ask each one to defend in detail why he or she deleted or retained the two disputed data points. You would decide whose testimony to accept on the basis of the reasons they give why the outliers *in this case* should be dropped or not. *You* would be making the decision based on reasons, none of which would be the general intellectual virtue of the two analysts. To do less would be intellectually lazy and fiscally irresponsible.

I won't rehearse the last two generic cases Johnson discusses[16] which involve appeals to intellectual virtue. In both, we see the same problem: they are vaguely described, and when you imagine specific cases that fit the generic description, they seem to be either cases in which the person is faced with expert testimony *simpliciter*, which the SA allows as a case in which examination of the speaker's character and background are relevant, or else would be cases in which the reasonable thing to do would be to seek more information, because you are competent enough to do so.

Further, in cases of testimony, when evaluating witnesses, rather than looking at general intellectual virtues '…such as methodological approach, willingness to consider evidence, extent to which one is willing to accept vague evidence, creativity of thought, perceptiveness, foresight of thought, and so on,'[17] the SA would advise looking to factors more observable to the person evaluating the testimony, such as the track record of success in cases like the one at hand, specific biases regarding the subject matter upon which he or she is testifying, number of publications in the field in which the testimony is being given, relevant degrees held, and so on. This is because typically only the experts in a field are competent to judge what count as intellectual virtues in that field and which researchers have them.

Johnson suggests that there are cases in which, while you are competent to look further into the facts, as a practical matter you simply don't have the time to look further into the topic. And in such cases, looking at the intellectual virtue of the arguer are then relevant.[18] There are three problems with this view.

The first problem is that in cases in which you feel your time is so limited that more evidence-gathering is impractical, you should at least be intellectually honest enough to recognize that in such cases, you are no longer evaluating someone's argument; you are only deciding whether to accept his or her testimony. One ought to be crystal clear on this difference. I will elaborate on this point later in this paper.

The second problem is that we ought also to recognize that the notion that whenever people feel they don't have time to exercise logical due diligence (i.e. when the evidence given by two arguers seems equally strong, to look for more evidence that bears on the issue at hand), they should just view the argument given as a species of testimony, is an invitation to intellectual laziness. For under the JVET, I can always say to myself at any time I face a factually and logically good argument for a conclusion I dislike, 'Well, I simply don't have time as a practical matter to evaluate this argument and find refuting evidence. Let me just look at the virtues of the arguer.'

I will elaborate on this objection later in the paper, but to see what it is more clearly, consider Johnson's own example of a child giving you an argument. Johnson says,

> There is more to arguments than the words that are used, especially when one is unable to verify their premises. This is easily seen when we compare an argument as put forth by a child and the same argument as put forth by an adult. There is credibility to the adult not borne by the child and this is enough to make us suspicious of what the child says.[19]

This seems to me to be debatable at best, and at worst an invitation to devalue whatever children say. Suppose at the market I encounter a friend with whom I enjoy discussing politics, and I say to him, 'I think that Smith will win the open

Senate seat in the election this Tuesday.' To our utter amazement, a young girl of say eight years of age (who is with her parents shopping) whirls around and says to me, 'Sir, I think that you are mistaken, because both the latest Zogby and Rasmussen polls have Smith down by eight percentage points, with a margin of error of only three per cent. And since the election is only a few days off, there is not much chance that the voters will shift enough in their opinions as to hand Smith the victory.'

Now, I may be shocked that a child would be so articulate; amazed that she is so interested in politics, or annoyed that she would intrude into a private conversation. But it would be intellectually lazy to think that because I cannot then and there verify the poll numbers she cites, I could just dismiss her argument out of hand because she is a child and these are 'adult matters'. It seems to me to be more reasonable to just suspend judgment until I get a chance to log on to a computer later and check the polling organizations websites myself.

The third problem is that while there may be rare cases in which one has to choose between little and no evidence, the result is still a fallacy, if an understandable one. Let's try to imagine a case in which you must choose between two claims, with truly no time or ability to gather more information or gather more information, and where the only difference is what you know of the intellectual virtue of one of the sides. Such a case is bound to be highly contrived and highly improbable. Let's imagine your spouse has had a major heart attack, and you have just arrived at the hospital. The hospital has only two heart specialists, Dr. Smith and Dr. Jones. Dr. Jones talks to you briefly and suggests that your spouse undergo a by-pass operation immediately. Jones then has to leave. A moment later, Smith comes in, and talks to you briefly and suggests a stent be inserted immediately, instead of a full by-pass operation. Smith then has to leave. You know absolutely nothing about heart disease and it treatments. You know nothing about Jones or Smith professionally, but happen to know that Smith is a great chess player (from a blurb in the paper). What should you do?

Well, you should talk to other doctors, to get a consensus. To rule this out, let us imagine that Smith and Jones are the only two doctors on duty that day (it is a small hospital!) Well, then you should ask for Smith and Jones to get together with you to each briefly explain their respective recommendations, hoping that you might be able to glean enough information to make an informed choice. To rule this out, let us imagine that both doctors are in surgery, and can't talk at all. Well, then you should go online quickly to one of the numerous reliable sites that briefly but accurately give medical information, such as 'WebMD.com'. Or you could Google search the two doctors to see their track records. To rule this out, let us suppose that vandals have destroyed the hospital's connections to the internet. Well, then you should talk to several nurses there (nurses know a good deal about medicine, and about which doctors have the best track records in operations). To rule this out, let us suppose that this hospital has a very strict (and unusual!) rule against nurses talking to patients about treatment modalities or doctors' records, enforced by the death penalty, so no nurses will say a word to you. Let us further suppose the rule applies to hospital staff and other visitors. Well, you should then simply call on your cell phone or one of the pay phones there to have a friend or relative to quickly Google search or WebMD research, or call other doctors for more testimony. To rule this out, let us imagine that terrorists have destroyed all telecommunication connections between the hospital and the outside world. In this (grotesquely rare) case, wouldn't it be 'reasonable' to choose Smith's recommendation, because there may be a 'correlation' between chess ability and general scientific competence? Doesn't that show that, at least here, the JVET is right, and examining intellectual virtue to decide which doctor to believe is reasonable?

It depends upon what you mean be 'reasonable'. Let us imagine an evidence scale ranging from 0% (total non-sequiturs) to 100% (deductive validity). Here you have let us say absolutely 0% evidence that Jones' plan is medically superior, and perhaps 3% evidence that Smith's plan is medically superior and you must choose. I suppose that, because 3% evidence is better than no evidence, yes, in that sense it would be reasonable to choose Smith. In the same way, if you didn't know anything at all about Smith either, it would be 'reasonable' to flip a coin. But the argument ('Smith's plan is better because he can play chess well') is still a howling fallacy. It can be prudentially reasonable to reason fallaciously in such incredibly unlikely situations as this. It would still be an *ad hominem* argument.

Let us now turn next to the example Johnson gives in which he feels that moral virtues are relevant in evaluating arguments. These are again not spelled out in any detail, but are cases in which he thinks it is plausible that moral and intellectual traits are linked. So he says that someone who is morally empathetic 'may be thought also' to be intellectually empathetic, someone who morally humble may also 'be thought to be' intellectually fair-minded, someone who is morally corrupt 'may be thought to be' intellectually corrupt, and if someone demonstrates moral courage may also 'be thought to be' intellectually courageous.[20] The phrase 'might be thought to be' indicates neither causal nor logical necessity, but rather 'correlation'.[21]

Johnson admits such correlations are 'tenuous'. He notes himself that moral absent-mindedness need not suggest intellectual absent-mindedness (an absent-minded professor can be forgetful of promises made to family but diligent about intellectual work), moral disloyalty need not suggest intellectual disloyalty (you could betray your spouse but remain loyal to your intellectual work), and one can be morally intolerant without being intellectually intolerant (you could be intolerant of foibles in your family but forgiving of mistakes made in creative research).

But he doesn't seem to see the same problems apply to the first four correlations, which he thinks are stronger. I can be morally empathetic from devout religiosity, but for that reason be lacking in intellectual empathy, especially as regards other religions. For the same reason I can be morally humble, yet intellectually close-minded. Again, I might be morally corrupt, let's say greedy, but be intellectually honest about my studies. And how often have we seen soldiers that are very brave, but intellectually cowardly — think here of Nazi and Soviet soldiers, brave in fighting, but unwilling to critically examine their regime's ideology.

Worse, it is not merely the tenuousness of such correlations that is a problem, but their specific relevance. Take the most plausible correlation (between moral and intellectual virtues) Johnson gives, viz., between moral corruption and intellectual corruption. Perhaps he has in mind a greedy used-car salesman who is pitching me on a car on his lot, citing alleged facts about the car, including its low mileage, Kelly Blue Book value, and its general condition. Now, let's assume for the sake of the discussion that most people who are morally corrupt (greedy, say) are also intellectually corrupted (inclined to lie or give bad arguments deliberately to deceive). Do I know that that correlation holds of this particular salesman? And even if it does, how does that make his reasons false (he may be corrupt enough to lie, but even liars don't generally lie if the truth will get them what they want). I certainly would not accept his *testimony* ('Believe me, pal, this is the car for you!'), as I would not accept the testimony of anyone with so obvious a bias in the matter, but here he is giving me reasons I can inspect independently. And if I don't have time to do so, why am I shopping for a car in the first place? Why don't I wait until I do have time to exercise due diligence in purchasing to buy a car?

Finally, Johnson considers correlations between non-moral character traits and intellectual virtues. He offers some examples: an interest in fine wine might suggest the intellectual virtue of attention to detail; experience in world travel might suggest the intellectual virtue of open-mindedness; an appreciation of abstract art might suggest the intellectual virtues of creativity and imaginativeness; and participation in sport might suggest the intellectual virtue of perseverance. Now, he concedes that many readers will find these correlations not merely tenuous, but fatuous.[22] One is tempted to reply, 'To say the least!' Kant never travelled outside of his home town, but it would seem odd to say he wasn't intellectually curious. And the athletes I have encountered in my teaching career have not tended to demonstrate exceptional perseverance in study (indeed, far from it). And it is hard for me to see how if you prefer impressionist to abstract art, you likely lack creativity.

Even less can I comprehend the notion that if one doctor recommends an operation, and a second recommends against it, that I should decide the matter by looking to see who had the better taste in wine.

Johnson, however, suggests that clusters of non-moral traits and moral virtues may be more reliable indicators of intellectual virtue.[23] So if a person is not just well-travelled, but has 'demonstrated' moral empathy and moral humility as well, then it 'might be' quite reasonable to judge him or her to be intellectually open-minded. But this cluster seems to be not much more plausible as a correlate to intellectual open-mindedness than the moral and non-moral traits taken singly, for a devoutly religious person might travel a lot (on missionary work), and be humble and empathetic, but completely close-minded (especially as regards other religions, evolutionary theory, and so on). And again, there is the question of whether there are really any situations in which you have enough time to investigate a person's moral humility and empathy, and find out the extent of his or her travel experience, yet not have time to investigate the evidence offered further, or consult more witnesses. Also again the question remains why knowing that someone is intellectually open-minded increases the likelihood that he or she is correct about a technical judgment, because an open-minded person (for example) might take some pseudo-science seriously, which may impair his or her judgment. (One thinks here of Alfred Russell Wallace, co-discoverer of the theory of evolution by natural selection, who wasted a good deal of his research time investigating spiritualism and other nonsense, compared with Darwin, who simply dismissed such matters.)

Having looked at his cases let me now spell out some arguments concerning JVET and the SA. I will first explore what I think are the most obvious problems the JVET faces, then I will offer reasons why the SA seems to be a stronger logical approach. (At no point will I inquire into other people's characters!)

The JVET faces four problems, which I shall call the conflict criticism, the vagueness criticism, the speech act criticism, and the self-defeating criticism.

The **conflict criticism** of the JVET is that it advises us to look (in various situations) to the speaker's intellectual virtues, moral virtues, and even non-moral character traits as well, to decide (sometimes) whether to accept his or her argument. But not only do these traits not always correlate, they often seem to conflict. If my doctor argues that smoking is bad, citing numerous large-scale observational cause-to-effect studies, should I accept her argument because of her intellectual virtue (she distinguished herself at Harvard Medical School, and has published a lot of papers in peer-reviewed medical journals)? But what if she is morally vicious in some way, say, is greedy or – depending upon what Johnson considers morally virtuous, he doesn't give us any list – is unchaste (chastity being considered a virtue at one time)?

Or what if she is intellectually and morally virtuous, but severely lacking in whatever non-moral character traits Johnson deems appropriate? Say she not only did well at Harvard, but she is a kind and caring person, full of love of humanity. However she simply has no sense of humor, has never travelled, drinks lousy wine, and has no flair for music. Johnson might say that intellectual virtue would trump other considerations, but then what about a case of someone low in intellectual virtue but very high in moral virtue? Could such a case ever call for accepting the argument? Or a case in which a person is low in intellectual and moral virtue, but is exemplary in whatever non-moral character traits Johnson esteems?

More generally, the history of ideas is full of people who were intellectually admirable in some ways but not others, and intellectual virtuous in some ways and morally vicious in others. You can have a highly diligent and creative scientist who is resistant to criticism. You can have a scientist who is brilliant, but is jealous of the success of others and ungenerous with credit (one might suggest Newton here).

In fact, one could argue that the things people have to do to achieve great intellectual virtue (studying hard, competing with others to be the first to discover things, spending endless hours in the lab, and so on) will usually work against the development and exercise of some important moral virtues (sensitivity to others, willingness to share time with others, desire to cooperate with others, and so on).

The SA faces fewer conflict problems. In a case of testimony or an employment application, only those character traits that directly relate to the primary question (should we believe Smith about his specific testimony on this specific matter, should we hire him for this particular job) together with specific background are relevant. In a witness, only moral virtues such as honesty and (in expert testimony) intellectual virtues such as diligence are relevant, while moral virtues such as benevolence or intellectual ones such as prudence seem almost always completely irrelevant.

In most other situations, in which a person is not testifying or being considered for a job, but simply arguing, background and character are again completely irrelevant.

The **vagueness criticism** of the JVET is that it gives us no criteria by which we can determine when a particular case of attacking someone's character is justified, and how far it is justified. Johnson tells us that, '…given our intellectual limitations and the pressures we are faced with it can sometimes be appropriate to appeal to character as a means of settling contention.'[24] This suggests that a key factor from the point of view of the JVET is the degree of pressure you face enters in to determining whether examining someone's character is logically appropriate.

But how much pressure is he referring to? Just a general shortness of time in your busy life? (And does merely believing yourself to be too busy to look into matters further really mean that you are truly too busy?) Or some specific emergency? And in the case of an emergency, what sort of emergency would make you decide to view the person's argument as merely testimony, and then reject it, as opposed to suspending judgment until you could verify the evidence yourself?

Again, when we look to 'correlations' of intellectual virtues with moral virtues and non-moral character traits, are these correlations that have been statistically established by cognitive psychologists, or merely correlations that I have personally come to believe? If the former, it would almost always take vastly more time to establish the correlation needed to justify looking at non-intellectual virtues of the arguer than simply investigating whether the premises of the argument are in fact correct to begin with. And if the latter, it would seem to allow all manner of prejudice – there are, for example, many people who will swear that moral goodness correlates with religious dogmatism, and moral viciousness with lack of religion.

Johnson admits, '…knowing how and when to judge that an appeal to the *ad hominem* is useful and justifiable is itself an intellectual virtue that must be developed to accommodate our limited capacities.'[25] I contend that this makes his account not very useful.

The **speech act criticism** of the JVET is that is lumps together markedly different sorts of speech acts. Testifying is not arguing in the ordinary sense of the term. Testifying is the act of conveying information (statements and judgments) based upon the speaker's (witness's) own credibility. When I tell you that I saw a duck drive a car, I am not arguing, but simply making an observational statement. That is characteristic of eye-witness testimony. In expert testimony, the witness may review the evidence that led to his or her judgment, but the listener isn't being asked to agree that the judgment follows from the evidence, for in cases in which experts need to testify, the listener is presumably incompetent to do that. The reason we typically want the expert to put forth the evidence that led to the judgment is so that other experts can evaluate what we cannot.

This is different from a standard argument, where the speaker is attempting to persuade the listener of a claim, not offering personal observation or professional expertise, but independent reasons. The speaker backs the claim with those reasons, not himself or herself. This is typically signalled by indicator words or phrases. Phrases such as 'Trust me, I know about these things,' 'Look, I saw it with my own eyes,' and 'In my professional opinion' indicate the speaker is backing an assertion personally. Phrases such as 'This seems to me to be true because of the following reasons,' 'Consider these facts,' and 'I think that if you reflect upon these facts you will come to see' indicate standard argument.

In standard argumentation, the speaker has the expectation, and rightly so, that the listener will focus on those reasons (if they don't accept them already), not attack the speaker personally. It is upon this conversational expectation that open, robust discussion is possible. Absent this conversational expectation, discussion becomes stifled – no one wants to argue, for fear of personal attack.

The point can be sharpened by recalling with my exchange with Hinman regarding Marxism (and similar ideologies and philosophies) which put aside criticism when the source is 'politically incorrect'. I made the point with Hinman that simply because Marxists feel that *ad hominem* reasoning is logically acceptable doesn't mean that it is. The point I would make to Johnson is that a generation after the collapse of a fair number of Marxist regimes, it is clear that the Marxists had few scruples about using 'class analysis' *ad hominem* attacks not to discover the truth, but merely to silence and dismiss (or even kill) their critics, whose criticisms were proven in the main to be reasonable in the light of history.

The **self-defeating criticism** of the JVET is that, if followed, it defeats or impedes the development of the very thing that informs it, viz., intellectual virtue. That is, the more you encourage me to look at the virtue (or lack thereof) of someone giving me an argument for some claim whenever I feel my time would be better spent than studying the relevant issues, the more you run the risk of destroying my own virtue (both intellectual and moral). This is true for several reasons.

To begin with, advising me to routinely examine the background of people giving arguments when I feel I have better things to do will encourage intellectual laziness. If I am given an argument, it typically takes real work to identify the argument (including filling in omitted thoughts in a charitable way), determining whether it is deductively valid or inductively strong, and then determining whether the premises are true – which may require considerable research and study. It is almost always easier to dismiss the argument by finding some real or imagined flaw, some lack of intellectual virtue, in the arguer. Given that actual human beings are never perfect paragons of virtue, finding such flaws is relatively easy.

Indeed, Bradley Smith has argued that this is a growing problem in American political discourse.[26] With the ease of internet search engines and the campaign donation disclosure laws, voters increasingly skip reading about the policy proposals put forward by candidates or presented as initiatives on ballots and instead just look to see who has gotten support from whom.

Additionally, the JVET approach would seem also to encourage the intellectual vice of close-mindedness. If I have an ideology or belief system I feel strongly about, I could deflect every criticism of it, no matter how powerful, by simply looking for intellectual vices in the source of the criticism, instead of wrestling with challenging arguments.

Again, I would remind the reader of the history of the 20th century, during which various self-reinforcing ideologies (Marxism, Fascism, even to a certain extent Freudian theory) were able to use *ad hominem* reasoning to dismiss legitimate criticism. This is by no means a theoretical problem.

Moreover, the JVET approach would also encourage intellectual shyness — the intellectual vice of not engaging others in the critical discourse so essential to maintaining a democracy. Why would I vigorously advocate positions, search for evidence and reasons to support my case, if I knew that my character and intellectual virtue would quickly become the focus of the discussion? I would instead likely withdraw from the marketplace of ideas.

Besides encouraging intellectual vices such as intellectual laziness, close-mindedness and shyness, the JVET would seem to me to encourage some moral vices as well. It would encourage distrust of others, in that it would encourage people to be looking for flaws in others, and also encourage manipulation of others, since a person would be encouraged to discredit an opponent's argument by making the audience see the opponent as flawed.

And it could lead to contempt for others (as well as a concomitant sense of personal superiority), as a person developed the habit of finding faults in people giving arguments whenever he felt his time was short or would be better spent elsewhere. Sophists are often arrogant that way, seeing how easy it is to demean others.

Let us now turn from critiquing the JVET to arguing for the superiority of the SA as a tool for understanding *ad hominem* argumentation. The considerations I will give are specific cases of the well-known criteria for evaluating competing theories, such as simplicity (i.e. whether the theory explains issues in its domain with few new constructs), generality (i.e. whether it explains a wide range of issues in its domain), consilience (i.e. whether it converges with other well-established theories in other domains), and fruitfulness (whether it explains new phenomena).

We will discuss in order the fit to legality argument, the fit to other fallacies argument, the fit to psychology argument, and the fit to political life argument.

The **fit to legality argument** points to the consilience between the evolution of American common law and the SA. Consider first a case where examining the background of someone might be allowable, even on the SA, a case of hiring. Suppose in a faculty hiring process for a new philosophy professor I decided to quiz applicants about whether they are married, and if not, whether they plan on getting married. The question at hand is who among the candidates is the most qualified, and marital status seems clearly irrelevant to that question. But the JVET would be 'more nuanced', meaning I take it that if there were evidence to support a claim like 'Married people are more productive', then I would be right to ask such questions. Now, some statistical studies of happiness may provide support for such a claim (viz., that there is a correlation between productivity and marital status), but the SA would view them irrelevant because the issue at hand involves the individual qualifications of the specific candidates, not those of general pools of candidates.

Now, consider a case in which a person, Prof. Smith, has written an op-ed advocating, say, a national health care system. I happen to know that Smith drinks heavily and has had some extra-marital affairs, which seems to me to show moral vices – intemperance and infidelity. I really don't have time to study the issues around national health care, so I tell everyone I know that Smith is morally vicious and should not be taken seriously on this matter. The SA would view this as clearly fallacious, for Smith is arguing for a policy, not testifying or applying for a job. (Indeed, even if he were testifying, the SA would view his foibles as likely irrelevant).

What does common law tell us in such cases? Precisely that society has come to take a dim view of looking at features of a job candidate's personal life and background, because it has come to view most of that as irrelevant to the narrow issue at hand. Asking such questions invites a lawsuit for discrimination or invasion of privacy, and rightly so. And even more in the case of my advertising Smith's failings, I am courting a lawsuit for slander. From the SA view, this is only logical. From the JVET view, this would seem perverse.

The **fit to other fallacies argument** invokes the idea of simplicity and generality of the SA account. To begin with, when Johnson talks about *ad hominem* arguments, he confines himself to the abusive form, where a person's character is attacked. So it is unclear how the JVET handles what are generally considered other forms of *ad hominem* attack, such as the circumstantial form (where you accuse your opponent of bias), *tu quoque* (where you accuse your opponent of hypocrisy), guilt by association (where you attack a person for his or her associates), and the genetic fallacy (where you attack an idea by criticizing the group that originated it).

Consider the circumstantial form. Suppose Sue proposes that we ought to build a freeway, and offers several reasons to support her view, for example that a freeway would dramatically easy congestion. But Sue is the owner of a highway construction firm that plans to bid on the project if it is approved. It is unclear what the JVET would say about this. Sue is self-interested here, so perhaps her argument should be discarded for the reason that she is not impartial, which could mean she is closed-minded, an intellectual vice. However, she *is* a highway contractor, so she is knowledgeable, an intellectual virtue.

But from the JA perspective, the question here is whether the freeway should be built, not whether Sue is biased. She may or may not be pushing her view out of self-interest – indeed, even she may not know her 'true' motive is, if (as some psychologists claim) many motives are unconscious – but her motive is irrelevant. We are best off if we just evaluate her reasons.

Next, suppose Sue is a climate scientist who opposes the freeway project, and offers a number of reasons, including that it will encourage people to use their cars more, contributing to air pollution and global warming. But Sue herself drives a large SUV. So her argument seems hypocritical. What to make of this under the JVET is again unclear. Doesn't hypocrisy indicate inconsistency – an intellectual vice? But Sue is knowledgeable, which again is an intellectual virtue.

But the SA is again quite clear: the issue is not whether Sue is consistent – she isn't testifying to us or asking us for a job – but merely whether building another freeway is a good idea, and the considerations of pollution and global warming are clearly relevant.

Next, suppose Sue favours the freeway, and offers reasons, but we discover she associates with drunkards and mobsters. Again, what does the JVET tells us here? Once again, it is unclear. Sue's associations could indicate a lack of discernment – an intellectual vice. But equally, it could betoken a great open-mindedness and aversion to being judgmental – intellectual virtues both.

But the SA is once again clear: the issue is not whether drunks and criminals are good people, or whether associating with such people is a good thing to do, but only whether her reasons are cogent.

Finally, suppose Sue argues against building a freeway, and gives as a reason that she opposes Nazism, and that in fact the first freeways ever built were built in Nazi Germany. Here the JVET seems even more unhelpful. Are we to look at the intellectual virtues of the Nazis? They were certainly extremely intolerant and closed-minded people – intellectual vices. But they did have tremendous engineering skills – especially when it came to weapons! – which is an intellectual virtue.

But under the SA, Sue's virtue is irrelevant here, and even more irrelevant would be the virtues of the Nazis.

More generally, the SA account of *ad hominem* attacks allows for a simple explanation of several other fallacies traditionally included as 'fallacies of relevance', viz., appeal to fear, appeal to pity, and appeal to the crowd. Under SA, these cases are rightly viewed as similar, for in each case, the fallacy consists not in invoking a feeling, but in invoking a feeling irrelevant to the specific question at hand. So, for example, if my doctor tries to get me to stop smoking by telling me about tobacco's role in causing cancer and heart disease, the fear she is arousing in me is not irrelevant to the issue at hand (to wit, whether I should stop smoking). But if she instead only shows me pictures of suffering cancer patients, that would be irrelevant, because the question at hand is not whether cancer is unpleasant, but whether my smoking significantly increases the chances of my getting it.

Again, if someone asks me to give to a children's charity by informing me that charity has a high 'pass through percentage' (that is, that most of the money will go to help poor children), it is not a fallacious appeal to pity. It the person instead only shows me a picture of a pitiful child, it would be irrelevant, because the question at hand is not whether this child (or poor children in general) need help, but whether contributing to this charity will in fact help the children.

The **fit to psychology argument** invokes the idea of consilience again, in that it points out that much work in the psychology of persuasion dovetails nicely with the SA. As Robert Cialdini notes in his survey of the psychology of persuasion, human beings (like all other higher animals) are subject to association – we associate things that may not be connected in reality.[27] We associate truth with physical attractiveness, like Pavlov's dogs associating food with the ringing of a bell. In just one of many psychological tests illustrating this, male subjects shown a picture of a new car with a scantily dressed beautiful model standing next to it will tend to rate *the car* as being higher in quality and performance than will a matched group of subjects who are shown a picture of the identical car *sans* model. Again, in studies of sentencing, it turns out that juries give harsher sentences to unattractive defendants than to attractive ones convicted of identical crimes.

This experimental psychological work complements nicely the SA. SA explains how such cases are illogical; the psychological literature explains them as being cases in which a psychological mechanism is triggered. Indeed, psychologists distinguish between positive association (an animal associates something pleasant with something else) and negative association (an animal associates something painful or negative with something else). Positive association would seem to explain why irrelevant appeals to the crowd and irrelevant appeals to pity succeed in persuasion, while negative association would explain why irrelevant appeals to fear and irrelevant attacks on persons succeed in persuasion.

So, for example, in appeal to the crowd, I get people to accept a claim by invoking a logically irrelevant but psychologically effective positive association with something about which they feel good (the flag, their family, their home town, or such like). In appeal to pity, I get people to accept a claim by invoking a logically irrelevant but psychologically effective positive association with something for which they feel sympathy or of which the feel protective (a cute puppy or child, for example).

On the other hand, in appeal to fear, I attempt to get the listeners to accept my claim by invoking a logically irrelevant but psychologically effective negative association with something they fear. And in attacking the person – which could be called in this regard 'appeal to hate' – I attempt to get the listeners to accept my claim by invoking a logically irrelevant but psychologically effective negative association with something or someone they hate, envy, or despise.

The **fit to political life argument** asks the simple question, what does observation show us about why and how people actually do look at the backgrounds of their opponents? What better place to look than the realm of political discourse, in which advocates for politicians and policies contend. When these advocates look at the character or other aspects of those with whom they disagree, are they honestly trying to assess intellectual and moral virtue, the better to ascertain the epistemic quality of the arguments their opponents offer?

Hardly. The actual behaviour of candidates and advocates shows something different: when they look at their opponent's background, they are only looking for whatever can be used to discredit the other side, i.e. to cause the audience to reject their opponent by creating a negative association with anything, no matter how irrelevant. Indeed, they hire 'opposition research' specialists to do this. Two features of this 'opposition research' show that this is their real motive.

First, if the opposition research team finds evidence of intellectual or moral virtue in the opponent, it certainly never mentions it. If Smith is running against Jones for the Senate, say, and Smith's opposition research team discovers that Jones was in fact a brilliant student when in college, the team will certainly not mention that. Only if Jones was a mediocre or poor student will his or her college record come up.

Second, the opposition research team will typically employ many private investigators – but few virtue epistemologists—to 'dig up dirt', any dirt they can find. Did this person ever use drugs, have an abortion, or have a same-sex affair? If so, that information will be leaked to the press, even though it could hardly be for the purpose of assessing truth via the evaluation of intellectual virtue, for such background is utterly irrelevant to intellectual virtue. No, it is clearly only exploiting popular prejudice to arouse negative association.

This practice can reach the depths of absurdity. In one recent American election, one candidate faced a massive amount of negative publicity when it was learned that *her daughter* had had a child out of wedlock. Another faced negative publicity when it was learned that *an acquaintance of his* had engaged in violent acts of protest decades earlier.

In this paper, I have argued that the SA account of *ad hominem* more plausible and useful that is the JVET. However, I hope that nothing I've said is taken as criticism of virtue epistemology in general, something I certainly did not intend to offer. Virtue epistemology has a number of strengths. Moreover, I have suggested it can easily accommodate the SA account of the fallacies of relevance by just incorporating them as cases in which the intellectual vice of settling issues by emotional manipulation occurs.

Notes

1. Johnson, Christopher M., 'Reconsidering the *Ad Hominem*' Philosophy 84 (2009), 251–266.
2. Johnson, op. cit. 252.
3. Hinman, Lawrence, 'The Case For *Ad Hominem* Arguments', Australasian Journal of Philosophy 60 (1982), 338–345.
4. Jason, Gary James, 'Is There A Case For *Ad Hominem* Arguments?', Australasian Journal of Philosophy 62 (1984), 182–185.
5. Johnson, op. cit., 257.
6. Johnson, op. cit., 263.
7. Jason, Gary, Critical Thinking: Developing an Effective Worldview (Belmont, CA: Wadsworth/Thomson Learning, 2001. See Chapter 8, sections 1 and 3.
8. Jason, op. cit. Chapter 3.
9. Johnson, op. cit., 253–254.
10. Jason, *Critical Thinking*, 232–236.
11. Johnson, op. cit., 254, says, 'When these optimal conditions do not obtain, though, as when we don't have the necessary time or facility to fully determine the correctness

of claims, *ad hominem* considerations can play a relevant role. In such situations they cease to be abusive and become appropriate means of evaluation.'

12. Johnson, op. cit., 257, mid-page.
13. Yaniv, Ilan, 'The Benefit of Additional Opinions,' Current Directions in Psychological Science 13 (2004), 75.
14. Yaniv, op. cit., 76.
15. Johnson, op. cit., 257–258.
16. Johnson, op. cit., 258
17. Johnson, op. cit., 259.
18. Johnson, op. cit., 259.
19. Johnson, op. cit., 259.
20. Johnson, op. cit. 260.
21. Johnson, op. cit. 261
22. Johnson, op. cit. 262.
23. Johnson, op. cit. 262.
24. Johnson, op. cit., 251.
25. Johnson, op. cit., 253.
26. Smith, Bradley 'In Defense of Political Anonymity', City Journal 20 (2010).
27. Cialdini, Robert B., *Influence: The Psychology of Persuasion* (New York: Morrow, 1993).

My thanks to the Cambridge University Press for permission to reprint this article. My thanks also to the journal *Philosophy* in which it first appeared.

Part Two

Epistemology, Philosophy of Science, and Philosophy of Psychology/ Cognitive Science

14

"The Concept of a Discovery"

(1979) first appeared in The Journal of Critical Analysis, Vol. VII, No. 4, pp. 109–118 (1979)

There has been considerable controversy in recent years about the "logic" of scientific discovery. Much of that controversy is due to the lack of clarity in the concept of "a discovery." Consider T. S. Kuhn's comment:

> Clearly we need a new vocabulary and concepts for analyzing events like the discovery of oxygen. Though undoubtedly correct, the sentence "oxygen was discovered," misleads by suggesting that discovering something is a single, simple act assimilable to our usual (and also questionable) concept of seeing. That is why we so readily assume that discovering, like seeing or touching, should be unequivocally attributable to an individual and to a moment in time. But the latter attribution is always impossible, and the former is as well. Ignoring Scheele, we can safely say that oxygen had not been discovered before 1774, and we would probably also say it had been discovered by 1777 or shortly thereafter. But within those limits or others like them, any attempt to date the discovery must inevitably be arbitrary because discovering a new sort of phenomenon is necessarily a complete event, one which involves recognizing *that* something is and *what* it is. Note, for example, that if oxygen were dephlogisticated air for us, we had discovered it, though we would still not know quite when. But if both observation and conceptualization, fact and assimilation to theory, are inseparably linked in discovery, then discovery is a process that must take time.[1]

Kuhn hits upon several very important points; however, much of the problem in figuring out the conceptual development of a discovery, the "process" of discovery, lies in the ambiguity and vagueness of claims about attributions of discovery.

In this article, I will give a preliminary analysis of the concept of "a discovery;" a complete analysis of this epistemologically important concept would require much more than an article. My analysis will concentrate on the ambiguities implicit in locutions used to express attributions of discovery.

Let's begin by considering the claim that the act of discovery is the act of somebody discovering something. The inadequacy of that claim is apparent if we consider these statements:

(1) John discovered his wife's body.
(2) John discovered that his wife had been murdered.
(3) John discovered the law of displacement.
(4) John discovered how to open his father's safe.
(5) John discovered the cause of her death.

Note that (1) involves (minimally) some person being the first to see some object (a body). But if we naively try to assimilate (2)–(5) with (1) – if we are deceived by their grammatical similarity to (1) – we wind up thinking that propositions, laws, theories, facts, techniques (methods), and causes are all objects which the discoverer stumbles across. Actually, (2) and (3) are eases in which John discovered *that* something is the ease; (4) is a ease in which John discovered *how* to do something; and (5) is a ease in which John discovered *why* something is the case. (These rough assertions will be amplified upon below.)

In picking our way through the types of discovery (discovering-how, discovering-that, discovering-why, etc.), we must critically examine examples of attributions of discovery, avoiding being misled by the surface grammatical structure. We must remember that we are operating on two levels in our analysis: we are working with examples – sentences – which are all locutions using the verb "discover," and we are directing our attention to the concept of discovery, inquiring into the types of discovery. We are operating on both the syntactic, the semantic, and even the pragmatic levels.

Discovering-It and Discovering-That

I indicated above that "the" concept of discovering something is really a cluster of concepts. Let me elaborate upon this point by distinguishing two elements of the cluster. Compare sentences (6), (7), and (8) with (9) and (10).

(6) Scheele discovered oxygen.
(7) Fleming discovered penicillin.
(8) Le Verrier discovered Neptune.
(9) Scheele discovered that oxygen is an element.
(10) Fleming discovered that penicillium mold gives off a substance which lyses bacteria.

Note that all the examples given so far, (1)–(10), are locutions with "discover" as the main verb. I shall call all such declarative sentences *discover-locutions.* If we look at (1), (6), (7), and (8), we see, on the one hand, that this type has the form [subject noun] + "discover" + <tense> + [object noun]. Let me call locutions of that form *discovering-it* locutions. On the other hand, examples like (2), (9), and (10) are complex declarative sentences of the form [subject noun] + "discover" + <tense> + "that" + [declarative sentence]. Let me call these *discovering-that* locutions.

Now let's look at what is being asserted by someone who utters (1), (6), (7), or (8). Clearly, the statement of any of them involves the notion that someone – John, Scheele, Fleming, Le Verrier – has observed (or detected) an object (or substance), and has been the first to do so. On the other hand, the statement of (2), (9), or (10) involves the notion that someone has learned the truth-value of some proposition, and has been the first to do so. The first concept, the concept of *discovering-it,* involves observation, whereas the second concept, the concept of *discovering-that,* does not necessarily involve observation. *Discovering-that* merely involves learning (method unspecified) the truth-value of a proposition. Thus the notion of A discovering X is at least two-fold ambiguous. If X is an object, we have in mind *discovering-it.* If X is a proposition, we have in mind *discovering that.*

Before looking more closely at the concepts of *discovering-that* and *discovering-it,* some remarks must be made about the use of locutions to express concepts. We generally use *discovering-that* locutions for attributions of the discovery that a certain state of affairs obtains, and *discovering-it* locutions for attributions of the observation (for the first time) of an object or substance.

But things are not always so pat. Reconsider (3), as well as:

(11) John discovered the fact of her death.
(12) John discovered the theory of natural selection.

While (3), (11), and (12) are all *discovering-it* locutions, we do not (as we have seen) use them to describe cases of *discovering-it.* After all, laws, theories, facts, and such like are propositional entities, not objects which John, stumbles across. What *do* we use the locutions to say? Well, (3) can be paraphrased as "John discovered that an object in water is buoyed up by a force equal to the weight of the water it displaces;" (11) as "John discovered that his wife had died;" (12) as "John discovered that species evolve via the mechanism of Natural Selection."

Thus, on the one hand, in many cases, we use a *discovering-it* locution to describe *discovering-that.* (Syntax may lead one into reification of all sorts of things – laws, theories, facts, etc.) On the other hand however, the situation in which a *discovering-that* locution is used to talk about a case of *discovering-it* seems not to arise.

Turning now to the concept of *discovering that,* we note that it includes as special cases *discovering-where, discovering-what, discovering-when,* and *discovering-why.* To discover where something is simply is to discover that it is in a certain location. To discover who did such and such is to discover that person P did it. To discover what object X is simply is to discover that X fits a certain category. To discover when some event occurred is to discover that the event occurred at time T. (*Discovering-why* will be examined in a separate section.)

Another thing to note about *discovering-that* is the complication caused by the nature of propositions.

Saying "A discovered that P" involves expressing P in your own language, or (if A speaks your language) in your own theoretical terms. A may not express P the way you do. Putting this point in terms of *discovering-that* locutions, one might say that *discovering that* locutions are referentially tricky. To say "John discovered that the carburetor was dirty" is not to say the John would himself say "I discovered that the carburetor was dirty." He may know little about cars, and may refer to carburetors as "gas goodies." More importantly, he may not know he is referring to the carburetor at all. This is a special case of the ambiguity of sentences involving definite descriptions. John may have said "The person who did this is a bum," thinking that Fred is the one who did it, whereas Ted is in fact the culprit. Depending on whether John is using the definite description "the man who did this" referentially or descriptively, he means either "Fred is a bum" or "Ted is a bum." I do not want to get bogged down in the confusing topic of reference; I want merely to point out that *discover-locutions* in general, and *discovering-that* locutions in particular, can be referentially tricky.

Putting this comment pragmatically, let me speak of the *preferred case of discovering that P* as being the case in which the discoverer would state P in the same way as our community would.[2] The upshot then is this: in considering cases of *discovering-that,* we must keep in mind that a state of affairs is one thing, a fact (a description of a state of affairs) is quite another. This is a misleading way of putting the point, in that it sounds as if there were theory-neutral states of affairs. I merely suggest that very few cases of *discovering-that* are preferred cases. (The question whether there is such a thing as theory-neutral observation is quite beyond the scope of this paper.)

Let's return to the concept of *discovering-it.* Reconsider example (1). What do we usually mean when we attribute the discovery of his wife's body to John? This sort of scenario comes to mind: John returns home from work, and smells gas. Running into his house, he finds his wife's body, and (perhaps) mourns. Discovering a body is not merely being the first to see it, but (in the usual case) to recognize it as a body, to see that the person is dead. *Discovering-it* typically involves *discovering-that.* Putting the point pragmatically, for our community to claim that a discovered object X generally involves our believing that A saw/observed/detected X, and was the first to do so, and further that A had knowledge about X. The recognition of this epistemic dimension of *discovering-it* is the basis of Kuhn's claim in the passage cited earlier, that discovering a new phenomenon "involves recognizing both that something is and what it is." What he should say instead is that discovering a thing generally involves possessing some knowledge which allows you to categorize that thing. This holds for even mundane discovery, and is not limited to cases of scientific discovery.

However, suppose – again thinking of example (1) – that John saw his wife's body, but erroneously supposed that she was asleep. Suppose, that is, that John saw the body without seeing that she was dead. It still seems quite correct to say John discovered his wife's body – although we are tempted to add that he didn't recognize it. It won't do to insist that John must have had some knowledge of the matter – that he must at least have recognized it as his wife, say, or at least as a woman. We can imagine John erroneously believing it to be an old rug (supposing his eyesight to be poor). Even here it seems correct to say that John discovered his wife's body. The point is, though, that John would use a different description to refer to the object from the one we would use. Thus, we might say that *discovering-it* locutions are also referentially tricky. To say that A discovered object X is not necessarily to say that A would refer to X by "X."

We can shed light on the relation between *discovering-it* and *discovering-that* by considering the claim that Scheele discovered oxygen. Kuhn's remarks lead one to view this claim as unambiguous, yet hard to assess, because of the complexity of the historical process. But the historical process is really quite simple.[3]

Scheele was a proponent of the phlogiston theory, which held that combustion involves the release of a substance "phlogiston" (denoted by the symbol ∅) into the air. For example, modern science views the change of a heated metal into calx as the combination of the metal with oxygen (combustion of the metal), producing its oxide:

Metal + Oxygen heat Oxide
→

But a phlogistonist would view this change as a decomposition of the metal (presumed to be a compound) into calx plus the hypothetical substance phlogiston:

Metal heat ∅ + calx
→

Guided by this theory, Scheele was investigating the release of phlogiston from various substances in confined volumes of air. He knew that when a substance burns in air, the volume of air decreases, leaving "foul air." He reasoned that the phlogiston released in the combustion must therefore combine with part of ordinary air and escape as heat. He called this hypothetical part of air "fire air." Thus air was a mixture of foul air and fire air, and he set out to isolate fire air by decomposing heat (fire air + ∅).

Scheele decided that to isolate fire air from heat he would have to absorb the phlogiston with a *better* receptor than fire air. He picked nitric acid, since it would separate the phlogiston from metals thus:

Metal (Calx + ∅) + Nitric Acid → Calx + red fumes (taken to be nitric acid + ∅)

So Scheele felt that heating nitric acid would give fire air via this reaction:

Heat (fire air + ∅) + Nitric Acid → Red fumes + Fire Air

Scheele fixed the nitric acid with potash, heated it, and absorbed the red fumes with slaked lime. He indeed isolated a gas, fire air, which we know to be oxygen. Scheele investigated the properties of "fire air," and found that it behaved just as he expected it would – it restored foul air to breathability, enabled a candle to burn brightly, and so on. But Scheele never abandoned the phlogiston theory, and always viewed "fire air" in those terms.

Now, our difficulty in assessing the claim "Scheele discovered oxygen" lies *not* in the complexity of the historical process that Scheele underwent, i.e., his conceptual evolution. The facts are clear, and common in the history of science. A researcher, possessing what we believe is a mistaken theory, carries out a line of research obviously suggested by that theory, and discovers an entity which we would refer to in one way, he another. It is the *claim* itself which is ambiguous. Do we mean that Scheele discovered the substance known to us as oxygen? Clearly true. Does it mean that Scheele discovered the substance (known to us as oxygen) and recognized that it is a separate element? Also true, although he did not have the modern concept of an "element."

The point is that *discovering-it* claims are vague, especially when (as in the case of scientific discovery) there are changes in terminology and conceptual schemes, leading to problems of reference. The attribution of discovery is an honor bestowed by a community, and the members of that community rarely state explicitly what concepts the putative discoverer must have possessed in order to receive the credit.

Discovering-How

In our discussion of Scheele's case, we can pick out yet another interpretation of the claim "Scheele discovered oxygen," viz., that Scheele discovered how to separate a substance, now known as oxygen. Under this possible construal, we have in mind that Scheele discovered a technique *without having the correct conceptual rationale for it.* The histories of medicine and engineering are replete with similar cases where a technique, the knowledge *how* to do something, is discovered without the discoverer being able to say why that technique works. Discovering a technique, learning a skill and being the first to do so, is what I mean when I speak of *discovering how.*

As we have seen before, the same concept may be expressed by different (and often misleading) locutions. Consider:

(13) Some primitive man discovered fire.

(13) uses a *discovering-it* locution, which may mislead one to view it as one views (1). But clearly, in saying (13) I don't mean that some early man stumbled across a fire. Rather, I mean that some early man mastered the art of starting, maintaining, and controlling fire for his purposes (such as cooking). In other words, discovering fire is really discovering how to start a fire and use it for various purposes. (13) is conceptually similar to (5), as well as:

(14) Paracelsus discovered how to treat syphilis with mercury.
(15) Carnegie discovered how to make inexpensive steel.

Let's define a *discovering-how* locution as being one of the form: [subject noun] + "discover" + <tense> + "how to" + [transitive verb] + [object noun]. The point of the foregoing is that not every case of discovering-how is described using a *discovering-how* locution. (The question whether *knowing how* – practical knowledge – is reducible to or equivalent to *knowing that* –propositional knowledge – is irrelevant here.)

Discovering-Why

Consider yet more examples:

(16) John discovered why his car was idling poorly.
(17) Freud discovered why people stammer.
(18) Pasteur discovered why juice ferments.

Asserting (16), (17), or (18) involves describing someone's discovery of why some proposition P is true, or more accurately, of his finding an explanation of its truth. *Discovering-why* is usually, but not always, expressed using a locution of the form: [subject noun] + discover + tense + why + [declarative sentence], which I will call *discovering-why* locutions. Cases where discovering-why is not expressed using a *discovering-why* locution are:

(19) Freud discovered the cause of stammering.
(20) Pasteur discovered the explanation of fermentation.

Clearly, if we credit a person A with discovering why p, we are presupposing that p is true. More pragmatically put, for a community to honor A by saying that A discovered why p, that community must believe p is true. More importantly, discovering why p involves discovering that q is true, where q explains p. Thus *discovering- why* is really a special case of *discovering-that.* This being so, we must be prepared for the usual referential trickiness.

Note that we generally mean, by saying that A discovered why p, that A not only discovered that q, where q explains p, *but also realized that q explains p.* This is not always true. Looking at (16), suppose John's car is idling poorly, and he sets out to discover why. He finds that the valve cover is dented, and replaces it under the misapprehension that this is the cause of the rough idling. At the same time he notices that the carburetor is dirty, and cleans it as well. Of course, the actual explanation of the rough idling is the dirty carburetor, but John doesn't recognize that fact. We (a community of auto mechanics) would say that John discovered (without realizing it) why his car was idling roughly.

Yet such cases are deviant. In general, discovering the explanation of a phenomenon involves recognizing that it is the explanation.

Let me conclude with a few remarks about the applicability of any logic of discovery (if one there be) to the history of science. We should not assume that the difficulty of assessing a historical claim arises from the difficulty in rationally reconstructing the past. Rather, the impreciseness and misleading structure of *discovering locutions,* and the cluster nature of the concept of discovery, make such historical claims ambiguous. Consider Kuhn's statement:

> Was it Priestley or Lavoisier, if either, who first discovered oxygen? In any case, when was oxygen discovered? In that form the question could be asked even if only one claimant had existed. As a ruling about priority and date, an answer does not at all concern us. Nevertheless, an attempt to produce one will illuminate the nature of discovery, because there is no answer of the kind which is sought. Discovery is not the sort of process about which the question is appropriately asked. The fact that it is asked is a symptom of something askew in the image of science that gives discovery so fundamental a role.[4]

It seems to be misleading because questions such as "Who discovered oxygen?" are inherently ambiguous. But a precise question (such as "Who first isolated the substance we know as oxygen?" "Who first recognized that that substance is consumed in combustion?" an the like) does admit of straightforward historical treatment, especially if one keeps the niceties of reference clearly in mind.

Notes

1. T.S. Kuhn, *The Structure* of *Scientific Revolutions* (Chicago: University of Chicago Press, 1962), p. 117.
2. This definition can be easily generalized to arbitrary linguistic/epistemic communities.
3. For a fuller account, see Aaron Ihide, *The Development of Modern Chemistry* New York: Harper & Row, 1964, pp. 51ff.
4. Kuhn, *op. cit.,* p. 116.

Permission to reprint courtesy of The Philosophy Documentation Center. I wish to thank *The Journal of Critical Analysis* as well.

15

My review of: *The Foundations of Psychoanalysis*

(by Adolf Grunbaum, Berkeley: University of California Press, 1984) first appeared in California Review, June 1985

Conservative and other rightist scholars have often been accused of misusing science for their hidden agendas. One thinks here, for instance, of recent attacks on IQ research, eugenics, and sociobiology by such writers as Steven Jay Gould, Carl Sagan, Ashley Montague, and so on. Indeed, movements like eugenics are often quite ugly and without scientific merit.

What has often gone unnoticed, however, is the abuse of science by liberal and leftist scholars. Steven Gould, so distressed by shoddy IQ research which has allegedly contributed to discrimination against blacks, is curiously unperturbed by Marxism, which surely has contributed to the killings of tens of millions of innocent people of every color. The social sciences have been especially useful for achieving leftist hidden agendas. It is clear by now that Margaret Mead's research on the Samoans was greatly distorted by her "progressive" political and social views. Sociology in particular has become the training camp for apologists of the Welfare State.

The reason one hears more often about rightist than leftist abuse of science is that the majority of historians, philosophers and popularizers of science are of left/liberal inclination. However, balance is being restored, although slowly and without much fanfare. The book under review contributes to the restoration of that balance.

It is almost impossible to overestimate the impact of Freudian psychoanalytic theory upon the intelligentsia and the public at large. Like Marxist theory, Freud's thought had great impact upon the thinking of writers, artists, and scholars in the first half of this century. Needless to say, the Freudian world-view is sex-oriented; from Freud's perspective, the lives of people, at their worst and at their best, revolve around sex. To be a well-adjusted person (the liberal equivalent of being a virtuous person) is to be sexually well-adjusted; to be badly-adjusted is to be "neurotic", i.e., to be sexually "hung-up."

Freud himself was arguably the first of the Great Psychobabblers. Not content to conduct a research program with empirical investigations, or (more daring) devise a method of treatment of psychological ailments, Freud did not hesitate to apply his ill-proven theory to other domains. He wrote, for example, that deplorable psycho-biography of Woodrow Wilson. And he certainly encouraged the use of his alleged insights in other disciplines. In no time at the entire world had to endure a parade of Freudian novels, poems, histories, movies, and even paintings (for instance, Salvador Dali—familiar to you younger readers from his recent phone company commercials).

However, Freudian theory has had from the beginning many critics, critics who have raised valid doubts about its scientific merits. Accusations have been made that Freud suppressed evidence or deliberately constructed a theory that is vacuous and untestable. Supporters have replied that Freudian theory is a genuine theory of the mind, and so brilliantly well-confirmed that Freud should be ranked in the Annals of Science with Newton and Einstein.

In the face of such radical disagreement about the status of psychoanalytic theory, Adolf Grunbaum has written a most valuable book. *The Foundations of Psychoanalysis* is a very clear, very probing examination of the theory in question.

Grunbaum is one of the most highly respected philosophers of science around today, and he has written many articles specifically about Freudian theory, so he is well-qualified to undertake the task of critically evaluating it. Actually, Grunbaum's work harkens back to the days when philosophers of science viewed themselves as sort of umpires, referees who had the job of critically examining various putatively scientific theories, and by open-minded probing distinguishing science from pseudo-science. The idea that philosophers of science can be neutral judges of scientific claims fell out of fashion in the 1960's, when logical positivism was eclipsed by the views of T.S. Kuhn, Paul Feyerabend, N.R. Hanson and others. I find Grunbaum's work a refreshing move back to a more normative, less purely descriptive philosophy of science.

Grunbaum's exploration of the epistemic nature and status of psychoanalytic theory is tremendously clear-minded. Much of his book consists of clearing away the obscurity and confusion surrounding that theory. To begin with, Grunbaum examines and obliterates the so- called "hermeneutic" construal of psychoanalytic theory, a view put forward by Jurgen Habermas, Paul Ricoeur, George Klein and others. These hermeneuticians (or whatever they please to call themselves) feel that mental phenomena call for a special sort of understanding: a person's motives and. intentions are not natural causes to be analyzed the way science normally analyzes causes. To attempt that would make one—dear me!—"scientistic," "crudely reductionist," "behaviorist" or some other such vile thing. Instead, a person's psychic life must be viewed as a text and "decoded."

Grunbaum dissects with surgical precision such arguments as are offered by the hermeneuticians, and calmly refutes them. He shows that there is no reason to deny that motives for actions can't also be causes of actions, and subjected to the normal sorts of causal analysis.

Moreover, a person can quite consistently maintain that mental causes are irreducibly mental—certainly a person need not be driven to behaviorism or any such view. Grunbaum has read Freud infinitely more thoroughly than the hermeneuticians have. Grunbaum shows that while Freud very early on equated his theoretical constructs (such as repressed desires or the id itself) with neuro-physical states, he very rapidly abandoned that quick reductionism for a less constrictive view, one that subjects mental phenomena to causal analysis without taking a stand on the metaphysical status of those phenomena. In short, the hermeneutic approach deals with straw men, and succeeds in "saving" Freud only by emasculating him, as it were.

Grunbaum likewise defends Freud from an unduly quick dismissal at the hands of the Popperians. Karl Popper has argued that there is no way to empirically test Freudian theory, and that therefore Freudian theory is vacuous and unscientific. Grunbaum has a devastating reply to the Popperian line of attack: he simply shows how Freudian theory can indeed be tested. To take just one example, Freud conjectured that repressed homosexual love is causally necessary for the occurrence of paranoid delusions. As Grunbaum notes, this is quite testable: we could simply determine whether or not the incidence of paranoid delusions is lower among openly practicing homosexuals. If paranoia proves to be virtually unknown among openly practicing homosexuals would confirm Freud's theory. If the rate of paranoia is the same for openly practicing homosexuals as it is for the rest of the population, then that fact would tend to disconfirm Freud's theory.

Having thus made sure that he is not setting up a straw man, Grunbaum turns to an examination of the evidence for Freudian theory, taking the theory as seriously as Freud meant it to be taken. Grunbaum shows quite convincingly that there is no substantial evidence for it at all. Essentially, Grunbaum argues that the chief evidence offered for psychoanalytic theory is clinical (the reports of Freudian therapists about their patients) as opposed to experimental (controlled experiments in laboratories or statistical studies of the population at large). (Grunbaum does note that some attempts have been made to experimentally prove the theory, but those attempts have not been very successful.) He established two points about clinical data: first, that such data is fatally flawed as evidence; second; that even if it were not fatally flawed, it would be inherently logically inadequate to confirm the theory.

Regarding the first point, Grunbaum points out something Freud realized, but was unable to refute: what a patient reports on the couch almost always is what the analyst wishes to hear. That is, clinical "data" is in fact the result of suggestion on the part of the analyst. Thus the theory is "confirmed" but only by the evidence its adherents manufacture.

Regarding the second point, Grunbaum points out that even if we could rely on the data produced in therapy sessions, such data would be logically insufficient to prove Freud's theory. It is a truism of elementary logic that simply adducing cases in which A and B occur together does not entitle one to infer that A causes B. For example, if we examine bald men and discover that every one of them has a mother, we cannot logically conclude that having a mother causes baldness. At the very least, we have to look at cases of non-bald men to determine whether or not there is some factor which is present in bald men and lacking in non-bald men. However, clinical data is data about people who have "neuroses"; well- adjusted people presumably don't go to the shrink. Thus even if every patient with neurosis N reveals to the therapist some repressed desire or memory R, and we accept the dubious claim that R was not an artifact (i.e.: the result of suggestion on the part of the therapist), it still would be fallacious to claim that R cause N.

I find only two faults with Grunbaum's fine book. To begin with, the prose is unfortunately rather dull and repetitious. That is unfortunate because it will limit the book's audience to academics, whereas Grunbaum's critique deserves to be understood by a much wider audience.

A second and more troubling problem is the rather subdued conclusion at which the book arrives. If Freudian theory is bereft of any significant evidential support, then why not just advocate that Freud be consigned to the dustbin of history—the history of failed sciences? There is no shame in being an alchemist in an era when alchemy seemed to be justified; but to be an alchemist today would be unreasonable. Should we not say the same thing about being a Freudian? The only reply one detects in Grunbaum's book lies in the comments he makes to the effect that Freudian speculations are "heuristic" and "brilliantly imaginative." But his own work shows that Freudian theory has not led to any significant psychological discoveries. And Poe had brilliant imagination, too—but so what? When I read *A Cask of Amontillado* I get a vision of what it is to have a thirst for revenge, but that hardly qualifies Poe as a great scientific genius.

I doubt that Freudian theory will lose its deceitful allure any time soon, despite the good work of Grunbaum and others to expose its glaring inadequacies. Far too many practitioners derive money and power from psychoanalytic theory. And far too many intellectuals enjoy the cheap and easy illusion of understanding that psychoanalytic theory gives them. What makes Freud's theory pseudoscience is not so much anything Freud did, as it is the way people now continue to believe it: in defiance of evidence, rather than because of evidence.

My thanks to *The California Review.*

16

"Science and Common Sense"

first appeared in The Journal of Critical Analysis Vol. VIII, No. 4, pp. 117–123 (1985)

There has been considerable disagreement in recent years among philosophers regarding what sort of cases to examine in doing epistemology (including philosophy of science). Some have preferred to examine ordinary language and mundane situations to draw their philosophic conclusions. Yet others – especially philosophers of science trained in the post positivistic period – prefer to examine historical cases of scientific discovery. In this article I will address this issue, one that is in fact part of the long-standing dispute about the relation between science and common sense.

Consider the cliché that science is just organized common sense. If this cliché is false (as clichés often are), the implications for epistemology are important. For then there would be several theories of knowledge, depending upon what is known (the realm of science versus the world of the common man). On the other hand, if the cliché is true, it also has important implications for epistemology. For then (again, it would appear) we could construct an adequate theory of knowledge by merely looking at simple, mundane cases of knowledge. The choice is an important one: In epistemology, do we look at cases drawn from the history of science in all their complexity, or do we allow ourselves the luxury of concentrating on the simple ("Jones owns a Ford")? Yet, for a question of such importance, the question of the difference between science and ordinary knowledge is rarely addressed explicitly.

We really should distinguish several questions here: What is the difference between the structure of scientific knowledge (organized into theories and laws governing various domains) and ordinary knowledge (if it has a structure at all)? What is the difference between scientific method and the techniques of ordinary learning? What is the goal of scientific research (perhaps pure truth) versus that of ordinary investigation (perhaps achieving some practical end)? I will focus on just one such question. It is the central one: Is the reasoning involved in scientific discovery essentially different from that employed in ordinary discovery?

The reader may wonder at the phrase "ordinary discovery." But what I'm referring to is clear enough. Many mundane occupations involve research. If that be too lordly a designation, then say instead sustained and rational investigations which (when successful) culminate in discovery. I have in mind, for instances: the auto mechanic trying to account for a car' s rough idling; the detective trying to figure out how a jewel disappeared from a room with all exits guarded; the TV repairman trouble-shooting a defective set; the gardener trying to decide why the dichondra won't grow; the doctor trying to determine the cause of a set of symptoms; and a hairdresser trying to restore body to bedraggled hair. Is there a difference between the reasoning of the scientist and that of those other people?

C. S. Peirce for one seems to have felt there isn't any logical difference between the reasoning in ordinary and scientific discovery. One thinks of his remark:

> I once landed at a seaport in a Turkish province, and, as I was walking up to the house which I was to visit, I met a man upon horseback, surrounded by four horsemen holding a canopy over his head. As the governor of the province was the only personage I could think of who would be so greatly honored, I inferred that this was he. This was an hypothesis.
>
> Fossils are found; say remains like those of fishes, but far in the interior of the country. To explain the phenomenon, we suppose the sea once washed over this land. This is another hypothesis.
>
> Numberless documents and monuments refer to a conqueror called Napoleon Bonaparte. Though we have not seen him, what we have seen, namely all those documents and monuments, cannot be explained without supposing that he really existed. Hypothesis again.[1]

Peirce adds that even our belief that our memory is veridical is hypothesis, put forward to account for our feeling that it is.

But others have disagreed, feeling that scientific reasoning is qualitatively (not just quantitatively) different. It will be instructive, I believe, if we examine one such view. I choose Toulmin's account as presented in his 1960 text, *Philosophy of Science*. He may not still hold this account after twenty-five years – I don't know. I would like to examine his view, and then present an observation about how we should use case studies in philosophy of science.

Toulmin begins the account by contrasting two cases of ordinary discovery with a clear case of scientific discovery, albeit of a low-level sort. He contrasts the reasoning involved in Robinson Crusoe's discovery that there was another man on his island (which Crusoe had hitherto thought deserted), and the reasoning involved in the discovery that swallows always migrate along great circles, with the reasoning involved in the discovery that light travels in straight lines.[2]

Beginning with the ordinary Crusoe discovery, Toulmin contends that it involves (shades of Peirce) an inferential step from the observation of a fresh footprint on the beach to the conclusion that there is another person around, via the assumption that "footprints mean man." Toulmin, that is, views Crusoe as inferring:

> Footprint!
> Footprints mean man.
> ______________________
> Therefore, man

Moreover, Crusoe can verify his inference by coming face-to-face with the man who caused the print. He is merely applying the old type of inference to fresh data.

On the other hand (Toulmin continues), the discovery that light travels in straight lines was *not* an inference from the data (namely, facts about light and shadows and the techniques-such as sundial construction-based upon them). He suggests several reasons why it isn't.

First, Toulmin claims that while Crusoe might meet his hypothesized person face-to-face, it makes no sense to speak of coming face-to-face with the light responsible for the shadows. "No single happening could establish the optical theory once and for all, in the way Crusoe's conclusion could be established."[3]

Secondly, Toulmin feels that the scientific discovery is one that we can use profitably even if it is only approximately correct. That is, the theory of the rectilinear propagation of light is not exactly correct – after all, light is diffracted, refracted, and scattered. But that doesn't stop us from profitably using the discovery to ask new and fruitful questions about light phenomena. This is not the case (Toulmin avers) with Crusoe's discovery or with the case of the swallows. The discovery here is that swallows always travel along great circles, and only that.

But the third difference Toulmin sees between ordinary and scientific discovery, a difference which surely proves that the latter involves non-inferential reasoning, is that in scientific discovery some of the key words are given new senses in the very statement of the discovery. This is not the case with ordinary discovery; the meaning of the term "man" for Crusoe doesn't change when he discovers that someone else has been walking on his beach. Yet the meanings of "light" and "travel'" do change with the discovery that light travels in straight lines.

Intertwined with his claim that the meanings of terms change in scientific discovery, Toulmin presents the claim that after making a discovery, scientists see the world in a different way, see (for instance) the shadows as effects of the blockage of light. (He also says that scientific discovery involves changing models.)

Now, Toulmin gives us quite a list of differences between ordinary and scientific discovery. The problem is that they aren't really persuasive.

Consider the first, that in the case of ordinary discovery, complete observational verification is possible, whereas such verification is never possible in true scientific discovery. This just isn't so. After all, the discovery that a bacterium causes a certain disease is surely a scientific discovery. Yet you can observe a bacterium directly.[4]

Conversely, even if Crusoe came face-to-face with the person who made the footprint, it is deceptive to talk about instant or conclusive verification of Crusoe's conclusion, at least as far as Crusoe is concerned. He can't be sure at first that he is faced by a man, as opposed to an unusual humanoid vegetable or a local robot.

Again, the claim that ordinary discoveries such as Crusoe's or the migration paths of swallows are either precise or else are uninteresting dead-end generalizations is dubious. Granted, the cases chosen to represent ordinary discovery are less interesting than the case chosen to represent scientific discovery. But the difference is a matter of degree, not kind. Swallows often stray off course a bit; hence *that* discovery is approximate, too. Moreover, this discovery *does* lead to interesting questions: How do they stay on course? What evolutionary purpose is served by such a migration pattern? And so on. Similarly, Crusoe's discovery suggests questions of great interest – to him, at least: Where did this person come from? Why is he here? What is the person's gender?

As to the welter of claims about meaning, perceptual and model change in scientific discovery, I want to point out that the same can be said to characterize ordinary discovery – at least when you go back early enough in a person' s training.

Consider this case of ordinary discovery. A young mechanic is given his first "patient," a car which has trouble accelerating from a full stop. The car can accelerate only in spurts – accelerating, then slowing, then reaccelerating. The novice, after examining the car's ignition system and carburetor, finally hits upon the idea of examining the fuel line. He finds a small hole in it, and begins thinking about whether such a hole could account for the car's anomalous behavior.

Before, (we may suppose) the novice had viewed the fuel line merely as a conduit for gas. Then he acquires an insight into the system. He begins to see it as a "suction conduit" which moves the fuel by suction, more gas being sucked as the car's engine speeds up. He hypothesizes that the hole causes the saltatory acceleration. As the car accelerates, the suction increases causing air to be sucked in. This cuts down the gas flow, which slows the engine, which reduces the suction, which increases the gas, which reaccelerates the car, etc.

After discovering why the car acted as it did, the novice *sees* the fuel line in a new way. The term "fuel line" has a new meaning for him.

Such a case may seem more like a parody than a serious counter-example to the claim that conceptual change characterizes only scientific discovery. But it seems like a parody only because we tend to forget that what we now know and the concepts we now employ were acquired very slowly. A young person making an ordinary discovery is in a very similar position to that of a scientist making a scientific one.

So in the end, none of Toulmin's putative "differences" seem to be real *qualitative* ones. Thus there seems to be no good reason to think that the reasoning involved in scientific discovery is essentially different from that in ordinary discovery, however deeper and more exciting the former might be. But are we to draw the conclusion that the philosopher can do his job just as well by examining simple cases of ordinary discovery (in the manner of those who do metaphysics by analyzing "ordinary language") instead of complicated cases from the history of science?

1 think we should resist making that inference for a very important reason: Cases drawn from the history of science, despite being less accessible initially, have the surprising advantage of clarity. Let me elaborate.

It is now universally recognized that scientific research (and ordinary investigation as well) takes place in some context. This has a bearing upon how that research evolves. That is, the social, economic, technological and cultural background (not to mention the prior history of research in that domain) enters into the scientist's program.

This is no less true in the case of ordinary "research." For example, the concepts that the auto mechanic has, his background knowledge and training, prior experience, and so on all enter into the way he trouble-shoots a given car. But the relevance of background factors is much less noticeable *precisely because* it is so familiar, shared as it is by most of us.

Putting the point another way, it is easier to spot the other fellow's presuppositions than your own. It is easier to see the complexity of reasoning in research (with the delicate interplay between background factors and new information) when the researchers are from an epistemic community different from your own. That is why introspection upon common-place investigation, and even retrospective reports by scientists about their own research, are (or at least tend to be) so much less revealing.

But something suggests itself here. If studying historical cases of scientific research is epistemologically important, not because of some essential difference between scientific and ordinary discovery, but because it is easier to detect the hidden background factors; and if such studies are inaccessible and have the drawback that the subject matter requires special training to understand what is happening in the research program; then, why not devise some approach that combines the best features of both ordinary cases (accessibility) and historical ones (clarity)?

One such compromise approach might be to study cases of ordinary investigation in times, cultures, and places far removed from our own. For instance, we could look at anthropological studies of magic and such like. (One thinks here of books like Horton's *Rationality and Magic*). But here again there may be problems of accessibility.

A better approach, it seems to me, is to design model games, with rules so clearly laid out that no questions of "presuppositions" or "background" will arise. Such model research games are now being investigated under the rubric "formal dialectic," and hold promise to be a middle course between science and common sense.

Notes

1. C. S. Peirce, *Collected Papers* 2.625.
2. Stephen Toulmin, *Philosophy of Science* NY: Harper & Row, p. 19ff.
3. *Ibid.* p. 19.
4. This claim is surely plausible, now that the theory/observation distinction as understood by the positivists has been shown to be dubious.

Permission to reprint courtesy of The Philosophy Documentation Center.
I wish to thank *The Journal of Critical Analysis* as well.

17

"Two Problems of Induction"

first appeared in Dialectica Vol. 39, No. 1 (1985), pp. 53–74

Introduction

Even the most casual reader of the voluminous writings on induction can affirm that there seem to be two basic problems about induction. These are, it should be noted, philosophical problems about an ongoing satisfactory practice, rather than practical problems about how to engage in it. The statisticians have brilliantly succeeded in devising probability theory and the attendant techniques of projective statistics—which seem to have endless fruitful applications.

The problems of which I speak are these. First, there is the logical problem of somehow "formalizing" (in a sense to be made clear shortly) traditional inductive argument forms, to put inductive logic on a par with deductive logic. Look at any introductory logic text and you will find the notions of "inductive-strength" and "deductive-validity" defined as if they were roughly similar properties; as for instance:

> An argument is *deductively-valid* if and only if it is impossible for the premises to be true and the conclusion false.
>
> An argument is *inductively-strong* if and only if it is not impossible but is unlikely that the conclusion would be false given that the premises were true.

Of course, the student later discovers the scandalous truth: that while there are agreed-upon inference rules for assessing validity irrespective of context, no such neat inductive logic exists. Instead, he is faced with a mélange of topics (Mill's methods, enumerative induction, eliminative induction, analogy, theory confirmation, and so on), with the probability calculus—a deductive system—hovering mysteriously in the background.

The second problem of induction is not so much logical as skeptical: given an intuitively satisfactory inductive logic, how can we justify its use or prove its adequacy? This second problem is what is called (with a note of exasperation) "the" problem of induction, and is one of Hume's enduring (if not endearing) legacies.

The thesis of this paper and its sequel is that both problems are pseudo-problems which arise out of mistaken presuppositions.

In Part I (this paper), I argue that the logical problem of induction (devising a formal account of induction which accords with the obviously satisfactory probability calculus) is resolvable if and only if we give up the presupposition that inductive reasoning is to be analyzed by a statement (assertoric) logic similar to deductive logic, and come to view such reasoning as being dialectical in nature. (The way is then open to use formal dialectic to explicate such reasoning.)

The flow of my arguments is as follows: first, to argue that there are no other evidential relations besides (at most) deductive-validity and inductive-strength; second, to argue that all traditional inductive argument forms are inter-derivable, and hence all are equally open to the same criticisms; third, to argue that construing induction as traditionally done renders context-free formalization impossible; fourth, to argue that if we give up the presupposition that there is such an evidential relation as "inductive-strength," the way becomes open for such context-free treatment via formal dialectic.

I will take up the skeptical problem of induction in Part II (the sequel to this paper).

Is There a Third Evidential Relation?

The traditional view of inductive logic has held that there are exactly two of evidential relationships, two different ways in which the premises of an argument can support its conclusion: inductive-strength and deductive-validity. But some prominent thinkers, C.S. Peirce and N.R. Hanson in particular, have felt that we ought to distinguish yet another type of evidential relation, that of retroductive-strength. That is, these writers have urged that just as we distinguish between certainty and mere probability, we ought to distinguish between probability and mere plausibility.

Delineating such a third evidential relation was the heart of Peirce's (and later Hanson's) search for a "logic of discovery." Peirce characterized the process of discovering any hypothesis as being an inference of the form:

1. Surprising fact F is observed.
2. If hypothesis H were true, then F would be a matter of course (would be best explained).

So H is plausible (worthy of investigation).

But this sort of argument form (which Peirce called variously "hypothesis," "retroduction" and "abduction," but which we will call the inference to the best explanation—the "IBE") equally well represents hypothesis/theory confirmation, except for the temporal order in which data-gathering and hypothesis-conceiving take place. And isn't theory confirmation just part of inductive logic after all? We as logicians are interested in the evidential relation between the hypothesis and the evidence for it, and isn't that relation the same whether the data suggests the hypothesis or tests one already conceived?

Since there seems offhand to be no compelling reason to distinguish a third evidential relation, the burden of proof rests on the man who claims that there is some inherent evidential difference between retroductive logic and inductive logic/confirmation theory. Several differences have been mentioned which I shall now review. None of them seems convincing.

(a) It is often said that induction generalizes, whereas retroduction explains. Or as Peirce put it, induction is reasoning from particulars to generals, and retroduction is reasoning from effect to cause.[1] But this confuses "broad" and "narrow" induction. Broadly speaking, an inductive argument is one in which the premises furnish good but not logically conclusive evidence for the conclusion. There are many types of inductive (in the broad sense) argument: analogy, the paradigm confirmation argument, induction by simple enumeration, eliminative induction, and so on. By narrow induction we mean generalization, induction by simple enumeration. Granted the IBE doesn't resemble enumerative induction—although we shall see in Section Three that the two argument forms are in fact related—still, the IBE is identical to the paradigm confirmation argument, which is certainly inductive in the broad sense.

(b) It is often said that retroduction goes from the observable to the unobservable. Peirce spoke this way when he said that induction infers phenomena similar to cases that have been observed, while retroduction is the supposition of something of a kind from what we have directed observed, and frequently something unobservable.[2]

This sort of claim again shows confusion between broad and narrow induction, for (to reiterate) the paradigm confirmation argument is a perfectly good broad inductive argument, and it certainly applies to theories involving unobservables. Moreover, consider narrow induction, simplistically put as:

$$\frac{\text{All known A's are B}}{\therefore\ \text{All A's are B}}$$

Do we need to stipulate that A's be observable, or that B be an observable trait? Surely not. All electrons ever examined have had spin ½, so, all electrons have spin ½.

(c) It is often said (in a manner similar to (b) above) that retroduction involves the introduction of new concepts, induction not.

This claim is only plausible if you view retroduction as being an inference from the data to the hypothesis. But the inference is really from the data plus the recognition that that hypothesis would explain the data, to confidence in the hypothesis, if it is an inference at all. (It isn't.)

It is, of course, quite true that inductive logic cannot mirror conceptual evolution. But neither can the IBE or any retroductive logic. No assertoric logic can analyze learning processes adequately; for that, one needs dialectic.

(d) It has been said that in induction (specifically theory confirmation), one begins with a theory and then gets evidence. In retroduction, one begins with the initial data, and finds a hypothesis to explain it. The temporal order of the processes is different.

But this is again misleading. A researcher, pondering in puzzling data, may have a *geistesblitz*—the sudden occurrence of an idea. But this (again) isn't yet hypothesis conception; the idea must be recognized as being such that it would (if true) account for the data. And the representation of that inference is the same as the representation of the typical inference involved in hypothesis testing. The temporal order in which the researcher's mind apprehended the premises is irrelevant to the logic of those situations, however much they differ dialectically.

(e) Many writers claim that retroduction and induction differ in the "strength" of the inference. As Peirce puts it,[3] induction is the stronger inference, plausibility being a weaker evidential relation than probability. And although the word "plausible" is often used as a synonym for "probable," we also quite often speak of something as being "only" plausible, not probable.[4]

Even if it were true that the strength of evidence in retroductive arguments is generally weak, it would not follow that the nature of the evidential relation in a retroductive argument is of some special sort. Why not just say the obvious: retroductive arguments are inductive arguments, but comparatively weak ones? Naturally, it takes more evidence to prove a hypothesis than to justify taking it seriously (worthy of testing), but the nature of the evidential relation is the same in proposing as in testing.

Consider this example. Suppose Fred's statement that he just saw Bob at home suggests to me that Bob is at home. I may verify my hypothesis (in the ordinary sense of "verify") by asking several other individuals who have just returned from Bob's house. If they testify that Bob is at home, my proof of the hypothesis consists not only of their testimony, but Fred's as well. The initial evidence (testimony) continues to be evidence for the claim, and forms part of the decisive proof (the totality of all the witnesses' testimony).

(f) One last attempt to distinguish retroduction from induction, retroductive strength from inductive strength, should be mentioned. Hanson drew a distinction between reasons for accepting a particular, minutely specified hypothesis from reasons for suggesting that the true hypothesis, whatever it turns out to be, will be of a certain kind.[5] In conceiving a hypothesis, we have reasons to think that it will be of a certain kind, before we have hit upon the precise hypothesis which succeeds in its predictions. In particular, said Hanson, there are reasons which suggest that the particular hypothesis H will be of a certain kind, yet which cannot establish H. Hanson gives us an example of Kepler's reasoning by analogy that since Mars had an elliptical orbit, and since it was a typical planet, then perhaps all planets have non-circular orbits of some sort (though perhaps not ellipses).

Hanson was fusing two distinct claims: first, that certain reasons (e.g., analogical ones) can be good enough to show a hypothesis plausible, yet cannot be good enough to establish its truth; second, that there could be evidence for a general hypothesis type which was not evidence for specific versions of that hypothesis. (The first claim has only incidentally to do with analogical reasoning—Hanson also mentions reasoning from considerations of simplicity or symmetry.[6])

Both claims are wrong. Consider the first. Why can't an analogical argument be strong enough to establish the truth of a hypothesis? Granted it can't ever be conclusive in the deductive sense—but then, neither can arguments from personal observation or any other inductive arguments. An analogical argument can have as high a degree of inductive strength as any other type of inductive argument.

Part of what Hanson had in mind is, of course, the point that often (indeed, typically) the evidence which suggests a hypothesis is weaker than the final evidence which establishes it. This point was examined in (e) above and found to be uninteresting.

But Hanson had more in mind: he felt (apparently) that certain "types" of evidence are never, by their very nature, able to prove hypotheses. Our earlier example can be modified to clarify this point.

Suppose my hypothesis that Bob is at home was suggested by Fred's testimony, but proved (not by other people's testimony but) by my own eyes. I simply go to Bob's house and see him sitting there. Granted, in some vague sense, the evidence which suggested my hypothesis was of a different type (testimony) from that which proved it (my own observation), but so what? Fred's testimony continues to be evidence for my hypothesis, but the evidence from my own eyes is (normally) so decisive that Fred's testimony is otiose. The testimony of others is not a *logically* different kind of evidence from personal observation (all of it is inductive); it is merely otiose given the latter.[7]

So it is with Kepler. Mars' orbit being elliptical is good evidence for (say) Jupiter's orbit being elliptical. But if we have decisive evidence in the form of the demonstration that all observed points of Jupiter's orbit fall on an ellipse, the original evidence is otiose. That it was analogic is beside the point.[8]

So Hanson's first claim is easily seen to be false, especially when you keep in mind that its plausibility rests on overlooking the fact that fairly good evidence can be rendered otiose, can be overshadowed by decisive evidence.

Also giving Hanson's first claim its air of plausibility is the fact—admitted in (e) above—that the evidence which suggest a hypothesis is usually weaker than that which confirms it. That, as we saw, proves nothing to the effect that retroductive arguments are not (as they seem to be) merely a subclass of inductively strong arguments.

Hanson's second claim, that there can be evidence for a general hypothesis which is not evidence for specific versions of it, is misleading if not false. Again, we can grant the point made in (e) that it takes more evidence to establish a specific version of a hypothesis than a general version, that sufficient or decisive for a general hypothesis is not usually decisive for specific versions of it. That is trivial and doesn't establish a difference between retroduction and induction.

No, what Hanson means is that there can be evidence for a general hypothesis which isn't evidence for each of the specific versions of it. This is not true, at least in those cases where there is not background information bearing on the various specific versions of the general hypothesis.

Consider a simple example. Suppose a fire occurs in a warehouse, and empty gas cans are found nearby. This, together with the fact that only humans are known to set fires, is evidence for (would suggest) the general hypothesis that a person set the fire. It is also—absent any background information—evidence for the hypothesis that a man set the fire. It is (again, absent any background information) equally good evidence that a woman did it. Of course, if you add in to the premises the fact that more men than women commit arson, then it is a stronger inference to conclude that a man did it. But that is just what I mean by background information.

As a general rule, it is not necessarily true that if E (some evidence) supports a general hypothesis, it supports every specific version of it. But it is true that if E contains no information against a given specific version, then E supports that version (given that it supports the general hypothesis). Thus, Hanson's second claim is, if not false, quite misleading. Hanson's claims thus do not succeed in distinguishing retroduction from induction.

Summing up this section, it appears that there is no reason to deny what most logicians take for granted, viz., that retroductively-strong arguments are just a subclass of inductively-strong arguments, and that the evidential relation of retroductive strength ("plausibility") is just inductive strength, usually to a lesser degree. To that extent, retroduction is induction.

Yet Hanson was right in his intuition that there is some difference between hypothesis conception and hypothesis testing, a difference he was never able to delineate. The key to the problem is the false dilemma he set for himself:

> Now, no one will deny that some differences exist between what is required to show H true, and what is required for deciding H constitutes a plausible kind of conjecture. The question is: are these logical in nature, or should they more properly be called "psychological" or "sociological?"[9]

Hanson meant by "logic" assertoric logic, and then—since he felt the distinction between hypothesis conception and hypothesis checking is more than merely a psychological difference—had trouble pointing out a difference in the logic of hypothesis conception (from hypothesis checking). In fact, there is no difference under that interpretation of "logic."

Yet there clearly is a logical difference if you construe "logic" broadly, to include dialectic. Reasons for proposing H differ dialectically from those for accepting H they play different roles in the learning process, even if they are logically indistinguishable from the point of view of assertoric logic. It is this insight I shall explore in Section Five of this paper.

Paradigm Inductive Arguments and Their Interrelations

It would be worthwhile at this point to review those argument forms traditionally pointed to as being inductively strong, with an eye to seeing if they are interrelated.

a) Enumerative Induction: This form of inductive argument is usually rendered (taking the special case of the "straight rule" where the ratio of m/n = 1):

$$Pa_1 \,\&\, Qa_1$$

$$\vdots$$

$$Pa_n \,\&\, Qa_n$$

$$\overline{\qquad\qquad\qquad}$$

$$(x)(Px \supset Qx)$$

This argument is subject to certain criteria or constraints. The most commonly cited constraints are that n be sufficiently large and that the sample a_i's have no biasing properties. Of course, making these intuitively obvious constraints precise, and stating with precision when these constraints are in fact satisfied, is a matter of some controversy.

Now, enumerative induction and the underlying straight rule have been dismissed by Ackerman as being simply fallacious, because the conclusion follows neither deductively nor by the probability calculus.[10] I think this view is essentially correct, as I shall explain later.

But of more immediate concern is this. As Mill noted, and as Goodman has emphasized, we must also stipulate that Q be a "projectable" property. If we check one bar of copper and find that it easily conducts electricity, we may well immediately generalize that all copper conducts electricity well.[11] But seeing a million grue emeralds won't justify us in saying that all emeralds are grue. Yet it seems that what counts as projectable depends upon our background knowledge and beliefs. Doesn't this mean that the assessment of enumerative inductive arguments depends upon pragmatic (i.e., extra-logical community based) factors? Doesn't that destroy any hope of an inductive logic, conceived of—following deductive logic—as a syntactic (formal) undertaking? This is just the problem of context-dependency which we must address in the next section.

Often overlooked is the fact that there is a sort of "second-order" induction by enumeration, where one generalizes on properties rather than individuals. One might, that is, infer from the fact that a and b have all observed properties in common, that they share all (relevant) properties:

$$\begin{array}{c} P_1a \;\&\; P_1b \\ \cdot \\ \cdot \\ \cdot \\ P_na \;\&\; P_nb \\ \hline (\Pi)(\Pi a \Rightarrow \Pi b) \end{array}$$

b) Analogy: Analogy is often rendered:

$$\begin{array}{c} Pa_1 \;\&\; Qa_1 \\ \cdot \\ \cdot \\ \cdot \\ Pa_n \;\&\; Qa_n \\ Pa_{n+1} \\ \hline Qa_{n+1} \end{array}$$

with constraints identical to enumerative induction. Russell[12] regarded this as a safer inference than enumerative induction, in that the conclusion in an analogical inference refers only to one individual. But this seems odd, in that the individual we refer to (the an + 1st) is arbitrary — we could just as well argue from the same premises to any other P-individual we run into. Thus, we can derive enumerative induction from analogy (assuming we can mix inductive and deductive inference) via universal generalization.

On the other hand, some argue that people really (as a matter of psychological fact) don't reason by analogy, but instead, generalize first, then instantiate next. The best rendering of this conjectured compressed inference would be as follows.

$Pa_1 \& Qa_1$ (premise)

.

.

.

$Pa_n \& Qa_n$ (premise)

Pa_{n+1} (premise)

$(x)(Px \supset Qx)$ (follows from simple enumeration)

$Pa_{n+1} \supset Qa_{n+1}$ (follows by universal instantiation)

Qa_{n+1} (follows by Modus Ponens)

Thus, first-order analogy and first-order enumerative induction are inter-derivable.

As in enumerative induction, we seem to have the problem of "background information" in figuring out what properties are relevant and which are not.

There is a second-order analogical argument, of course. If a and b share all relevant properties so far examined, then they will share the next relevant property. Again this seems inter-derivable from second-order enumerative induction, assuming the embeddability of second-order deductive rules of inference.

c) Eliminative induction: Eliminative induction, which Keynes and C.D. Broad took to be basic, involves gathering evidence of different sorts, from different areas, in generalizing. Thus, for example, the generalization "all frogs are green" is best supported by looking at frogs from many different regions of the earth (as opposed to looking at the same number of frogs, but all from the same area). Clearly, eliminative induction has the same form as enumerative induction, but with the constraints stated differently (the demand that the sample be stratified instead of "sufficiently" large).

d) Inference to the Best Explanation: Finally, there is the IBE. As before, we have an argument from which can be put syntactically, and constraints which cannot be so stated:

F

H would, if true, best explain F

H

where the constraints center around what it is for a hypothesis to be better than another. One usually sees listed various virtues that a hypothesis should possess: simplicity; consilience (the ability to account for evidence in various domains);

conservativity (not conflicting with established theories); generality (having the most content); and so on.

Again, none of these virtues can be stated purely formally, or so it seems after intensive work. And, like moral virtues, they are at tension with one another (as generosity is at tension with prudence).

How does the IBE fit in with the other traditional inductive argument forms? Well, as Harman points out enumerative induction (and by extension analogy) can be viewed as a special case of inference to the best explanation. For when do we generalize from the fact that all observed P's are Q's to the hypothesis that all P's are Q's? We do so just when that hypothesis is the best explanation of what we have seen, i.e., when there is no evidence that our sample was insufficient or biased.[13]

On the other hand, we can represent any reasoning characterizable as IBE as an analogy as well. For consider a situation where I hypothesize that this F case was caused by an H — say, where I hypothesize that these footprints were caused by a man walking on the beach. Presumably, if that is the best explanation (at least, in my opinion), then in the majority of cases like this footprints are caused by men (or at least that is what I would believe).[14]

But then my mental act, my inference, can as well be represented as an analogy:

This is an F
Most F's are H's

This is an H

as it can by the IBE:

This is an F
Were this an H, its being an F would be explained

This is an H

Thus it seems that all of the traditional forms of inductive arguments are "inter-convertible," in that any inference representable by one can be represented by any of the others. The question of which is "basic" is for our purposes irrelevant. It is irrelevant if one means by that to ask "what argument form actually represents how we, in fact, mentally process information inductively, " since that is a question for cognitive scientists to answer empirically. (We shall soon show how to represent "inductive" reasoning dialectically.)

The question is also irrelevant if by it one means to ask "which form plays the role in axiomatized formal inductive logic that Modus Ponens plays in the typical deductive logistic?" That question is not interesting because—as I will point out next—those traditional forms are not formalizable at all.

Traditional Inductive Arguments and Context-Dependency

We say that a rule is *formal* if it can be stated without reference to any particular reasoner or group of reasoners. Of course, the modern approach to formulating logical rules involves constructing artificial language schemata which incorporate in their rules of transformation the logical rules. Thus, in a symbolic system, the rules being purely formal (in my sense) amounts to their being formulatable on the syntactic level only.

The very nature of logic thus being to formulate general rules, it is clear that logicians should in theory seek formal rules where possible. After all, a formal rule, a rule not limited to person or group, is more general than informal rules.

What are some of the ways a logic, or a set of logical rules, can be said to be pragmatic, community—or context—dependent? Well, a logical system may be said to be pragmatic if its application by the logician to represent certain reasoning involves consideration of context (of whatever sort). Let us call this "application pragmaticity" or "application context-dependency."

Clearly, such context-dependency is not very disturbing. After all, classical, extensional deductive logic is "pragmatic" in that sense: I must use contextual clues and psychological conjectures to determine if your argument (say) is an instance Modus Tollens:

$$\begin{array}{c} \sim A \\ B \rightarrow A \\ \hline \sim B \end{array}$$

or is instead a case of contraposition followed by Modus Ponens:

$$\begin{array}{c} \sim A \\ B \rightarrow A \\ \sim A \rightarrow \sim B \\ \hline \sim B \end{array}$$

A second way a logical rule may be said to be pragmatic (not fully formal, context-dependent) is for the rule's validity to depend upon the possession (by the reasoner) of certain concepts or beliefs ("background information"). This sort of pragmaticity is not easily brushed aside.

In the foregoing section I repeatedly hinted at the "context-dependency" (of the pernicious sort) of inductive evidential relations, as exemplified by those traditional argument forms. Indeed, this problem is not only constantly referred to in the professional literature, but is apparent to even the neophyte logic student.

Consider in some detail traditional argument forms and the ways they depend upon background beliefs. In the case of enumerative (and eliminative) induction, what properties you generalize upon (i.e., what predicates you project) depend upon your background. What sample you consider large enough and unbiased enough depends upon your background information (or similarly, how you stratify your sample depends upon the background information you possess). Crucial in that background information would be your assumptions about how that property is distributed in the population.

But if a simple enumerative argument is good or bad depending upon background information (or else "upon the way the world is"), doesn't that mean that assessing such arguments is impossible? The traditional answer is to float some version of the "requirement of total evidence," that is, to require that inductive arguments contain within their premises all relevant evidence, so that we can assess the argument without worrying about background or the way the world happens to be.

Alas, the requirement of total evidence is not a very good way out. Does it mean "all possible relevant evidence?" If so, it's unhelpful because the human race will never have all the evidence possible. Does it mean "all relevant evidence possessed at the present time?" Then the assessment of any argument is open to revision later. As Ackerman puts it,

> This (the total evidence requirement) gives the statistical syllogism (i.e., the straight rule) a kind of temporal validity. Surely this is a very obscure piece of advice. Is one to run off all relevant experiments before computing a probability? Otherwise one apparently doesn't know when to stop gathering information, since to stop gathering it he must estimate the probability of finding further relevant information at zero, and this seems to involve the requirement of a paradox...[15]

Indeed, Ackerman claims that the requirement of total evidence, intended to enable us to assess the argument by inspecting only it, has the opposite effect.

> We cannot look at an inference and know that the premises embody the total evidence except by considerations outside the argument. Now it is usually thought in traditional logic that the validity of an inference should be determinable from an examination of its premises and conclusion. In inference forms involving the requirement of total evidence, this feature is absent… .[16]

To be fair, however, the proponent of the requirement might reply that such inductive arguments contain a premise of the form "There is no other evidence relevant to the matter"—and, while determining the truth of that premise would involve outside considerations, assessing the relation between those premises and the conclusion does not. (Of course, such a premise is in fact unknowable.) But we still have the problem: what counts as "relevant?"

With analogy, to compare two things is to say they are like each other in all "relevant" or "significant" respects. But again, what counts as relevant? (Projectability problems.) And how many similarities does it take to establish the analogical conclusion? (Sample-size problems.) As before, it all depends upon background considerations.

Needless to say, the IBE falls prey to these attacks, these allegations of context-dependency. To say a hypothesis is (say) simpler than another is to make a claim the acceptance of which depends upon one's having certain ideas about simplicity, about what aspects (number of entities posited? Length of formuli? Number of new predicates introduced?) are relevant.

If one reviews the literature and these various accusations, he sees that they are all variants of two fundamental criticisms. Consider the inductive evidential relation "E therefore C." One problem stressed is that this relation is not invariant with respect to translation, whereas the relation of deductive-validity is. Hence the valid argument "all emeralds are green; thus this emerald is green" remains valid when translated into Goodman English (English, but with Goodman-type predicates): "all emeralds are grue; thus this emerald is grue." But the inductive argument "all emeralds up until now have been green; so the next one I see will be green" loses its strength when translated (after the year 2000) "all emeralds have been grue, so the next emerald I see will be grue."

The second problem stressed in the literature is that the strength of "E, so C" is not knowable by inspection, as is the validity of an argument. For example, "This child has fever, congestion and pains, and all his family currently has the flu, so he has the flu" seems strong, but if the child has suffered from bouts of malaria over the years, the argument is not, in fact, strong. The observer can't tell just by inspecting the argument. (Compare any valid argument; there, the matter can be settled by inspection alone.)

The usual reply is to add a "total evidence has been given" premise. But again, aside from the puzzling nature of such a premise (it deals, not with the conclusion being discussed, but with the argument itself), it could never be known. And saving the inspectability of an argument by adding a premise which is by its nature unknowable seems a pyrrhic victory indeed.

Dialectic and Induction

Matters stand thus. If we assume that there is some evidential relation called "inductive-strength," and seek an inductive logic consisting of paradigmatically acceptable argument forms (rather like inference rules), we run up against the stone wall of context-dependency of a very pernicious sort. Is there some other way to view inductive reasoning, one that does not put it on a par with deductive reasoning, a view which gets around the problem of context-dependency and also allows us to more naturally bring in the probability calculus? I think there is—a view that utilizes formal dialectic. To get an intuitive feeling for this sort of view, let's consider Mill's methods for a moment.

Mill's five rules of scientific method are usually greatly misunderstood, not least because of the way they are stated. They are stated as if they are argument forms, but in fact they are something quite different. Mill's five canons purport to be rules of discovery of explanatory hypotheses—hypotheses about the causes of phenomena being investigated—as well as rules for proving those hypotheses. Let's focus on the Method of Agreement, my remarks applying equally well (mutatis mutandis) to the other four canons as well.

Mill's method of agreement is (bluntly stated) this: If all E type events (or phenomena) have factor F in common, and only factor F in common, then F causes E. For example, for the fact that the only thing bald men have in common is a deficiency in zinc, the hypothesis that zinc deficiency causes baldness in men suggests itself. But at the same time the hypothesis is proved by the very data which suggest it.

As it stands, then, this rule seems to be a deductively valid (and quite unhelpful) rule, if we mean by "cause" a necessary and sufficient condition (or set of conditions) for the occurrence of E. This rule seems unhelpful, since the antecedent (that the only factor E events have in common is F) can never be known in practice, since the number of factors is infinite.

But in reality, what the Millian has in mind is this. We begin our investigation with an idea of what factors are relevant, what factors could possibly be the cause of E. We begin, that is, with a list of possible candidates. Then we begin checking E case after E case, eliminating possible candidates by the deductively valid rule "if F is not present in any given E case, F cannot be the cause of E."

Thus the method of agreement is indeed a method, an interactive process for learning the answer to a question, and not an argument form at all. The iterative process, of course, involves the repeated application of an argument form, but to new information each time. (This situation is similar to the trial- and-error method of solving a problem, which consists in repeatedly applying the rule of Modus Tollens.) To logically represent such methods, we need dialectic, not merely assertoric logic.

It might be wondered why the method of agreement, which involves the iterative use of a *deductive* argument form, is included in writings on inductive logic. The usual answer is that the initial hypothesis about what factors are relevant is the result of some inductive inference or other. But this means that Mill's methods begin after induction is done!

Actually, "induction" as it applies to Mill's methods really amounts to deductive reasoning on the basis of *causal* assumptions—which suggests that we don't need any other evidential relation besides just the relation of deductive validity. What we *do* need is a formal dialectical system that has built within it both causal axioms *and* probability axioms (in addition to the axioms and inference rules of deductive logic).

I will outline such a system. I cannot completely review all the concepts of formal dialectic—the reader should perhaps look at Hamblin [1970] and [1971], as well as Jason [1979].

Dialectic is the study of dialogues or conversations. But we need only concern ourselves with *information-oriented dialogs*, by which I mean dialogs whose sole purpose is the acquisition and transmission of information. We can then more precisely define *formal dialectic* as the symbolic study, involving explication and evaluation, of information-oriented dialogs.

Such dialogs can be represented by matrices of locutions:

$$\begin{matrix} L_{11} & \cdots & L_{1n} \\ \cdot & & \cdot \\ \cdot & & \cdot \\ \cdot & & \cdot \\ L_{m1} & \cdots & L_{mn} \end{matrix}$$

where each L_{ij} is either a question, a statement or an imperative.

It should be noted that the matrix is *normally* assumed to represent a conversation between n participants, each of which speaks in turn, or at least "passes" by saying "pass." Yet it is quite conceivable for a person to have a dialogue with himself.

Note also that any L_{ij} may be of the form "(P_1 & ... & P_n) therefore C," representing (normally) one participant giving an argument for C.

We take m to represent the number of *rounds*, i.e., the number of sets of locutions-and-responses. For the sake of simplicity, we will assume that the first round begins with "start," so that L_{11} has the form "start: p," where p is either a statement or a question. Again for simplicity we will assume that the dialogue ends with all the participants except the last (the nth) passing, and n^{th} participant saying "pass and over." Thus (turning from our normal interpretation of the matrix to the matrix itself) the mth row is (pass, pass ... pass and over).

Note that, when we speak of locutions, we are presupposing an underlying assertoric grammar, plus an underlying erotetic extension thereof. Dialectic is, in reality, only an extension of assertoric and erotetic logic. We select as the underlying assertoric and erotetic grammars ordinary classical quantificational calculus plus identity, supplemented by causal and ordinary modalities (as discussed by Burks[17]), and erotetically extended (as discussed in Belnap/Steele[18]).

An important concept, especially from the point of view of this study, is that of the "commitment-store" of any participant at any time. (This is Hamblin's phrase.[19]) The commitment-store of participant p at round r (abbreviated "$C_{p,r}$") is that set of statements that he is committed to at that point. As Hamblin notes, to be committed to a statement is not quite the same thing as to believe it, but the difference need not concern us. Typically, in the cases Hamblin considers, the commitment-store begins empty, save perhaps the axioms of symbolic logistic.

We can now lay out part of our formal dialectical system. We begin with the vocabulary and the intended semantic interpretations.

Symbols	Intended Interpretation
A, B, C,..., Z (subscripts allowed)	These are propositional constants, intended to express non-compound statements
p, q, r, s, t	These are propositional variables, intended for the usual purpose
$A^1, B^1, \ldots, Z^1; A^2, \ldots, Z^2; \ldots$ (subscripts allowed)	These are predicate constants, intended to designate particular properties and relations
a, b, c,..., o (subscripts allowed)	Individual constants intended to denote particular individuals

Symbols	Intended Interpretation
u, v, w, x, y, z (subscripts allowed)	Individual variables, intended as usual
p^1,q^1,r^1,p^2,... (subscripts allowed)	Predicate variables, intended as usual
~,v, [],[c], =	Logical constants
(,),[,],{,}	Brackets, intended as punctuation devices

Next, the derived symbols:

Derived symbols	Note that α and β are metalinguistic variables
&	$(\alpha \;\&\; \beta) =_{def} \sim(\sim\alpha \text{ v } \sim\beta)$
$\supset$	$(\alpha \supset \beta) =_{def} (\sim\alpha \text{ v } \beta)$
$\equiv$	$(\alpha \equiv \beta) =_{def} [\alpha \supset \beta) \;\&\; (\beta \supset \alpha)]$
<>	$<>\alpha =_{def} \sim[]\alpha$
<c>	$<c>\alpha =_{def} \sim[c]\alpha$
$\rightarrow$	$(\alpha \rightarrow \beta) =_{def} [](\alpha \supset \beta)$
$\Rightarrow$	$(\alpha \Rightarrow \beta) =_{def} [c](\alpha \supset \beta)$
$\leftrightarrow$	$(\alpha \leftrightarrow \beta) =_{def} [](\alpha \equiv \beta)$
$\Leftrightarrow$	$(\alpha \Leftrightarrow \beta) =_{def} [c](\alpha \equiv \beta)$
$\exists$	$(\exists x)\alpha =_{def} \sim (\forall)\sim\alpha$

Finally, the non-assertoric symbols:

Non-assertoric symbols	Linguistic function
?	The erotetic operator
$\cup$	The addition operator
\	The deletion operator
$\varnothing$	The passing operator
!	The imperative operator

We next stipulate the rules of construction. (These include rules for constructing statements, questions and commands). Here, "wff" abbreviates "well-formed formula."

- RF 1: If α is a propositional symbol, then 'α' is an assertoric wff ("awff").
- RF 2: If α^n is an n-ary predicate symbol, and $\sigma_1, \sigma_2, \ldots, \sigma_n$ are individual symbols, then '$\alpha^n(\sigma_1,\ldots, \sigma_n)$' is an awff.
- RF 3: If α is an awff, then '$\sim \alpha$' is an awff.
- RF 4: If α is an awff without any modal operators, then '$[]\alpha$' and '$[c]\alpha$' are awffs.
- RF 5: If α and β are awffs, then '$\alpha \vee \beta$' is an awff.
- RF 6: If α is an awff and x is an individual variable, then '$(\forall x)\alpha$' is an awff.
- RF 7: If $\alpha_1, \ldots, \alpha_n$ are all awffs, then '$?({}_{\upsilon}{}^{\mu}\forall-)(\alpha_1, \ldots, \alpha_n)$', '$?({}_{\upsilon}{}^{\mu}--)(\alpha_1, \ldots, \alpha_n)$', '$?({}_{\upsilon}{}^{\mu}\forall\neq)(\alpha_1, \ldots, \alpha_n)$', and?$({}_{\upsilon}{}^{\mu}-\neq)(\alpha_1, \ldots, \alpha_n)$' where $(1 \leq \upsilon \leq \mu \leq n)$ are all ewffs (erotetic wffs).
- RF 8: If $\alpha^1{}_1, \alpha^1{}_2, \ldots, \alpha^1{}_r$ are all one-place predicates and $\sigma_1, \sigma_2, \ldots, \sigma_n$ are all individual variables, and α^n is an n-place predicate, then '$?({}_{\upsilon}{}^{\mu}--)(\alpha^1{}_1\sigma_1, \ldots, \alpha^1{}_r\sigma_r, \sigma_{r+1}, \ldots, \sigma_n \parallel \alpha^n\sigma_1\ldots\sigma_n)$', '$?({}_{\upsilon}{}^{\mu}\forall-)(\alpha^1{}_1\sigma_1, \ldots, \alpha^1{}_r\sigma_r, \sigma_{r+1}, \ldots, \sigma_n \parallel \alpha^n\sigma_1\ldots\sigma_n)$', '$?({}_{\upsilon}{}^{\mu}-\neq)(\alpha^1{}_1\sigma_1, \ldots, \alpha^1{}_r\sigma_r, \sigma_{r+1}, \ldots, \sigma_n \parallel \alpha^n\sigma_1\ldots\sigma_n)$', and '$?({}_{\upsilon}{}^{\mu}\forall\neq)(\alpha^1{}_1\sigma_1, \ldots, \alpha^1{}_r\sigma_r, \sigma_{r+1}, \ldots, \sigma_n \parallel \alpha^n\sigma_1\ldots\sigma_n)$' are all ewffs.
- RF 9: '$!\varnothing$' is an iwff (imperative wff).
- RF 10: If α is a wff, then '$!(\sim\alpha)$' is an iwff.
- RF 11: If α and β are iwffs, then '$!(\alpha \vee \beta)$' is an iwff.
- RF 12: If α is an awff or an ewff, then '$!\cup\alpha$' and '$!\backslash\alpha$' are iwffs.
- RF 13: If $\lambda_{11}, \ldots, \lambda_{mn}$ are all awffs, ewffs, or iwffs, then

$$\begin{matrix} \lambda_{11} \ldots \lambda_{11} \\ \cdot \\ \cdot \\ \cdot \\ \lambda_{11} \ldots \lambda_{11} \end{matrix}$$

is a wfd ("well-formed dialog").

Next we lay down the axioms, taken to be stored in the commitment-store. These include some typical axioms of quantifier calculus (with identity), augmented by Burks' modal axioms, plus (and this is most important from the point of view of this paper) the axioms of the probability calculus.

- AS 1: $\alpha \supset (\alpha \,\&\, \alpha)$
- AS 2: $(\alpha \,\&\, \beta) \supset \alpha$
- AS 3 $(\alpha \supset \beta) \supset [\sim(\beta \,\&\, \gamma) \supset \sim(\alpha \,\&\, \gamma)]$
- AS 4: If x is not free in α, then $\alpha \equiv \alpha(x)$ is an axiom.
- AS 5: $(\forall x)(\alpha \supset \beta) \supset [(\forall x)\alpha \supset (\forall x)\beta]$

- AS 6: Let β be the result of substituting y for all free occurrences of x in α. If β has exactly as many free variables as does α, then $(x)\alpha \supset \beta$ is an axiom.
- AS 7: $(\forall y)\{\alpha(y) \equiv (\exists x)[(x \equiv y) \,\&\, \alpha(x)]\}$

The following six axiom schemata are restricted to non-modal a's.

- AS 8: $[]\alpha \supset [c]\alpha$
- AS 9: $[c]\alpha \supset \alpha$
- AS 10: $[](\alpha \supset \beta) \supset ([]\alpha \supset []\beta)$
- AS 11: $[c](\alpha \supset \beta) \supset ([c]\alpha \supset [c]\beta)$
- AS 12: $(x)[]\alpha \equiv [](x)\alpha$
- AS 13: $(x)[c]\alpha \equiv [c](x)\alpha$
- AS 14: If α is an axiom, so is $(x)\alpha$.
- AS 15: If α is a non-modal axiom, so is $[]\alpha$.
- AS 16: $Pr(\alpha) = 1$if $\alpha$is a tautology; $Pr(\alpha) = 0$ if α is a contradiction.
- AS 17: If $[](\alpha \equiv \beta)$ then $Pr(\alpha) = Pr(\beta)$.
- AS 18: If α and β are independent, then $Pr(\alpha \,\&\, \beta) = Pr(\alpha) \times Pr(\beta)$.
- AS 19: If $[]\sim(\alpha \,\&\, \beta)$, then $Pr(\alpha \vee \beta) = Pr(\alpha) + Pr(\beta)$
- AS 20: $P_r(\sim\alpha) = 1 - Pr(\alpha)$
- AS 21: If there is no set of elements in L such that any element of $[E_1,\ldots, E_n)$ is entailed by it, and if $[](E_1,\ldots, E_n)$ then $Pr(Ej) = 1/n$ all j.

Delineating the rules governing legitimacy of dialogs (akin to inference rules or rules of transformation in assertoric logic) is trickier.

First, we ought to distinguish between logical rules governing dialogs and strategic rules. Rules of strategy are rules which any participant is free to break, but which he would do well to follow if he wishes to maximize his information gain. On the other hand, logical rules are rules which no participant is free to break. Compare standard draw poker: rules like "you may draw up to four cards after the first round of betting" define the game, and breaking them (cheating) will perhaps get the participant shot. On the other hand, a rule like "never draw to an inside straight" can be broken, but habitually doing so will very likely cause the player to lose over the long run. Indeed, the analogy extends to deductive logic: any good logic textbook will contrast the rules for justifying the steps in a proof (the inference rules) with the rules of strategy for divining those proofs.

Among the logical rules of dialectic, we ought to distinguish between those which arise out of, or are a part of the assertoric and erotetic underpinnings of the dialectical system, and those which are peculiar to the system as a whole. The former I call structural (logical) rules, the latter I call procedural (logical) rules, for no particular reason.

Clearly, the structural rules of dialectic are just the rules of the underlying assertoric and erotetic grammars:

Rules of Structure:

- SR 1: From α and $\alpha \supset \beta$ to infer β.
- SR 2: The rule of substitution.

Erotetic Rules (where '**Q**' is a question and '**I**' an answer to it):

- ER 1: If **Q** has the form '$?({}_{\upsilon}^{\mu} - -)(A_1, \ldots, A_n)$' then **I** must have the form 'B_1 &... & B_p' where each of the B_i is an element of $(A_1, \ldots, A_n)$ and $\upsilon \le p \le \mu$.
- ER 2: If **Q** has the form '$?({}_{\upsilon}^{\mu} - -)(C_1x_1, \ldots, C_rx_r, x_{r+1}, \ldots, x_n \,||\, Ax_1 \ldots x_n)$' then **I** must be '$(Aa1_1 \ldots Aa1_n \,\&\, \ldots \,\&\, Aap_1 \ldots Ap_n)$ where $\upsilon \le p \le \mu$.
- ER 3: If **Q** is of the form '$?({}_{\upsilon}^{\mu} \forall -)(A_1, \ldots, A_n)$' then **I** must be '$(B_1 \,\&\, \ldots \,\&\, B_p \,\&\, {\sim}C_1 \,\&\, \ldots \,\&\, {\sim}C_q)$' where $\{B\} \subset \{A\}$ and $\{C\} \subset \{A\}$ and $\{B\} \cap \{C\} = \varnothing$ and $\{B\} \cup \{C\} = \{A\}$ and $\upsilon \le p \le \mu$.
- ER 4: If **Q** is of the form '$?({}_{\upsilon}^{\mu} \forall -)(C_1x_1, \ldots, C_rx_r, x_{r+1}, \ldots, x_n \,||\, Ax_1 \ldots x_n)$' then **I** must be '$\{[Aa1_1 \ldots a1_n \,\&\, \ldots \,\&\, Aap_1 \ldots ap_n] \,\&\, (\forall x_1) \ldots (\forall x_n)[(C_1x_1 \,\&\, \ldots \,\&\, C_rx_r) \supset (Ax_1 \ldots x_n \supset ((x_{1,n} = a1_{1,n}) \vee \ldots \vee (x_{1,n} = ap_{1,n}))))]$' with $\upsilon \le p \le \mu$.
- ER 5: If **Q** is of the form '$?({}_{\upsilon}^{\mu} - \neq)(A_1, \ldots, A_n)$' then **I** must be '$B_1$ & ... & B_p' where $\upsilon \le p \le \mu$, and where for all i,j with $1 \le i, j \le p \sim (B_i \Leftrightarrow B_j)$.
- ER 6: If **Q** is of the form '$?({}_{\upsilon}^{\mu} - \neq)(C_1x_1, \ldots, C_rx_r, x_{r+1}, \ldots, x_n \,||\, Ax_1 \ldots x_n)$' then **I** must be '$\{[Aa1_1 \ldots a1_n \,\&\, \ldots \,\&\, Aap_1 \ldots ap_n] \,\&\, [\boldsymbol{\&}_{(1 \le I \le I \le p)} \mathbf{V}_{(1 \le k \le n)} (ai_k \neq aj_k)]\}$'.
- ER 7: If **Q** is of the form '$?({}_{\upsilon}^{\mu} \forall \neq)(A_1, \ldots, A_n)$' then **I** must have the form $\{[B_1 \,\&\, \ldots \,\&\, B_p] \,\&\, [\sim C_1 \,\&\, \ldots \,\&\, {\sim}C_q] \,\&\, [\boldsymbol{\&}_{(1 \le I, j \le p)} {\sim}(B_i \Leftrightarrow B_j)]\}$ subject to earlier restrictions.
- ER 8: If **Q** is of the form '$?({}_{\upsilon}^{\mu} \forall \neq)(C_1x_1, \ldots, C_rx_r, x_{r+1}, \ldots, x_n \,||\, Ax_1 \ldots x_n)$' then **I** must have the form '$\{[Aa1_1 \ldots a1_n \,\&\, \ldots \,\&\, Aap_1 \ldots ap_n] \,\&\, [\boldsymbol{\&}_{(1 \le i, j \le p)} \mathbf{V}_{(1 \le k \le n)}(a_i \neq a_j)] \,\&\, [(\forall x_1) \ldots (\forall x_n)((C_1x_1 \,\&\, \ldots \,\&\, C_rx_r) \supset (Ax_1 \ldots x_n \supset ((x_{1,n} = a1_{1,n}) \vee \ldots \vee (x_{1,n} = ap_{1,n})))))]$'.
- ER 9: If **Q** is of the form '? Why p' then **I** must be '$[L_1 \,\&\, \ldots \,\&\, L_n \,\&\, C_1 \,\&\, \ldots \,\&\, C_m]$' where $[L_1 \,\&\, \ldots \,\&\, C_m] \Rightarrow p$, and where each L_i is of the form $[(\forall x)(\alpha x => \beta x) \,\&\, <> (\alpha x \,\&\, {\sim}\beta x) \,\&\, <> ({\sim}\alpha x \,\&\, \beta x) \,\&\, <c> \alpha x \,\&\, {\sim}[c]\beta x]$ and where all the L_i's and C_i's are elements of the commitment-store.

However, what about the rules of procedure? What do they look like? Well, in contrast to the rules of strategy, these rules are part of the essence, the definition of rational conversation (that is information oriented). Yet, in contrast to the structural rules, these rules govern the evolution of the rounds, the relation between responses to a given move and the moves prior to it. A few simple examples come to mind: never ask a question which presupposed the negation of a previous answer; never repeat the same statement twice.

More directly, it seems that the procedural rules can be stated in terms of how the commitment-store should evolve. These seem to be the most obvious such rules:

Rules of Procedure:

- PR 1: If $\alpha r_{(i+1)}$ is of the form '?Why αr_i' then $\alpha r_{(i+2)}$ must have the form '(P_1 & … & P_n) $\Rightarrow$ αr_i', where each P_i is a statement in the commitment-store or else is of the form '!\ar$_i$'.
- PR 2: If the rth round is of the form (!$\cup\alpha$, !∅, ..., !∅) then $C_{r+1} = C_r \cup \alpha$.
- PR 3: Let {P_1, …, P_n) be the set of direct answers to question **Q**. Then **Q** must occur in round r only if (P_1 v … v P_n) $\in C_r$.
- PR 4: If P $\in C_r$, then '?Why P' is permitted.
- PR 5: '!∅' can occur anywhere except after a challenge.
- PR 6: If '!(α & β)' occurs, where α and β are iwffs, then both α and β must be responded to.
- PR 7:. If '!(α v β)' occurs, then either α or β must be responded to.
- PR 8: If the rth round is of the form (!\P, !∅,..., !∅), then $C_{r+1} = C_r - P$.

With this sort of formal system, we can more naturally and more accurately reflect inductive reasoning. We represent such reasoning not as arguments with some weird kind of evidential relation obtaining between premises and conclusions, but rather as dialogues in which probabilistic deductive inferences take place against the backdrop of changing elements of the commitment store.

Notes

1. Peirce, 2.636. (All citations from the *Collected Works of Charles Sanders Peirce*). See also 2.642, where Peirce says that induction is classification, retroduction is theorization. Again, this confuses broad and narrow induction; theorization involves, after all, theory confirmation.
2. Peirce, 2.640. See also 6.3: "The things that any science discovered are beyond the reach of direct observation. We cannot see energy, nor the attraction of gravitation,

nor the flying molecules of gases, nor the lumineferous ether, nor the forests of the carbonaceous era, nor the explosions of nerve cells. It is only the premises of science, not its conclusions, which are directly observed."

3. Peirce, 2.642.
4. Brian Skyrms argues that plausibility amounts merely to probability. See pp. 172–3, also p. 182ff of his *Choice and Chance* (Belmont, California: Dickenson Publishing Co., 1975), 2nd edition.
5. Norwood Russell Hanson, "Is There a Logic of Discovery," in *Current Issues in the Philosophy of Science*, ed. Herbert Feigl (New York: Holt, Rinehart and Winston, 1961), pp. 20–42.
6. *Ibid.*, p. 26.
7. This is normally the case. But, of course, occasionally the testimony of others can overrule one's own observation.
8. Carmichael made a similar point. See R.D. Carmichael, *The Logic of Scientific Discovery* (Chicago: Open Court, 1930), p. 21.
9. Hanson, op. cit., p. 22.
10. Robert Ackermann, "Some Recent Problems of Inductive Logic," in *Philosophical Logic*, ed. J.W. Davis, D.J. Hockney and W.K. Wilson (Dordrecht, Holland: D. Reidel Publishing Co., 1969), p. 143.
11. Indeed, some have claimed (F.E. Abbott and Dretske, among others), that we directly or immediately *see* general facts. When looking at that particular bar of copper, we just see that copper conducts electricity well, sans inference. Whether this psychological claim is true or not, as Peirce noted, is really unimportant; we can in any case represent non-inferential seeing as an inference.
12. Russell, Bertrand *Problems of Philosophy* (London: Routledge & Kegan Paul, 1909).
13. Gilbert Harman, "Inference to the Best Explanation," *JOP*, 1964.
14. For a more complete justification of this point, see K.A. Fumerton "Induction and Reasoning to the Best Explanation," *Philosophy of Science* 47 (1981), 589–600.
15. Ackermann, op. cit., p. 142.
16. *Ibid*, p. 142.
17. Arthur Burks, *Chance, Cause and Reason* (Chicago: University of Chicago Press, 1977).
18. Nuel Belnap and Thomas Steele, *The Logic of Questions and Answers* (New Haven: Yale University Press, 1976).
19. See C.L. Hamblin, *Fallacies*, (London: Methuen, 1970), p. 257.

Permission to reprint courtesy of John Wiley and Sons. I wish to thank the journal *Dialectica* as well.

18

"Epistemologies and Apologies"

first appeared in Dialectica Vol. 40, No. 1 (1986), pp. 45–58

Quite a bit of recent work by epistemologists can be viewed as being part of a struggle between two theories of knowledge, viz., foundationalism and fallibilism.

Foundationalism is the older of the two epistemologies, being most commonly associated with Descartes. Fallibilism is somewhat younger, being most commonly associated with Peirce. I would like to examine the difference between these two views from a certain angle, namely, the angle of the justification of the principles of reasoning. Specifically, I would like to present the thesis that while foundationalism leads to the traditional problem of induction, fallibilism, which does not face that problem, faces a functional analogue. This "functional analogue," which I shall call *the problem of convergence*, seems to be nearly as difficult as the traditional problem of induction. The epistemology you hold will dictate the apology you must make for the principals of reasoning you employ.

The terms "foundationalism" and "fallibilism" are notoriously hard to define. In what follows, the definitions I give will be guided by the vision of Descartes and Locke as paragons of foundationalism, and Peirce as a paragon of fallibilism. But the labeling of figures is at best procrustean, and at worst misleading or even erroneous. So take my definitions as arising from, but not necessarily describing, certain historical positions. In particular, I think it is most profitable to look at the motivation behind each view.

The foundationalist is concerned with skeptical doubt. We intuitively feel that we do indeed have knowledge about many things. By "knowledge" we will mean true justified belief. (Gettier-type problems will not be of relevance in what follows.) But here skeptical doubt enters in. How can I tell if my beliefs are true and justified? How do I know that I am not completely deceived by them all? (Descartes' image of the Evil Demon serves to make this doubt systematic). We all know the skeptical doubt game: I ask you for your justification of claim p_1 and you cite evidence p_2. I then ask for your evidence for p_2, and you can only cite some other evidence p_3. And so the regress goes.

The traditional foundationalist response is to stop the regress at some set of beliefs which are held to be self-evident. Traditional foundationalism, which I shall call *strong foundationalism*, held that:

(1) There are foundational beliefs $\{f_1, f_2, ...\}$ which can be/do form the basis for all other beliefs which can/are known.[1]
(2) The $\{f_i\}$ are all incorrigible/indubitable/self-evident/certain.[2]
(3) A person can truly claim to know *p* if and only if he can prove *p* on the basis of some of the $\{f_i\}$.
(4) A person can truly prove a belief if and only if he can know by inspection that his proof is logically adequate.

The research program which grew out of strong foundationalism accordingly focused upon the nature of the $\{f_i\}$, and sketching out the rational reconstructions of beliefs. Were the foundations general truths known by the light of reason (as the rationalists believed), or instead particular truths known by direct observation (as the empiricists held)? Did the reconstruction involve only deductively valid inferences or probabilistic ones as well? Should we reconstruct beliefs about minds in terms of the overt behavior of the body, or reconstruct beliefs about observable objects in terms of mental images?

Problems arose in carrying out the strong foundationalist research program. Fallibilism arose more or less in reaction to the failures of the old theory, and while characterizing fallibilism is more difficult (if for no other reason than the philosophy is still evolving rapidly), we can characterize it tolerably well by opposing it to strong foundationalism:

(1*) The starting points for any justification of beliefs are those beliefs $\{s_1, s_2...\}$ held to be self-evident by one's community.

(2*) No beliefs, not even the $\{s_i\}$, are ever incorrigible, or "certain"/"self-evident" in any community-transcendent sense. Rather, the $\{s_i\}$ are those beliefs that are held by the community to be not worth questioning.
(3*) A person can legitimately claim to know *p* in a community if and only if he can prove *p* on the basis of some of the $\{s_i\}$ of that community.
(4*) A person can legitimately claim to have proven *p* in a community if and only if his proof is in accordance with the logical canons of that community.

The differences between the (strong) foundationalist and the fallibilist are profound. To begin with, reconsider the question of motivation. While the motivation for the foundationalist is theoretical—answering *skeptical* doubt, the motivation for the fallibilist is ultimately economic—answering *real* doubt. To use Peirce's term for it, the "economics of research" dictate that we actually spend our effort in answering real doubts, real questions set for us by our community. Skeptical doubt isn't the spur to scientific research, but real doubt is. Part of the training of a scientist is to learn both the questions and the methodology for answering those questions in his domain of research. (Naturally, the questions and ever the methodologies change over time. This is a point to which we shall return.)

The point about the difference in motivations brings up another difference in perspective. While the foundationalist typically seeks certainty in all knowledge via the certain reconstruction of beliefs upon incorrigible foundations, the fallibilist seeks reasonable security rather then certainty. We can, the fallibilist claims, have true knowledge, but we can't ever be certain about anything we believe—at least, we can't have the absolute certainty sought by the foundationalists. Everything is open to later revision.

This latter point (that everything is open to later revision) is no minor difference. For the fallibilist, even the laws of logic are potentially open to revision; indeed, Peirce spent a good deal of time investigating many-valued logics. To the fallibilist, deciding which logic is "the true logic" is a question that calls for detailed empirical (psychological, anthropological, historical and sociological) research and is not a question of absolute self-evidence. Peirce's analogy with geometry is apt: for many centuries people supposed Euclidean geometry to be indubitable, but the work done by Gauss, Riemann, Bolyai, Lobachevski et al. proved otherwise.

However, from the point of view of this paper, the most important difference between the two theories of knowledge is that between (4) and (4*). For the strong foundationalist, knowledge is solitary: knowledge is something an individual sees that he has or lacks, depending upon whether he can actually carry out the justification and verify its adequacy. For the fallibilist, knowledge is social: knowledge is something a person claims, his claim's merit being dependent upon whether the community assents to his starting points and his logical methodology, i.e., the validity of his canons of reasoning. (Of course, he can "lead the community" as in a scientific revolution, that is, he can get his community to reject or modify some of the starting points or even some of their canons of reasoning, but only by appeal to the remainder of the beliefs or canons.)

As I said earlier, the fallibilist research program is still relatively young, and there does not seem to be widespread agreement among fallibilists about (for instance) how one individuates epistemic communities (by beliefs, language?), whether the fallibilist needs to reject the KK thesis, and so on. But I want now to return to strong foundationalism, because what I will later say about fallibilism grows out of what I will now say about foundationalism.

The strong foundationalist faces a problem, growing out of his acceptance of (4): you can truly prove a belief if and only if you can know by inspection that your proof is logically adequate. Knowing that your proof is adequate involves two things. First, you must know that the steps connecting p (the belief in question) to the foundation statements f_i, f_j,... upon which it is based must be in accordance with the canons of logic, and second you must know that your logical system is valid (or acceptable or adequate). Waiving problems about the possible corrigibility of your belief that your steps are all instances of your rules, you still have the problem of knowing that your logic is adequate. Traditionally, strong foundationalists have automatically assumed that demonstrative (deductively valid) inference is self-evidently adequate, whereas the principles of non-demonstrative inference are not self-evident, and need some justification. But, as Hume so well indicated, this leads to a problem.

The problem is this. To be justified in using an inductive logic N (according to the strong foundationalist view), you must be able to prove that N is adequate, i.e., that the arguments to which N assigns a high degree of inductive probability lead from true premises to true conclusions most of the time.[3] But how can this be done?

The reader is no doubt familiar with most of the attempts to justify induction; is not, the second chapter of Skyrms (1975) has an excellent survey.[4]

Obviously, we cannot give a deductively valid proof of the adequacy of N. For we have in the premises of such a proof only information about how well N has worked in the past, and that information cannot logically entail any statement to the effect that N will work in the future. Yet to prove N is adequate, we must show that the arguments which it sanctions lead from true premises to true conclusions most of the time past, present and future.

One the other hand, how would one construct an acceptable inductively strong proof of the adequacy of N? If one proves N is justified by using N, doesn't that beg the question? It seems to.

Of course, those who seriously attempt to meet the challenge do so in ways more subtle, though in the end no more satisfactory than those indicated above. For instance, a more sophisticated attempt at an inductive justification of induction would be this.[5] Begin by distinguishing *levels* of arguments, with *level 1* arguments being arguments about individual things and events; *level 2* arguments being arguments about level 1 arguments (such as: "Some level 1 arguments are valid; all level 1 arguments which are valid are explicable formally; therefore, some level 1 arguments are explicable formally"); *level 3* arguments being arguments about level 2 arguments, etc. Then we can distinguish between levels of inductive logic, with N_1 being that inductive logic which evaluates level 1 arguments, etc. Now, we can justify induction by showing that N_1 has been adequate in the past, and arguing that it will therefore be adequate in the future. That is, we justify N_1 by giving a level 2 argument which is sanctioned by N_2. If the skeptic has doubts about N_2 we can justify it by a level 3 argument sanctioned by N_3 and so on.

Alas, this layer-cake approach isn't satisfactory. After all, one could play the same shell-game with a counter-inductive logic N^c, which sanctioned arguments of the form "such and such happened in the past, therefore, it will not happen in the future". You could justify such level 1 arguments by appeal to N^c_1. But, of course, given the way our world works, level 1 arguments sanctioned by N^c_1 will lead to inaccurate predictions. Fine, because we can then formulate a level 2 argument to the effect that that arguments sanctioned by N^c_1 have not led to true predictions in the past, so they will in the future; and this level 2 argument is sanctioned by N^c_2. Thus (quite proper) skeptical doubts about N^c_2, doubts about N^c_2 by N^c_3, and so on.

Again, Reichenbach and Feigl floated a more sophisticated deductive defense of induction. Very crudely put, the defense consists of showing that, if any inductive logic will work, N will. (Here the precise formulation of the logical system N becomes crucial.) But we must use some system of inductive logic, even if it is only spinning a bottle. So we are justified in using N.

Unfortunately, this sophistication buys us little. The essence of the defense amounts to recognizing that even if some crazy system of making predictions (say, spinning a bottle of Jack Daniels whiskey) works (makes accurate predictions) on the level of individual objects and events, then scientific induction N will have at least one accurate prediction, namely, the prediction that that crazy system will continue to work. Put another way, the essence of this deductive justification of induction is the recognition that to even say that a method "works" and to advocate its continued usage involves generalization in accordance with N.

Yet this insight is too feeble to do the job required. As Skyrms puts it:

> Now this is quite different from showing that if any method works on any level then scientific induction will also work on that level, or even from showing that if any method works on level 1 then scientific induction will work on level 1. Instead what has been shown is that if any other method is generally successful on level 1 then scientific induction will have at least one notable success on level 2; it will eventually predict the continued success of that method on level 1.[6]

And as Skyrms notes, this is quite compatible with the possibility that scientific induction (system N) doesn't work at the level of ordinary world of things (as opposed to arguments).

The problem of induction is nothing new. But what is somewhat more recent is the recognition that the same sort of problem faces any logic, deductive logic not excepted. To be justified in using any system of deductive logic L (on strong foundationalist grounds), one must prove that L is adequate, i.e., that the arguments L sanctions lead from premises to true conclusions all of the time. But as Haack observed, it is no less difficult to justify deduction (in the sense required) than it is to justify induction:

> ... we cannot justify deduction inductively, because to do so would be, at best, to show that usually, when the premises of a deductive argument are true, the conclusion is true too—which would be too weak; and we cannot justify deduction deductively either, because such a justification would be circular.[7]

And, as before, increased sophistication gets us no closer to meeting the challenge. For instance, we might distinguish between levels of deductive arguments, and justify (say) modus ponens on one level by using it at a higher level. But Haack devises a counter rule, Modus Morons ("From $A \supset B$ and B to infer A"), which can be justified on one level by using it on a higher level.[8]

Of course, the strong foundationalist might throw up his hands in frustration and insist that the steps in any proof are directly knowable by inspection. But any particular step is valid only if any step of the same form would be valid (otherwise, the difficulty would be compounded: he would have to say why *this* step is allowable for him and not for others). But this gets back to the notion of a logical rule.

Perhaps the strong foundationalist might allege that the rules of logic (of whatever variety) are simply self-evident. But this seems very dicey, indeed. For millennia Euclidean geometry seemed self-evident, but it isn't. In the realm of deductive logic (to elaborate upon a point mentioned earlier), the classically valid *Tertium non dater*" (i.e., "$p \vee \sim p$") is not valid in threshold logic, nor is the law "$p \rightarrow (q \rightarrow p)$" valid in relevant logics.[9]

If the laws of demonstrative inference are thus not knowledge by inspection, then how much more dicey such a claim (that the steps of reasoning are knowable by direct inspection) is when applied to non-demonstrative inference! For example, consider the rule dubbed by Haack "Modus Morons", more usually called the Fallacy of Affirming the Consequent:

$$\begin{array}{c} p \supset q \\ q \\ \hline \therefore p \end{array}$$

This argument is deductively invalid. But great controversy surrounds this argument form regarding its status from the point of view of inductive logic. Put in terms of confirmation the rule

$$\begin{array}{c} T \rightarrow O \\ O \\ \hline \therefore O \end{array}$$

(the arrow representing "predicts" in any way you care to take it—as material implication, strict entailment, or whatever) is held to be inductively strong by corroborationists: successful predictions serve to establish a given hypothesis. Again, put the argument form in terms of explanation:

$$\begin{array}{l} F \\ H \rightarrow F \\ \hline \therefore H \end{array}$$

(Where now the arrow now symbolizes "is the best explanation of"), and you have an argument form held to be good (either inductively strong or else good in some other sense). Peirce and Hanson called this form of reasoning variously "retroduction", "abduction", and "hypothesis". Harman has called it the "inference to the best explanation".

Now, some writers (such as Popper and Lauden) think the inference to the best explanation is simply bad reasoning. Some (such as Fumerton[10]) view it as either confused or enthymematic for some other sort of reasoning. Some view it merely weak. And some (Hanson, Peirce, Harman and others) view it as acceptable. Similar controversy surrounds reasoning by analogy as well as enumerative induction (the straight rule).

In sum: thesis (4) (and (2)) of strong foundationalism lead to skepticism. Strong foundationalism has as its chief motive the defeat of skepticism, but has as its chief result the creation of an even more powerful skepticism.

Lately, some philosophers have tried to devise a foundationalism which does not face the problems of justifying either foundations or the principles of reasoning from those foundations. For example, Alston has floated a version of foundationalism much weaker than the traditional sort I have discussed above.[11] Essentially, this weak foundationalism only holds:

(1) There are foundational beliefs $\{f_1, f_2 \ldots\}$which form the basis of all other justified beliefs;
(2) A person can truly know *p* if and only if he can justify *p* on the basis of the $\{f_i\}$.

This form of foundationalism is indeed clearly weaker than the traditional form. Unlike the strong foundationalist, the weak foundationalist is not committed to the incorrigibility of the foundations in any sense of the term "incorrigible". And under the weak foundationalist view, a person may be justified in believing something, yet not be able to "justify" his justification in the strong sense of proving adequate the logical system used.

One the other hand, weak foundationalism seems utterly useless. The major motivation for foundationalism was to refute skepticism, and all that remains of the original anti-skepticism is a nostalgic attachment to the concept of "foundations". One has no assurance that either the foundations or the derivations are sound.

Perhaps the fallibilist is no better off—we shall see. But weak foundationalism still involves an empirical thesis—that knowledge is based upon a fixed type or set of foundations.[12] In the face of the abandonment of the anti-skeptic motivation, why bother holding on to such a dubious claim? The claim is certainly not empirically attractive: can you name these community-transcendent foundations? Sense-data, perhaps? But theory-neutrality is no longer in vogue, to say the least.

Why not accept instead the more empirically adequate fallibilist claim that in any research setting there are some agreed upon starting points, which may well be highly theoretical or subject to revision? Such a view seems much more plausible: one's belief in rain tomorrow is really based more often on the word of the weatherman than some set of sense-data or such.

To be fair, however, we haven't spent much time criticizing the fallibilist perspective. Lest I be accused of special pleading, I would like to turn now to the problem of convergence, the problem which I view as the functional equivalent (in fallibilism) of the problem of induction.

To begin with, it is clear that in any epistemology one needs some principle governing the use of justification techniques, if not the strong on discussed above. Otherwise, any proof technique, any logic would be acceptable. And so anybody could prove or justify any belief he wanted to. It is not a good bargain to swap skepticism, the view that nobody knows anything, for pan-sophia, i.e., the view that all people know everything. And indeed, the fallibilist does have a restriction built in regarding the logical rules employed in justifying a belief: those rules must be accepted by the community of which one is a member.

Yet this restriction seems hardly enough. Remember that the fallibilist is not a special type of skeptic—a skeptic, say, with a particular sociology of knowledge. The fallibilist, while perhaps not motivated by the goal of answering skeptical doubts, in fact does assert that knowledge is actually achievable. In reviewing the fallibilist theses (1*)–(4*), we see only the preconditions for people being justified in thinking that they know. My belief in p may be based upon my community's starting points, my proof may be acknowledged by one and all to accord with the canons of reasoning my community (including myself) accepts, and there may be no real reason to doubt those canons or starting points. Yet one hundred years later, my claim—however legitimate—may be seen to be false, along with the whole basis upon which it rested. May not that be true of every possible community of researchers?

So far as theses (1*)–(4*) are concerned. I believe the answer is—yes. The fallibilist position so far defined only establishes that people are often justified in claiming to know—something quite compatible with skepticism. It seems clear that what is required to demarcate fallibilism from skepticism is something like:

> (5*) There has been, is now or will be some community whose starting points are true, and whose canons of reasoning are valid. (Call this *the ideal community*).[13]

With such a principle, it becomes rather easy to demarcate fallibilism from skepticism. I have, truly have, knowledge if my proof is such that it is acceptable in the ideal community. (By "ideal" I by no means imply that that community is somehow unachievable; rather, this postulated community is "ideal" in the sense of being perfect for the job of defining genuine knowledge.)

The concept of the ideal community, whatever its drawbacks, does enlighten us in just the way fallibilists want to enlighten us. To take just one instance, we can (from this expanded fallibilist perspective) better understand the history of science, which is full of people who were justly honored in their times as having discovered (or known or established) some alleged fact or theory later found to be wrong, and full of people treated with scorn for their beliefs or methodologies, later found to be correct. (Such historical phenomena are notoriously hard for foundationalists to account for: if there are absolute foundations and obviously correct logical principles, why did intelligent people of times gone by not recognize them?)

But I just did something sly. In describing the historical cases, I assumed that our community is the ideal one. But surely that is epistemologically debatable, not to say arrogant. Which community or communities are ideal? Might not (say) Aristotle and his followers have been the ideal community? Or Hitler and his minions?

If we don't want to arrogantly assume that our community is the ideal one, and we don't know which if any of part communities is the ideal one, we have to resort to some sort of open-ended characterization such as:

(6*) The ideal community is the community whose beliefs and logical practices are those which would be the result of an infinite long run of research.

More succinctly, genuine knowledge is belief converged upon in the infinite long run.

Fallibilist writings contain expressions of this view, sometimes expressed as a theory of truth, other times—more recent times—expressed as a version of realism. Some sample quotes:

> Truth is a character which attaches to an abstract proposition, such as a person might utter. It essentially depends upon that proposition's not professing to be exactly true. But we hope that in the progress of science its error will indefinitely diminish, just as the error of 3.14159, the value given for π will indefinitely diminish as the calculation is carried to more and more places of decimals. What we call π is an ideal limit to which no numerical expression can be perfectly true. If our hope is vain; if in respect to some question—say that of the freedom of the will—no matter how long the discussion goes on, no matter how scientific our

methods may become, there never will be a time when we can fully satisfy ourselves either that the question has no meaning, or that one answer or the other explains the facts, then in regard to that question there certainly is no truth. But whether or not there would be perhaps any reality is a question for the metaphysician, not the logician. Even if the metaphysician decides that where there is no truth there is no reality, still the distinction between the character of truth and the character of reality is plain and definable. Truth is that concordance of an abstract statement with the ideal limit towards which endless investigation would tend to bring scientific belief, which concordance the abstract statement may possess by virtue of the confession of its inaccuracy and one-sidedness, and this confession is an essential ingredient of truth. A further explanation of what this concordance consists in will be given below. Reality is that mode of being by virtue of which the real thing is as it is, irrespectively of what any mind or any definite collection of minds may represent it to be. The truth of the proposition that Caesar crossed the Rubicon consists in the fact that the further we push our archaeological and other studies, the more strongly will that conclusion force itself on our minds forever—or would do so, if study were to go on forever. An idealist metaphysician may hold that therein also lies the whole reality behind the proposition; for though men may for a time persuade themselves that Caesar did not cross the Rubicon, and may contrive to render this belief universal for any number of generations, yet ultimately research—if it be persisted in—must bring back the contrary belief. But in holding that doctrine, the idealist necessarily draws the distinction between truth and reality.[14]

... all the followers of science are animated by a cheerful hope that the processes of investigation, if only pushed far enough, will give one certain solution to each question to which they apply it. One man may investigate the velocity of light by studying the transits of Venus and the aberration of the stars; another by the oppositions of Mars and the eclipses of Jupiter's satellites; a third by the method of Fizeau; a fourth by that of Foucault; a fifth by the motions of the curves of Lissajoux; a sixth, a seventh, an eighth, and a ninth, may follow the different methods of comparing the measures of statical and dynamical electricity. They may at first obtain different results, but as each perfects his method his processes, the results are found to move steadily together toward a destined center. So with all scientific research. Different minds may set out with the most antagonistic views, but the progress of investigation carries then by a force outside of themselves to one and the same conclusion. This activity of thought by which we are carried, not where we wish, but to a fore-ordained goal, is like the operation of destiny. No modification of the point of view taken, no selection of other facts for study, no natural bent of mind even, can enable a man to escape the predestinate opinion. This great hope is embodied in the conception of truth and reality.

The opinion which is fated to be ultimately agreed to by all who investigate, is what we mean by truth, and the object represented in this opinion is the real. That is the way I would explain reality.

But it may be said that this view is directly opposed to the abstract definition which we have given of reality, inasmuch as it makes the characters of the real depend on what is ultimately thought about them. But the answer to this is that, on the other hand, reality is independent, not necessarily of thought in general, but only of what you or I or any finite number of men may think about it; and that, on the other hand, though the object of the final opinion depends on what that opinion is, yet what that opinion is does not depend on what you or I or any man thinks. Our perversity and that of others may indefinitely postpone the settlement of opinion; it might even conceivably cause an arbitrary proposition to be universally accepted as long as the human race should last. Yet even that would not change the nature of the belief, which alone could be the result of investigation carried sufficiently far; and if, after the extinction of our race, another should arise with faculties and disposition for investigation, that true opinion must be the one which they would ultimately come to. "Truth crushed to earth shall rise again," and the opinion which would finally result from investigation does not depend on how anybody may actually think. But the reality of that which is real does depend on the real fact that investigation does not depend on how anybody may actually think. But the reality of that which is real does depend on the real fact that investigation is destined to lead, if continued long enough, to a belief in it.[15]

But all this requires a conceived identification of one's interests with those of an unlimited community. Now, there exist no reasons, and a later discussion will show that there can be no reasons, for thinking that the human race, or any intellectual race, will exist forever. On the other hand, there can be no reason against it; and, fortunately, as the whole requirement is that we should have certain sentiments, there is nothing in the facts to forbid our having a hope, or calm and cheerful wish, that the community may last beyond any assignable date.

It may seem strange that I should put forward three sentiments, namely, interest in an indefinite community, recognition of the possibility of this interest being made supreme, and hope in the unlimited continuance of intellectual activity, as indispensable requirements of logic. Yet when we consider that logic depends on a mere struggle to escape doubt, which, as it terminates in action, must begin in emotion, and that, furthermore, the only cause of our planting ourselves on reason or that other methods of escaping doubt fail on account of the social impulse, why should we wonder to find social sentiment presupposed in reasoning?[16]

> As to reality, one finds it defined in various ways; but it that principal of terminological ethics that was proposed be accepted, the equivocal language will soon disappear. For "realis" and "realitas" are not ancient words. They were invented to be terms of philosophy in the thirteenth century, and the meaning they were intended to express is perfectly clear. That is real which has such and such characters, whether anybody thinks it to have those characters or not. At any rate, that is the sense in which the pragmatist uses the word. Now, just as conduct controlled by ethical reason tends toward fixing certain habits of conduct, the nature of which (as to illustrate the meaning, peaceable habits and not quarrelsome habits) does not depend upon any accidental circumstances, and in that sense may be said to be destined; so, thought, controlled by a rational experimental logic, tends to the fixation of certain opinions, equally destined, the nature of which will be the same in the end, however the perversity of thought of whole generations may cause the postponement of the ultimate fixation. If this be so, as every man of us virtually assumes that it is, in regard to each matter the truth of which he seriously discusses, then, according to the adopted definition of "real," the state of things which will be believed in that ultimate opinion is real.[17]

Matters stand thus. A fully articulated foundationalism, one that faces squarely the problem that prompted it, faces the problem of induction, or more broadly, the problem of justifying the principles of reasoning (and for that matter, the incorrigibility of the foundations). A fully articulated fallibilism escapes that problem, since the truth of my claim that I know something grows out of whether the ideal community would accept my principles and starting points, and I may not be able to show that it would.[18]

But as I said at the outset, I think the fallibilist faces a problem analogous to the (generalized) problem of induction. The problem of convergence can be stated as three nested questions:

(a) How can convergence be defined and measured?
(b) (assuming (a) has been answered) How do we know there will be convergence to some limit?
(c) (assuming (b) has been answered) Why would there be convergence?

We can get some insight into the first question by thinking about theoretical terms of temporally successive theories. In what sense are theories converging? Laudan has argued that the history of science is replete with cases of theories that were successful during their time, but are now (i.e., our community's perspective) seen to be non-referential with respect to the central theoretical terms. He mentions such examples as 19th century aether theories, the crystalline spheres of ancient and medieval astronomy, the phlogiston theory, theories of spontaneous generation and so on.[19] But if historically successive theories may not even refer to the same things, how can we speak of convergence of belief? Convergence of belief in what? How can we tell of two communities are converging in belief, as opposed to talking about different things entirely?

Thus the question "how can convergence be defined and measured?" leads one into a hornets' nest of difficulties (about the nature of reference, of "approximate truth", of the incommensurability of theories, and so on). Perhaps one way to answer the question yet avoid the hornets' nest is to focus, not upon the convergence of theories, but instead the convergence of belief in theories. That is, one might shift focus from explaining how one theory can be said to be more approximately true than another (a syntactic/semantic issue) to explaining how one can identify how a community comes to agree to reject one theory and adopt another theory in any given domain (which is more of a pragmatic issue).

Even assuming that there can be some way to detect convergence, we still face the problem of uniqueness. Isn't it possible that even faced with all possible data, there might still be alternative theories that fit? Quine aptly speaks of the "under-determination of theories by data", and says of Peirce's theory:

> Peirce was tempted to define truth outright in terms of scientific method, as the ideal theory which is approached as a limit when the (supposed) canons of scientific method are used unceasingly on continuing experience. But there is a lot wrong with Peirce's notion, besides its assumption of a final organon of scientific method and its appeal to an infinite process. There is a faulty use of numerical analogy in speaking of a limit of theories, since the notion of limit depends on that of "nearer than" which is defined for numbers and not for theories. And even if we by-pass such troubles..., still there is trouble in the imputation of uniqueness ("the ideal result"). For ... we have no reason to suppose that man's surface irritations even unto eternity admit of any one systematization that is scientifically better or simpler that all possible others. It seems likelier, if only on account of asymmetries or dualities, that countless alternative theories would be tied for first place. Scientific method is the way to truth, but it affords even in principle no unique definition of truth. Any so-called pragmatic definition of truth is doomed to failure equally.[20]

Again, I don't mean to suggest that the difficulty here is an impossibility. We might argue that convergence would be reached on matters of beauty or elegance, if not on the basis of data alone. That is, even given that explanatory power and simplicity might not ensure uniqueness of final theory, perhaps there is some set of virtues that would, a set including beauty, consilience, and so on.

More cogently, Quine's objection ignores the fact that the limit is reached by an historical route. Even supposing that we looked at all data on the day of final judgment and decided that we could devise other theories, the community might have converged on one single theory just as a matter of fact. This agreed-upon theory would (we are imagining) account for all the data equally simply, elegantly, and so on as any other theory anybody could devise, so there would be no temptation to switch. Remember the difference in motivation between the foundationalist and the fallibilist: the fallibilist is not interested in skeptical doubts about his theory—so long as it works well, so long as there is no real reason to doubt it, he doesn't change it. And in such a scenario as we are imagining, there would be no such doubt.

The third difficulty seems like the least bothersome, but I suspect that it is in reality the most profound. This objection, you will recall, is that it is unclear why these would be convergence of opinion at all. Assume we can measure convergence, assume that such convergence would be convergence to but one point of view, still, *why would there be convergence at all?* You almost automatically say: because there is one real world out there that forces (or would force) eventual agreement. But on what basis do we know there is "one world" "out there"? An empiricist foundationalist would say "we just see it!", but (waiving the problems inherent in such a view) that is not really a reply the fallibilist can make. There is no certainly in perception, even if my community agrees with my perceptual claims. The only reply open to the fallibilist seems to be: the statement "there is one world out there" is true because a community of researchers would converge to agreement upon that claim.

When Descartes had finished *The Meditations*, he sent the work out to a number of philosophers for comment. Arnauld pointed out what has since come to be known as "the Cartesian Circle". Descartes argues early on that whatever we clearly and distinctly perceive is true, then uses this criterion to prove that God exists, and then proves that the criterion is correct because God's existence (somehow) guarantees it. This, as Arnauld recognized, is circular.

The fallibilist similarly faces a circle: we know that in the ideal community, there will be eventual convergence because there is a real world out there, and we know there is a real world out there because the ideal community will converge in belief that there is. It is not clear to me how the fallibilist can reply.

One reply to the problem of convergence might be to weaken fallibilism. If we call theses (1*)–(4*) weak fallibilism and theses (1*)–(6*) strong fallibilism, the argument might run as follows. Since the problem of convergence arises only when we move from weak fallibilism to strong, why not just stick to weak fallibilism? Granted, weak fallibilism isn't incompatible with skepticism, but we fallibilists don't have exaggerated worries about skepticism anyway. We leave the hyperbolic doubt to others.

In a curious way this argument is reminiscent of the argument for weak foundationalism, and is open to the same sort of reply: The weak theory of knowledge can't do the job for which the strong version was intended. In particular, the fallibilist theory was devised to shed light on the economics of research: why some questions are investigated rather than others, why some research programs and not others are undertaken, and so on. But the weak fallibilist has no basis for doing any normative work, he can only describe. This physical theory is preferred by physicists today, but I (the weak fallibilist) can't really say that that theory is any better or closer to the truth than its predecessors. This community checks for lung cancer by chest X-rays, that community by reading chicken guts. There is no right or wrong about the matter.

A close reading of one of the earlier quotes by Peirce suggests another reply to the dilemma of circularity or weakness. The start of the quote which reads:

> ... all the followers of science are animated by a cheerful hope that the processes of investigation if only pushed far enough, will give one certain solution to each question to which they apply it...

The phrase "are animated by a cheerful hope" originally read "are fully persuaded", indicating that Peirce weakened the claim that we are sure there is an ideal community to the claim that we hope there is one. We might accordingly say that we fallibilists don't know for certain that there is a single world out there that will force a unique convergence, but we have no real reason to doubt what seems so obvious to us, and until we do, we ought to keep that conviction. In short, perhaps the way to answer the problem of convergence is to be a more consistent fallibilist.

In sum, the weakened versions of foundationalism and fallibilism seem altogether ad hoc and uninteresting. Thus faced with a choice between strong foundationalism and strong fallibilism, I am inclined to choose fallibilism.[21] There are reasons for this choice. An empirical approach to logic and related matters (such as theory choice) allows the epistemologist to learn more from his colleagues in the cognitive sciences (cognitive psychology, history of science, artificial intelligence, and so on). Also, the fallibilist perspective is more conducive to a diachronic approach as Glymour's "bootstrapping" view of theory confirmation, and more generally to epistemological theories which stress learning and discovery, as opposed to the retrospective justification of the already learned.

Finally, there might just be a solution to the problem of convergence. There might not be such a solution, of course. But I take it as being an inescapable feature of the act of choosing a research program that there be is no guarantee of success.

Notes

1. Quite often foundationalists offer their epistemology more as a program for reconstructing our beliefs to achieve true knowledge than as an analysis of how our belief systems are in fact structured.
2. There are of course important differences between various concepts of certainty, incorrigibility, indubitability, and so on. Those differences will not be important in what follows.
3. Note that the skeptic here is *not* (as is sometimes charged) trying "to turn induction into deduction." The skeptic does not demand that we show that the arguments which N sanctions.
4. Skyrms, Brian *Choice and Chance (2nd ed.)*, Belmont, CA: Dickinson Publishing Company, 1975.
5. *Ibid* pp. 41–47.
6. *Ibid* p. 46.
7. Haack, Susan "The Justification of Deduction," *Mind* 85 (1976), pp. 54–62.
8. Haack, op. cit., p. 57.
9. This is a bit quick. The "→" connective is not the same as the material implication symbol "⊃". "$p \supset (q \supset p)$" is still valid in most, though not all, relevant logics. In any case, the point still remains that the ordinary language statement "if p, then if q then p" may well not be a law of logic.
10. Fumerton, R.A. "Induction and Reasoning to the Best Explanation" *Philosophy of Science* 47 (1980), pp. 589–600.
11. Alston, William "Two Types of Foundationalism" *Journal of Philosophy* Vol. 78 No. 7 (1976), pp. 165–185. Alston does not commit himself to the view he calls "simple foundationalism" which is equivalent to the view I call "weak foundationalism". See also James Van Cleve "Foundationalism, Epistemic Principles, and the Cartesian Circle" in *The Philosophical Review* 88, No.1 January 1979.
12. Or, at least, weak foundationalism involves the normative claim that knowledge *should* be based on the $\{f_i\}$.
13. Strictly speaking, we might want to speak of "an ideal community." But if there were two ideal communities, we could be led to contradictory ascriptions f knowledge unless both communities in fact were one (meaning, shared belief systems). In my argument, I assume that the law of non-contradiction is held to be true by the ideal community.

14. *Collected Works of Charles Sanders Peirce* Vol. V, Section 556.
15. *Ibid.*, Vol. V, Section 407–408.
16. *Ibid.*, Vol. II, Section 264–265.
17. *Ibid.*, Vol. V Section 430.
18. But then again, maybe I could. Richard Feldman, in "Fallibilism and Knowing That One Knows" (*Philosophical Review* XC, No. 2 April 1981) argues that the KK thesis may be compatible with fallibilism.
19. Laudan, Larry "A Confutation of Convergent Realism" *Philosophy of Science* 48 (1981) p. 33. Note that Landon's concern is with convergent realism, rather than the convergence theory of truth, and note also that his objections are somewhat different from the one I am discussing here (viz., that convergence is hard to define). For a reply to Laudan, see Clyde Hardin and Alexander Rosenberg "In Defense of Convergent Realism" *Philosophy of Science* 49 (1982) pp. 604–615. Laudan's counter response to Hardin and Rosenberg is to be found in *Philosophy of Science* 51 (1984) pp. 156–162.
20. W.V.O. Quine *Word and Object.*
21. Coherentists may resent me for not having mentioned their theory of knowledge as an alternative. But regarding the thesis of this paper, I think the coherentist will face the same sort of problems as the foundationalist and fallibilist/pragmaticist. The coherentist believes that beliefs are justified by being part of a coherent web. That is, beliefs don't usually require justification, but require it only when coherence demands. But, how can we define and measure coherence? How do we know that there would be one coherent web (as opposed to an infinity of webs)? And why would there be coherence anyway?

Permission to reprint courtesy of John Wiley and Sons.
I wish to thank the journal *Dialectica* as well.

19

My review of: *The Myth of Neurosis: Overcoming the Illness Excuse*

(by Garth Wood, New York: Harper & Row, 1986) first appeared in Chronicles of Culture, October 1986

Psychotherapy is big business. America employs perhaps a half million professionals and paraprofessionals (psychotherapists, psychiatric technicians, drug/alcohol counselors, clinical social workers, clinical psychologists, psychiatrists, psychiatric nurses, and family therapists) in the field, and the talk therapy industry as a whole is worth about $17 billion. Yet many scholars and laymen are uneasy at the sight of the tower of psychobabble. Himself a psychiatrist and philosopher, Garth Wood has written a fascinating book, which is at once a critique of psychoanalytic therapy (and theory) and a sketch of an alternative form of therapy Wood calls "moral therapy."

To help the reader see the difference between real mental illness and phony "disorders" and "neuroses," Wood provides a detailed appendix which helps you decide whether or not you are truly psychotic. (As he notes, chances are good that if you worry about being insane, you aren't insane.) Moreover, Wood does not criticize all forms of therapy—he readily concedes that some forms of behavioral therapy are quite effective in modifying undesirable behavior. But he denies that either "talk" therapy (Freudianism and all its descendants) or drug therapy ("mind candy") are effective. His critique of those standard psychiatric therapies is both philosophic and scientific.

On the scientific side, Wood lays out the evidence against psychotherapy and psychoanalytic theory in detail. Wood reviews the classic theoretical criticisms of Freudian theory by Sir Karl Popper and Sir Peter Medawar. Even supporters of Freudian theory such as Adolf Grunbaum (the eminent philosopher of science) and Arnold Cooper (past president of the American Psychoanalytic Association) admit that its theoretic underpinnings are weak. A number of empirical studies have likewise shown psychoanalytic therapy to be ineffective and even harmful. One early critic, Hans Eysenck, analyzed 19 reports on the effects of psychotherapy and discovered that the patients who had no psychiatric therapy improved the most, those with "eclectic" (non-Freudian) therapy improved less, and the patients with Freudian therapy did the worst. Wood concludes bluntly that the therapeutic claims of psychotherapists no longer have scientific or moral credibility and that practitioners are shamelessly "taking money from the gullible."

Wood's criticisms ring true, especially if you have ever known someone who has been "in analysis" for years. Wood is caustic on this point:

> [Psychoanalysis] may be rubbish, but it is dangerous and demeaning rubbish, tending to rob us of our natural belief that we are in control of our mental and physical behavior, fostering the illusion of our lack of responsibility, of our passivity. As the tentacles of this pernicious doctrine reach out to embrace the arts, politics and education, nothing remains untouched by the poison of its determinism as it degrades creativity, debases ambition and reduces the value of human aspiration.

More philosophically, Wood criticizes the whole concept of neurosis. He puts forward the view, so obvious that it has escaped the masters of arcane psychiatry, that aside from clear cases of psychotic illness, much of what passes for "mental illness" is in fact not illness at all. So called "neuroses" and "personality disorders" are just pseudoscientific terms for behavior that is self-destructive, self-centered, imprudent, eccentric, noble, or evil. Thieves and murderers must not be stigmatized as "evil men" but treated as mentally ill "sociopaths."

When Wood turns from his trenchant critique of psychotherapy to propounding his own method of "moral therapy," things are less satisfactory. The goal of the moral therapist (friend, minister, priest or whatever) is to help the other person gain self-respect. The doctor/patient relationship gives way to friendship between equals, and "therapy" can take place at the ball-park or bar as well as in an office or hospital. The moral therapist helps his troubled friend grow in self-respect in three ways: (1) recognizing and living up to his own value system; (2) confronting problems squarely; (3) exercising.

The problem lies in getting past the first step, which sounds suspiciously like the "values clarification" strategy now touted by too many professors of education. Wood goes so far as to tell us that if a mentally troubled man's own ideals lead him to acts that society would regard as "terrorist," then the "individual's mental health" should take priority over "the standards and rules of society." Sending one letter bomb may indeed provide as much catharsis as several hours on the couch, but does Wood really want to replace Freud with Sorel?

Perhaps the problem is simply that Wood has spent so much time demolishing Freudianism that he hasn't worked out his own views enough. Currently at work on a new book, Wood may yet help us escape both the ersatz professionalism of the psychoanalyst and the chummy relativism of the "moral therapist."

My thanks to *The Chronicles of Culture.*

20

My review of: *The Mind's New Science: A History of the Cognitive Revolution*

(by Howard Gardner, New York: Basic Books, 1985. 423 pages) first appeared in Philosophia Vol. 17, No. 2 (1987) pp. 209–216

Cognitive science is one of the success stories of the past decade, with departments sprouting like mushrooms. The discipline is a hybrid of AI (artificial intelligence), cognitive psychology, anthropology, philosophy, linguistics, and neuroscience, and as such it has a fascinating (if young) history. Howard Gardner has written a history of this new science. It is fair to say that as a popularization of cognitive science the book succeeds extremely well, though as serious history of science the book does not succeed as well.

Gardner does a nice job of surveying this very broad field. In Chapter One he characterizes cognitive science as involving four tenets: a commitment to intentionality as an explanatory construct at the psychological (as opposed to the neurophysiological or social) level; the view that the digital computer is central to understanding the human mind; the view that any successful cognitive science must draw upon the resources of many fields; and the view that the agenda of cognitive science has on it the classical epistemological questions.

Chapter Two contains a concise history of psychology from the cognitivist perspective. Early in this century researchers wanted to investigate scientifically traditional epistemological concerns such as the nature of thought, language and rationality. But their empirical approach rested upon introspection. The behaviorists rebelled against that: methodologically, behaviorists have a commitment to overt observable behavior as the only sort of evidence allowable in psychology; metaphysically, behaviorists oppose positing mental entities (plans, desires, ideas, and so on), as explanatory factors in psychology. Gardner rightly acknowledges that in a real way behaviorism was progressive: it did counteract a tendency to very vague and speculative theorizing about "will" and "faculties." But the price was high: the baby of cognitive phenomena (language acquisition, inference, planning and so on) went out with the bathwater of introspection.

Gardner picks as the opening shot of the cognitive revolution Karl Lashley's talk before the 1948 Hixon symposium (attended by von Neumann and a number of other luminaries). Lashley challenged behaviorism. He urged that intentional factors had to be taken into account in any adequate explanation of language acquisition and use. In arguing that linguistic behavior can not be explained by the behaviorist S-R model Lashley anticipated the Chomsky/Skinner debates. Lashley put forth a view of the central nervous system as an ever active system composed of interacting subsystems. Again, Lashley was anticipating a later crucial concept: the concept of modularity. Gardner finishes the chapter with a sketchy but adequate review of the key early inputs to cognitive science: mathematical logic (especially Turing's work); McCullock's neuronal model; von Neumann, Weiner and Cybernetics; and Shannon's information theory.

In Chapter Three Gardner continues his sketch of the early history of cognitive science. He sets the September 1956 symposium on information theory held at MIT (attended by Chomsky, Simon, George Miller, and others) as the birthplace of the subject. The late fifties and early sixties were a time of intellectual ferment: AI emerged as a discipline, and key work was being done in neurophysiology. In 1960 the Center for Cognitive Studies was founded at Harvard by Jerome Bruner and George Miller, and there was a shift away from behaviorism to a frank embrace of "plans," "goals," "images," and other highly mentalistic entities. One sign of a maturing discipline is the appearance of texts, and the first text in cognitive psychology was Ulrich Neisser's *Cognitive Psychology* in 1967. In 1972 Newell and Simon published *Human Problem Solving.* In the late sixties and early seventies there was an explosion of literature in cognitive science, and the journal *Cognitive Science* was founded. In 1975 the Sloan Foundation decided to fund the nascent science, and the influx of funds established the field's independence.

Gardner then begins to survey the various cognitive sciences. In Chapter Four, philosophy is surveyed. There is a quick and reasonably accurate summary of the views of Descartes, Kant, the logical positivists, Russell, the ordinary language philosophers, and especially useful discussions of Rorty, Fodor, Dennett, and Putnam. Gardner treats philosophy, it is comforting to note, seriously if a bit patronizingly: "Rather than being the ultimate arbiters, or the ultimate victims, of scientific work, philosophers have been (and will continue to be) important handmaidens in the scientific study of cognition." (p. 54) But his view that philosophers need to be more sensitive to empirical findings is surely not implausible.

In Chapter Five Gardner gives a more detailed account of recent trends in psychology. He covers the work by Miller in the mid-1950's which indicated that there are limitations to human information storage (with short-term storage capacity as low as seven). He also discusses the work of Colin Cherry and Donald Broadbent in the late 1950's, who were influenced by information theory, and who showed by some very pretty experiments that the intake and storage of information by the mind is limited. Broadbent was the first to use flowcharts to describe the information flow in the human being, (i.e., the flow from the senses to a short-term store, to a selective filter, then to a limited-capacity channel, to an output system and a long-term store). Jerome Bruner's 1956 classic *A Study of Thinking* is also discussed. All of this work was as empirical and experimental as behaviorism, but in this work the participants are viewed as active information processors and problem solvers, not mere SR engines.

Gardner then jumps backwards in time to give a thumbnail sketch of the history of psychology from the 19th century (Helmholtz, Brentano) to Piaget. He views Brentano—who emphasized intentionality as the mark of the mental—as the spiritual ancestor of all cognitive scientists. Wundt's laboratory is discussed, as is the work of Ebbinghaus (who shifted research from how the subject feels to how he performs in an objectively measurable way). Also discussed is the Wurzburg school, which focused on information structuring in perception, a topic of much current interest. Of course behaviorism is covered, but only briefly. More attention is paid to Gestalt psychology and how it differs from today's cognitive psychology. Gardner also discusses the work of Frederick Bartlett (on memory and the transmission of stories) and Jean Piaget (whose "genetic epistemology" is very congenial to cognitive scientists, although the details of Piaget's view have not held up to the test of experiment).

The work by Gestalt psychologists and others like Bartlett and Piaget was more or less isolated from the mainstream of psychological theory, which was predominantly behaviorist especially from the thirties to the late fifties. What got cognitive science moving was the rise of computer science and information theory. Gardner discusses the recent work by Roger Shepard and others. He finishes the chapter by discussing some of the recent criticism raised against the whole enterprise of cognitive psychology.

Chapter Six is in my opinion the best in the book. It summarizes the history of AI, work which is probably unfamiliar to most philosophers. Again, Gardner starts by describing a seminal conference: the 1956 seminar at Dartmouth, attended by John McCarthy, Marvin Minsky, Herbert Simon and Allen Newell. He notes an important distinction between the weak and strong conceptions for AI. The weak conception of AI is that the goal of AI should be to devise computer programs that mimic the ways human beings carry out cognitive tasks. The strong conception is that the programmed computer actually has cognitive states. It is the strong conception of AI to which philosophers such as Hubert Dreyfus and John Searle object.

After giving a short history of the digital computer, Gardner discusses some of the key successes in AI. Early on, Newell and Simon devised the Logic Theorist program which proved theorems from Whitehead and Russell's *Principia Mathematica.* (Indeed, the Logic Theorist devised a proof of a theorem even more elegant than the original proof). Gardner also discusses the General Problem Solver, a more ambitious program that, while not ultimately successful, generated a fruitful line of research. Less well known to the general public is Marvin Minsky at MIT, who has been the mentor of many AI researchers. One is T.G. Evans, who devised a program that solves analogical puzzles at the level of the average high school student. Another is Daniel Bobrow who did the same for algebra word problems.

Gardner reviews other AI successes: DENDRAL (a program for analyzing chemical compounds); ELIZA (a program that mimics dialogues between therapists and patients); and SHRDLU (the first "expert system"—a program that focused on a limited domain). SHRDLU was a new paradigm in AI—it marked a change from looking for general problem solvers to looking for narrowly focused problem solvers for particular domains.

Gardner also considers attacks on AI research. Joseph Weizenbaum's view is that AI technology is dangerously seductive, tempting us to abdicate our responsibility for decision-making. Hubert Dreyfus, a phenomenologist, has a different criticism, viz., that human knowledge is wrapped up with the human biological and social condition, and that any rules-based epistemology is bound to fail. But phenomenology is not a very compelling point of view, so Dreyfus' criticisms are not widely regarded as conclusive. A third sort of critique of AI is offered by James Lighthill, who criticizes the disparity between the initial hope and the actual success of AI.

Although the early high hopes were disappointed, by the late seventies AI was flourishing. Economically, AI is now very big business. And scientifically, AI has scored notable successes in the realm of perception of decision-making. These recent developments are covered well.

Gardner finishes the chapter by discussing the recent criticisms of AI raised by Searle.

In Chapter Seven there is a solid review of modern linguistics, mainly focused on the work of Chomsky. Chomsky's 1957 classic *Syntactic Structures* and his attacks upon Skinner and behaviorism are reviewed. Especially nice is the discussion of the implications of Chomsky's views for psychology: Chomskian psychology is innatist and unabashedly mentalistic.

Gardner reviews earlier linguistics, including de Saussure, Roman Jakobson and the Prague School, Leonard Bloomfield, Edward Sapir and his student Benjamin Lee Whorf, and Zellig Harris. The chapter finishes with a discussion of the evolution of Chomsky's thought (from the 1957 *Syntactic Structures* to the 1965 *Aspects of the Theory of Syntax* to his more recent work on universal grammar) and the impact of his work on other areas of cognitive science.

Chapter Eight is devoted to a review of Anthropology as a cognitive science. Gardner begins with Lucien Levy-Bruhl, who wrestled with the question whether primitive people are "pre-logical," i.e., think in a different way from moderns, or whether instead of difference between primitive and modern thinking is merely a matter of degree. There follows a concise history of modern anthropology: Edward Tylor, Franz Boas, Radcliffe-Brown, Malinowski, Levi-Strauss, and Sperber are all discussed. Especially crucial from Gardner's point of view is Levi-Strauss' insistence that to understand social reality we need to understand the way the human mind organizes experience. Levi-Strauss felt that there are only a limited number of ways the human mind can work, that it comes equipped with "custom universals" that get combined in various ways. This sort of thought underlies his treatment of mythology. Gardner respects Levi-Strauss' work as a cognitive scientist, but acknowledges that many others doubt its value.

Gardner concludes the chapter with a discussion of cognitive anthropology and ethno-science.

Chapter Nine is another outstanding chapter. It covers the history of modern neuroscience. The review starts with Karl Lashley, who explored the use of the lesion method of experimentation, in which an area of the brain is destroyed and then the resulting impairments are identified and observed. Lashley's 1929 classic *Brain Mechanisms and Intelligence* attacked the view that specific areas of the brain are tied to specific skills, memories, thoughts, and so on. His work posed a challenge for localization theories and reductionism generally. Lashley's view was one of equi-potentiality: the ability of other areas of the brain to take over when one area is destroyed. Lashley argued against a naive equation of the brain with the digital computer, or neurons with switches. Instead, he argued that the brain is more analog than digital and that we need to think statistically to understand neuronal behavior. Lashley was especially critical of the behaviorist view that there are "reflex arcs" or specific neural ties between stimulus and response.

More recent work has shown the brain to be more localized than Lashley believed. But Lashley's tendency to reject simple reductionism and his willingness to use concepts such as "plans" or "structures" cleared the way for cognitive scientific concepts.

Gardner spends a fair amount of time on the history of early neurophysiology from Descartes to Broca, based on a very nice distinction between localism and holism, with those of the localist perspective being most inclined to reductionism. By the 1940's researchers were looking for a compromise between localism and holism. One such attempted synthesis was Donald Hebb's *The Organization of Behavior*. But despite Hebb, in the late 1950's the issues began to be resolved more in the favor of the localists. David Hubel and Torsten Wiesel conducted experiments (which later won them the Nobel Prize in physiology) on perception in cats. They were able to isolate sets of cells in the cortex that identify horizontal and vertical movement. Again, Roger Sperry's work on brain lateralization is evidence for localism. And the recent research by Eric Kandel on learning in snails is very reductionist in spirit. (Some learned behavior in snails is traceable to as few as 50 neurons. Learning seems to involve altering the effectiveness of preexisting pathways).

Gardner finishes the chapter with a defense of the view that even if localism is closer to the truth than holism, reductionism should be resisted so as to keep open lines of fruitful research.

In Chapter Ten Gardner takes up the recent history of work by cognitive scientists on perception. He quite rightly focuses upon the path breaking research by the late David Marr. Marr was trained in neurophysiology and in the late sixties studied the function of the human cerebellum. In 1973 he joined the AI lab at MIT where he worked until his death in 1980. Marr rejected the notion of direct perception in favor of "symbolic descriptions." Under his theory of vision, the brain does not construct an image (say, of external objects in space) all at once. Rather, the brain computes a series of symbolic representations or "sketches": a primal sketch, which represents only basic geometric features and shading; a "2.5-D" sketch, which represents surface features such as shape, depth, and the position of the object from the viewer's frame of reference; and the finished 3-D sketch, which represents volume, solidity, and the coordinate system from the objects point of view. Marr held a very modular view of vision, with different modules being responsible for computing motion, color, depth, and so on.

Gardner finishes the chapter by discussing the research done by Marr's competitors such as James Gibson.

In Chapter Eleven the research on mental imagery is reviewed. Cognitive scientists are more inclined than are philosophers to believe that mental images exist and are worth studying. Especially interesting is the work by Stephen Kosslyn, who is concerned to prove empirically the existence of mental imagery, and delineate the major properties of the imaging system. Gardner also presents the criticisms of Kosslyn's views by Zenon Pylyshyn and others. There is a vital issue at stake: do cognitive scientists need to postulate imagistic knowledge as well as propositional? And yet if we accept the criticisms of images, then why stop there? Propositions are not much less dubious from the philosophical point of view.

The last few chapters cover theories of classification and of rationality. I found the review of the literature testing Whorfs hypothesis enjoyable (it turns out that the hypothesis doesn't hold up very well). Johnson-Laird's and Amos Tversky's research on how far people depart from standards of rationality is well explained, although the review is less useful to philosophers only because they are familiar with that body of literature already.

It should be clear from the foregoing summary that Gardner has produced a very useful popularization of a rapidly evolving new field. However, as serious history of science the book is inadequate. For one thing, the book jumps from recent history to current theoretical disputes to distant history in a very abrupt and disjointed fashion. Far too many topics are introduced to allow proper historical development. And the book's quality is very uneven, with some chapters (especially the ones on AI and neuroscience) being of much higher quality than others.

Most disturbing is the Whiggishness of the work. Certain tenets are laid down which define cognitive science, and researchers are assessed on the basis of how much they contributed to the field so defined.

Yet, I don't wish to be churlish. Gardner's book is fascinating and clearly written. It is especially useful to those philosophers who wish to quickly survey an important new field.

Permission to reprint courtesy of Springer. I wish to thank the journal *Philosophia* as well.

21

"The Role of Error in Computer Science"

first appeared in Philosophia Vol. 19, No. 4 (1989), pp. 403–416

The aim of this paper is to explore the concept of error as it applies to computer science. Now, it is customary in computer science (hereafter "CS") to distinguish between hardware (the actual computing equipment) and software (the programs which run on that equipment). We will not be concerned with error in hardware, since that is a matter of engineering design and manufacturing quality control. We are specifically interested in the notion of error in software. For the purposes of this paper, CS will be synonymous with software science. There are a number of interesting features to error avoidance in software that bear examination.

We can distinguish various levels of software. At the most basic or micro level, there are algorithms, that is, step by step logical procedures, which become elements of programs when implemented in a programming language. Next up in the hierarchy are the medium sized programs that function to accomplish specific tasks such as (say) sorting personnel files or computing the trajectory of a rocket. We can call this the mini level. At a third or macro level are large-scale integrated programs, such as air-traffic control or commercial word-processing programs. These high level programs generally are produced by teams of computer programmers and analysts over months or even years, and usually involve very sophisticated "user-interfaces" (i.e., elements which allow untrained data entry clerks or businessmen to be able to run the software successfully). Finally, at a "meta" level are programs in Artificial Intelligence which seek to mimic human reasoning.

The distinction made above (between micro, mini, macro, and meta level software) is of course somewhat arbitrary, and leaves out much of out much of the story (such as the sorts of data structures and programming languages used). But it will do to allow us to frame our survey of techniques of error analysis and avoidance. I will allow the term "error" to remain only implicitly defined for now; after we survey some material we will be able to define the term more precisely.

Let's start at the micro level, i.e., at the level of algorithms. The study of the efficiency of algorithms is a highly mathematical branch of theoretical computer science called *computational complexity.* Computational complexity applies mathematics to the measure of the time and space requirements of algorithms, that is, it aims to determine precisely how much running time and how much memory a given algorithm will need. Let's review computational complexity analysis briefly.

Simplifying considerably, and speaking somewhat imprecisely, we say that a function g(n) is "on the order of" some other function f(n) if g(n) grows no faster than Kf(n) after a certain value of n and for some positive value K. For example, the function $3x^2 + 2x + 5$ is on the order of x^2, since it grows no faster than (say) $4x^2$ after x = 5. Typically, the complexity analyst uses the following 0-notation to characterize classes of running times:

constant	0(1)
log log	0(log log n)
logarithmic	0(log n)
linear	0(n)
n log n	0(n log n)
quadratic	$0(n^2)$
cubic	$0(n^3)$
exponential	$0(2^n)$

(Here, n represents some basic measure of the size of the task the algorithm is meant to accomplish, for example, the number of positions in a table to be searched, or vertices in graph to be examined). Algorithms are evaluated as to their complexity by determining into which classes they fall. An algorithm that runs in linear, logarithmic, or log log time is considered to be fast. An algorithm that runs in exponential time is considered to be hopelessly slow. To get an intuitive feeling for these classes, Standish (1980, p. 14) gives this table:

f(n)	n = 2	n = 16	n = 1024
log log n	0	2	3.32
log n	1	4	10
n	2	16	1,020
n log n	2	64	10,200
n^2	4	256	1.05×10^{12}
n^3	8	4,100	1.07×10^{18}
2^n	4	65,000	1.80×10^{38}

By way of comparison, consider two algorithms for searching a list of names, one of which runs in linear time and the other in exponential time. In the time it takes the exponential time algorithm to search a list of forty-four names, the linear time algorithm could search a list of thirty thousand *billion* names.

Determining the actual time (or space) complexity of a algorithm usually requires subtle mathematical argumentation. For one thing, a distinction must be made between worst case, best case and average case time/space complexity. Also, a distinction must be made between the running time and the preprocessing time of an algorithm. But while the technical details of such proofs are not of much interest to the philosopher, the existence of such techniques should be. For it occasionally occurs in the literature of Artifical Intelligence that an author will claim to have devised a program which supposedly mimics some aspect of human reasoning, yet which turns out to be exponential in time complexity. When run on tiny ("toy") data sets the program does the job, and much fanfare is raised about AI growing closer to achieving full machine intelligence. Such a claim can be resisted if the inherent limitations of the underlying algorithm are recognized, since obviously the human mind does not operate exponentially slowly.

Let us move next to the level of mini scale programs. At this level, work on error avoidance has focused on the formal specification of programs. Considerable effort has been spent developing techniques for specifying formally the requirements for a program, i.e., for specifying what the output and input should be, and verifying whether in fact it will produce that specified output given that specified input. The formal approach to program verification was first explored by Floyd and Hoare in the 1960's (see Floyd (1967) and Hoare (1962)). A brief review of this work is worthwhile.

We begin with the concept of a specification, consider small routine to compute $x^2 + 2$, given that $x = 2$:

Start

[X: = 2]

a

[Temp: = X]

b

[X: = X^2]

c

[X: = X + Temp]

d

[end]

At point a, after assigning 2 to X, we require/specify that X = 2. At point b, temp should have the value 2 as well. At c, X should have the value 4. At d, X should have the value 6. These statements about the values of the program variables at each stage in the program are called assertions. We can specify the conditions before and after any statement in a program by assertions, and (since a program is a sequence of simple or compound statements), we can specify the input and output of any program by assertions. Precisely defined, the specification {P} S {Q} specifies that if the computer executes instruction S in any state described by P, then if S terminates, it will be in a state described by Q. P is called the pre-condition and Q the post-condition. Thus, looking at post-condition C in our earlier example, we can write (X = 2) X: = X^2 (X = 4).

Now, again, a program is just a sequence of simple or compound instructions, so we can represent a program with the pre-and post-conditions of the statements as a tableau (with the program input as the first precondition and the program output as the post-condition). In our simple example, the tableaux would be:

(true)
X: = 2
(X = 2)

$$
\begin{gathered}
\text{temp:} = X \\
(\text{temp} = 2) \\
X: = X^2 \\
(X = 4) \\
X = X + \text{temp} \\
(X = 6)
\end{gathered}
$$

Such a tableau is valid if (a) when a triple (P) S (Q) occurs in the tableaux, it is true; and (b) whenever a pair of the form (P) (Q) occurs, assertion P implies assertion Q. We can utilize inference rules to establish the validity of proofs. A few of the standard rules are:

Assignment:

$$\{P|^{E}_{X}\}X: = E\{P\}$$

where $\{P|^{E}_{X}\}$ stands for the result of substituting E for X in P.

Compounding:

$$\frac{\begin{gathered}(P)\ S_1\ (Q) \\ (Q)\ S_2\ (R)\end{gathered}}{(P)\ S_1S_2\ (R)}$$

Strengthening Precedent:

$$\frac{\begin{gathered}P \rightarrow Q \\ (Q)\ S\ (R)\end{gathered}}{(P)\ S\ (R)}$$

Weakening Consequent:

$$\frac{\begin{gathered}Q \rightarrow R \\ (P)\ S\ (Q)\end{gathered}}{(P)\ S\ (R)}$$

Of course, more rules are needed for a complete set. But with these we can work through a simple example:

$$\begin{array}{c} (X < 5 \;\&\; X > 1) \\ Y{:} = 3X \\ (Y < 15 \;\&\; Y > 3) \\ Z{:} = Y \\ (Z < 15) \end{array}$$

Step 1:

$$\frac{}{(X < 5 \;\&\; X > 1)\ Y{:} = 3X\ (Y < 15 \;\&\; Y > 3)}$$

by assignment.

Step 2:

$$\frac{}{(Y < 15 \;\&\; Y > 3)\ Z{:} = Y\ (Z < 15 \;\&\; Z > 3)}$$

by assignment.

Step 3:

$$\frac{\begin{array}{c}(Z < 15 \;\&\; Z > 3) \rightarrow (Z < 15) \\ (Y < 15 \;\&\; Y > 3)\ Z{:} = Y\ (Z < 15 \;\&\; Z > 3)\end{array}}{(Y < 15 \;\&\; Y > 3)\ Z{:} = Y\ (Z < 15)}$$

By completing the above set of rules with rules for if-then and do-while statements, proofs of program correctness are readily obtainable.

The formal specification and verification of programs has been welcomed by most software engineers. In fact, computer scientists have extended these techniques in a number of ways. Some have used temporal logic for the verification of concurrent programs. It also may be possible to use erotetic logic to specify and verify database queries. And a number of programs (such as GYPSY) or extensions to existing programming languages (such as ANNA, i.e., annotated Ada) have been devised which allow the inclusion of assertions into the code and the automatic verification of programs.

At the macro level of software, the concern for error avoidance is central to the discipline called *software engineering*. (For a good overview of software engineering, see Pressman (1984)).

Basically, the field of software engineering generally, and the "structured revolution" in particular, grew out of the software crisis of the 1970's. In the 1950's and 1960's, hardware developed rapidly, but as it grew in complexity and power, software costs grew even more rapidly. By the early 1970's software became the biggest cost in computer systems, and cost/time overruns became rampant. "Horror stories" abounded of software projects disastrously gone awry, such as the multimillion dollar rocket which had to be destroyed when it strayed off course due to a simple programming error (viz., the truncation of a real number by default). (For a classic discussion of a case of a software project that led to a crisis, see Brooks (1975)). Moreover, the gap between what was needed and what was available kept widening rapidly.

The first (and narrow) response to the software crisis was the rise of "structured" programming languages and "top down" design methodologies. Specifically, it was proven (in the 1960's) that any possible program could be constructed out of just three structures: if– then- else (i.e., simple branching), do-while (i.e., simple looping), and sequence (simple direct instructions such as move and store). This led to a movement to eliminate "go-tos" in programs, that is, to write programs in which the program flow was linear, so could be followed easily (as opposed to jumping all over the place, making error detection difficult). To facilitate "go-to-less" programming, new languages such as Algol and Pascal were developed, and older languages such as COBOL and FORTRAN were revised. Moreover, it was recognized that programs could be more reliably designed and more collectively written if the tasks in a program were modularized, i.e., segregated into separate blocks of instructions. Again, the structured programming languages were created with an eye to encouraging the top-down decomposition of a program into modules.

Consider an example. Suppose we are writing a "program" for making an omelet. The major subtasks are: get the ingredients from the refrigerator; get the utensils; mix the omelet; and cook it. We can "code" this task top-down:

```
         ___________________
        | start
        | <get ingredients >
make    | <get utensils>
omelet  | <mix omelet>
        | <cook omelet>
        | stop
        |___________________
```

We can then "program" the modules:

```
                         ______________________________
                        | enter module;
                        | open refrigerator;
        get             | take out the eggs;
        ingredients     | take out the butter;
                        | take out the cheese;
                        | return to the higher module;
                        |______________________________
```

and so on. To see how if-then and do-while loops can be employed, consider the manner in which we mix the ingredients. We have in mind using a certain number of eggs (say, six, if we are ravenous or cooking for two). We use a counter variable to keep track of the number of eggs in the bowl. We might also check the cheese to see if the end is dry, and if so, cut off the dry part before grating the cheese.

```
          ____________________________________________________________
         | enter the module;
         | set the egg-count to zero;
         | inspect the cheese;
         | if the cheese is dry
         |                                  ________________________
         | then                            | cut off the dry end;
         |                                 | grate the cheese;
         |                                 |________________________
mix      |                                  ________________________
omelet   | else                            | grate the cheese;
         |                                 |________________________
         |
         |                                  ________________________
         | do while the egg -counter < 6   | crack an egg;
         |                                 | split it over the bowl;
         |                                 | add one to the egg-count;
         |                                 |________________________
         |
         | pick up a fork;
         | mix the ingredients with the fork;
         | return to the higher module;
         |____________________________________________________________
```

The idea of using a top-down approach and structured languages was first extensively tried and empirically evaluated in The New York Times IBM project in the late 1960's, and it was shown that programmers who used structured programming techniques were many times faster at producing error-free code than programmers who did not use the structured approach. This result was well publicized, and contributed to the rapid spread of structured programming.

But the structured revolution proved to be insufficient to solve the software crisis. A more broad set of techniques had to be developed to address software inadequacies. Software engineers came to realize that software has a "life cycle" that needs to be understood. Specifically, the development of any piece of software takes place in stages, and the development of error-free software requires the application of techniques appropriate to each stage.

To be more concrete, let us look at commonly accepted model of the software life cycle (although it is not the only accepted model, and in fact is a bit out of date):

```
Requirements analysis
            |____design
                  |____coding
                        |____testing
                              |____maintenance
```

This simplified model, often called "the waterfall model", views the typical development of software as beginning with a clear determination of the needs for which the software is to be designed to handle. Then the software is designed at a highly abstract level, with the implementation details left out. Only after the design is reviewed and clarified does the actual coding (i.e., programmers writing the detailed machine- executable code) begin. After the program is written, it is tested in hopes of removing all the major defects ("bugs"). Finally, the software is installed on the customers computer system, and long-term maintenance gets under way: small bugs that surface when the software is running full-time are corrected, and modifications needed because of the customer's changing requirements are made.

The point I want to make is that for each stage of the software life-cycle, techniques have been developed to minimize error. At the stage of requirements analysis, the goal is to produce a "software requirements specification," which is a precise statement (either informal or formal) of what the proposed software is to do. Many requirements analysis techniques have been developed, some manual and some automated (i.e., computerized), and a number of companies market these tools. One popular group of techniques involves the use of data flow diagrams. For example, we might specify the requirements for a program to do payroll for a small company as follows:

Level 1:

[Payroll Clerk]---hours worked--->{Payroll Program}---paycheck amounts--->
[Paycheck Generator]

↑ ↑

<Employee Records>------------exemptions---hourly wage

Here the rectangles represent sources of external inputs or outputs, the circle a process which transforms data, the double line a data repository, and the arrows the transfer of data.

Level 2 (decomposes the payroll module further)

Hours worked------>{Gross Pay Calculator}----gross pay------->{Tax Calculator}---net pay---->

↑ ↑

Hourly wage Exemptions

Notice that all we are trying to do is to specify exactly the requirements of the system, before we even try to design it. We can keep drawing specifying the requirements to any degree of precision desired. And again, computer-aided software engineering (CASE) workstations exist which allow the software teams to devise the data-flow diagrams automatically.

At the stage of design and coding, all the concepts of structured programming discussed earlier apply. Warnier diagrams, flowcharts, decision tables, and a dozen other devices are used commonly in the design of programs. And coding is done typically in structured high-level languages.

Techniques for improving the efficiency of the testing and maintenance phases also have been developed. One important class of these is techniques, called *metrics*, for measuring the amount of errors in a piece of software. For example, the eminent software engineer McCabe devised a metric that, when applied to the control flow graph for a program (a graph similar to a data flow diagram), estimates the complexity of the program. This, in turn, indicates the testing difficulty and (ultimately) the reliability of the software. Another class of useful software engineering techniques which apply at the latter phases of the software-life-cycle is the set of strategies for testing (such as "black-box", "white-box", top-down and bottom-up testing strategies). I will not go into those strategies here as they would lead us far afield. Suffice it to say that the software engineer has a tremendous number of tools which allow him to minimize errors at each stage of the software life cycle.

At an even higher level, and complementary to the work outlined above in software engineering, there is a whole realm of diverse work which might be called "social impact engineering" for lack of any commonly accepted term. One long-established area of social impact work is computer ergonomics, which aims to design hardware which minimizes negative impact upon the workers who use those systems. For instance, non-glare screens have been developed to reduce eye strain, and special ergonomic chairs have been developed to reduce back strain in the data entry clerks who must spend all day in front of the computer. Similar to ergonomic design, but more relevant to the topic at hand is the recent work in design of user-oriented (or "user- friendly") software is software designed to minimize the problems of the user using it. For example, one user-oriented consideration is the degree to which the software "forgives" improper data entry (such as entering negative instead of positive amounts when recording payments at a bank).

More broad still is the design of fault-tolerant software. Software now impacts not just the user but society at large. Software controls the running of nuclear power plants, air traffic control systems, ICBM's and so on. Since the social consequences of software failure in such cases can be profound, a growing concern is to design the software so that minor faults or errors result in the least social harm possible.

Let us move lastly to what I have termed the "meta" level. I have in mind here work in Artificial Intelligence ("AI") which seeks to design software which can "reason" under uncertainty or in the face of error. (I put the scare quotes around the word "reason" since I don't want to get embroiled in the controversy about whether machines can think.) This level is "meta" in the sense that the researchers are not seeking to design methodologies for minimizing software error, but are instead designing intelligent software that can itself deal with error.

I will not attempt an extensive review of the AI literature on the topics of reasoning under uncertainty and error. About reasoning under uncertainty, I will just mention the major approaches. One very well known way of dealing with uncertainty is to utilize Bayesian inference, which involves assigning prior probabilities and altering them in the light of new information. Another approach utilizes fuzzy logic, which allows vague statements (such as "Chester is balding") to be expressed formally as partial class membership. Still another approach is the endorsement model, in which decisions are reached on the basis of pro or con endorsements. For example, uncertain about whether or not I should buy a Ford Bronco, I might call all the people I know who have owned similar cars, and ask each of them to give his opinion of the car. (For more detail on these approaches to uncertainty, see Cohen (1985)).

Regarding reasoning in the face of error, an AI approach of great interest is non-monotonic logic. Non-monotonic logic was developed to handle situations in which initial assumptions have to be retracted in the light of new information. For example, I might initially order an expensive meal in a restaurant, assuming that is accepts credit cards. Upon learning from the waiter that the restaurant does not accept credit cards, I may decide to revise my order to a less expensive meal. The term "non-monotonic logic" refers to the fact that, whereas in standard logic the addition of new axioms cannot decrease the set of theorems (so the set grows monotonically), in this new logic the set of theorems can shrink in size. Again, I will merely mention the major lines of attack. One line of research focuses on reasoning by default, that is, cases in which a rule is assumed to hold unless an exception is explicitly involved. For instance, the rule "birds can fly" applies by default to any bird, unless it is explicitly mentioned that the bird is a penguin. A second line of research focuses on reasoning by circumscription, that is, cases in which it is assumed parsimoniously that only the objects and relations mentioned explicitly are relevant to the problem at hand. For instance, in the simple algebra word problem

> A car is travelling at 60 KPH towards a town 120 Km. away. How long will it take to reach the town?

it would be natural to assume that the car is not going to be vaporized by a bolt of lightning.

The four-fold hierarchy of software I have used to frame the discussion in this paper is, as I admitted at the outset, simplistic. There are sorts of software which fall between levels. Thus for instance I have not explored the realm of "domain algebra," which is an area of applied mathematics of great use in database theory. Specifically, domain algebra is a formalism directed at resolving anomalies which arise in the management of large stores of data (such as the information kept by a large insurance company on its policy-holders). Databases are of great and growing interest to computer scientists, and the programs which manage them (called "database management systems") are of special importance. But I trust that our survey has been complete enough for us to draw a few broad conclusions about the nature of software error and its role in computer science.

To begin with, what is of interest to computer scientists (as opposed to professional programmers, systems analysts, and computer operators) are not particular pieces of software *per se*, but rather the methodologies by which software is produced. That is, part of what makes a computer scientist a scientist is that he is interested in the process of producing error-free software, rather than in maintaining a particular product or system. Naturally enough, the failures or successes of particular products of a given software design process are grist for the mill of improving software methodology, but the focus is still on process rather than product. Note that philosophers who distinguish between discovery and justification, and view only the latter as being of epistemic importance, are ill-suited indeed to appreciate the essence of computer science.

A second point is that the evaluation of rival methodologies in computer science is usually attempted empirically (or at least mathematically). For example, the claim that the structured approach is a better approach to programming than the unstructured approach has been tested repeatedly by empirical studies. Again, various software metrics have been compared against test programs to see which metric has the best predictive power. This tendency to test empirically is again the mark of a science.

A third point to note is the desire of the computer scientist to move to higher orders of design. That is, no sooner is a methodology for designing software enunciated then some computer scientist is attempting to automate that methodology. If data flow diagrams prove useful in stating the overall requirements for a software project, well, then, it is not long before a computer program is written which produces data flow graphs from a statement of the basic data sources, transforms and data items. If a metric which estimates the number of errors in a given program from the number of key words in it proves useful in testing and maintenance, it is not long before a program is written which estimates errors (using that metric) given other programs as input.

To summarize the thesis of this paper, in the realm of software science, an *error* is a failure of a given piece of software to perform as required in a given context. This includes errors in the narrow sense of algorithms which fail to terminate or terminate with an erroneous result, to the broader sense of software systems which fall short or the performance specified in the approved requirements analysis documents, to the very broad sense of software whose functioning involves unacceptable social risks. The role of error in computer science is in fact positive:

software errors are what fuel the search for better methodologies for detecting and eliminating error. In this latter trait, computer science is not unlike other sciences, in which theorizing often is driven by observed failure of prior theory.

Bibliography

1. Aho, A.V., Hopcroft, J.E. and Ullman, J.D., *The Design and Analysis of Computer Algorithms*, Reading, MA: Addison-Wesley (1974).
2. Brooks, F., *The Mythical Man-Month*, Reading MA: Addison-Wesley (1975).
3. Cohen, Paul, *Heuristic Reasoning about Uncertainty:. An Artificial Intelligence Approach*, Marshfield, MA: Pitman Publishing (1985).
4. Floyd, R.W., "Assigning Meanings to Programs," in *Mathematical Aspects of Computer Science*, ed. J.T. Schwartz, *Proceedings of Symposia in Applied Mathematics* 19, AMS, Providence (1967).
5. Gries, David, *The Science of Programming*, Berlin: Springer-Verlag (1981).
6. Hoare, C.A.R. (1962) "An Axiomatic Basis for Computer Programming" CACM 12 (10).
7. Pressman, Roger *Software Engineering: A Practitioner's Approach*, N.Y.: McGraw-Hill (1987).
8. Reynolds, John, *The Craft of Programming*, London: Prentice-Hall International (1981).
9. Standish, Thomas, *Data Structure Techniques*, Reading, M.A.: Addison-Wesley (1980).

Permission to reprint courtesy of Springer. I wish to thank the journal *Philosophia* as well.

22

My review of: *A Skeptic's Dictionary*

A Collection of Strange Beliefs, Amusing Deceptions, & Dangerous Delusions (by Robert Todd Carroll, New York: John Wiley, 2003, 446 pages) first appeared in Liberty, October 2005

Robert Todd Carroll's enjoyable new book is a concise dictionary of pseudosciences and other nonsensical belief systems and the people who promulgate them. Carroll, who is chairman of the Philosophy Department at Sacramento City College, is well versed in critical thinking and logic, having published a critical-thinking text (*Becoming a Critical Thinker: A Guide for the New Millennium*).

In this book, Carroll takes on trendy tabloid pseudo-sciences and cults. We meet relatively recent absurdities, such as hollow Earth theory, alien abduction, creation science, Falun Gong, the indigo children, SRA (Satanic ritual abuse), biorhythms, holistic medicine, transcendental meditation, Uri Geller, and reverse speech. And he includes many favorite oldies, such as palmistry, Nostradamus, the Loch Ness monster, astrology, numerology, Gurdjieff, haunted houses, Bigfoot, the Illuminati, reincarnation, Noah's Ark, fairies, vampires, zombies, phrenology, the shroud of Turin, mesmerism, and parapsychology—not to mention Roswell (we all know what happened there!). Well represented too are various pop therapies, such as EST, dianetics, New Age psychotherapies, NLP (neuro-linguistic programming), and orgone energy, which never acquired scientific respectability, along with some that have gotten some mainstream support, such as the Myers-Briggs Type Indicator (used to classify personalities), the Rorschach inkblot test, RMT (repressed memory therapy), and TFT (thought field therapy). There are nearly four hundred entries, a veritable grab bag of the inane, the insane, the asinine, and the delusional.

If all Carroll did was debunk the usual suspects, his book would not be better than similar books, such as James Randi's excellent primer, *An Encyclopedia of Claims, Frauds, and Hoaxes of the Occult and Supernatural.* But Carroll covers some more recent and interesting specimens of intellectual dreck. He includes the nasty phenomenon of Holocaust denial, for instance. He also discusses the much-hyped use of subliminal messaging and mind control (brainwashing), both of which have been proven ineffective, despite popular fears to the contrary.

Even more valuable are his pithy essays on logic and scientific method, which identify the nature of pseudoscience as well as logical fallacies (such as begging the question) that underlie it. For example, he succinctly discusses the Forer effect (also called the Barnum effect), which is the use of such vague language (in psychological surveys or predictions by astrologers) that it describes everyone. His discussion of entrenchment, or what he calls the sunk-cost fallacy, is a delight—we keep flying the Concorde not because it makes a profit but because we don't want to admit our initial investment was wasted. He discusses confirmation bias (the tendency to seek only evidence which will support one's theory), *ad hoc* hypotheses, positive-outcome bias (the tendency to publish positive outcomes rather than negative outcomes), the post hoc fallacy, control-group experiments, memory (false and veridical), the placebo effect, pseudo-history, pseudoscience, and Occam's razor. All these make the book a good reference book for a critical-thinking class.

My admiration for his book is lessened by omissions that in my view are all too characteristic of contemporary academic skeptics. There are dozens of books lampooning the usual suspects such as astrology and parapsychology, but these books (including Carroll's) never mention, say, Marx or communism. Now don't get me wrong—astrology and parapsychology are nonsense, of course. But so is Marxism. I've been in philosophy departments where astrology is ridiculed ("Oh, the stupidity of the plebs is so hard to endure!") but where Marx is held in high esteem ("A soaring genius!"). Yet while the devotees of astrology haven't killed anyone, devotees of Marxism were responsible for as many as 100 million deaths in the twentieth century. Again, while Carroll's book has entries on such obscure figures as Edward Bach (a British physician who devised a therapy using flowers) and Frederic Lenz (a Zen entrepreneur who calls himself Rama), you don't see an entry on Margaret Mead, whose pseudoscientific anthropological research (based upon a hoax by her key source) helped persuade people that all gender differences are culturally constructed. Nor is there any entry in Carroll's book on Alfred Kinsey, the poster boy for bias in sampling. Again, one searches in vain for any mention of Black Athena (or its author Martin Bernal), which propounded the theory that the Greeks (the ultimate in dead white males) stole philosophy, math, art, and science from Africa. Again, I surely commend Carroll for discussing the oft-forgotten Lysenko affair, in which a rank pseudoscientist was able to exploit political ideology to destroy genuine biological science in the Soviet Union, but what about the current attempt by feminists to stamp out research on gender differences in cognitive psychology?

My suspicion is that skeptical academics are more apt to debunk the belief systems of the *hoi polloi* than deal with the absurdities so prevalent in contemporary academia for a number of reasons. First, although the average man is usually modest about his intellectual abilities, academics are usually less modest, if not positively hubristic.

Second, the degree of vapidity of belief is often greater with academics. As Orwell observed, there are some ideas so stupid that only intellectuals can believe them. Suppose someone tells me he believes in reincarnation. While I think this belief is silly, I confess that nothing in my experience directly refutes it, so my mind simply rolls along. But to hear someone—with a PhD, no less—argue that paying everyone equally will maximize workplace production, or there are no innate differences between men and women, or criminals don't choose to commit heinous crimes but commit them because of ignorance, so profoundly offends my daily experience that my mind boggles.

Third, there is simple pusillanimity. Tell believers in astrology that they are fools, and nothing happens. But if a university professor tells feminists or diversity scholars that their arguments are specious, they will demonstrate outside his office or torment feckless administrators until he is sacked.

Finally, there is sympathy. As Solzhenitsyn observed long ago, if you're a left-liberal, you have to have a sneaking sympathy for socialists, so in turn for communists. If you believe social justice requires confiscating most of what a productive person earns, why not all? The vast majority of academics are politically and socially liberal, as well as secular, and this colors even their skepticism.

Carroll's book is delightful but not revolutionary.

Reprinted by permission of Liberty Magazine.

23

My review of: *Unauthorized Freud*

Doubters Confront a Legend (ed. by Frederick C. Crews. New York: Viking Penguin publishers, 1998, 301 pages) first appeared in Philosophia Vol. 33, Nos. 1–4 (2005) pp. 343–349

Over the last twenty years what has come to be called "the Freud Wars" has raged with considerable ferocity. Critics such as Adolf Grunbaum, Hans Eysenck, Edward Erwin, Frank Cioffi, Ernest Gellner, Jeffrey Masson, Frederick Crews and numerous others have nearly toppled the edifice of Freudian Psychoanalytic Theory. I think it's fair to say that what was widely considered even fifty years ago as revolutionary science on a par with Darwinian and Copernican science is now widely suspected of being, well, pseudoscience. For those whose academic focus may have been elsewhere, Frederic Crews has edited a very accessible collection of essays reflecting the major angles of criticism of classical Freudian theory.

Crews, in his preface, indicates clearly that he regards Freudian Theory as hopelessly flawed (page x):

> The chapters and editorial comments below not only take the full measure of Freud's well-documented conceptual errors, relentless apriorism, disregard for counterexamples, bullying investigative manner, shortcuts of reasoning, rhetorical dodges, and all-around chronic untruthfulness; they also show that

> contemporary analysts possess no reliable means, internal to 'clinical evidence,' of locating and correcting their own misconceptions.

He is motivated in his critical efforts in great part because of the deleterious effects of the "suppressed memory recovery movement," a topic upon which he has written another book (*The Memory Wars*).

In the introduction, Crews draws the reader's attention to where Freud's originality laid the better to assess it. Plenty of thinkers explored "the unconscious" well before Freud, most notably Nietzsche. And the existence of unconscious mental functioning is undisputed and demonstrable. No, the specific and unique contribution of Freud is: (a) his postulation of a psychodynamic unconscious that plans, lusts, atones, remembers, represses, quarrels with itself, symbolizes, and so on; (b) his view that this psychodynamic unconscious causes all manner of ailments—"neurotic" ones, such as paralysis, rashes and sores, phobias and compulsions, and even psychotic ones such as schizophrenia, paranoia, and bipolar disorder (manic-depression); and (c) his view that the psychodynamic cause for these ailments can be understood and the ailments cured by examining slips of tongue, free association, and dreams. This core theory, psychoanalytic theory, and its application to anthropology and history, is what Freud developed, and is that for which he ought to be assessed. Rightly, Crews points out that we should assess this theory on the basis of empirical evidence, which is hardly overwhelming in the corpus of Freud's own writings. It won't do to merely assert, as some philosophers have done, that Freudian theory is merely a plausible way of extending our common sense way of inferring motives from observing behavior, because most of the characteristic claims of Freudian Theory are at variance with common-sense intuitions. And indeed, there is something problematic about the notion of using the testimony of patients under analysis as evidence for the truth of the theory, since the theory allows the analyst to take patients' reports as literal or as requiring interpretation, depending upon the whims of the analyst.

Crews finishes the extended introduction by considering several strategies Freudians have employed to rebut criticism of the lack of observational support or even the possibility of clear observational support for their theory. First, some rehash relativistic claims (usually citing Kuhn) that all scientific observation is theory-laden. But the fact that observation is theory-laden does not mean that it is laden with precisely the specific theory being tested, rendering all experiment an exercise in begging the question. Second, some argue that psychoanalysis is not meant as science, but rather as a hermeneutic activity, so should be judged on intuitive and empathic, as opposed to empirical, grounds. But Freud certainly viewed his theory as science. And it is hard to see how to take his claims about the etiology of various phenomena (such as psychosexual development, mental structure, the formations of dreams and so on) as interpretive principles, when they seem so clearly intended to be causal mental laws. Third, some argue that while Freud's specific psychoanalytic theory is flawed, psychoanalytic theory has subsequently developed into an empirically adequate scientific theory. To this tack, Crews has two replies. First, which of the myriad of post-Freudian theories has made this great scientific progress? Second, all these novel psychoanalytic theories "appeal to the same knowledge source—namely, the clinical interaction between therapist and patient, with particular stress on the two features that remain virtually universal, the analysis of free associations and the analysis of the transference." (Page xxx.)

The articles in the anthology are grouped into four sections, each preceded by a detailed overview by Crews. In the overview to the first section, Crews lays out in summary form the legend of how Freud originated his theory, from his early association with Charcot in 1885 to his self-analysis and final break with Fliess just prior to 1900. The selections in the section each are intended to tell the real story of the origins of psychoanalysis. The first selection, by Mikkel Borch-Jacobsen, examines the case of Anna O., where the idea was born in the minds of Breuer and Freud that that there is a disease, "hysteria," that it is caused by traumatic memories, and that it can cured by taking the memory away under hypnosis. Freud later changed key elements of the theory, taking the memory causing hysteria first to be an actual childhood sexual assault, then to be a childhood sexual fantasy, then finally to be an oedipal fantasy, and moving from hypnosis to free association, to the analysis of resistances and transference. But despite the claim that the talking cure worked miraculous wonders for Anna O., it appears clear that the treatment Anna O. received did nothing to alleviate, much less cure, her symptoms. The second selection, by Peter J. Swales, examines the case of "Frau Cacilie M.," whom Swales was able to identify as Anna von Lieben. As in the case of "Anna O.," we see a case of a patient presenting an ever-changing array of symptoms, who is treated by drugs and hypnotism in the hope of exposing the repressed, and thus eliminating the symptoms. But she underwent treatment by Freud and other physicians for over thirty years, and despite the "cathartic" methods, she never got better. Freud neglected to mention in his discussion of his patient that she had been addicted to morphine for years, and that Freud, after applying his cathartic methods, would also give her an injection of morphine, after which her symptoms would vanish, but only for a day, whereupon Freud would be called back! The third selection, Frank Cioffi's seminal BBC radio talk from 1973, explores the anti-empirical nature of Freud's hypothesis of repressed Oedipal fantasy (the theory he moved to when he abandoned his seduction theory). Additionally, the Cioffi selection and the fourth selection (by Mikkel Borch-Jacobsen) argue that Freud suspected but refused to confront the likelihood that the real problem with the seduction theory was that the "memories" of the patients were in fact induced by the therapist (Freud) himself. The fifth selection, by Frank Sulloway, argues that Freud's theories were much more tied to the thinking of Wilhelm Fleiss than Freudians care to acknowledge.

The second section of readings concerns the epistemic basis for Freudian theory—specifically, the ability of techniques such as free association, dream interpretation and the analysis of slips of tongue to empirically ground claims about mental causation. The first selection, by Adolf Grunbaum, argues strongly that the data obtained from free association are hopelessly unreliable because of the selection biases of the analyst—the patient is prompted to continue until producing precisely the responses needed to validate the analyst's diagnosis—and the suggestiveness of the patient's reports. The second selection, by Rosemarie Sand, casts doubt upon Freud's theory of dream interpretation, arguing that the common-sense view of dreams (which takes the "manifest" dream to be a reflection of waking concerns) is more in line with modern scientific work on dreaming than Freud's theory (which postulates a "latent" dream in which unacceptable wishes are repressed and expressed symbolically as the manifest dream). The third selection, by Sebastiano Timpanaro, casts doubt upon Freud's analysis of slips (parapraxes), arguing that from the point of view of a linguist, the sort of associations (phonetic and semantic similarities of words) used by Freud can connect any slip to any cause the analyst chooses. The fourth selection, by Barbara Von Eckhardt, argues that Freud's methodology was flawed in that it relies on mere explanatory power as a mark for truth, and the data adduced for its support are theory-laden in a pernicious way. A good theory not only explains data, it is superior to other theories explaining the same data. And while all data are theory-laden, a good test of a theory does not involve producing data that presuppose the theory being tested. The fifth selection, by Frank Cioffi, argues that persistent flight from criticism and counterevidence is so characteristic of Freudian psychoanalysis as to make it a pseudoscience. In the sixth selection, by Malcolm McMillan, the deficiencies in Freud's account of female sexuality are explored in detail.

The third section of readings focuses on the inadequacies of the case studies cited by Freud as evidence for his views. Crews, in his introduction to the section, contends that even waiving problems with placebo effects and long-term relapses, Freud could not document even one unambiguously effective treatment of a client. The first selection, by Allen Esterson, examines the case of Dora, and argues persuasively that Freud's preconceptions led to a radical misdiagnosis and bullying treatment of a hapless young woman. The second selection, by Joseph Wolpe and Stanley Rachman, examines the case of "Little Hans," and argues that the child never accepted the Freudian interpretation of his fear of horses, but rather had words put in his mouth by his interrogators (mainly his own father, a devotee of Freud), and in any case there was no relation between the abatement of his symptoms and the interpretations he was given. This case is especially chilling, in that we get a glimpse of the current "recovered memory" therapists' use of questionable tactics to interrogate children. The third selection, by Frank Sulloway, makes the case that Freud systematically distorted his reports of his case studies to give the appearance of medical/scientific success, in order to build his personal legend. The fourth selection, by Stanley Fish, attempts to analyze Freud's rhetoric to exhibit its power to charm the reader into overlooking the weakness of the empirical evidence being presented. The fifth selection, by David Stannard, looks at the psychoanalysis Freud gave of Leonardo da Vinci, the first in a series of works in which Freud sought to analyze people whom he never met, and argues that Freud's historical understanding was limited at best, and his conclusions about Leonardo are totally unsupported.

In the fourth and final section, Crews takes up the issue of why Freudian theory was so successful, despite its faulty methodology and lack of empirical or medical success. It certainly satisfied the desire, among people who are inclined to spurn religion-based traditionalism, to replace priests and ethicists by mind-doctors. And to Freudian initiates it delivered no little power, money, and prestige. But the selections point to other factors as well. The first selection, by Ernest Gellner, sets forth the view that psychoanalysis is the transmission of a faith, in which the patient first gives up independent judgment while being swamped with a lot of attention, and then is rehabilitated in terms of the Freudian belief system. The second selection, by John Farrell, argues that Freud's view of himself and his intellectual creation had a paranoid slant, which led him and his followers to promulgate their system more in the manner of a cult than a science. The third selection, by Francois Roustang, explores the unscientific and vicious squabbles among the disciples of the aging Freud to become sole heir to his legacy, reinforcing the image of a cult. The fourth selection of the section (and the final one of the book), by Lavinia Edmunds, explores the case of Horace Frink, an emotionally unstable disciple picked and cynically used by Freud as a tool to spread psychoanalysis to America.

This anthology is a good place to start to survey the various lines of criticism of Freudianism that have grown over the last quarter century. The survey does leave out some topics one would like to see addressed. In particular, one very important reason for the rapid demise of psychoanalytic theory has been the rise of biological understanding of behavior. It is hard to maintain the Freudian view of the cause of psychoses such as bipolar disorder and schizophrenia, given the efficacy of drugs such as lithium and the studies of twins reared apart, showing a high degree of inheritability of these ailments. Even so-called neuroses such as depression and obsessive-compulsive disorder are readily yielding to drug therapies. But despite that limitation, Crews book is a valuable one.

Permission to reprint courtesy of Springer.
I wish to thank the journal Philosophia as well.

24

My review of: *Remembering Trauma*

(by Richard J. McNally, Cambridge, MA: Harvard University Press, 2003) first appeared in Philosophia (2006) 34: 477–481

Over the last decade, few psychological topics have attracted as much attention as how and how extensively people remember trauma. Besides its intrinsic importance in both psychology and philosophy, it has practical ramifications in both the therapeutic and the political realms. We are fortunate that Richard McNally has produced a fine, thorough survey of what has been learned on this subject in recent years.

McNally starts with a discussion of why the topic of trauma memory is so politically charged. Traumatic memory is tied to the sexual politics of the twentieth century, especially in the last decade with the rise of recovered memory therapy (in which patients, mainly women, suddenly remember childhood sexual abuse during therapy). Here, you have a maelstrom of ancillary issues, such as the rise in diagnoses of Multiple Personality Disorder, the formation of False Memory Syndrome foundations around the world, not to mention the lawsuits directed at parents by patients who have recovered memories of sexual abuse, as well as lawsuits directed at therapists by accused parents and by patients who have retracted their stories. Also, it is tied in with the rise in diagnoses of Post-Traumatic Stress Disorder (PTSD), which is often linked to antiwar politics.

McNally then moves on to survey current psychological research on how memory works in general. While research on memory is a hot topic in psychology and cognitive science, a certain consensus seems to be emerging. Psychologists distinguish short term or working memory from long term memory. There are two ways scientists conceptualize long term memory. Long term memory is divided into declarative memory (essentially verbal), such as episodic memory of life experiences and semantic memory of facts, and non-declarative memory (essentially behavioral), such as knowing how to ride a bike. Second, long term memory is divided into explicit (essentially, conscious or intentional) and implicit. The key point here is that while implicit memory is unconscious, it is not "unconscious" in the sense of "repressed into the unconscious mind." As McNally notes (p. 34):

> Indeed, the concept of the unconscious of contemporary cognitive science must not be confused with the psychodynamic unconscious of Freud, with its buried memories of childhood trauma and its forbidden sexual and aggressive urges struggling to burst through into awareness. The two are entirely different concepts. The unconscious of cognitive science, exemplified by research on implicit memory, simply refers to information that occurs outside awareness…

Regarding autobiographical memory, i.e., long term personal memory (both episodic and semantic), what is clear after much research is that it is a reconstructive rather than a reproductive process. That is, when we remember an event from our past, we don't simply replay an internal videotape, but rather we reconstruct it from various encoded elements distributed throughout the brain. Generally speaking, recent genuine memories are more vivid than are memories of childhood: memories to tend to fade, although thinking or talking about them can prevent details from fading. But it is similarly true that thinking or talking about an *imaginary* event makes a person more likely to confuse it with a real one. *Pace* Descartes, the vivacity of a memory is no guarantee of its accuracy. McNally notes that people who score high on measures of imagery ability and dissociation are especially apt to confound imagined with real events. Moreover, the empirical research that has been done on memory points clearly to the conclusion that emotional stress enhances rather than impairs memory, although it may cause the focus to be on the central features of the event rather than the peripheral. As McNally notes, this is what one would expect on evolutionary grounds: how adaptive would it be for members of a species to rapidly forget life-threatening situations? Finally, McNally reviews the large amount of recent work in the creation of false memories, which shows fairly conclusively that many (if not most) people can come to have memories of stressful events that never in fact happened, indeed, never could have happened.

McNally then considers the notion of psychological trauma itself. This is a tricky and controversial issue. The rise in interest in psychological trauma has an economic component: diagnoses of PTSD can be the basis of disability payments. Trauma has two sides: the objective (does the stressor constitute a real threat to life or of serious injury?) and the subjective (does the stressor humiliate or terrify the individual?). Research seems to show that there is no simple relation between the degree of objective trauma and the symptoms that may result (people do differ in how a given stressful event impacts them psychologically), and it is hard to measure the degree of objective trauma. Most researchers have relied on reports from patients relying on memories of past trauma, but such reports are in great part a function of the patient's current clinical state, and most people who undergo severe trauma do not develop PTSD.

Regarding the memory for trauma, the recent research has upheld part, but only part, of "clinical lore." Nightmares and flashbacks, especially for those suffering PTSD, are (again) not like videotape replays, although there is the vivid illusion of reliving the initial trauma. In flashbacks, what is experienced often differs from what really happened in the initial traumatic experience, and indeed, some people experience vivid "flashbacks" of events that never occurred. Moreover, very recent research indicates that people who were unconscious during the trauma (e.g., knocked out in an auto accident) have recurring emotional reactions to it, although it is still unclear whether those reactions are due to some kind of conditioning while unconscious or just learning about the event afterwards (say, from reading police reports or talking to family members).

McNally turns next to the mechanisms for traumatic memory. Here he notes (p. 156) that recent experimental research has debunked various assumptions about memory, trauma, and the mechanisms underlying traumatic memory. PTSD patients, despite anecdotal reports to the contrary, do not in general show memory impairment on standardized tests. And studies do not support the idea that high levels of the stress hormone Cortisol shrink the hippocampi of PTSD sufferers: first, the levels of Cortisol are not typically higher in PTSD sufferers, and second, smaller hippocampi are likely genetic in origin. (A smaller hippocampus in fact may be a risk factor for PTSD, rather than an effect of it.) And experiments into the notion that trauma survivors (especially those who suffered childhood sexual abuse) develop skills for suppressing such memories have failed to support it, indeed, tend to indicate the opposite, i.e., that experiencing trauma impairs your ability to forget disturbing material.

McNally then gives a fair and comprehensive review of theories of repression and dissociation. He covers Freud's seduction theory in detail, as well as

Lenore Terr's theory, Jennifer Freyd's Betrayal Trauma theory, up through Bessel van der Kolk's theory (a fusion of neuroscience with the theories of Pierre Janet). Such theories posit that: people can have traumatic experiences as children; they then repress/dissociate explicit memories of those traumas; they will express those memories in emotion and behavior; they can subsequently recollect as adults those memories with a high degree of accuracy; and recovering in narrative form those repressed or dissociated memories is therapeutically beneficial to them. Any such theory is posited as a best explanation of cases in which a person undergoes traumatic experiences, does not think about them for years, and then begins to think about them again, say, under therapy.

In reply, McNally makes what ought to be obvious points. First, again, what evolutionary scenario could we possibly imagine that would confer selective advantage upon members of a species that didn't remember severe threats? Second, such theories attribute "traumatic amnesia" to either repression or dissociation, overlooking the obvious explanation of ordinary forgetting of unpleasant memories. Amnesia means that you *cannot* remember, it is an *inability* to remember, and that is quite different from simply not constantly refreshing your memory at each moment. There are unpleasant, shameful or humiliating incidents in my life which I am perfectly capable of remembering at any given time, but which I avoid remembering because of the attendant pain they bring. In a word, suppression of unpleasant memories is different from repression or dissociation. Moreover, if the traumatic incident is perceived by the person to be shameful, even if he brings it to mind, he certainly will not be inclined to discuss or reveal it. Amnesia is different not only from suppression, but from silent remembering. Conflation of suppression with repression is not a minor problem, but is on the contrary a deep methodological flaw in theories of repression. As McNally notes (p. 184):

> We cannot tell the difference between unavailability of the memory trace and refusal to disclose the abuse. To discriminate either of these alternatives from repression or dissociation, we would have to establish a way to detect and measure the operation of these inhibitory mechanisms independent of the facts they are adduced to explain: the person's failure to report abuse. That is, we cannot invoke the mechanism of repression (or dissociation) to explain memory failure if the only evidence for the operation of the mechanism is the very data the mechanism is invoked to explain. Trauma theorists must establish methods for measuring repression and dissociation independently from recall failure itself.

McNally then surveys the studies regarding traumatic amnesia, i.e., inability to remember trauma. Retrograde amnesia is the inability to remember events that occurred before the precipitating event (such as an auto accident or brain surgery), anterograde amnesia is the inability to remember events that occurred after the precipitating event. Organic amnesia is amnesia caused by events that damage the brain; psychogenic amnesia is amnesia caused by events in which some psychological or emotional components result in memory loss without brain damage. Organic amnesia is relatively common, but psychogenic amnesia isn't, popular belief notwithstanding. The issue of psychogenic amnesia is complicated by the fact that psychological stressors can trigger retrograde amnesia in people with preexisting brain damage, and –worse yet—some people (such as criminals) will pretend to have psychogenic amnesia.

The sort of amnesia hypothesized to explain why a person would not remember childhood sexual abuse can't be psychogenic amnesia, because standard psychogenic amnesia starts right after the triggering episode, and involves sweeping retrograde memory loss (and loss of personal identity as well). This is quite different from the traumatic amnesia claimed by recovered memory therapists and others, where a single event is repressed for many years, but all other memories remain intact, as does personal identity, and the memory gets recovered in therapy (thus isn't a case of permanent amnesia). So the rare reports of true psychogenic amnesia do not support the peculiar "amnesia" supposedly operating in repression/dissociation and recovered memory theories. Similarly, the DSM-IV PTSD symptom "Inability to recall an important aspect of the trauma" is ambiguous: as Elizabeth Loftus and others have shown, during a traumatic event (such as, say, an armed robbery) the victim may focus on some features (like the gun the robber is holding) rather than others (such as the color of the robber's belt). This is hardly true amnesia.

McNally again surveys the literature attempting to establish traumatic amnesia in general and in particular amnesia for sexual abuse, homicide, genocide, torture, disasters, and combat. Moreover, he looks at various oft-cited studies of recovered memories. He cites numerous flaws to be found in these studies: simple failure to distinguish inability to remember from not remembering at a given time or for a long period of time; failure to grasp that some people molested as children didn't perceive what happened to them as sexual abuse at the time; failure to verify (or even to bother trying to verify) that the trauma really happened (or just accepting at face value the subjects' claims that corroboration exists); failure to distinguish the inability to remember an event from the lack of desire to talk about it; failure to rule out other possible explanations for not remembering besides traumatic amnesia (such as head injury, sleep deprivation, or outright lying); and failure to conduct follow-up interviews to ascertain why the subject didn't mention the traumatic event initially.

McNally considers next the recently highly researched topic of false memories (a topic the aforementioned Elizabeth Loftus has done so much to investigate). Among other criticisms, he points out the dark side underside of the recovered memory movement: reports of abduction by aliens from outer space, of torture and rape by roving bands of satanic worshippers, and of ritualistic sexual abuse of children. These reports are all incredible, in the face of the lack of any solid independent evidence of satanic cults and space visitors. He rightly quotes the sociologists Richard Ofshe and Ethan Watters that such bizarre reports put recovered memory therapists in a dilemma: either go along with those who believe E.T. is a real being with outrageous sexual habits, or admit that the methodology for supposedly recovering repressed memories is hopelessly flawed because it creates false memories in significant numbers of patients. A few such therapists have grasped the first horn of the dilemma, and have said that space molesters exist, and a few others have backed off from their therapeutic techniques. Woefully many, it seems to me, have simply failed to face the issue.

McNally finishes up by first sketching his own experimental research into some of these contentious areas, such as the rise of current therapeutic techniques like guided imagery, the Deese/Roediger/McDermott (DRM) paradigm, directed forgetting, the emotional Stroop Task, as well as alien abduction. He states an important conclusion of his work on alien abduction (p. 273):

> Some psychotherapists have claimed that recovered memories of childhood (or other) trauma must be authentic because the emotional intensity of recollection is so great. Our study indicates the fallacy in this argument. Indeed, the abductees we studied evinced objective signs of emotional, psycho-physiologic reactivity while recollecting memories of traumatic events that almost certainly had not happened.

McNally closes by suggesting some areas of emerging controversy, such as whether some people are pretending to be PTSD-afflicted combat vets for the disability pay (he cites in this regard the recent expose *Stolen Valor,* by B.G. Burkett and Glenna Whitley), whether the very concept of trauma has been inflated beyond all reasonable bounds, and whether PTSD is itself a social construction.

Besides its obvious appeal to psychologists, McNally's book is extremely important for philosophers. The nature of memory is (and has traditionally been) a topic of much interest to epistemologists, and so McNally's literature review of current work on memory is certainly useful to epistemologists. In particular, this book is one more nail in the coffin of the video-recorder theory of memory. For those of us who work in the area of critical thinking, this work on the nature and reliability of memory is very applicable, indeed. In my own critical thinking classes, I utilize this recent work in discussions about the criteria for determining whether testimony is credible.

For philosophers working in the history and philosophy of psychology, or the philosophy of cognitive science, McNally's is timely as well. McNally's book is of course important in the ongoing critical assessment of Freudianism. But it is also of interest to those working in cognitive science generally. Memory is one of the hottest topics of research in cognitive psychology and cognitive neuroscience.

In sum, *Remembering Trauma* is an indispensable work for anyone interested in Freudian theory, current therapeutic methods, and the recent history of psychology generally. It is also useful for those interested in the epistemology of memory (and its application to critical thinking), as well as issues in the philosophy of psychology. I have seldom read as clear an exposition of a complex scientific topic, all the more remarkable because it is written by a highly respected, active researcher in the field. McNally has done us all a great service.

Permission to reprint courtesy of Springer.
I wish to thank the journal Philosophia as well.

Part Three

Ethical Theory, Applied Ethics, and Social/Political Philosophy

25

"Deontologism and Dialectic"

first appeared in The Journal of Value Inquiry 17: 119–131 (1983)

The central issue in modern moral philosophy is the question of what acts are morally right, and why. An answer to this question is a theory of the right, and such theories have fallen into three groups.

We may distinguish, in rough terms, between motive theories, results theories and deontological (rule) theories. That is, some moral philosophers hold that an act is right if and only if (iff) it is done from certain motives. Other moral philosophers hold that an act is right iff it leads to the best results. And yet other philosophers say that an act is right iff it possesses certain 'intrinsic' features.

As examples of motive theories, we can cite agapism and existentialism. *Agapism* is the view that an act is right if it is done out of love. The rightness of an act (under this theory) consists not in any features of the act itself, but rather in a feature of the agent: his love for those affected by his act.

Similarly, *existentialists* tend (so far as I can tell) to hold the view that an act is right iff it is undertaken with full commitment, 'authentically,' not 'aesthetically,' or some other such notion. Here again, the rightness of the act depends upon a feature of the agent, to wit, his wholeheartedness.

Rather different are results theories, which include (for example) egoism and utilitarianism. The *egoist* believes that an act is right iff it produces the maximum balance of good over evil for the agent himself. The *utilitarian* holds that an act is right iff it produces the maximum balance of good over evil for everyone affected by the act (including, but not limited to, the agent himself). In both these theories, the rightness of an act lies not in features of the act itself, but rather in features of the consequences of the act i.e., later events to which the act gives rise—namely, the desirability (in a non-moral sense) of those results.

Thus, in both motive and results theories, while the question addressed focuses upon the rightness of the act, the answer involves shifting our gaze away from the act and to either the agent or else later events. In contrast, the deontologist asks us, when assessing an act, to 'look to the act itself,' to focus upon features intrinsic to the act per se.

As examples of deontological theories we should mention four. First, there is *legalism*, which is the theory that an act is right iff it accords with the laws of the agent's society. Next consider *divine command theory*, which holds that an act is right iff God would approve of it. Neither of these forms of deontologism has had many philosophic adherents, but I mention them anyway because discussion of their drawbacks will aid the construction of our alternative theory.

More philosophically respectable is the third deontological theory, Kant's *Categorical Imperative*. An act is right iff the agent can consistently will and would be willing to see the maxim under which his act falls become universal law. Also respectable is *Ross' deontological theory*. Ross' theory consists of an enumeration of a number of putatively self-evident *prima facie* duties (which arise from the nature of the agent and his past interactions with others). An act is right if and only if it accords with the *prima facie* duties (in some fashion never quite made clear).

Of course, the deontologist's focus upon 'intrinsic features of the act' generally takes the form of devising a rule or rules, whose obligatory ('deontic') nature is independent of the consequences of the actions permitted by those rules. Deontological theories are *rule* theories.

This stands to reason. For, if an act's moral lightness consists in its having a certain special feature F, then a rule suggests itself: Always do F-acts. (An act is right if and onlynif it is an F-act.) Similarly, if an act's moral rightness consists of its having some combination of features F_1,.. ., F_n, then this rule suggests itself: Always do acts which combine F_1,..., F_n (in such and such a way).

Now I believe that the deontological approach has a certain a priori plausibility, but spelling this belief out is not easy.

As we have contrasted the results, motive and deontological approaches (to devising an adequate theory of the right), the deontological approach seems clearly the most plausible precisely because it focuses upon the act itself. After all, consider the relation between a person's actions and his motives, and the relation between his actions and their consequences. Both these relations seem tenuous in a way that militates against rational appraisal of our actions, in that the links between act and motive and between act and result are beyond what the agent can completely know or control. And this would make moral decision-making inherently adventitious; one's judgments being objectively correct or incorrect would become something he could not be even reasonably sure about.

To make the matter plain, consider again motive theories. They ask us to decide what to do (or—and this amounts to the same thing for our purposes—how to assess another person's decision) on the basis of motives (love, say, or wholeheartedness) and motives alone. But does the possession of a given motive really guarantee the lightness of an act? Can't one imagine, for instance, an authentic/committed/wholehearted Nazi? And can't one imagine a person who hurts others out of love—say, a mother who forces her son into a life that she erroneously thinks is best?

And again, such theories assume that we can be very sure of other people's motives, or at least of our own. But when I see someone (say) being charitable, I have no way of knowing whether his true motive is love or (say) self-aggrandizement. I may see him be charitable when nobody else is around, but does he believe that nobody will ever see his act of charity?

The situation is no less problematic with my own self. Given the undeniable capacity of people for great self-deception, for denying to themselves their true motives, does it not seem unlikely that a motive theory of the right will enable us to make moral judgments and decisions with even a fair chance of being objectively correct?

A similar objection can be raised against results theories. Suppose I wrestle with a decision, thinking about all aspects of the act and its content, and finally deciding upon a course of action. But now suppose wholly new events (unforeseeable at the time of my decison-making) intervene to cause my act to have unpleasant consequences. According to the results theories, my act is wrong, morally wrong—though not through anything I was responsible for or had control over.

But again, doesn't this make it unlikely that I could ever make decisions and judgments about other people's decisions with reasonable hope of being sure of objective correctness? Surely it is more plausible to peg decision-making to the act itself. We can then say of the above situation: "Look, I did the morally right thing. It just didn't work out."

In sum, if deontological theories really do focus on the intrinsic features of the act itself, then they are likely (not automatically, mind you, just likely) to be more conducive to secure moral judging than the results and motives theories, which focus on things only adventitiously connected with it.

The problem is: deontological theories do not focus on the act itself.

Consider the divine command theory, for instance. In looking at God's approval or disapproval, we are manifestly not looking at a feature intrinsic to the act, but instead one intrinsic to God. Again, in legalism, in looking at the agreement between the act and the laws of the agent's society, we are not viewing a feature of the act so much as a feature of that society (its collective approval, codified more or less explicitly in some legal code) or of that society's legislators.

To carry the point further, Kantian theory in the end asks us not to view any feature of the act per se, but instead asks whether the situation in which the maxim under which that act falls is universally adopted (supposing it can be) would meet with the agent's own approval. The point applies as well to Ross' theory, which in the end ties the rightness of an act to the approval of plain men of common sense.

Indeed, the foregoing suggests that so-called deontological theories are more aptly named *approval* theories: an act is right if and only if it is approved by some group or other. This group—whom I shall refer to as 'the arbiters'—may be an actual group of people, or merely an imaginary group, and may be mortal or divine, depending upon the particular deontological/approval theory in question.

Thus unmasked, do deontological theories still retain an a priori plausibility over results and motive theories? I believe that they do, but the explanation of this a priori plausibility requires a bit more discussion of the notion of 'approval.'

After all, consider the paradigm of practical reasoning: a case being decided in a court of law. The arguments, the reasons pro and con, are presented to a set of arbiters for their ultimate approval or disapproval: the judge and the jury. It is not necessarily a bar to our being able to take the moral point of view—i.e., to judge seriously and with the prospect of our careful deliberation leading us to objective truth—that our deliberations and our decision must meet with the approval of a certain group. Indeed, quite the contrary: that our judgments must meet with the approval of others can be an aid to our securing certainty, if the arbiters provide help in checking any errors in our reasoning.

But this depends crucially upon who is to do the approving. For instance, the reason that legalism is untenable as an ethical theory is that it is very possible that the legal system of the agent's society is wicked. Hence, from the legalist point of view, any German who harbored a Jewish family in the time of the Third Reich would have been behaving immorally; but such is clearly not the case.

Put another way, the legalist theoretician tells us that an act is right if and only if it meets with the approval of the actual society of which the agent is a member. Yet it is clearly possible and not historically uncommon for a total society (or at least its legislators) to be completely wrong in their ethical beliefs. This makes the equation of the approval of the agent's existing society to the rightness of his acts not a plausible line of ethical research.

So it appears that while it is certainly agreeable to common sense that making a reasoned judgment in some way involves appeal to the approval of others, this way must be spelled out. Otherwise, the relation between the approval and the rightness of the act would be as accidental as the relation between (say) the act and its consequences.

Thus, the key to carrying out a satisfactory deontological research program is figuring out who it is our moral reasoning and resultant decisions must meet the approval of. To address this problem, let us examine in detail the more plausible deontological theories, focusing upon the arbiters posited by each.

The divine command theory holds that an act is right iff it is approved by God. But of course this theory faces a number of large problems.

There is the metaphysical problem of establishing God's existence. After all, if God does not exist, then this theory entails that all things are permitted—not a pleasant prospect to imagine. There is also the practical problem of figuring out what God approves of—which prophet or holy book do we select?

Most important from our point of view, however, is the objection raised long ago by Socrates. If an act's being morally right simply amounts to its being approved of by God, then God cannot be said to be moral, except in the trivial sense that He approves of what He approves of.

Now, Socrates' objection is generally felt to be devastating, but only against the divine command theory. However, the same objection can be generalized into a probe which can be used to examine any deontological theory. The general Socratic challenge is this: if an act is right iff it meets with the approval of a certain set of persons [P_1,..., P_n], then it makes only trivial sense to say that these persons are themselves agents who choose the right. For to say that P_1,..., P_n are themselves moral (that they choose the right) is only to say—if the theory is adopted—that they approve of what they approve of.

We can put this probe another way. Suppose Socrates had been a Manichean, that is, had believed that God and the Devil were equally powerful, omniscient, and so on. Then he might have asked the holder of the divine command theory: Why select God and not the Devil to be the arbiter in your theory? (It can't be because God is good.)

In a like manner, we might demand of any approval theorist: Why do you select the group [P_1,..., P_n] and not some other group as the arbiters of right conduct? And you cannot reply that you selected them because they choose the right.

Kant's theory is as subtle as it is famous. I assume that it is familiar to the reader, only stating it here in rough terms. An act is right, this theory goes, iff the maxim under which it falls is such that the agent is both able to will consistently, and is in fact willing, to see it adopted by society as a universal law.

The problems with such a theory are profound. To begin with, the agent may have certain peculiarities which may lead him to will maxims into universal law of an undesirable sort. For instance, a sadomasochist might will "hurt others when you can get away with it" into universal law; a very arrogant man might will "never help others" into universal law.

Moreover, acts can be described in different ways, hence fall under different maxims—some of which may be universalizable, and some of which may not. Thus the act (e.g.) of taking someone else's car may be variously described as "stealing" or as "teaching others not to get too attached to physical objects."

Kant's theory is an approval theory, but where the person who does the approving is the agent himself, or more exactly, a counterpart of the agent, a person exactly like the agent except for having a desire to create universal law.

Viewing Kant's theory as an approval theory allows us to restate the first objections to it thus: Why pick this person (the counterpart of the agent, the agent as universal lawmaker) rather than another as the arbiter of the decision? What reason can be given? (Certainly not that the counterpart agent chooses morally, chooses the right.) And this, we see, is just the Socratic probe.

We finally consider the theory of W.D. Ross. This theory is deontologism with a vengeance, the heart of the theory being the enumeration of an indefinite number of prima facie rules of obligation. One's actual duty is to be determined by examining the situation and those prima facie rules in a manner Ross did not clearly elucidate.

Indeed, this latter feature is the standard objection to the theory: we are given no way to pick our actual duty out from amongst the conflicting and contending prima facie duties. Thus Ross' theory fails the first requirement of a theory—it doesn't tell us which acts are right and which are wrong.

But a second objection can be brought to light if we ask in what way Ross' theory is an approval theory. Ross, after all, focuses almost all his exposition on the delineation of the *prima facie* rules.

However, the notion of an arbiter emerges in his discussion of how the prima facie duties are discovered. Ross held that the "plain man," the average person (and the philosopher who is able to set aside his conditioning, and rely on his common sense), will immediately agree on certain general duties as being self-evident, as needing no proof.

Thus Ross regarded the plain man's moral judgments about prima facie duties in the same way positivist philosophy of science regarded direct observation statements; viz. as being the incorrigible foundations upon which any theory had to build. The arbiters here are in fact the set of plain men, to include the reader if he but stick to his common sense.

Now the Socratic challenge can be posed again: Why choose this group as arbiters? Why say that the common man's opinions are constitutive of the right? (Again, we are forbidden the circular reply, "because his judgments are morally right.")

More precisely, what the common men of a society take as self-evident definitely changes over time. Ross himself, for instance, took it as self-evident that we have a prima facie duty to ensure that wealth is distributed according to merit. But I very much doubt that the ordinary man of today would even regard that position as being true, much less self-evident.

Reviewing what we have said about the divine command theory, Kant's theory and Ross' theory, it is clear that any deontological theory must deal with two problems. First, it must give us some understanding of 'practical reasoning'. That is, it must tell us how we are to arrive at our moral decision on the basis of rules or morality. Kant owes us a description of how we are to describe our contemplated action, and under what maxim it falls. Ross owes us a description of how we are to arrive at the actual duty, given the prima facie duties.

The second problem any deontological theory must address is the Socratic challenge. Given that a deontological theory is an approval theory, a theory which selects some actual or imaginary set of arbiters (whose approval makes our decision morally right or wrong), what justifies our choosing that group as arbiters? This second problem is all the more pressing because it is one that tends, to get overlooked. It is my intention to outline (in what follows) such a theory.

Let us begin by asking what set of arbiters we should choose. Our theory selects as the set of arbiters the set of ideal researchers. That is, we select the set of ideal counterparts of the human race, fictional investigators who are bereft of all motives except for the desire for truth and justice—or more precisely, the truth about what is just. Further, we conceive these counterparts to be blessed (or cursed?) with an infinite life span and have sufficient resources to support their moral inquiries.

That such a group of judges is nonexistent is no more a mark against our theory than is the fact that people don't as a rule seek universal law a mark against Kant's theory, or than is the fact that everybody has been corrupted by at least a little philosophy (so that there are no truly 'plain' men) a mark against Ross' theory.

The reader should note well that this imaginary group (of ideal moral researchers) is the counterpart of the entire human race in its entire history, including the future. The only differences between the imaginary arbiters posited by our theory and the actual human race are that real humans are possessed by a number of drives besides seeking justice (indeed, some lack that desire altogether), and secondly that the real human race will probably manage to make itself extinct, bringing to a rapid end all research, moral and scientific.

To be fair, there is yet another difference between the human race and the arbiters dreamt of in our moral philosophy. Our arbiters are conceived of as continuously existing through an infinite span of time. The human race, even if it manages to survive indefinitely, would still be composed of different individuals as time passed—new persons being born and coming of age of reason, older ones dying off. Since beliefs evolve over time, this means that our arbiters can compare their beliefs at any time with their beliefs at any earlier time. But actual humans are notoriously unable to comprehend the belief systems of earlier people, a phenomenon any historian of science is well acquainted with. The human race (alas) does not have a collective memory; in its stead we have at most feeble written remnants of earlier periods, ill preserved and imperfectly understood.

Having selected our set of arbiters, we must next address the Socratic challenge, why that set and not some other? Perhaps the answer will emerge if we contrast our set of arbiters with the sets posited by other deontological theories. To begin with legalism, we say that that theory chose as arbiters either the actual society of which the agent is a member, or else the set of legislators of that society. But of course the problem is that the moral views of a whole society (and still more of the legislators of that society) may be wrong.

However, in our theory the arbiters are not some members of some particular society in some particular epoch of its history, but rather what that (or any) society would be were it to be composed of ideal researchers inquiring over an indefinite period of time. And the errors of one epoch would eventually be recognized as errors in some later epoch.

Or consider the divine command theory. It posits an omniscient being as the sole arbiter. But there is the problem of conceiving of such a being. (Note that there is no analogous problem for our theory; it is quite easy to imagine people just like ourselves, who always have a goal that we only sometimes have, and who live indefinitely.) Moreover, there is the problem (the original Socratic challenge) of why we would worship (as opposed to merely fear) God if the divine command theory were adopted.

Our theory faces no such problem, because we don't say the arbiters are good, or right, or even that they would be good or right were they to exist. Much less do we worship them—they don't exist anyway, and our theory frankly admits that.

As against Kantianism our theory has merit. The problems with Kantianism we said were twofold. First, Kant's theory does not tell us why the arbiter selected (the counterpart of the agent, i.e., the agent as willing his maxim into universal law) could be depended upon to judge right—he might, after all, be a very strange individual (irrationally overconfident, say, or sadomasochistic). The second problem is that Kant's theory does not tell us how to describe acts and how to decide which of the many maxims under which a given act falls is the one to which we apply the universalizability test.

About the second problem, more will be said later. But as regards the first, note that our theory doesn't face any analogous problem, because our arbiters include the counterparts of everybody who now exists, has ever existed or will in fact exist. Thus we don't have to worry about a strange person who is willing to see a maxim universalized that nobody else would, for it is the interactive judgment of all the arbiters (not just one) which counts.

Finally, reconsider Rossian theory. Again, we saw that there were two basic problems, one Socratic and theoretical, and the other practical. To begin with the former, why assume that the plain men of a given society (or all the people of that society stripped of all philosophic preconceptions) would be right in their judgments? The second problem is that of deciding what our actual duty is among the contending *prima facie* duties.

As before, I defer discussion of the second (the practical) problem until later, when I discuss practical reasoning. About the first, however, we can quite readily show that it does not arise from our own theory. This is because our theory does not concern itself with the moral deliverances of the common sense of any particular epoch in the history of any particular society, but rather with the moral deliverances of the collective common sense of mankind itself—or (to repeat), what mankind would be like were it solely concerned with moral judgments, and could it but live forever.

Having thus compared our theory with the other chief approval theories, we are now in a position to answer the Socratic challenge directly. Why select the set of arbiters we did? Precisely because there is no other set to choose. We can select subsets of this set, as legalism, Kantianism and Rossianism have done, but there is no assurance that the subset will not be quite atypical. The only way to guarantee that the arbiters' various idiosyncrasies are checked, balanced out as it were, is by including all of them in the set.

On the other hand, there is no authority beyond the collective judgment of the ideal counterpart to the human race. For truth—if the notion makes sense at all—is something which the human race could eventually have (or discover.) Not, mind you, 'will have': the human race is in actuality not much interested in truth, scientific or moral, nor will it survive forever. We may collectively never reach the truth on any given matter. But 'the truth' on any given matter must be something that creatures like us, except being more serious and more lasting, could reach collective agreement upon.

Having selected our set of arbiters, we now need an account of what Aristotle and Kant called "practical reasoning." I equate practical reasoning with dialectic—for reasons which will become clear as we go along—and I believe that recent work done in formal dialectic gives us a way to approach these matters.

I beg the reader to put aside any negative connotations he may associate with the term "dialectic." The word surely does smack of turgid Hegelian metaphysics, not to mention sinister Marxist politics. But as I (and a number of other recent writers) use the term, it merely refers to the logical analysis of information-seeking dialogues. That is, formal dialectic is just the study of interactive research reasoning, the dialogues that take place between researchers in a given domain of science.

By way of fleshing out the phrase 'formal dialectic,' let's examine a few of the basic concepts thereof.

Two such notions are fundamental: the notion of a **commitment-store** and the notion of a **rule of procedure**.

We visualize an information-seeking dialogue as the product of a research game in which the goal of the participants is to maximize their information about the subject at hand, to be achieved by obeying certain rules. But research into anything, be it a trivial matter such as (say) the location of an object hidden in a room, or a deep matter such as the structure of subatomic particles, requires that the participants in the game initially share certain beliefs, and change these shared beliefs during the game only in a way jointly agreed upon. People who share absolutely no beliefs couldn't even begin to engage in research.

As the game proceeds, beliefs get added or deleted from the shared belief system, which we call *the commitment-store*. These additions and deletions are governed by certain rules, the investigation of which constitutes the soul and essence of dialectic.

Actually, there are two sorts of rules governing any dialogue/research game. Within any round, i.e., at any point during the dialogue, the participants are governed by the cannons of logic, of course. A participant may not assert something and at the same time assert its negation. If a participant establishes 'α' and 'if α, then β,' he may rightly conclude 'β;' and so on for the other rules of logic.

However, governing the evolution of the rounds are other rules, "logical" only in a very broad sense. These rules, which we term *procedural rules*, can be formulated in terms of what can be added to or deleted from the shared commitment-store. For information-seeking dialogues, such truly dialectical rules include:

- No participant can ask a question which presupposes the denial of anything in the commitment-store.
- A statement may be stored in the commitment-store only if all participants agree to it.
- A statement can be established only by a logical (in the narrow sense) argument, the premises of which must be elements of the commitment-store.
- The same question cannot be raised again after it has been answered.
- If a legitimate question has been raised, the participants must answer it, either on the basis of elements of the commitment-store, or else on the basis of new information jointly agreed upon.

The delineation of all the rules of governing research is a task which will require a considerable amount of scholarly work, and such work is only just getting under way.

But as interesting as formal dialectic is, how does it apply to practical reasoning? After all, formal dialectic analyzes the product dialogues of a number of researchers seeking to maximize information about physical reality. How is that similar to the practical reasoning involved in determining your actual duty in any given situation?

The answer is that practical reasoning is like research reasoning in its goal, structure and character, however dissimilar the content of each. In other words, while interactive research involves reasoning about scientific matters, and practical reasoning involves reasoning about moral matters, the two types of reasoning are similar in those three key aspects.

After all, what is the goal of all practical reasoning? It is to ensure that justice for all be done, to "give every man his due." Ross' key insight serves us well here: a human being is not some kind of moral atom, unrelated to other people (as the egoist has it) except perhaps as neutral beings whose well-being he ought to promote equally (as the utilitarian has it). Rather, a man is part of a web of social relations to others that makes him the unique person he is. He is an atom only to the extent he is bonded to a multiplicity of other atoms.

And Ross is right that out of these relations (teacher to student, mother to daughter, friend to friend, and so on) arise certain *prima facie* duties which it is the function of practical reasoning to reconcile. That is the *raison d'etre* of the moral point of view.

We might note here that results theorists disagree with our thesis about the goal of moral judgments. Results theorists often urge that the institution of making moral judgments about ourselves and other people is just a social institution like any other, and so exists for the same reason that any other social institution exists: to promote the well-being of society.

This objection is fallacious. It confuses the goal of the participants in an institutional activity with the social goal of (or reason for) having that institution and hence is a kind of genetic fallacy. The purpose of the institution as a whole may indeed be (as the results theorist has it) to promote the well-being of society, but the goal of any participant in any particular act of moral decision-making is to judge correctly, which means giving each person involved his due.

This goal, to wit, discovering which action will best give each person his due, is in fact just the goal of discovering the truth of justice. And discovering truth is the goal of scientific research as well.

Similarly, the character of practical reasoning is the same as that of research reasoning: interactive, rather than solitary. We tend to talk to others and seek to bring their past experiences to bear on our present dilemmas. One would no more be able to make a reasonable moral decision without consulting others (or at least reviewing the work of others) than he could do worthwhile scientific research entirely by himself.

The point is entirely general. Both the concept of 'knowledge' and that of 'obligation' are societal notions. I learn what I know from—or at least with the help of—others. And I owe what I owe because of my interactions with others. Moreover, my claims to knowledge of this or that are meaningless unless society eventually honors me (or would eventually honor me) with the credit. And my claims about what I owe (or don't owe) are not my subjective property, but instead must meet the eventual approval of society.

Finally, practical reasoning is similar to research reasoning in that very dialectical structure we examined earlier. In moral reasoning, no less than scientific research, we must begin with some shared beliefs. And we store or delete statements in our shared belief in accordance with shared rules—some logical (in the narrow sense), some procedural. And it is these rules which the scholar ought to analyze.

To gain some insight into practical reasoning, let's examine two mundane cases. The first is an imaginary traffic-court case in which a man accused of speeding has a dialogue with a judge. I talk about this case to bring to the fore certain features of the commitment-store and rules of procedure. (Indeed, it seems to me generally true that legal proceedings are the very epitome of practical reasoning.) I will then look at a dialogue between two salesmen to see how similar features arise in ordinary life.

Case 1: A man S has been cited for speeding near a school. He is contesting the citation, feeling that since the students were all within locked gates, he was justified in travelling at the speed he was.

Initially, the joint commitment-store of S and the judge J contains (among other things) these laws concerning proper speed:

- L_1: Never travel faster than road conditions permit.
- L_2: Unless otherwise posted, the speed limit is 25 mph on all surface streets.
- L_3: Near a school in session the speed limit is 15 mph.

Of course, these laws are all defeasible. One cannot exceed 25 mph on a surface street not otherwise posted; however, if one is bleeding to death and must get to a hospital, or has been ordered to pursue another vehicle by a uniformed officer, or some other such unusual event, the law is defeated.

In addition to the commitment-store, J and S share a lexicon which governs how events may be described. All speeds are given in miles per hour, and that phrase is operationally defined by both speedometer and radar gun. Note that this lexicon can change. For instance, it might be discovered that radar guns are inherently inaccurate, in which case that device would no longer be used to establish vehicular speed.

J and S also share a principle of law (not a law, but a rule governing the application of the laws). Namely, if several speed-limiting laws apply in a given case, one is obliged to travel at the lowest indicated speed. We might then see the following exchange (divided into rounds) take place.

(R_1) J: Where were you when you received the citation?
S: I was cited for speeding driving north on De Soto Avenue, near Sutter Grade School, for doing 25 mph.

(R_2) J: The citation indicates that you measured by radar as going 30 mph.
S: But my speedometer read 25 mph.

(R_3) J: Was there any traffic sign posted?
S: None.

(R_4) J: Was school in session?
S: Yes, but Sutter is one of those new reform schools which lock all the gates during the school day.

Note that in R_1, S attempts to store his statement that he was traveling at 25 mph, but J will not agree to it (in R_2). In R_3 on the other hand, the statement that S wants to store actually does get stored (becomes a 'fact'). This suggests a rule procedure: a statement will be stored in the joint commitment-store if and only if all the participants agree.

(R_5) J: In cases such as this, we normally allow a variance of 5 mph in the accuracy of your speedometer. We shall establish your speed as having been 25 mph, not the 30 that the citation reads.
S: Thank you.

(R_6) J: However, there is ample precedent for denying your claim to exemption from L_3 because the school had locked gates. Several other courts have held that even in such situations, because of the possibility of the children scaling the fences, the 15 mph limit is valid. Fine will accordingly be set on the basis of exceeding the speed limit by 10 mph.
S: Thank you.

In R_5, the key fact of the speed travelled is established (stored). But in R_6, the judgment goes against S anyway, since the facts in his case are seen to be similar to other cases in which L_3 was held to not be defeated. The rule used here is just an inductive rule of analogy—after the facts have been established.

This is a paradigm of practical reasoning. The participants in that dialogue first try to agree on the facts and relevant rules (laws), then search for similar cases that have been decided in a consistent and reasonable manner. Next, consider this dialogue between two car salesmen, A and B.

(R_1) A: My last sale is really eating at me.
B: Why? You sold that guy a turkey nobody else has been able to unload, and the boss was really impressed with your salesmanship.

(R_2) A: Yeah, but the car was a real lemon. That guy has a couple of kids and he needed a better transportation car—but what I talked him into buying is really going to cost him.
B: Look—the guy had eyes. He could see what he was buying.

(R_3) A: Ah, c'mon. I blew so much smoke at him he couldn't tell night from day. Then I took him into the closing tank where Mike and Pat worked him over till he bought the damn thing.

B: Yeah, I see your point. But that's the way any car gets sold. You really have to make the fish bite. No tuna ever volunteers to jump into the boat by himself!

(R_4) A: Oh, I know that. I know that to sell any product you have to manipulate the buyer. But I really stuck this guy...

B: Then I guess what's bugging you is the fact that the car was trash.

(R_5) A: Yeah, that must be it.

B: Maybe you should do what Joe did—start selling news. I mean, if it really bothers you to sell trash, move over to the showroom. They're looking for a good salesman anyway.

(R_6) A: You know, that's not a bad idea. Looks like I owe you a beer.

Here, A and B initially share the belief that the car was a lemon. B attempts (in R_2) to store the statement that the customer knew what he was doing, and hence (presumably) A shouldn't worry about the situation. (This indicates that A and B share a background belief, a rule to the effect that if a person knowingly buys an inferior product, the seller is excused from responsibility.) But A refuses to store B's claim (R_3). A and B then tacitly agree to store the statement, that A manipulated the customer into buying the defective car.

In R_3 and R_4, A and B explicitly agree to store the statement, that manipulation of prospective customers is not wrong. The other feature of the act—that the car was known by A to be defective—begins to dominate the deliberations, prompting B's suggestion that A change over to selling new cars only. (Note that A and B both assume that the new cars the dealership sells are not defective.) Here again, a past case enters into the decision, B's suggestion being based on analogy with "what Joe did."

While A and B have hit upon a resolution of A's moral dilemma, it is only against the shared background beliefs that manipulation of others is not inherently immoral, and that the new cars sold at the dealership where they work are in fact good quality products. A can become more sure of his choice by discussing it with others with a less similar background. To the extent A seeks to expand the dialogue, A approaches more closely the ideal moral arbiters postulated by our theory. He would be seeking to correct any defects in his commitment-store by isolating them in dialogues with others.

Indeed, this sort of dialectical process provides a new way of understanding Kant's notion of making one's moral decisions '*sub specie aeternitatis*.' For to the extent one widens his moral dialogues to include more and more diverse participants, seriously attempting to use their insight to augment his own and their foibles to counterbalance his own, the more likely it is that his decisions would indeed be such that an ideal community would tend to converge to agreement with them. And it is precisely that which constitutes eternal truth.

Permission to reprint courtesy of Springer.
I wish to thank The *Journal of Value Inquiry* as well.

26

"Dialectic and Desiderata"

first appeared in the Journal for Value Inquiry 18: 139–144 (1984)

In a previous issue of this journal I began a sketch of an ethical theory.[1] This ethical theory is broadly pragmaticist in spirit, in that it emphasizes the social nature of moral judgments and decision-making. Specifically, I outlined a theory of the right (a theory of moral obligation) that was deontological in nature, i.e., one that does *not* tie the moral rightness of acts to either the moral nature of the motives of their agents or else to the desirability of their consequences.

Instead, my theory of the right ties the rightness of an act to the approval in the indefinite long run by the set of ideal researchers. By "the set of ideal researchers" I mean the set of counterparts to the human race, imaginary persons who are like actual persons except that they have unlimited time to engage in moral research, are motivated solely by the desire to reach true judgments, and live forever with memory intact.

I then argued that one could be reasonably secure in the correctness of his moral decisions if he made sure to involve as many other people in the dialogues regarding his choices as possible, and made sure to obey the rules of logic and dialectic. The more numerous the participants and the more diverse their backgrounds, the more secure the decision-maker can be that his act is objectively morally correct. All this is governed in practice, of course, by what Peirce called "the economics of research": one simply doesn't have the resources or time to seek out all kinds of people to aid in the dialectical rendering of a judgment about trivial matters.

An important feature of my theory of the right, then, is the equation of practical reasoning with dialectic. (As I indicated in my earlier article, by "dialectic" I only mean the study of information-seeking dialogues such as arise in interactive scientific research.) I equate the two because they have identical goals and character. Practical reasoning is like research reasoning in having truth as its goal, albeit truth about morals rather than about physical nature. They are alike in character because both are interactive rather than solitary. You learn and you judge (decide) only with the help and guidance of others, bringing to bear their relevant experiences on the issue at hand, and using their idiosyncrasies to counterbalance your own.

In this article I want to extend this pragmaticist approach to ethical theory by developing a theory of non-moral worth.

A theory of non-moral worth is a theory about what things a person should desire in life—desire intrinsically rather than merely extrinsically, as ends rather than mere means. A theory of non-moral worth is an answer to the question, "What is happiness?"

Much confusion can be avoided if we reflect upon what sort of state the term "happiness" denotes. I daresay most writers take it to refer to a single mental state (typically, pleasure). But such a view has problems with it. First, it automatically stacks the deck in favor of hedonism, where in fact hedonism is a dubious theory that needs to be argued for. Worse, it seems phenomenologically implausible to suggest that the happy new mother, the happy musician, the happy politician and the happy mystic all share the selfsame mental state.

So what does the term "happiness" refer to? I suggest it denotes a single *behavioral* state—the state of not seeking to change one's life fundamentally even when free to do so. It is that which the happy mother, politician, mystic and so on share. (The clause about being free to change is important, since we wouldn't want to say of a prisoner in a slave-labor camp who despairs of escape that he is happy.)

Viewing happiness as a behavioral state allows us to seriously consider the hypothesis that several quite different mental states can give rise to this single behavioral state, much as several quite different disease organisms (allergens, flu viruses and pneumococcal bacteria) can give rise to the same disease symptoms (coughing, fever and so on).

Let's consider now the most common theory of nonmoral worth, hedonism. *Hedonism* is the view that the only mental state which can give rise to happiness is the sensation of pleasure. While there are many different kinds of experiences that are pleasurable, it is the pleasure-sensation and that alone which makes them intrinsically worthwhile.

The difficulties this view faces can be seen by looking at a problem hedonist theorists themselves debate. If pleasurable experiences are all desirable only because of the attendant pleasure-sensations they create, and if pleasure-sensation is one single determinate mental state, then it follows that the desirability of quite different activities (pushpin and poetry, swilling beer and doing theoretical physics) differ only in the quantity of pleasure-sensation produced. But some hedonists (most notably Mill) feel uneasy about this hardline hedonism, and try to float a softer version of it by distinguishing "qualities" of pleasure.

What such soft-line hedonism amounts to is unclear. We can of course distinguish between the *moral* worth of various pleasure-experiences (saying for instance that sado-masochistic sexual acts are immoral even if pleasurable), but so what? That is not the issue. The hard-line hedonists can reply that the pleasur*e-sensation* is the same irrespective of the moral quality of the pleasure-experience.

The only alternative open to the soft-line hedonist is to distinguish between pleasure-sensations as being irreducibly different types of mental states. And it does seem phenomenologically correct to do so. The pleasure-sensation gotten from sensual experiences (food, drink, perhaps sex) is simply a different mental state from the aesthetic pleasure-sensation involved in (say) listening to music. Indeed, even more phenomenologically accurate is to view sensual-sensations as being a family of more or less closely related mental states. Similarly, we ought to view aesthetic pleasure-sensations as a family of mental states.

We ought to cleave off the family of recreational pleasure-sensations as well. This family consists of the more or less closely related mental states occurring in sports of various sorts; and perhaps the pleasure-sensations involved in solving problems belong in this category.

But now the wall has been breached. For if we come to say (with the soft-line hedonist) that many quite different mental states can give rise to the same behavioral state, why stop with just sensations? After all, there is a doctrine—no less true because of its antiquity—of the tripartite division of the human soul. We have "feelings" in the sense of *sensations*, but we also have "feelings" in the sense of *emotions* and also in the sense of *thoughts.* ("What are your feelings about Reagan's economic policies?")

In accordance with this ancient doctrine, we should ask whether other types of mental states besides sensations play a role in happiness.

Consider first the emotional aspect of man. Could a person be happy who never felt loved? I seriously doubt it. The emotion of love (as contrasted with the sensation of sex) both for others and by others seems clearly to be an intrinsically desirable mental state, i.e., one of those mental states that helps (in a sense explained shortly) create happiness. And we ought to view love as a whole category of intrinsically desirable emotions. The mental states of romantic love for another, nonromantic love for friends, family, and God, as well as the feelings of being loved in various ways by various people, are all slightly different mental states that bear a strong enough family resemblance to each other that they form a category which ought to be distinguished from the other categories of intrinsically desirable feelings delineated earlier (sensual, aesthetic, and recreational pleasure-sensations).

But there are yet other categories of intrinsically desirable emotions as well. Besides desiring love, we also desire some degree of *control.* We naturally seek power over others, responsibility for certain tasks, mastery of certain skills and subjects and so on. To see this, just ask yourself whether a person could really be fully happy as a pampered slave. Again, I doubt it. Eating well, listening to good music, loving and being loved can't suffice to make a slave happy (or more precisely, shouldn't make him happy). He needs to feel free, to feel control over his life and to feel he has some measure of power over others and over his society.

On the other hand, we ought not, in rejecting hedonism, to go to Nietzschean extremes of declaring power to be the only good. The emotion of feeling in control is just one feeling among many that are intrinsically worthwhile.

Again, we should note that "the" emotion of control is really a family of mental states: control of self, power over others, a voice in government, practical mastery of the physical world around us, and such like.

Another category of intrinsically desirable emotions is the category of *recognition.* The rational man should want to include in his life a measure of recognition, admiration and respect by his fellows. (Respect and love are by no means the same emotion.) No child can be happy who is ignored—the reader may verify this for himself by ignoring a small child and observing the result. It is acutely distressing to one's sense of self not to have others recognize him and pay him at least some respect.

Of course, we ought again to avoid philosophic extremism, and resist the view (held by many performers and politicians) that fame is the only desideratum. It is but one among many.

Turning now from the sensational and emotional aspects of the mind to the rational or cognitive, we can again delineate several quite distinct categories of inherently good feelings. (I shall use the term "joy" to mean any intrinsically desirable cognitive mental state, however quaint that term may be.) There are the joys of learning, a family of good feelings of understanding, learning, contemplating, achieving insight, meditation. A totally unexamined life, we would all agree, wouldn't be worth living, no matter how full it was of pleasure, love, fame and power. (To see this, imagine a pampered prince who had all those yet could not understand any features of the world and himself or others.)

The desire for understanding is what leads scientists and philosophers to forgo pleasure in order to inquire into theoretical matters—even without *any* assurance that engineers will eventually find profitable applications for the theories discovered.

Once again, I ask you to avoid the extremist view that knowledge is the sole thing a person should be after in life. A person influenced by Aristotle might argue that we *should* hold such a view, because the only thing that makes man unique among the animals is his rationality. Let us not (as is usually done) focus upon the logical inadequacy of such an argument. What is striking is precisely the factual inaccuracy. Animals differ from men no less in their emotional and sensual limitations than in their cognitive ones.

Consider sex. Even the highest nonhuman primates engage in coitis only when the female is in estrus. Humans are able and generally willing to engage in sex at virtually all times. Similarly, no animal matches man's intense focus on the taste of food, much less has any animal applied even its limited rationality to mixing foods to improve taste.

A similar point can be made regarding emotions. Konrad Lorenz's graylag geese notwithstanding, no animal can match man's ability to love deeply. And few animals are concerned with fame.

The joy of understanding, then, is not the sole desideratum.

Another family of rational joys is the group of feelings of creative expression, those mental states that occur with the act of creating anything beautiful. The feeling of the artist, musician or mathematician when he creates a new form is not the same as the feeling the observer gets when he appreciates the work, the first feeling being a rational joy, the second feeling being an aesthetic sensation. Although nothing prevents the artist from feeling both joy in his act of creation and pleasure from contemplating what he has created, nothing guarantees the artist will feel both—one can, after all, readily imagine a blind artist.

The usual cautions apply here: "the" joy of creation/accomplishment really denotes a family of related feelings, and one ought to avoid the extremist view that all there is to being happy is being creative.

It seems to me that there is one other category of intellectual good feeling: feelings of moral worth. Part of leading a maximally happy life is feeling good about yourself, feeling that you are a basically decent person. Even those most inclined to neglect this aspect of happiness—to wit, businessmen—often adhere to an ideology (libertarianism) which helps them retain their positive moral self-image while maximizing their power, prestige and pleasure. That even businessmen try mightily to maintain their picture of themselves as moral individuals indicates that that feeling is necessary for happiness.

Of course, there are those who carry the search for moral distinction to extremes. Susan Wolf has pointed out that life of a moral saint is not something that a person should seek to lead.[2] From my view the reason is clear: a maximally moral person will likely have a life high in feelings of moral self-esteem, but (since such a life would almost certainly focus on helping others) be noticeably lacking in pleasures, feelings of powers and creativity. We may admire saints in one sense (i.e., view them as leading morally good lives), but we wouldn't want to see anyone we love become one, because when you love someone you want that person to be happy.

I have delineated nine categories of mental states which contribute to happiness, which any rational person should desire intrinsically. But I want to emphasize that there is nothing sacred about the number nine, and that this plan for a theory of non-moral worth can only be implemented by carrying out a detailed phenomenological mapping of the many mental states which people desire intrinsically. Such a detailed map may uncover a number of other broad categories of good feelings beside the nine mentioned above.

More important for us now is the question, how does practical reasoning enter in? It's pretty clear that it has to do with the satisfaction of those nine needs, but in what way?

Practical reasoning enters into choosing personal courses of action aimed at satisfying all nine desiderata first because those desiderata are in principle impossible to reconcile completely, and second because social and psychological conditions constrain the decisions.

That the nine desiderata are theoretically at tension is fairly obvious. To the extent that one seeks power over others, to that extent he will be drawn away from creative accomplishment and moral worth. To the extent he tries to perfect his moral persona, to that extent will he forgo power and pleasure. One of the main reasons for the existence of practical reasoning is to find a course of action which best satisfies desiderata which are inherently mutually at odds.

The second reason for the existence of practical reasoning is the constraints reality imposes upon us in deciding what will make us happiest. It may well be that the life of a successful theoretical physicist is the happiest of all, combining as it does the elements of financial reward (allowing sensual pleasure), close friendships, recreational and aesthetic pleasure in constructing and contemplating theories, the joy of understanding, and the admiration of society. But not everybody has the opportunity to be a theoretical physicist. Most lack the brains, most who have the brains are born into unfavorable social and financial surroundings, and many of those favored by genes and circumstance are hobbled by psychological problems. (Thus while one feels strongly that Einstein must have led a supremely happy life, Newton—an extremely solitary and mentally troubled man—was probably quite unhappy even in his glory.)

So even more than balancing goals that are mutually at tension, practical reasoning involves trying to achieve those goals in the face of (sometimes shifting) constraints: inopportunity, inabilities, social impediments and psychological flaws.

How can we here employ the insight that practical reasoning is interactive dialectic? It is simple enough. We come to realize that the way people should (and usually do) choose courses of action in their unceasing attempt to find happiness is by working with others. We need the help of others for several reasons.

To begin, the essence of practical reasoning—in science, ordinary life or a court of law—is the comparison of the present problem-situation with past precedent. In choosing a course of action (a career, "a lifestyle," or whatever), we want to know of comparable choices made by others and how they turned out (whether the agent was happy afterwards). As an example, many people—myself included—have been influenced in their career choice by observing representatives of various professions, "role-models" in the argot of the psychologist.

Moreover, we need other people to help us see our limitations and come to grips with time. We need the mentor who assures us of our exceptional ability in a field and gives us the confidence to proceed. But we need as well the honest counselor who tells us what we either don't know or won't face—that we are in the wrong line of work, that our abilities are not powerful enough to garner a fair measure of success.

Finally, we need others to point out and (to the extent possible) help correct the psychic impediments to happiness. In matters of the soul no less then the body, self-diagnosis and self-treatment are not likely to succeed.

In the final analysis, our judgments about non-moral worth—like our judgments about moral rightness—must be arbitrated by the set of thinking people in the indefinite long run.

Indeed, we ourselves—whether we achieve happiness or fail miserably in the attempt—provide precedents for others, becoming (as it were) grist for the mill of human decision-making.

Notes

1. "Deontologism and Dialectic," *Journal of Value Inquiry*, Vol. 17, No. 2 (1983): 119–131.
2. "Moral Saints," *Journal of Philosophy*, Vol. 79, No. 8 (1982): 449–439.

Permission to reprint courtesy of Springer.
I wish to thank *The Journal of Value Inquiry* as well.

27

"On the Nonexistence of Computer Ethics"

first appeared in Social Philosophy Today, Vol. 4 (1990), pp. 197–206

So-called "applied philosophy" has been something of a growth industry over the last decade. There has been a rapid proliferation of journals, books, conferences and so on, devoted to medical ethics, animal rights, philosophy of ecology, philosophy of sport, business ethics, and philosophy of sex and love. The most recent addition to this growth industry is "computer ethics". In this paper I will defend the curmudgeonly thesis that there is no such subject as computer ethics. Specifically, it is my view that while computers may, or may not, be of professional interest to epistemologists and metaphysicians, they should be of no particular interest to moral theorists.

Let me draw what I think is the crucial distinction in these matters, viz., a distinction between what is of direct and what is of merely indirect concern to philosophers. I say something is of indirect concern to philosophers if it merely serves as an occasion for philosophic inquiry into what is of direct concern. What is of direct concern is a matter I shall discuss below.

Pretty clearly, anything can be of indirect concern to philosophers, because anything can be an occasion for philosophic thought. The lowly cheeseburger can be an occasion for philosophy, since it might prompt someone to wonder on what basis he knows the bread is nutritious rather than poisonous, and thus to face an issue of direct philosophic interest (to wit, the problem of induction). Similarly, a particularly vivid nightmare might possibly be an occasion for philosophy, and may actually have been the occasion for the *Meditations* of Descartes.

The striking thing to note about things that are merely of indirect interest to philosophy is that while they are sufficient to prompt direct philosophic inquiry, they are never necessary for that inquiry. Returning to our humble cheeseburger, we see that while it may well be the start of my philosophic reflection, a hot dog, a real dog, or a prairie dog would serve as well. What is directly relevant is the problem of induction; what is of only indirect interest is the historical occasion for the inquiry. Dispensability is the mark of indirectness.

I don't mean the distinction between direct and indirect interest to be some kind of profound or absolute distinction. But it is useful enough to help understand the issue at hand. Let's take a clear ease. I trust that not even the trendiest of philosophers would want to see a specialty spring up called "The Philosophy of Automobiles". But why not? The answer clearly has to do with the indirectness of the ways automobiles lead to philosophic inquiry. A car crash which injures people brings up the problem of evil, but so does a boat or a plane crash. A car crash that leaves the driver clinically brain dead brings up the mind/body problem, but so does brain damage caused by falling off a log. Automobiles create pollution which threatens (so it is claimed) the delicate ecosystem, but so does the pollution from power plants and volcanoes. The genuine philosophic issues that arise from the usage of automobiles are only very indirectly related to automobiles.

What, then, is of direct concern to philosophers? To give a precise characterization of that would require considerable meta-philosophical theorization, far beyond what is needed here. Suffice it to say that the traditional concerns of philosophy are clearly, indeed paradigmatically, of direct interest to philosophers. Of direct interest to moral philosophers are the concepts of right, just, good, and virtuous, and the judgments people make concerning the application of those concepts. Typically, the moral philosopher attempts to construct, elaborate, or criticize a theory which captures the broadest range of true judgments in a given domain. Computer ethics (as well as other "applied" ethical disciplines) does not involve broad-based theory construction, and we would do well to consider why.

With those preliminary remarks out of the way, let us turn to the main issue. Are there any aspects of computers that are of reasonable direct interest to moral theorists? Several such aspects have been mentioned: the dangers posed by computers to our privacy; the responsibility or liability of computer programmers for damage caused by their software, along with questions of property rights for software designers; and finally, the threat of dehumanization wrought by computers and (specifically) robots. We need to look closely at each of these to see whether any ethical issues are directly (not merely indirectly) involved. The answer, I will suggest, is no.

Computers and Social Relationships

A number of writers have raised alarms about the possible negative impact of computers upon our social relationships. For instance, Sherry Turkle (in *The Second Self*) has troubled us with descriptions of fanatic hackers, who spend all their waking moments glued to computers and are utterly unable to have normal social intercourse with their fellow beings. And a number of writers have expressed the fear that Computer-Assisted Instruction (CAI) will rob children of the necessary interaction with their teachers and stunt their emotional growth.

I find such concerns hyperbolic and premature. Hackers are like any other people totally absorbed in an avocation or vocation. Scholars often spend *their* waking hours reading and writing books on a tiny area (say, the history of the Trucial States), yet nobody makes a big deal about *that*. Scholars often wind up being socially inept yet manage to get along reasonably well and usefully in society. As for CAI, it has all the earmarks of an educational fad: heavy on hype, light on results. Computers hardly seem likely to replace teachers, despite what the computer magazines say.

But even if the doubts are not exaggerated, my point here is that they are not of direct philosophic interest. Television has had a vastly wider impact on young people, one much more clearly harmful to their social and intellectual (not to mention aesthetic!) growth, but that hardly makes television of direct philosophic importance.

Computers and Privacy

The aspect of computers which is perhaps most frightening to the average person is the threat computers seem to pose to privacy. One indication of the depth of popular interest is the fact that one of the most popular investigative reporters around today, David Burnham, confidante of Serpico and Silkwood, has written a best-selling book on the subject (*The Rise of the Computer State*). We all know that a significant amount of information about us is kept on various computer tapes. It is now possible to track a person's movements by looking at "transaction records" (of phone calls, car and hotel room rentals, meals charged, etc.). TRW and other credit agencies keep track of who pays bills and who does not. The microprocessors in some cars can tell the dealer how many times the car has been driven over the recommended maximum speed or started with warning lights on. Medical records are being computerized.

Again, my reply is twofold: these fears are exaggerated, and in any case that computers are only tangentially involved in the issue of privacy. To begin with, computers can enhance privacy as well as diminish it. Microprocessor-controlled detectors allow us to leave the college library without having to have our brief-cases searched (as was once required). Computerizing records, especially medical records, can dramatically increase their security and hence increase the privacy of the people whose data is contained therein, and even where privacy is diminished, a commensurate gain in other freedoms may result. For instance, computer-controlled equipment for searching passengers may diminish their privacy, but increase their freedom of mobility (by decreasing the chance of hijacking).

But again, suppose computers do indeed threaten privacy and even that they do so in a way not compensated for by gains in other freedoms. What makes that directly relevant to philosophy? It is clearly true that privacy is a philosophic issue. But computers only add one more possible technology to a wide panoply of existing technologies that pose a threat to privacy: radio-transmitting devices (hidden microphones); standard cameras; television cameras; fingerprint files; spy satellites and even spy helicopters; and so on. Here as before, computers are not of direct relevance.

Software Ownership and Liability

Some writers have felt that issues surrounding the ownership of and liability for software are of direct relevance for philosophy. For instance, Johnson and Snapper in their recent anthology *Ethical Issues in the Use of Computers*[1] include sections of readings on responsibility for software errors and property rights of software designers.

But it is very unclear why computers are particularly relevant to the philosophic issues of property rights and responsibility. The usual response from those who believe in computer ethics is to sketch an interesting scenario or two where responsibility for software errors is ill-defined. For example, imagine a case where a team of computer programmers designs a program that controls the administration of radiation to cancer patients and the program has a bug in it which is detected only after a patient has been harmed by an overdose of radiation. Who is to blame (it is asked provocatively): the hospital, the computer company, or the programmer who actually made the design error?

Does answering such a question really directly involve philosophic inquiry? If so, then a similar sort of point could be made about automobiles. Suppose a person buys a car with defectively designed emergency brakes. He parks the car on a hill, and while he is buying a cheeseburger the emergency brakes give way, and the car rolls over a bystander. As before, it is a nice question indeed, who is liable (the owner? car dealer? manufacturer?) But does that mean we should write about "Ethical Issues in the use of Automobiles"? Hardly. The questions in such cases are purely legal ones, which is, of course, not to deny their importance or trickiness. And one notes that many of the selections in the Johnson and Snapper book are from law journals.

A similar point obtains regarding property rights and software. There is very little there of direct philosophic importance, although copyright and patent lawyers have much difficult (and lucrative) work to do. Who owns software designed by a company, and under what conditions should individuals be allowed to copy it? One may ask in reply: who owns the "product" (i.e., the movie) put on a videotape, and under what conditions should they be allowed to copy it? I am not denying that these are economically vital legal questions. I am denying that they are, in any interesting sense, philosophical questions.

Computers and Dehumanization

We all have seen or at least heard about Fritz Lang's classic *Metropolis*, a movie which depicts a totally dehumanized world. We also all have seen any number of movies in which malign computers attempt to take over the planet, from HAL in *2001* to Colossus in *The Forbin Project*. As usual, movies tend to present, in a vivid and exaggerated way, concerns shared by a large portion of the public. Critics have suggested that computers are dehumanizing people, replacing wisdom and judgment by calculation of subjective utilities or whatever. (This is a point made by David Burnham, Joseph Weizenbaum and others).

But again, where is the new philosophy in all of this? It is indeed an interesting question whether man is just a machine, but that question was more occasioned by the Scientific Revolution of the 17th century than by recent computer developments. It is indeed an interesting question whether judgment can be replaced by calculation, but that question was more occasioned by the rise of classical economics and mathematical statistics than by computers. It is indeed an interesting question whether machines are dehumanizing and alienating people, but that question was occasioned more by the industrial revolution than by recent trends in robotics.

A Possible Criticism

I can imagine some readers thinking to themselves, "Jason's set up a straw man here. Of course, computers and computerization aren't themselves of direct philosophic importance; rather, the philosophy of computers is really the use of philosophy to understand the impact of computers on our lives. People trained in academic philosophy have much to add to that discussion." So, for instance, Deborah Johnson (in *Computer Ethics*) attempts to utilize classical theories of moral obligation (e.g., utilitarianism, Kantianism, and so on) to help understand such things as privacy, the status of professional codes of ethics, and so on.

But I am skeptical of this weaker view of computer ethics as well. For it seems to me that the social impact of computers is better studied by social science than philosophy. Consider, for example, the professional codes of ethics of various organizations of computer scientists (such as the Association for Computing Machinery) Such codes contain rules markedly at variance with actual professional practice, such as proscriptions against a consultant over-representing his expertise (whereas, in reality, the consultant who is most modest is least employed!). In Johnson's book, such codes are "justified" by showing that the rules accord with utilitarian and Kantian moral theories. (Oddly enough, no attempt is made to show that those codes accord with the principles of Ethical Egoism!). But does this really help us understand such professional codes? Hardly.

To understand why such codes exist, we must get clear on the purposes they serve—for example, whether the association is promulgating the code of ethics to improve its public image, or achieve higher salaries for its members. But that is an exercise in political science, not moral philosophy. And to understand why such codes should be followed—assuming that they should be followed requires only common moral intuition.

Perhaps it might be said that the role of moral philosophy with regard to professional codes of ethics is to help professionals become more ethical. Under this view, computer ethics (or applied ethics more generally) is rather like psychotherapy or education—a professionally trained ethicist helps his clients become more ethical. But I am skeptical. It seems to me that what inclines a doctor truly to care about his patients, or an engineer/computer specialist sincerely to want his creations to help people, or a salesman genuinely to want to be honest with his customers, is not some professional code of ethics, or advice from Ph.D.'s in philosophy. Instead, it is a set of values either inculcated at an early age (typically in the context of religious training) or else innately present. If those codes of values are present, codes of professional ethics are obvious. If those values are absent, those codes are ineffective.

Conclusion

I fear that the reader may misunderstand what I am saying. Let me point out a few things I am not saying.

First, I am not denying that there is some kind of "computer revolution" going on. The computer is having a significant impact upon society. So has the automobile, television, radio, DDT, penicillin, nuclear weapons, motion pictures, contraceptives, and so on. Whether computers will have the profound impact on society that the printing press or the assembly line have had remains to be seen, however. The point is, though, that not everything of great social importance is of great philosophic importance.

Second, I am not saying that moral theorists should not write essays about the social impact of computers. All men and women of letters should be encouraged to write on whatever topic they feel is important. Just don't call it philosophy, or pretend that training in ethics gives one any special expertise in the legal or social issues surrounding computers.

Third, I don't deny the possibility that computers may be directly relevant to metaphysics and epistemology. I am agnostic on that score. After a great deal of work on the question of whether machines can think, I'm not sure that much has emerged which helps answer the mind/body problem. I suspect—but only suspect—that the question of whether microchips can think is no less puzzling than the question of whether neural tissue can think. And while I suspect research in Artificial Intelligence may have some direct epistemological relevance, that point is not at all clear (as Herbert Dreyfus has argued so vigorously). But whether or not computers are directly relevant to metaphysics and epistemology, they are not directly relevant to moral theory.

One last point is worth noting. A colleague of mine, who specializes in the social impacts of computing, when she heard my skeptical ruminations about computer ethics, replied "Then what is philosophy good for?" That is a fair question, and we would do well to think about it for a moment. For this sort of feeling (that for philosophy to be valuable, it must be applicable to the various realms of daily life) seems to lie behind much of the demand for "applied ethics".

I do not believe that philosophy is valuable only to the extent that it is "relevant". Philosophy has both intrinsic and instrumental value. Intrinsically, it is simply good that we understand our moral judgments, that we organize them and search for deeper principles that underlie them. Theorization in ethics (or philosophy more generally) is no less inherently worthwhile than theorization in natural or social science.

Instrumentally, philosophy has value in a way not understood by those who ask for relevance. Getting clear on how we universalize moral maxims, for example, gives us great insight into human judgment, and that may well be useful in artificial intelligence. That is, Kantian moral theory may be instrumentally valuable irrespective of whether it can be directly "applied" to "justify" some professional code of ethics.

So it is that my skepticism about computer ethics does not grow out of a feeling that ethics as a discipline is useless. It is inherently good and practically useful—but not in the naive way envisioned by people who seek to "apply" it as they would some engineering technique. Philosophy is, in the end, a Humanistic enterprise: it is about understanding, not application.

Notes

1. Johnson, Deborah and John Snapper, *Ethical Issues in the Use of Computers*, Belmont, CA.: Wadsworth Pub. Co., 1985.

Permission to reprint courtesy of The Philosophy Documentation Center. I wish to thank the journal *Social Philosophy Today* as well.

28

My review of: *Libertarianism For and Against*

(Craig Duncan and Tibor R. Machan, Rowman & Littlefield, 2005) first appeared in Liberty, January/February 2008

The book under review is a lively exchange about the merits of libertarian political philosophy between one of its leading exponents, Tibor Machan, and one of its critics, Craig Duncan. Each participant provides an original defense of his political philosophy, then reads the other person's paper and critiques it; then each rebuts the other's critique. This makes the book a model of balance and clarity. It is also a model of civility: the debaters actually address each other in a reasoned and intellectually honest manner.

Its most important virtue, however, is its clear presentation of a host of basic issues that divide libertarians (a variety of "classical liberals") from modern ("progressive") liberals. The multitude and importance of these issues justifies a detailed consideration of the authors' arguments.

Machan starts off the exchange by enunciating his view of libertarianism, which he equates with classical liberalism and finds embodied in the Declaration of Independence. It is a philosophy of minimal government, in distinction to the governments of monarchist, socialist, fascist, and welfare states. He characterizes such states as "top-down" hierarchies seeking to impose their own goals on the citizens, as opposed to the "bottom-up" approach of genuine classically liberal states, in which the only goal of government is to enact laws the people desire;

government is the employee of the people. This view of government stresses the fundamental rights of the Declaration: life, liberty, and the pursuit of happiness (really, just property in Lockean terms). This leads Machan to the Harm Principle: "everyone is authorized to carry on his or her chosen activities and pursue his or her objectives, if doing so does not violate others' rights" (p. 5). Government is restricted to guarding those rights. This is the ideal of civil society: no conquest, oppression, or other coercive means are to be inflicted upon others. The distinction Machan draws is the standard libertarian one between "force" (which can be legitimate if applied to defend citizen rights) and "coercion" (which is, by definition, illegitimate force used to further state goals).

But Machan argues that the rights so important in this view of legitimate political governance do *not* give the notion of "rights" a fundamental priority in political theory. Instead, he views them as "derived from the requirements of the ethics of individuals flourishing within the context of human communities" (8). Here, the libertarian vision is that of a society in which people take care of themselves, forming and using voluntary mediating structures such as families, churches, social clubs, and companies. The government acts as a referee to ensure basic rights by using the courts, police, and military.

Nevertheless, Machan rejects a consequentialist approach to grounding libertarianism, one that regards libertarianism as moral because in a state of maximum (negative) liberty, people are going to make the best choices and the best social consequences will result. His libertarianism is based on respect for human choice, which can be and often is self-destructive. His libertarians reject vice laws, not because they like vice, but because they respect choice—a point one wishes libertarians would make more often.

To the charge that libertarianism involves an atomistic individualism that views human beings as isolated and self-sufficient, Machan replies that it need not do so. He notes that you *can* found individualism on a naturalist view of humans as a species of social animals with rationality as a central attribute, or you can found it on a Christian view that each person is a unique child of God, possessed of innate rights (17). In any event, he argues, individualism accounts for the superiority of free markets over controlled (statist) economic systems.

He draws some libertarian policy implications: government shouldn't regulate business or private conduct unless it demonstrably violates (or threatens to violate) individual rights; granting people "positive rights" (such as the right to health care) violates the real rights ("negative rights") of others and ought to be opposed; redistributionist schemes by government are inherently morally wrong (essentially enslaving some people to benefit others); government affirmative action is also morally wrong; and government should not punish people for using drugs (absent harm to others). Along the way, ironically, he marshals a large number of consequentialist arguments for these policy prescriptions: affirmative action programs increase racial tension and fail to help the very people targeted for help; the War on Drugs has increased organized crime while not helping those with drug problems; and so on.

Duncan begins by noting that he also bases his political philosophy on "respect for human beings' distinctive capacity for choice" (45). He puts forward four basic (and common) objections to libertarianism. The first, which he calls the "unanchored property" objection, is that in reality what a person receives from any market transaction is not just the product of his or her own efforts but is highly dependent upon a governmental structure of supporting institutions and activities (police and court systems, banking insurance, monopoly prevention, government currency, transportation infrastructure, et cetera). All of these morally obligate people to pay for them in taxes.

For Duncan, taxation is not a kind of theft but a cost of doing business. He does think that some kinds of taxation systems can be unfair (too heavy on high-income earners, or too light on them), and we need to be guided by a principle of reciprocity: "there should be at least some rough balance between the benefits one gains and the burdens one shoulders in contributing to society" (47–48). But he gives no specifics about how that rough balance is to be calculated, or who will do the calculation. So what is rightfully yours is what the government leaves you after taxes. Also—an aspect of this critique that Duncan mentions but doesn't explore—to talk about keeping what's yours overlooks the dicey origins of property: "your" farm may be the land that was originally stolen from some native tribe by colonists centuries ago.

Duncan's second objection, which he calls the "inadequate defense of liberty" objection, is that minimal government can't protect people's freedom. The libertarian view allows government to use be treated unfairly. For example, "fair access to economic opportunity will require some system of publicly funded education so that ignorance does not radically reduce the opportunities open to children of poor or negligent parents" (52). But fairness rights aren't open-ended "positive rights" such as a general "right to be made happy," because they deal with equality of opportunity, not equality of result. Duncan says that these fairness rights are fundamental, not just something based upon the consent of the governed.

The third objection, which Duncan calls the "dilemma of consent" objection, applies to the Lockean basis that Machan cites for his libertarianism, i.e., to the notion that a government is legitimate only to the degree to which it is based upon the consent (at least the tacit consent) of the governed. What is consent? Will mere continued residence do? If you don't consent, will you have to leave the country whose laws you do not consent to? As Hume objected, the high cost of emigrating makes this an unrealistic option for most people; and anyway, what if no other country is willing to take you in? (Whether Hume's practical objection is still true in this era of low-cost travel is debatable.) And of course, if consent is the basis of legitimate government, Sweden's welfare state is as legitimate as a purely libertarian one.

"Insufficiency of charity" is the fourth objection. Duncan argues that absent governmental coercion, people will not give enough charity to provide the poor with education, health care, food, energy, and so forth. He bases this argument on some brief historical comments about how bad working conditions were at the start of the industrial revolution: the rich lived very well, while masses of people lived poorly, working (in England) 65-hour work weeks, etc. These conditions were, allegedly, ameliorated only by the rise of the welfare state. (This history is debatable. For example, before the 1930s there was little in the way of a welfare state in America, but people certainly didn't starve en masse—charity did seem to work.)

Duncan offers the standard collective action problems. In a libertarian society free of government coercion, the charitable factory owner who provides safe and comfortable working conditions to his employees will lose out in competition to the Grinchy one who doesn't, because the charitably run factory will have higher costs. Thus there will be (as the cliché holds) a "race to the bottom." Moreover, if we don't force everyone to contribute, we wind up with the "free rider" problem: if the police force (say) is paid for voluntarily, then those who don't pay stand to benefit just as much as those who do, so there will be a diminishing number of voluntary contributors.

Machan doesn't reply to these objections. He begins by noting the obvious, to wit, that most academic political thinkers are egalitarians, not libertarians. He holds that they, including Duncan, take equality to be the core value, whereas libertarians take freedom to be. And he makes the consequentialist point that the result has been an extensive and ever-increasing redistribution of wealth. The rates of progressive taxation are high here and even higher in Europe. (Machan ought to have gone farther and noted the cost in slower growth that this high taxation causes.) He traces the prevalence of egalitarianism in academe to two causes: first, a denial of free will; second, an intuitionist approach to ethics.

Regarding the first, he notes that many philosophers are unsympathetic to the idea that the hard-working entrepreneur deserves his money, because they view that person as just conditioned to be ambitious. Given that, the person doesn't deserve to be rewarded more than other people, who happened to lack those inborn talents or social conditioning. Regarding the second, Machan says that the principle that everyone ought to be rewarded equally is just intuitively "true"—and hastens to add that intuitionism is a dicey basis upon which to base ethical views.

A more serious objection to individualism is that people are not social atoms; they are parts of a larger group, be it a nation, tribe, society, or community, and thus owe loyalty to that group. Socialists such as Marx and communitarians such as Charles Taylor say in effect that classical liberalism rests on a mistaken view of human nature, viz., that of atomistic individualism, the view that human beings can live without any society at all, like solitary animals.

To this Machan replies that communitarians take Aristotle's insight that man is a social animal way too far. He thinks they deny the idea that people are self-governing even while living in groups. Being social doesn't mean that we enjoy (for example) the condition of servitude: "there is an essential individuality to our lives as well, and this requires for our flourishing that we enjoy sovereignty in how we live" (68). That means (here Machan leaps) that it isn't unfair for some to be better off than others. Machan suggests that the expectation of "fairness" may be a socially conditioned impulse—in our affluent society, parents bend over backwards to treat their kids equally.

This strikes me as armchair psychology at its worst. Desire for equal treatment seems innate not just in humans, but in lower primates as well, as experimental psychology has shown. Give one chimp a piece of cucumber, and another a piece of banana, and the chimp given only the cucumber will be very angry. Now, one must hasten to add that not all our innate desires are good; we all innately prefer a diet high in sugar and fat, but that hardly leads to physical flourishing in today's world. However, the psychological desire for equality does seem to be real, and libertarians ought to deal with it.

Machan closes by making a couple of nice points. One is the observation that the mere fact that you don't deserve something doesn't mean that you deserve to have it taken away. Another is that people—often even libertarians—hold the rich in real contempt. About this, Machan is puzzled: it makes sense for the French people to have hated Marie Antoinette, since royalty do nothing to earn their money, and get it by taxing ordinary folk (who in her time were desperately poor); but these days the ultra-rich (e.g., Bill Gates) get their wealth by their own work and have to *pay* huge taxes, while average people are well off in absolute terms, and certainly well off when compared to average people of the past, and typically don't have to pay heavy taxes. Yet Machan should not be puzzled: envy is a constant of human psychology.

In chapter 4, Duncan lays out his case for what he calls "democratic liberalism," i.e., modern (as opposed to classical) liberalism. He contrasts the "wergild" system of feudal England, under which it was a greater crime to kill a king than a nobleman, and a greater crime to kill a nobleman than a serf, with the egalitarian idea that all human beings have equal dignity and worth. This, he avers, is the basis for his political philosophy.

For Duncan, the source of the human dignity arises from our powerful mental capacities and our ability to articulate values and make choices. It is upon this mental capacity that we base our concept of moral responsibility. He notes that his view of politics—based on a respect for dignity and the capacity for rational choice—goes back to the ancient Stoics and was most forcefully articulated by Kant. He then analyzes respect for this capacity for choice as involving three things: not impairing it; not constraining it; and not ignoring it.

By impairing a person's ability to make rational choices, Duncan means crippling his or her mental capacities. This can be done in a myriad of ways, by physically or psychologically abusing people, or terrifying them, or addicting them to some powerful drug. By constraining a person's ability to make rational choices Duncan has in mind such things as physical restrictions (keeping a person locked up in a cell, for example), or threats that incapacitate a person (as when a mugger demands your wallet at the point of a gun). Here the person's dignity isn't reduced so much as thwarted.

The third way of failing to respect people's dignity is treating them as incapable of rational choice. This is "insulting a person's dignity." One way to do it was classically stated by Kant—treating someone as a means, a tool, for your own purposes. Duncan's spin here is that in treating people as means, you are treating them unequally. He points out that we are social animals, meaning that we cooperate to obtain the necessities of life. Society should respect the dignity of its individual members, but this leads to a dilemma: society is necessary for the development of the capacity for choice (hence for human dignity), but society requires rules and sanctions for getting its members to comply, which in turn threaten freedom and equality, and hence human dignity.

Duncan deals with this dilemma as so many modern liberals do, by appealing to John Rawls' "liberal principle of legitimacy." In this view, "the basic rules of society should be chosen so as to create a reasonable balance among the various inevitable threats to human dignity, chief among which are the threats of constraint and insult" (89). So, Duncan says, it is unreasonable to suppose that people will freely adopt constraints on their choices of occupation, spouse, number of children, and so forth, but it is reasonable to suppose that they will adopt "lesser" constraints on income, pollution, driving, etc. This gives him his key opening: he says that choice must be real, which means (to him) that a poor worker faced with options such as "do this or you will be fired" is like a person facing a mugger who demands at gunpoint "your money or your life."

Under this concept of dignity-based liberal democracy, people have civil rights (rights to free expression, association, and so on); personal rights (rights against personal assault, murder, and so on); economic rights (to personal property, to freedom from discrimination); and political rights (voting, due process in legal proceedings, etc.). Restrictions on these rights are allowed when and only when "it would be reasonable to expect free and equal members of society to accept" them (94). Of course, this leaves a lot open to question. Does it mean that members of society must be equal to begin with? Are we talking about all members, or a majority? And do they operate from ignorance, or do we suppose that they are knowledgeable about basic economics, psychology, and history?

But… on to practical proposals. Duncan favors a democracy based on proportional representation, so that smaller parties have an easier chance of being part of the debate and of the legislative process. He does not mention the obvious problems that such democracies face, such as the increased difficulty in forming legislative majorities. He favors publicly funded campaigns, so that big money contributions don't dictate elections, but he doesn't address the major problems of such systems, either. Doesn't denying me the right to contribute all the money I can to defeat a candidate I view as evil count as a denial of free speech, and dignity as well?

In the economic system, Duncan's dignity-based democratic liberalism favors some form of property rights, but not "absolute" ones. He thus predictably focuses not on whether property rights are guarded but on whether people have "adequate opportunity" to shape their lives. This means we must go beyond a system that gives people merely "formal" equality of opportunity to one that requires everyone to be given the opportunity to acquire the skills needed to succeed. Middle-class people should thus pay more in taxes so that inner-city schools can achieve financial equality.

Duncan doesn't consider the option of vouchers, which would give all students an equal share of tax revenues to attend a school of their choice. Even in a poor urban district such as Washington, D.C., this would amount to $14,000 per year per child. And he doesn't offer evidence that there is real underfunding of education in America—indeed, that claim is a progressive shibboleth, as Jay P. Greene shows in his recent book, *Education Myths*.

Besides, as Duncan himself notes, equal funding will hardly equalize education, because differences in genetics, subculture, and family enter in. He notes (103–4) that there have to be "sensible limits" to the ideal of equality. One can just imagine the radical leftist response: then why *not* abolish the private family? And it's unclear how Duncan can reply to this obvious extension of his own principles. One thinks here of Solzhenitsyn's point made decades ago, that contemporary liberal principles of egalitarianism can't resist extension by socialists, and ultimately by communists.

Addressing market outcomes and just deserts, Duncan makes the common leftist point that in our society, your economic reward doesn't just reflect what you "rightly" deserve, or your "contribution to society." Luck is also involved, as well as other people's ideas of your contribution. A pornographer may earn what 20 nurses do. Janitors (as Duncan avers) may be underpaid, while CEOs (whom, Duncan feels, owe their status more to cronyism than to performance) may be overpaid.

Because the market is bad at rewarding people either for their effort or their contribution, and because (as Duncan readily concedes) governments in planned economies have been lousy at setting wages, he suggests that government *help to set morally correct wages.* Further, because "the power that employers have over employees is problematic from the point of view of respect for human dignity" (112), this power needs to be held accountable by a welter of laws prohibiting sexual harassment, ensuring worker safety, and setting a livable minimum wage. (He cites one study that alleges that minimum-wage laws do not increase unemployment, but one doubts that even 1 in 20 economists would agree.) He of course advocates social security, unemployment insurance, health insurance affordable by everyone, and a "maintenance" income for those in poverty. To all of this he adds that we shouldn't micromanage the economy.

He might have considered the effects of the welfare states of Europe, which apply all the programs he advocates—effects such as chronically high unemployment, low economic growth, massive population decline, and lower real wealth. He might also have projected the financial consequences of the entitlement programs we already have, which will, if not reduced, absorb *all* the federal budget within a couple of decades. And he might have investigated libertarian alternatives to safety net programs. Even if we agree that social security is needed, why can't we have the fully privatized system that the Chileans enjoy?

In his rejoinder, Machan accuses Duncan of basing his fundamental concept of equality on his own intuitions. Machan urges that his own version of egalitarianism rests instead on the objective facts of human nature. From this naturalist rather than intuitionist approach, democracy can clearly be seen to threaten liberty. Machan focuses on a particular point: libertarians value freedom, not merely democracy. Yes, complete freedom requires people to be able to choose their leaders, but freedom, liberty, also requires that rights be observed. The fact that the majority of people may vote to renounce liberty doesn't make it just. A country can lose its freedom democratically. (Machan cites the case of Hitler). Indeed, some non-democratic countries are freer than democratic ones: a dictator may allow his subjects substantial liberty, just not the liberty to vote him out. In short, "A free country is one the members of which do not have burdens to which they have not given their full consent imposed on them by others" (133). And by that definition, America is not free. To Machan, the sort of taxation Duncan advocates is just extortion. To fund the legitimate functions of government, only voluntary means—such as user fees, fees on contracts to fund the courts, and perhaps lotteries—ought to be used. Machan doesn't address the free rider problem involved in such taxation.

But Duncan replies with a *tu quoque*, claiming that his theory rests on intuitionism no more than Machan's. Because different natural rights and natural law theories have been offered during the history of philosophy; Machan's is not the only, objective one. Duncan also says that Machan's theory would lead to judicial tyranny—an unusual charge for a modern liberal to make. In a libertarian society, he claims, "libertarianism is not up for debate" (149). No matter how much the people in an ideal libertarian society might want (say) minimum wage laws, those laws would be struck down by the judges. Here Duncan simply begs the question. He assumes that the majority *should* be allowed to pass such laws, which is precisely what Machan denies, because he holds that the majority should not be permitted to violate the rights of the minority.

Duncan concludes by pointing to passages in Jefferson and Paine that he thinks indicate that the Founding Fathers were not libertarians. His case would require a much fuller defense: a couple of quotes are unconvincing, and in any case Paine's views were considerably different from those of the real Founding Fathers.

Here, as elsewhere in this book, one comes away with the feeling that the case laid out on each side is shaky. Let's start with Machan's case for libertarianism. First it seems "too skinny"; it doesn't seem to legitimize enough power structures to enable a society to survive in a world (such as the real world) with other societies that are not equally constrained. It is hard to see how Machan's principles could, for instance, justify having much of a military, or the kind of spy agency that could avert war or terrorism. Machan is also inconsistent in discussing the basis of libertarianism. He bases it now on Lockean rights theory, then on Kantian dignity and respect for free agency, then again as neo-Aristotelian flourishing. He says he is not a consequentialist, but his arguments are often consequentialist in form. As to his attempt to base his libertarianism on the dignity of rational agents, how secure can this foundation be if ultra-statist liberals such as Duncan can also base their view on it? And the natural rights/natural law tradition that Machan occasionally employs can also be used as a foundation for modern statist liberalism, as recently argued by Christopher Wolfe (in "Natural Law Liberalism").

In addition, doesn't basing libertarianism on a Kantian ethic of the dignity of all rational agents downplay the fact that not every person is a rational agent? What does a libertarian do about orphaned children? Rely solely on private charity? I agree that over the history of this country private charity has watched out for the destitute—more than Duncan acknowledges—but if hypothetically there were a shortfall, can the state not act? After all, a dead child cannot exercise rationality. And suppose a person wants to take a drug that destroys rationality itself: doesn't respect for dignity say that we must stop him?

Machan never really addresses Duncan's point about the reality of wealth creation. Suppose I make my fortune in real estate. Are not the institutions of society—fire departments, police departments, well-regulated banks, state-supported infrastructure (sewers, roads, etc.), court systems, and a myriad of others—contributing factors in my success? Can we disaggregate those factors from my own efforts and contributions? Even if many of the functions can be privatized, can they be freed of all governmental supervision?

Finally, Machan, like many other libertarians, appears to believe piously in freedom of the will. But what if we don't have contra-causal free will after all? Does the libertarian approach to political governance then fail? Can we have political libertarianism without metaphysical libertarianism?

Duncan's contemporary (i.e., "progressive"—or, better—statist) liberalism is also shaky. The first problem with his account is one that Machan hits on nicely: if we all have a right to support from others, doesn't this lead to the tyranny of the majority, with the majority voting to support itself by plundering the minority? Duncan tries to put a limit on this with his principle of reciprocity. But don't systems that allow free taxation to equalize opportunity degenerate into an equality of income? Here Duncan faces his own free rider problem: in a democracy where 70% can tax the 30% to pay for everything, the 70% are completely free riders. And his point that such redistribution should be limited by the requirement that the (comparatively and temporarily) wealthy minority get a "rough" balance of return for its lost income is meaningless, since *the balance must be determined by the free riders themselves.* This is not merely an abstract issue: at present, the upper 5% of American income earners pay 57% of all federal income taxes, while the bottom 50% pay a negligible 3%. The economist Gary Shilling estimates that 53% of all Americans now receive much of their income from government. And this is in "capitalist" America—in the European welfare states, this disparity if worse.

Also, Duncan's concept of "desert" is simply too strong. We ought to distinguish positive from negative desert. If I find a diamond, I don't positively deserve it, since I didn't make or earn it, but I negatively deserve it, in that it was I, not someone else, who found it. The fact that I don't positively deserve it doesn't mean that it should be taken from me.

Machan locates another problem with Duncan's argument: there seems to be a contradiction between saying that you respect the dignity of rational agents, but then saying that they are not responsible for their actions or their state of existence. Machan traces this—rather unclearly in my view—to the problem of free will and materialism (compatibilism) (140). I view it instead as resulting from Duncan's inability to face the key fact about modern history: the welfare state that inspires him has created and perpetuated the social problems that distress him. Duncan tosses out a brief comment (116) that, yes, the plight of the poor is sometimes the consequence of their own bad choices, but he afterwards ignores this fact as if it were only a tiny fraction of the problem. I would argue that at this point in American history it is the predominant part of the problem.

Consider the 1960s Great Society welfare programs. Did they not directly cause an explosion of illegitimate births? And is it not clear that the absence of fathers has proven a major factor in the chances of children becoming destitute, criminal, or substance dependent? In Duncan's footnotes I saw many references to Rawls, whose work is the most popular *theoretical* justification for the welfare state, but no reference to the work of the social scientist Charles Murray, whose *empirical* work shows that the effect of these programs was to halt the historical reduction of poverty and make it far more socially catastrophic (see, for example, his masterful book, *Loosing Ground*).

Duncan has the usual one-sided modern liberal view that what I earn is enhanced by the actions of an always benign government. But what about the costs imposed by the government or the harms it causes? For example, if an ob/gyn has his income dramatically cut because of our disgraceful tort system, doesn't that balance out the benefits "given" to him by the state, such as his partially subsidized education? Again, if the government debases the currency, am I not absolved of some of my moral obligation for the good things government delivers?

Considerations like this make determining the degree of reciprocity virtually impossible.

Even worse, Duncan doesn't spell out how the lack of equal opportunity for education and other services is due to "unequal power." Is it really the case that, during the industrial revolution, the poor were *made* poor by the rich or had money *stolen* by the rich, or that the wealth of the rich *prohibited* the poor from becoming wealthy (as in some zero sum game)? You would have a very hard time proving those assertions.

Likewise, Duncan's critique of reward and merit in a capitalist system is very dubious. To begin with, he conflates moral with non-moral goodness. While it is true that the pornographer renders a less morally meritorious service than a nurse, his service may still be desirable in a non-moral way: he provides a type of pleasure. Moreover, Duncan overlooks the difference between "rule" and "act" utilitarianism. It may be that the practice of rewarding people purely on the basis of the free market is generally the best rule to follow, even if in *particular cases* it isn't. He also overlooks the role of pricing as a mechanism of information. The fact that philosophy professors earn dramatically less than engineering professors helps to inform would be philosophers that either there is an over-supply of their profession, or that society has less desire or need for it than it has for other things. (That society may have morally wrong preferences, from Duncan's perspective, is another matter.)

Looking at the presentations of both authors, one feels that finding a secure ethical basis for libertarianism (or for modern liberalism) is still an open question. There is a wide spectrum of ethical theories, from ethical egoism, to utilitarianism, to Existentialism, to Christian agapism, to Kantianism, to Rossianism, to virtue ethics, all of which are arguably compatible with a libertarian social and political philosophy. Political libertarians have often been ethical egoists. But the same Mill who wrote "On Liberty" was a utilitarian. Machan bases his libertarianism mainly on Kantian respect for rational agents, but he notes, you could base it as well on Christian ethics. While the most influential existentialist writer Sartre was as politically leftist as you can get, his philosophy emphasizes the radical freedom of human choice, and so surely could be used as a basis for political libertarianism. Similarly, the multiple rule deontologism of W.D. Ross could easily be used as a basis for a libertarian political philosophy.

But my suspicion is that while these various ethical theories are compatible with social and political libertarianism, and can be used in some sense as bases for the libertarian perspective, the best approach would be one of virtue ethics.

In particular, I have doubts whether appealing to what rational agents would do in a hypothetical state of nature or veil of ignorance is the best way to proceed.

Human beings are not generally exemplars of shining rationality. Never mind that children, adolescents, many of the elderly, and many prime age adults are mentally impaired. Normal adults aren't fully rational, either—as Daniel Kahneman and Amos Tversky demonstrated decades ago, in work for which Kahneman was recently awarded the Nobel Prize in Economics. A more plausible case could be made for the idea that we need to focus on the role that large-scale, centralized, coercive government plays in destroying virtue, and the role that nongovernmental, self-organizing groups play in creating and sustaining it.

Such a "virtue libertarianism" would, I believe, be more biologically realistic than other flavors of libertarian philosophy, some of which—if I may speak with brutal frankness—read as if they were written by perpetual adolescents, people who never married or had children, or were ever likely to. If we are truly naturalist—which we ought to be—we should never forget that humans are evolved hominids, and as far back as we can see they formed families for reproduction and child-rearing, and groups for mutual protection. Libertarians need to take such realities into account as much as they do the debating points of abstract theories, however attractive and inspiring and partially explanatory they may be.

Reprinted by permission of Liberty Magazine.

29

"The Market for Body Parts"

first appeared in Liberty on October 2007

The federal government prohibits the sale (as opposed to the donation) of human organs. Under the National Organ Transplant Act of 1984 (NOTA), it is a felony to give or receive compensation for them. Legalizing sales has been discussed in some circles, but proposals to let people sell their own organs as they see fit do not appear at the top of the list of most discussed issues or anywhere close to the top.

Yet the issue of organ sales (sales of body parts, bone, skin, and tissues of any sort) is becoming ever more urgent. One reason has been noted by Laura Meckler:[1] for many years, organ transplants were rare, dangerous, and costly; and the supply of donated organs from the deceased was enough to cover demand. But now that organ transplants are relatively routine, relatively safe, and covered by many insurance plans, the number of organs available from donor corpses is insufficient. Patients either have to wait or turn to living relatives for donations.

The problem will become more dramatically evident over the next decade, when for the first time in our history elderly people will be upward of a third of our population. And the notoriously narcissistic baby boomers will hardly be squeamish about replacing their faulty organs. Look how many have embraced Botox injections and cosmetic surgery, procedures that have nothing to do with keeping you alive.

So the proposal to legalize organ sales is well worth discussing—but with some care.

Certainly, from the libertarian perspective, there is a compelling moral case for it. Being a free agent means that I control my own body. If my body isn't my property, what is? The idea goes back to one of the founding documents of libertarianism, John Locke's "Second Treatise on Government." Even if you draw the line at suicide, as Locke did, selling a kidney won't kill you, at least in normal cases. This is all the more true if we are talking about my agreeing *while alive* to sell my kidneys *after I am dead.* Another idea that has been influential on libertarianism, the harm principle, enunciated very clearly by John Stuart Mill, tells us that rational people ought to be allowed to do whatever they please, so long as it doesn't harm anyone else. Well, what harm is done to anyone else if I decide to sell Fred one of my kidneys? *Prima facie,* there doesn't seem to be any—indeed, it will likely save Fred's life.

Utilitarian ideas also seem favorable. If I benefit from the money Fred pays me for my kidney, and he is better off, then everyone directly affected by my action benefits. As a rule, allowing organ sales would increase the wealth of the poorer and the longevity of the wealthier. It would obviously encourage more donations of life-giving organs. Consider how many more people would put codicils in their wills allowing the extraction of their body parts upon their demise if the sales money could be passed along to surviving spouses and other heirs.

If the philosophical case seems defensible, add to it a reason drawn from precedent and current practice. People are free to sell their blood, and many regularly supplement their income by doing so. And people are free to *donate* their body parts. If people are rationally capable of and morally entitled to give away their body parts, why can't they profit by the transaction? That is, if my autonomy as thinking, choosing human being allows me to grasp the risk and pain of an operation to give a kidney to my child because I love her, then why not allow me to sell my kidney to a stranger for love of money? Remember that money is typically desired instrumentally as a tool to get other things; it is seldom loved intrinsically for itself. Suppose that the money I get from selling my kidney will be used to help my family—give them, say, better food or a better house or a better education. Is that not also a case of giving my kidney to save my family, albeit indirectly?

Now consider the practical benefits of organ sales. One of the most important of them is that it addresses the shortage of organs available for transplant. Meckler puts the number of living *donors* (usually kidney donors) at about seven thousand a year. Most of them are people who give organs to keep family members alive. Those willing to donate to strangers are much more limited. Several internet sites have been developed to make it easy for willing donors to connect with those who need organs; matchingdonors.com is one example. But the last I checked, there were fewer than four thousand such persons. This is woefully inadequate. One recent estimate is that there are over ninety thousand Americans already waiting for body parts. Other estimates are of seventy thousand waiting for kidney transplants alone. The shortage has several consequences.

To begin with, people die. A few years ago, Brian Doherty estimated that every day, seventeen Americans die waiting for organs. No doubt the figure is higher now. The shortage has also created a black market, with all the unpleasant side effects that it brings. There have been cases in which people have purchased organs of uncertain provenance, only to find out that they were taken from people who died of syphilis or hepatitis B. Finally, the shortage has produced the bizarre result, nicely explored by Kerry Howley,[2] that in this black market, everyone pockets good money except the donors. This is extremely unfair compensation.

Why, then, would anyone object to organ sales? There are three broad reasons: first, worries by medical ethicists about the nature of the choice; second, concerns about the potential for abuse, as suggested by some recent horrific headlines; and third, concerns raised by some religious ethicists about the sanctity of the human body. Let me briefly examine these areas of concern.

You can get an idea of what troubles medical ethicists by looking at an article by Papadimos and Papadimos[3] that opposes allowing women to sell their ova to pay their college tuition. The Papadimos paper raises a number of objections to the practice, objections that apply equally well if not more forcefully to organ sales in general. Ironically, all the objections are considerations of autonomy.

The authors view autonomy as involving "voluntariness, competence, capacity, understanding, and disclosure…" And they feel that decisions to sell ova fail to meet the standards of real autonomy. One of their arguments is that since college students need the money, they are under the influence of the buyers. They are being exploited. Another argument is that the age of the students (typically, twenty to twenty-five) makes their mental capacity questionable and renders suspect their ability to understand risks. As the authors put it:

> Persons may comprehend information, but do not or cannot accept the information. For example, if a twenty year old female is told she has a 1% chance of hemorrhaging, a 1% chance of having a post-operative infection, and a remote chance of death with an egg donation procedure; can she accept this? Can she understand the long-term risk of fertility drugs, including the risk of cancer? This young woman may very well understand these risks, but can she actually accept the fact that she has a remote, yet possible chance of getting cancer or dying?

These theoretical worries strike me as hyperbolic. Again, look at actual practice. We allow young women to take birth control pills and elect for surgery of all sorts, from abortion to cosmetic surgery. All involve significant risk. We allow young men and women to drive cars, not to mention volunteer for combat; this also involves significant risk and with far less disclosure required. As to the idea that the need for money invalidates a person's autonomy, that would seem to disallow any trade of any sort in any economic realm.

Turning next to the potential for abuse of a free market in organs, recent horrific headlines suggest major problems. There have been cases of sophisticated grave robbing. A recent New York case is illustrative:[4] seven funeral home directors pleaded guilty to plundering corpses for body parts. They removed bone, skin, and organs from hundreds of corpses, pocketing millions by selling the tissues to biomed companies. A recent AP report announced the apprehension of a former director of UCLA's Willed Body Program. He was arrested for appropriating parts of the bodies donated for research and selling them to an outside company for tens of thousands of dollars. The owner of the company was also arrested; he had made over a million dollars by reselling those body parts to various hospitals and medical research companies.

News stories have also been generated by the aggressive harvesting of organs by certain authoritarian regimes, most notoriously China. Recent stories—see, for example, Coonan and McNeill[5]—indicate that the Chinese are systematically harvesting organs from executed prisoners and selling them to rich Japanese and Americans, who pay about $50,000 per kidney and $110,000 per liver. This is a significant inflow of foreign currency to a country that executes eight thousand people yearly, more than all other countries combined. Even more ominous are recent reports that China now targets groups it dislikes, such as political dissidents and Falun Gong, for arrest and execution, in part because the trade in human organs is so lucrative. Even more alarming are reports that the organs are being harvested from prisoners who are still alive.[6]

The Chinese government heatedly denies these various reports. China's foreign ministry has conceded using some organs from prisoners but only with prior permission. Its spokesman, Qin Gang, said, "It is a complete falsification, a lie or slander to say that China forcibly takes organs from the people convicted of the death penalty for the purpose of transplanting them." Still, China has announced it will start requiring donors to give permission in writing before allowing transplants. Moreover, this is the same government that denies it has carried out any military buildup, that Tibet was ever an independent nation, and that anyone died at Tiananmen Square. Its credibility is hardly compelling.

But in any case, the danger is clear: allowing an unrestricted market in organs runs the risk of giving incentives to totalitarian regimes to violate people's rights in the most horrible ways. From a tyrannical government's psychopathic point of view, it's a perfect "twofer": it gets rid of annoying groups *and* makes a ton of money.

However, it is easy to draw the wrong conclusion from such claims. I would argue that what is driving people to go to totalitarian regimes or other black markets is precisely the growing unmet demand for organs by people who face certain death if they don't get them. If you don't let these people obtain what they need legally, don't be surprised when they do so illegally.

The third set of concerns—those of religious ethicists—centers on feelings that the body is sacred, not to be tampered with lightly or for base motives. Some people suspect that legalizing organ sales will somehow be like legalizing abortions—it will cheapen life and encourage an ungodly practice.

Again, I find such worries understandable but overblown. There is little comparison between abortion, the killing of a new life-form, and selling an organ, which is someone's existing tissue, for the purpose of moving it to another's body. While many religions hold that the fetus has a soul (at some point in its development), no religion of which I have ever heard views my liver as having a soul. Moreover, abortion is not generally done to save someone's life, whereas that is the whole point of organ transplants.

In any event, why would giving some of your body to save someone else's life defile your body? And if giving it wouldn't defile your body, why would selling it? Even if one believes that giving tissues defiles his body, what gives him the right to impose that view on others who don't share it—and, in so doing, condemn many others to early deaths?

I suspect that the general aversion to a free market in organs –an aversion shared by even some classical liberal economists (such as James Buchanan)—like the general aversion to allowing creative entrepreneurs from amassing billions of dollars and allowing open immigration. Many of our moral intuitions arise from our evolutionary past. We are disposed by our origins as a species to fear the other tribe (hence our atavistic aversion to immigration), to desire that all tribe members get an equal share of the hunt (hence our atavistic aversion to great disparities of wealth), and to avoid touching the dead (hence our aversion to trade in body parts).

While I find the three broad types of concern generally unpersuasive and the theoretical, practical, and moral case for allowing a free market in organs compelling, there are some legitimate issues that must be addressed—in other words, practical problems that must be addressed by some legal mechanism.

One set of problems involves fraud and misrepresentation. If we are going to allow rational people to sell parts of their bodies, there has to be real informed consent. Downplaying the risk and pain would be an attractive ploy for any sales agent: "Look, kid, what's your worry? You have two kidneys, so you won't even miss one of them. We'll pop it out of you—no hassle! Just think of all the cool stuff you can buy with the ten grand we're giving you!"

Another set of problems involves the limits of people's rationality. The reason we wouldn't want to allow a twelve-year-old to sell one of her kidneys is the same reason we don't allow her to drink or have sex: adolescents are not fully capable of making such choices. But what about cases that aren't so clear? What about drug addicts or the clinically depressed or people with early Alzheimer's? We need more than a simple age limit here.

Even more worrisome, in my view, are problems of coercion, problems involving people who are executed to harvest their organs or have their organs stolen after death. Of course, it seems likely that if we were to allow *legal* sales of body parts, the illegal sales would be less attractive since the price would drop. But we still need appropriate safeguards to minimize the chances of theft, fraud, manipulation, and coercion.

My proposal is to allow free trade in organs, with certain tight restrictions. We should begin by requiring that all purchases of body parts be from sellers who are United States citizens. The market could be expanded to sellers from other countries but only on a case-by-case basis and only when we can assure ourselves that the country in which the sellers live is free and has the same controls on the organ trade that we do. And in exchange for seeing legal organ sales within this country, citizens ought to be willing to prohibit fellow citizens from buying transplants from abroad. That would help stop the kind of abuse going on now, with growing numbers of Americans buying organs from corrupt, totalitarian regimes, where organs are obtained at the cost of liberty.

Second, an organ sale must be accompanied by a contract between the buyer and a named seller, be it an individual or a hospital. This contract would have to be drawn up to legal standards, just like an incorporation or will, by a licensed legal practitioner. And it would have to be accompanied by a sworn affidavit by an independent licensed medical professional that the seller of the body parts was an adult, apparently of sound mind, and provided blood tests showing him to be free of the influence of drugs or alcohol at the time of signing. At the time of transplantation, the DNA of any purchased body parts should be verified against the DNA of the seller, as listed on the contract.

Third, the contract would have to be accompanied by a signed statement of disclosure, in which the known risks and health consequences of the procedure, as stated by the AMA, would be listed fully and clearly. The statement would have to be signed by a neutral medical professional, not someone who was a party to the financial transaction. I envision doctors and nurses working pro bono, or being paid by charitable organizations, to apprise sellers of all the consequences of their decisions, without any manipulative sales pitches.

Fourth, when setting age requirements, we should distinguish between sales of organs while the seller is still alive from sales of organs after death. Put the minimum age at eighteen for the latter (perhaps with special provisions for parents who wish to donate the organs of their deceased child) but twenty-one for the former.

Fifth, there should be a requirement that any organ available for purchase be checked by a lab for the presence of HIV, hepatitis viruses, or other dangerous communicable diseases.

Sixth, the sales of all body parts must be completely recorded and available for inspection on the Internet so that the market will be transparent to all interested parties—potential sellers and potential buyers, as well as journalists and other investigators. In this way, sellers and buyers will know the going price for various body parts, and investigators can monitor sales for patterns of abuse. This will make it less likely that a naive or ignorant person can be tricked into selling his organs at some absurdly low price. We require such transparency for other markets, such as cars (for example, sites such as KellyBlueBook.com) and real estate (for example, sites such as Zillow.com), and the organ market would need it even more.

There is a clear and growing need for organs and other tissues. Now there are occasional stories about "cloning organs" (i.e., taking a stem cell from a person and growing, say, a replacement liver from it). Of course, were such a procedure to exist, the whole issue of whether we should permit organ sales would be rendered moot—nobody would pay to buy another's organs if he could get new ones based on his own DNA, which would eliminate the problem of tissue rejection and the need for immunosuppressant medications. But no such procedure seems even remotely close to becoming available, so our choices remain either keeping organ sales illegal or making them legal under practical regulation. The case for the second option is far stronger than for the first.

I think there is growing recognition in DC that something needs to be done soon to solve the shortage of organs created by an ill-considered federal law—Lord, how often do we see the government working at any given time to clean up the damage it caused by its stupid laws of a prior time? Recently, the U.S. House of Representatives passed the Charlie W. Norwood Living Organ Donation Act, which aims to make it easier for donors of kidneys to switch recipients with other donors in cases of biological incompatibility. That is, if I want to donate a kidney to *X*, and Fred wants to donate a kidney to *Y*, and my tissue is incompatible with *X*, but not *Y* (and vice versa for Fred), the law would allow us to switch recipients. That should result in a fair rise in the number of available kidneys, but it will still be way short of what is needed. We need to open up the process fully and make it transparent by repealing the NOTA and crafting more realistic and less atavistically idealistic laws.

Notes

1. Laura Meckler, "The High Price of Keeping Dad Alive," *The Wall Street Journal*, January 20–21, 2007, A1, A12.
2. Kerry Howley, "Who Owns Your Body Parts?" *Reason*, March 2007, pp. 22–31.
3. Thomas Papadimos and Alexa Papadimos, "The Student and the Ovum: The Lack of Autonomy and Informed Consent in Trading Genes for Tuition," *Reproductive Biology and Endocrinology* 2 (2004): 56.
4. Tom Hays, "Seven Plead Guilty in Stolen Body Parts Case," AP, October 18, 2006.
5. Clifford Coonan and David McNeill, "Japan's Rich Buy Organs from Executed Chinese Prisoners," *The Independent*, March 21, 2006.
6. Randi Kaye, "Ailing Americans Seek Chinese Organs," *Anderson Cooper 360 Blog*, June 15, 2006 cnn.com.

30

"The Ethics of Tort Reform"

first appeared in Liberty on June 2008

In this essay I want to advance the view that the American tort system needs reform, and advance it by appealing to several different ethical perspectives. I will briefly sketch out the reforms that appear to be the most ethically reasonable.

Since the institution which we will critique is a branch of law, perhaps the most natural place to start is from the consequentialist one. Specifically, what costs does the quirky American tort law system impose on society?

This question has occurred to almost everyone who has ever run a business, but it is not a question that seems to interest many academic economists or other social scientists. Nor is it of absorbing interest to political leaders. Trial lawyers, who profit mightily from the present system, are also mighty contributors to political campaigns. Indeed, one of the major candidates for the Democratic nomination, John Edwards, made mega-millions from tort cases. It is especially hard for Democratic politicians, who get the majority of trial-lawyer money, to see trial lawyers, not as heroes, but as participants in an institution that (like any other) has socioeconomic costs.

So it is a welcome development that a group of scholars at the Pacific Research Institute have investigated precisely this neglected issue. The PRI is an independently funded free market think tank. The group was headed by distinguished economist Lawrence McQuillan, and included Hovannes Abramyan and Anthony Archie. The McQuillan group has written a solid report on the costs of our tort system, with remarkable findings. The report, entitled "Jackpot Justice: The True Cost of America's Tort System," is downloadable in full from the PRI website.[1]

The document is meticulously researched and extremely detailed. It looks at the various economic costs of lawsuits aimed at giving an injured party compensation for damages suffered through the negligence of another ("tort" is French for "wrong"). The study focuses on class actions, medical malpractice suits, and product liability suits. It aims, in the investigators' words, to provide "a conservative first approximation of the total costs, both direct and indirect, as well as the total excess costs of the U.S. tort system."[2]

The McQuillan group is not attacking tort law itself. It stipulates that a good tort system is essential to the free market, because it helps ensure that businesses take care to make safe products and refrain from harming the environment and that people who are truly harmed by some trade or industry—as inevitably happens in any economic system—are appropriately compensated. When critics of the tort system miss this point, their prose turns into mere lawyer bashing, complete with the line from *Henry VI*: "The first thing we do, let's kill all the lawyers."

Yet a bad tort system is a burdensome tax on the economy, killing jobs, lowering income, and increasing prices. Additionally, it exacts opportunity costs: every nickel a company has to plow into fighting lawsuits is a nickel less that it can plow into research and development, higher salaries for its employees, or lower costs for consumers. And to the extent that America has an unnecessarily burdensome tort system it will be at a disadvantage in the global economy.

The authors find that the direct and indirect cost of the current tort system was, in 2006, an astonishing $865 billion: "To put the annual social cost of the U.S. tort system into perspective, it is equivalent to an 8% tax on consumption, a 13% tax on wages, the combined annual output of all six New England states… The annual price tag, or 'tort tax,' for a family of four in terms of costs and foregone benefits is $9,827."[3]

In comparison with other industrialized nations—which seem to be protecting their consumers well enough—the U.S. tort system is grossly excessive. We spend 2.2% of our GDP on direct tort expenses; the other advanced nations spend 0.9%. That 1.3% difference suggests that as much as 59% of U.S. tort costs are excessive. This means that about $589 billion annually is drained uselessly from the American economy—about $7,850 per family of four.

The McQuillan group unfortunately does not compare the number of lawyers in the United States to those in other industrialized nations. Back in 2000, the *Economist* pointed out that the United States had 281 lawyers for every 100,000 people, versus 94 for Britain, 33 for France, and only 7 for Japan;[4] and the percentage of lawyers in the United States has increased even more since then.

Along these lines, in a now-classic study done in 1992,[5] economist Stephen Magee, using international data sets comparing growth rates and relative numbers of lawyers as a percentage of white-collar workers, concluded that there was an optimum of the percentage of lawyers in a population. Too many lawyers hurt the economy, *as do too few.* By his estimate, the United States had something like 40% too many lawyers.

It's a depressing subject. The McQuillan group does its best to leaven dry economic analysis with illustrations of crazy tort actions, but these tend to be depressing too. In one case, a small pharmacy owner was sued in a class action against a diet drug (fen-phen) that had been approved by the FDA and was sold by the pharmacy only by prescription. The lawyers targeted the small pharmacy because it was in a county known to be "plaintiff-friendly," even though the drug maker was located in an entirely different state. The stress of the legal shark attack apparently induced a heart attack in the owner, killing him. His wife subsequently had to sell the pharmacy they had built. She was sued over a hundred times before the sharks had their fill.

And these things don't stop. Since the report was issued, several even more egregious examples of tort law abuse have made the headlines. For instance, there is an administrative law judge by the name of Roy Pearson, who sued his dry cleaners for fifty-four *million bucks* for losing his pants. He also lost his case, but he plans to appeal, putting the defendants (Soo and Jin Chung) through a living hell.

In another big news story, William Lerach, one of the most famous and successful class-action lawyers in the country, pleaded guilty to several felonies for his role in bribing people to become plaintiffs in big-buck lawsuits.[6] Lerach won billions by suing major corporations, including AT&T, Enron, Lucent, Microsoft, and Prudential Insurance. His firm, Milberg Weiss, had paid over $11 million in kickbacks to get people to be plaintiffs in lawsuits that netted the firm over $250 million. (Lerach will do only one or two years, alas, but will have to disgorge the better part of $8 million. Other partners in the firm have been charged, including cofounder Melvyn Weiss, who faces up to forty years in jail.)

A third case of trial lawyers gone wild occurred recently in Kentucky.[7] Three tort lawyers—Shirley Cunningham Jr., William Gallion, and Melbourne Mills Jr.—got a settlement (in 2001) for a group of 440 consumers who had purchased a diet drug containing fen-phen. The settlement was for $200 million, from which the attorneys were to collect a third for their contingency fees. The lawyers kept $106 million for themselves and put another $20 million into a charity that they set up. So the plaintiffs got $74 million rather than the $132 million they were due. The judge who presided over the original settlement, Judge Bamburger, retired in 2004 and was promptly appointed director of that selfsame charity, at a hefty salary. Complaints by the plaintiffs led to a federal investigation, and the lawyers have all been indicted. The federal judge overseeing the case has even jailed them as flight risks. And the plaintiffs are suing to get the rest of the money. The Kentucky Bar Association has yet to disbar the crooks.

In a fourth recent case, Mississippi tort-meister Dickie Scruggs (an apt moniker, indeed) was indicted for attempting to bribe a judge, presiding circuit court Judge Henry Lackey.[8] Scruggs' law firm had obtained massive settlements from insurance companies for Katrina victims, and Scruggs fell into a dispute with another attorney in the firm (John Griffin Jones) about how to divide the $26.5 million in attorneys' fees. The *Jones v. Scruggs* suit was due to be heard by Judge Lackey.

According to the indictment, Scruggs sent an emissary (an outside attorney named Timothy Balducci) to offer a bribe to Judge Lackey. Lackey, however, refused to fulfill the promise of his name and went to the FBI. Working undercover and likely wearing a wire, he agreed to take a $40,000 bribe. Balducci then allegedly handed over $20,000 in cash up front and the rest later on. Scruggs and his four cohorts—lawyers all, remember—face thirty years in prison.

If you want to read other outrageous cases, the estimable American Tort Reform Association has a page on its website[9] listing some of the more ludicrous ones. It also has a downloadable annual report on the areas of the country that have the worst record of judicial rulings in tort cases. These are called, appropriately enough, Judicial Hellholes.

To return, however, to the McQuillan study, as useful as it is, it does not include the costs of other areas of civil law, such as employment, securities, the Americans with Disabilities Act, or contract lawsuits. So the study's "conservative first approximation" of the total costs of our tort system is very conservative indeed.

More importantly from the philosophic point of view, the study explores only the utilitarian (or more broadly) consequentialist case against tort law abuse. That case is fairly obvious, so long as one does not suffer from any of the biases listed above. Yet there are also ethical perspectives to be invoked.

Begin with the Kantian perspective—the injunction to treat people as ends, not as mere means to our own ends. That would surely rule out suing someone (or some company) not because he actually harmed you, but because you can convince a jury that he did and thereby take his assets. It would also rule out the "deep pockets" strategy employed by not a few trial attorneys, that of suing persons or companies that were only tangentially involved in a tort and truly blameless of the harm, simply because they have more assets or because they are located in a jurisdiction favorable to trial attorneys. And it would rule out juries' occasional practice of awarding damages to a plaintiff not because he was really harmed by the defendant but because the jury felt sorry for him and viewed the defendant (a large corporation, typically) as having the resources to help him. Such a Robin Hood approach clearly treats wealthy defendants as if they were cows to be milked.

There is also the natural rights perspective. If all people have unalienable rights, surely they have the right to be free from harassment by other people, from having their property wrongfully taken, and from having their privacy violated by unjust legal actions.

Finally, the recently regnant "virtue ethics" perspective would encourage us to look at the role of institutions in building or destroying character. From such a perspective, one must view with alarm a tort system so loose that it encourages people to steal legally from others. Ironically, it has been economists rather than moral philosophers who have been most aware of the moral hazards (especially rent-seeking) that come from a loose tort system. Moral hazard (in philosophic terms) is making people vicious by offering them perverse incentives to become so.

In sum, a number of consilient moral considerations argue for systematic tort reform.

The McQuillan study does not suggest how this might happen, though several approaches come to mind. I want to start, however, by reviewing some ideas for controlling tort abuse with which I do not agree. One is the general idea of limiting what people can gain from lawsuits, with an eye to lowering incentives for them to file frivolous ones.

We could cap noneconomic damages (awards for pain and suffering over and above economic loss). There is some evidence that noneconomic damage caps work to curtail tort abuse. For example, a recent article in the *Investor's Business Daily*[10] shows that since Texas, four years ago, passed a state constitutional amendment capping noneconomic damages in medical malpractice cases, it has seen a 21% drop in medical malpractice insurance premiums. This, of course, helps health care consumers (a.k.a. patients) in two ways.

Directly, it lowers doctors' charges since any health care provider builds insurance costs into the price of services. Indirectly, in Texas it has led to a flood of doctors moving from states that have runaway tort systems. Since awards were capped in 2003, applications for medical licenses have skyrocketed, from 8,391 in the four years before the cap was passed, to 10,878 in the four years since.[11]

Nevertheless, capping noneconomic damage awards is less appealing than some other approaches. For one thing, it limits the freedom of juries to address a proven harm as they see fit. While individual juries can behave irresponsibly, we still have to judge the institution as a whole.

Moreover, while the function of the tort system is primarily to compensate, "make whole," the person injured, that is not its sole function. In some unusual cases (say, where people are permanently disabled or disfigured through extreme recklessness), punitive damages may well be just, both to punish the defendant and to deter future recklessness by others. In this regard, we should note that since 2003, Texas has witnessed a rise in investigations of doctors (up by 40%), complaints by patients (up by 25%), and disciplinary actions against doctors (up by 8%), though this could also be caused by closer regulatory scrutiny.[12]

We can agree that the punitive function should be kept strictly for egregious cases, not for ordinary negligence, but it seems legitimate in theory. There is recklessness that does not rise to the level of outright criminality. In fact, courts tend to peg the amount of punitive damages to the actual damages suffered by the plaintiff, and they require a greater burden of proof for punitive as opposed to other damages.

A second approach is to limit or even prohibit contingent fees, fees that lawyers get only if they win a suit. Contingent fees are not allowed in most European courts and were not permitted in early America. Yet this again is an approach I do not favor, for the same reasons that the American legal system eventually decided against it.

We should be reluctant to tell autonomous agents engaged in negotiating a price for some service what they must agree to. The practice obviously violates their rights to negotiate freely. More specifically, there are some cases in which a person who has truly been harmed could not afford a lawyer, if a contingent fee arrangement were not available.

Besides attempting to limit awards for damages or fees for trial lawyers, reformers have suggested that we simply eliminate the jury system for tort cases and rely on the judges instead. This is the norm in Europe and makes a certain amount of sense. After all, judges are trained in law and are (arguably, at least) less susceptible than juries to the irrelevant emotional appeals and flowery rhetoric—especially class warfare rhetoric—that trial lawyers too often dish out.

But trial by jury in common law suits of over $20 is guaranteed by the Seventh Amendment to the United States Constitution, so at least at the federal level the change would be practically impossible to make. And I think the reasons for putting that right into the Constitution still apply. Not only are juries a check on the power of government but, except in a headline-grabbing minority of cases, jurors also tend to be reasonable. I don't think they are the core of the problem.

My preference is for a number of other approaches, some rather narrow and one very broad, that focus on making the tort procedures themselves (as opposed to the lawyers and jurors who work under the procedures) more rational and fair.

To begin with the narrower approaches, we first need to pass laws that limit liability for torts to agents who have the main direct causal role in the tort. (These laws to limit tort exposure will likely have to be industry-specific). Dragging into lawsuits people who had no real hand in the commission of the harm surely violates their rights. Remember the case of the pharmacist who was sued for selling an FDA-approved drug. Since the pharmacist didn't manufacture or prescribe the drug, he should have been held legally harmless in the matter. Pharmacists should be responsible for torts that occur in the normal specific practice of their business, such as mistakes in filling prescriptions or selling drugs that are past their declared shelf life, not for things they weren't involved in, such as the manufacturing of the drugs they sell.

For this reason I support attempts to hold gun manufacturers liable only for damages that occur from defects in their products (such as guns that can explode when fired), as opposed to liability for the wrongful use of their products (such as the use of guns in criminal activities, unless the manufacturer had knowledge that the person buying a gun was criminal or mentally incompetent).

Second, a number of states (such as California) have enacted statutes that require compulsory arbitration in certain cases, and many contracts (especially for medical, legal, and other professional services) already contain arbitration clauses. But we need to get creative in setting up even more venues for compulsory arbitration.

Third, we need to follow a suggestion by Peter Huber, who argues in *Galileo's Revenge: Junk Science in the Courtroom*[13] that the dropping of the Frye rule about the "general acceptance" of professional ideas has led to a proliferation of dubious cases in which clearly bogus science was allowed into the courtroom. For example, the aforementioned John Edwards won a lot of money from convincing juries that obstetricians caused cerebral palsy in the infants they delivered by failing to perform caesarian sections, a claim the vast majority of medical scientists would view as pseudoscience.

I will be brief, referring the reader to Huber's fine book for further details. In 1923 a federal appellate court ruled that expert testimony would be allowed in a trial only if the testimony was based on theories and methods generally accepted by practitioners in the field. However, in 1975 this rule was weakened at the federal level, and in 1993, the U.S. Supreme Court (in *Daubert v. Merrel Dow*) rejected it and put in its place a requirement for independent judicial review of the scientific testimony. But absent the Frye rule or some other tight standards, judges (who are trained in the law but typically not in science or statistics) and juries (who are ordinary folk, not trained scientists from relevant disciplines) are put in the position of having to decide which scientific theories and practices are scientifically correct.

Fourth, we need to require that any person filing a lawsuit must actually have been harmed by the person or company he is intending to sue. Believe it or not, there are some states (such as my beloved state of California) that actually allow attorneys to sue companies for various consumer law or other infractions (such as infractions of ADA codes) despite the absence of an actual consumer even alleging harm. A recent case became notorious for this—a legal firm sent its employees out to various small businesses, studying the width of parking stalls, the accessibility of bathrooms, etc. The firm then filed hundreds of lawsuits against the businesses, usually settling for roughly what it would have cost them to contest the cases in court. This firm was living parasitically upon the small business community, and living well.

Fifth, we need sharp limitations on discovery during the early phases of the tort complaint. Allowing the plaintiff's attorney freedom to trawl through a defendant's records, searching for anything that might be damaging, is an invitation to frivolity and injustice. Most other legal systems in the industrialized world limit discovery to what is reasonably relevant to the alleged tort.

Sixth, and more broadly, we should move to the system of "loser-pays." Under this system—sometimes called "fee-shifting," and sometimes "the English Rule," although it is the norm throughout Europe—if Jones sues Smith for any reason and loses, Jones has to pay Smith's legal fees. This would be a constant guard against frivolous lawsuits, such as the infamous $54 million lost-trousers action.

From the ethical point of view, the loser-pays rule seems imperative. We need to remember that every frivolous lawsuit against an innocent person or company is itself a tort. It causes stress, a kind of pain and suffering for the wrongfully sued person. It often hurts the reputation of the person sued, potentially causing a large loss of income. (Indeed, precisely because being sued often results in tremendous amounts of bad publicity, lawyers are often able to extort money from public corporations.) The time and trouble of putting up a defense is an opportunity cost, because that time could be spent more profitably elsewhere. Worse, even if the victim prevails, he still typically pays his own legal fees, which complete the punishment of the innocent.

Let's return to the Kantian perspective for a moment. Kant had a second formulation for his ethical theory, one he termed the categorical imperative. I view this theory as essentially a demand for consistency in ethical reasoning. In his formulation, we should act under those, and only those, rules that we could will to be universally adopted. This is (as often noted) an abstract formulation of the Golden Rule: do unto others as you would have them do unto you.

Well, what are the reasons typically given for the tort system? That it makes people who have been harmed whole (i.e., compensates them fairly for their loss), that it acts as a deterrent to negligence or reckless behavior, that it helps to motivate those who have caused harm to negotiate in good faith with those they have harmed (or face a lawsuit).

If consistency has any meaning, these reasons should apply to the tort system itself.

If one reason for a rightful tort case is to compensate the victim appropriately, then in a wrongful tort case the victim (the defendant) should be compensated appropriately. He or she has lost money in legal fees, and so having the plaintiff reimburse those fees would make the defendant whole.

If we accept the need to deter negligence and recklessness, then we also need to deter lawyers from carelessness or, worse, in bringing lawsuits. The loser-pays system would be such a deterrent. Why suppose that the tort law business needs any less deterrence against malfeasance or negligence than any other business? I don't believe that lawyers on average are any more prone to unethical behavior than (say) people in the housing industry, but it beggars the imagination to suppose that they are less so.

And if we agree that the threat of a tort lawsuit can motivate those who have caused harm to negotiate fair compensation for those whom they have harmed, then consistency should tell us that the threat of having to pay the defendant's legal fees, as well as one's own, should one lose, will encourage plaintiffs to seek reasonable settlements first or accept binding arbitration to begin with.

That loser-pays is a moral imperative becomes even clearer when you reflect upon the fact that in a tort case, the level of proof is only "the preponderance of evidence," nothing near the high standard of "proof beyond all reasonable doubt" that is required in criminal trials.

I would anticipate a few objections to the loser-pays system but none that strike me as morally compelling.

One is the objection that if we move to a loser-pays system, the average person harmed by defective products will not be able to get legal representation at all, because his attorney will be up against a huge team of lawyers for the evil Big Business that produced the defective product.

But the counterarguments are as obvious as they are numerous. To begin with, scaring off potential plaintiffs who have weak or frivolous cases is the whole idea. Next, most business in America is small- to medium-sized business, so in most cases where someone is genuinely harmed by a defective product or service, the legal representation will be roughly equal. In cases of genuine harm caused by truly big business, other plaintiffs could join in a class-action lawsuit. Finally, the management of any business that has to employ a large team of lawyers to face a plaintiff in the loser-pays system will have motivation to enter into settlement negotiations in good faith. After all, it faces huge legal bills just from its own lawyers, and it knows that the plaintiff and plaintiff's counsel are, almost surely, sincerely convinced that they have enough evidence to prevail.

Another objection is the contrary argument: under loser-pays, poor plaintiffs will be more inclined to sue, knowing that they have nothing to lose, whereas the other side does have something to lose.

This is weak. Under the current system, that's precisely what we have for everyone: nothing to lose! More importantly, while any poor plaintiff inclined to a frivolous lawsuit has nothing to lose, his attorney certainly does.

A third objection: what about cases in which a person is harmed by a product or service, not by negligence but by mere bad luck? That is, what about harms for which the company that produced the product or rendered the service was in no way really negligent and in no way could have foreseen the harm but still caused it? If such consumers can't collect from the company, aren't they forced to pay for their own medical bills? Is that just? And what about people who can't pay medical bills at all?

My reply is that the vast majority of people have health, auto, home, and other insurance for just this reason: to protect against what are, in effect, the acts of nature. And if I am harmed by a product that I chose to buy, a product that was not negligently designed or produced, and turned out to harm me through no fault of the producer, it is as if an act of nature caused the harm.

But what about all those people who can't afford health and accident insurance? Well, the pricing and financing of health care is a serious social problem (and the topic for another essay), but social problems require social solutions. In the meantime, it is simply unjust to allow juries to force an innocent party to pay.

It is worth reiterating that one U.S. state and virtually all the major nations in Europe already have the loser-pays system. Yet I must admit honestly that getting it enacted into law in this country is a daunting task.

There are two major barriers.

The first is the power of the chief rent-seekers in this field, the trial lawyers. They are articulate, skilled in using the law to their own ends, well-connected politically, and in danger of losing a great deal of income if reform triumphs. This power explains why only one state (Alaska) has enacted loser-pays (although Oklahoma and Oregon both have some form of loser-pays in a few areas of their tort systems).

The second is that tort reform needs to be passed on both the state and the federal level, because the U.S. Congress—under the Erie doctrine—has limited power to mandate state court rules and procedures.[14]

Any meaningful, just tort reform will face a long struggle, state by state and nationally. Is it worth it? Yes, it is.

Notes

1. www.pacificresearch.org.
2. Op. cit., x.
3. Op. cit., xii.
4. *The Economist* (December 16, 2000): 35.
5. Stephen P. Magee, "The Optimum Number of Lawyers: A Reply to Epp," Law & Social Inquiry 17 (Autumn 1992): 667–93. This article is downloadable from the website jstor.org.
6. AP report in the *Orange County Register* (Oct. 30, 2007). See also the AP report in the *Orange County Register* (Sept. 19, 2007).
7. "Kentucky Trial Derby," *The Wall Street Journal*, August 20, 2007.
8. "The Trial Bar on Trial," the *Wall Street Journal* (Nov. 30, 2007).
9. www.atra.org.
10. "The Doctors Are In," *Investor's Business Daily* (July 13, 2007).
11. Ralph Blumenthal, "More Doctors in Texas After Malpractice Caps," *The New York Times*, October 5, 2007.
12. Blumenthal, *op. cit.,* 2.
13. Peter Huber, *Galileo's Revenge: Junk Science in the Courtroom* (New York: Basic Books, 1991).
14. The Erie Doctrine originated in a 1938 Supreme Court decision, written by Judge Louis Brandeis, which requires federal courts to follow the state common law when deciding issues concerning that state's law.

31

"The Ethics of Closed Shops"

first appeared in Liberty on January 2009

Defining terms

While the Taft-Hartley Act of 1947 outlawed "closed shops," it allowed two closely related entities: "union shops" and "agency shops." A union shop is a workplace in which all new hires are required to join the union (usually after a short period of time), and the company is required to fire any employee who refuses to pay dues (though not employees kicked out of the union for other reasons). An agency shop is a workplace in which new hires are not required to join the union but *are* required to pay union dues. The comments in this essay apply generally to union and agency shops as well as to Taft-Hartley "closed shops."

The essay

In American parlance, a closed shop is one in which a union has a contract with an employer requiring all employees to be union members. Although this is, strictly speaking, a private contract, various forms of the closed shop are sanctioned by law; and the two big political parties constantly squabble over the laws surrounding these entities.

From the natural rights view, closed shops clearly require justification, because they seem at least a prima facie violation of freedom of association. If people want to unionize and collectively bargain a contract with management, that is their right. But why should they be allowed to force others to join them?

Several arguments are offered to justify closed shops. The first two are broadly consequentialist while the third takes more of a natural rights course. We can call them the free-rider argument, the unequal power argument, and the freedom to contract argument.

The free-rider argument, such as found, for example, in Joseph DesJardins' *An Introduction to Business Ethics*,[1] holds that employees who join a unionized company without joining the union are free riders. They are reaping the benefits of collective bargaining—presumably, higher wages and better benefits than they could get on their own—without paying their dues, literally and figuratively. This, on the face of it, appears unfair. As DesJardins puts it:

> If one receives benefits from a process that entails costs, it seems only fair that you share the costs. Especially if there is evidence that workers would receive lower wages and benefits without the union, mandatory union membership allocates the benefits and burdens of union membership in a fair and equal manner.[2]

Proponents of this argument often cite statistics to buttress the claim that unions are able to negotiate better contracts. Twenty-two states are "right to work" states (i.e., they have laws prohibiting closed [and union] shops). The U.S. Department of Labor statistics are often cited to show that workers in right-to-work states earn less than workers in union-shop states (4% was the figure given by the Economic Policy Institute in 2001, controlling for differences in living costs) and that they also have more workplace fatalities.

But the free-rider argument is unconvincing for a number of reasons. First, it is unclear why I should consider myself obligated to share the costs of some process that benefits me if I don't want to be a part of that process. Suppose I live in a crime-plagued neighborhood and some of my neighbors form a vigilante group that kidnaps gang members and lynches them. Even if it does lower crime, thus benefiting me, why am I obligated to support it, when I consider its actions reprehensible?

Second, the free-rider argument applies, at best, only to the average worker. What about workers who are exceptionally talented, well-educated, or hardworking? Such people might well be able to get a better contract on their own.

Third, and more generally, what compelling evidence is there that unions *always* negotiate the best contracts? It may well be true that unions historically have often gotten higher wages and better benefits, but they have also, in many cases, put companies out of business because they saddled them with such high labor costs that they couldn't survive competition or forced them to close under the pressure of a prolonged strike. Workers may get more short-term benefits but at the cost of long-term security. So if workers can be compelled to pay dues to a union under the theory that the union gives them benefits, shouldn't a union be compelled to pay workers when its actions cost them their jobs or other things they value?

The comparative data are interesting on this point. For example, Census Bureau statistics indicate that during the period of 1982–2001, the number of manufacturing companies grew by 7% in right-to-work states while shrinking by 4.9% in union-shop states. Moreover, data from the Department of Commerce (Bureau of Economic Analysis) indicate that during the period of 1993–2003, real personal income grew by 37% in right-to-work states, compared to only 26% in union-shop states.

Fourth, we have to consider other factors besides wages, benefits, and job security when assessing the consequences of union activity to the workers involved. In particular, unions spend (and have historically spent) much of their members' dues on political campaigns. The argument here is that unions are providing such good benefits that allowing them to compel all workers to belong is justified, but it doesn't take into account this other cost: the union may elect politicians who increase the workers' taxes, abridge their right to own weapons, deprive them of choice about their children's education (by opposing voucher and charter schools), or deny their children equal opportunity (by supporting affirmative action schemes that give other children preference).

This is no purely abstract point. In recent elections, unions have spent 60% of their members' dues on lobbying, political donations, and other political activities. And 90% of those political donations go to Democratic Party candidates, even though up to 40% of union members vote Republican in any given election. Much of the opposition to closed and union shops comes from this opposition to dues being used to further projects that workers despise. Doesn't compelling someone to pay for causes that he religiously, economically, or philosophically opposes violate that person's rights in a profound way?

Granted, in 1988, the U.S. Supreme Court ruled (in the *Beck* case) that employees have a right to refuse to pay that portion of their dues that is used for political purposes. But unions have been very successful at blocking implementation of the *Beck* ruling. Typically, a union will demand that any dissident employee wanting a dues rebate put his or her request in writing, which is an inconvenience and subjects the worker to the possibility of reprisal. Several states have passed "paycheck-protection" acts that put the burden of getting worker approval for spending dues on political campaigns squarely on the union. When Colorado and Utah passed paycheck-protection laws that required unions to get written permission from members before using their dues for political campaigns, dues collections dropped by more than two-thirds.

Needless to say, unions that have ties to organized crime have an especially poor argument for the closed or union shop. Any benefits the union delivers must be balanced against the costs of criminal activity.

The unequal power argument rests on the idea that management is typically in a position to say "take it or leave it" to the individual worker, and the worker will have to submit to a bad deal. Only if there is a union to represent the workers will they have a fair chance in negotiation, and unions can exist only when there is solidarity.

The truth of this argument is debatable. Even if unions always, or typically, negotiate the best deals, why would that require total "solidarity," that is, total membership of the workforce? Why couldn't a union representing (say) 80% of the workers still have the power to negotiate a good contract?

But even if we answer "it could," there is a problem with the logic—it is an *ignoratio elenchi.* At most it shows that unions are generally necessary for empowering the worker. If this is true, it only shows that workers ought to join the union for their own good, not that it is morally permissible for them to be compelled to do so as a condition of employment.

By far the most philosophically interesting argument, and the one that is bound to be most interesting to libertarians, is the freedom to contract argument. It seeks a reversal of sorts: to use classical liberalism, viewed by the political Left as a pro-business ideology, to justify a practice that greatly benefits unions. Under classical liberal economic principles, employers are free to offer any compensation package they want, and potential employees are free to accept or reject the package or counter with any proposals they want. As long as no coercion is involved, the government should stay out of the matter. Why, then, should unions not be able to contract with employers for a closed shop?

Before critiquing this argument, I want to make two observations about it. The first is that, as economist Charles Baird has noted,[3] the same argument would equally support the view that the government should not—as it currently does—prohibit yellow-dog contracts, contracts that require employees to surrender their right to form unions as a condition for employment. Needless to say, union supporters never advocate permitting *those* contacts.

The second is that the key qualification, that the employer (and employee) not be coerced, is seldom honored in the real world. To get a closed-shop contract from a company, unions historically have threatened or resorted to strikes (which typically involve the breaking of an earlier agreement to work, in the classical liberal view) and have in many cases harassed or even assaulted dissident and replacement workers, sabotaged equipment, vandalized property, or committed other coercive acts. The presence of a closed-shop agreement has often signified the fact that coercion has been used to get it.

But let's waive these points and focus on the argument itself. Must someone who holds classical liberal principles necessarily accept the legitimacy of closed shops? I think not.

We need to remember that, from the classical liberal point of view, agreements that limit the parties' later rights and freedoms are inherently suspect, even if entered into freely. A classic example is the one given by John Stuart Mill in *On Liberty*, where he argues that the law should not allow a person to sell himself into slavery. For the same reason we look askance at free elections in which one of the candidates clearly intends to eliminate free elections if he wins. We derisively, and rightly, refer to such elections as "one man, one vote, once." For a similar reason, Congress is barred from passing laws that restrict later congresses' powers, such as a law that would require future tax bills to get a two-thirds vote to be passed.

In a similar vein, it is morally questionable that I should be encouraged to join an organization that will not allow me to quit—which is what a union shop amounts to. While it makes sense, in general, to say that I should be free to enter into contracts, this is not the same as entering into contracts that limit my freedom to make new contracts. To put it another way, while I am ethically bound by prior agreements (that is, my freedom is limited to some degree by the contracts I've entered into), that doesn't apply to my freedom to make new agreements, going forward.

Something like this principle is found in the common law on contracts. For centuries, common law has held that contracts to compel someone to perform some job cannot be enforced; this smacks too much of slavery. Suppose an opera singer agrees to sing on a given night, signing a contract to do so and accepting partial payment and then refuses to perform. The managers of the opera house cannot sue to compel the singer to sing. They can sue the singer to get their advance back, to get compensatory damages for lost revenues, and perhaps even to get punitive damages—but they cannot compel the singer to perform.

One might reply that if a person doesn't want to work for a closed shop, he or she can just go elsewhere—as can the worker who doesn't want to work for a company that has a yellow-dog contract banning unions. But the problem with this reply is that it allows for the possibility of clearly coerced choices. It is possible that in some future place or time, open shop companies may not exist (if, for instance, a union manages to get closed shop contracts from all the companies in a worker's field). In such a scenario, the employee would either have to join a union or go without work: join or starve. That is hardly the paradigm of free choice. (The same holds for yellow-dog contracts: if all companies in the economy managed to get them, then any worker who wanted to be allowed to join a union would either have to give up that right or starve.)

This is not merely a theoretical problem. Admittedly, in the contemporary private-sector economy, we are far from that scenario. The percentage of private-sector workers who are members of unions has dropped steadily, from 35% in the 1950s to 20% in the '80s to about 7.4% today. Meanwhile, however, the percentage of public-sector employees who are members of unions has been growing apace.

Suppose I want to be a college instructor in California. Public colleges in California are, generally speaking, agency shops. (The University of California is not, insofar as ladder-and-rank faculty is concerned, but it is in respect to its vast army of teaching assistants, "instructors," and "lecturers.") So if I go to work for a public California college or university, I have to pay dues to the teachers' union. Well, someone might ask me, are you compelled to work for a California public college? Why don't you just go to work for a private college?

My rejoinder is that because of the power of taxation, the public sector of education has virtually crowded out the private sector. The California Community College system has 109 campuses and 2.5 million students. The California State University system has twenty-three campuses and upward of a half million students. Two hundred thousand students are enrolled in the ten campuses of the University of California system. By comparison, the Association of Independent California Colleges and Universities, which has as members the vast majority of California private colleges, represents only seventy-five campuses and about two hundred fifty thousand students. The state's power of taxation ensures that the billions poured into the public system dwarf employment opportunities in the private college system. If this crowding out continues to increase, the theoretical problem of a totally closed (or at least union) shop society is not so theoretical after all.

Even stronger examples might be given. Perhaps, as libertarians argue, roads and road building should be privatized; but right now it is virtually a monopoly of the state and can easily be made a monopoly of closed-shop employment practices.

I have examined the most common arguments used to justify closed shops and found them wanting. But are there compelling ethical reasons that support the view that closed shops should not be allowed? I believe there are.

Obviously, we have the natural-rights consideration raised at the beginning of this essay. Closed shops (as well as union and agency shops, but also yellow-dog contracts) manifestly violate freedom of association. Absent compelling ethical reasons to the contrary, a person should be able to join or not to join, support or not to support, any group at any time. And as mentioned above, there are consequentialist reasons to regard closed shops as undesirable.

But I also want to sketch a neglected line of ethical thinking on this issue—the line that might be taken by "virtue ethics," that is, by the method of evaluating practices by asking how they support or hinder the development of virtue. On this ground, there is a very good reason to criticize closed shops. Simply put, they corrupt unions.

Unions, no less than businesses, flourish as socially useful organizations when they aim to produce something that people want. This only reliably occurs in free markets, because the force of competition requires the organization to take seriously what the consumer wants and deliver it.

But with unions no less than businesses, the temptation is always present to "compel rather than sell," that is, to coerce consumers rather than letting them choose a good or service freely—enticing them with a superior product or service. A well-run union can play a valuable economic role. It can help many workers negotiate better wages and benefits than they might get on their own, enhance job security, and provide other services (such as pension options, banking services through credit unions, and discounts from merchants). When workers are free to belong or not or to choose among competing unions, these organizations are forced to focus on the workers' preferences. Allowing unions the power of coercion makes them more interested in enhancing their political power. It also makes them lazy and neglectful about improving their services.

The push for closed, union, or agency shops is just one of a variety of inherently coercive tools that are too often favored by organized labor. Organized labor's efforts to coerce membership (or at least the paying of dues) use member dues to further the union leaders' political agenda (in violation of the workers' *Beck* rights) and get Congress to end secret ballots in votes to unionize workplaces, all ultimately corrupt the unions. In their attempt to achieve such coercive powers, unions come to resemble those desperate businesses that try to save themselves by protectionism.

In sum, there is a strong case based upon converging lines of ethical thought that closed shops are inherently bad. My hope would be to see all states adopt right-to-work laws, not just the twenty-two who do so now. Given the stranglehold organized labor has on many states, this will probably require a federal law.

To those who (understandably) distrust the federal government to make such a major change in labor contract law, I would make several points.

Both state and federal law already set the conditions in which contracts are allowable and enforceable. The federal government, through Wagner, Taft-Hartley, and other acts, sets conditions for the unionization of workplaces, conditions that are generally helpful to unions (although Taft-Hartley disallows closed shops in the narrow sense). Over twenty states have right-to-work laws, and the state governments have had no problem enforcing them, ordinarily with good results.

Modifying the Taft-Hartley Act to disallow union and agency shops as well as closed shops, narrowly defined, would certainly not end federal interference in the marketplace; but it would impart more balance to patterns of government action that are often skewed in favor of unions. It would implement the freedoms vouchsafed to workers by the Supreme Court under its *Beck* ruling, it would increase freedom of association, and it would bring labor law closer to common law principles of contract. Those would be real gains.

Notes

1. Joseph DesJardins *An Introduction to Business Ethics* (4th ed.) New York: McGraw-Hill 2011.
2. DesJardins, *Op. Cit.,* p. 125.
3. Charles Baird, "Hayek on Closed Shops and Yellow Dogs," in *The Freeman,* Vol. 57, Issue 3, April 2007.

"The Ethical Case for Boycotting Chrysler and GM"

first appeared in the American Thinker on June 10, 2009

In business ethics, the typical way one makes a judgment about the morality of a business action or practice is to consider the facts surrounding it in the light of four major ethical perspectives. These four ethical theories have been the ones considered most plausible in over two millennia of moral philosophy.

The first perspective is the natural rights view, or what I will call the *rights perspective.* This view judges an action or practice by asking whether it flows from the rights of those doing it and, more importantly, if it violates the rights of others.

The second perspective is the *consistency perspective.* This view judges an action or practice by asking what would happen if it were done or practiced by everyone, not just those involved in this situation. It is the view expressed by the Golden Rule, a rule common to most major religions.

The third perspective is the *virtue perspective.* This view asks whether the action or practice corrupts or enhances people's characters.

The fourth perspective is the *utilitarian perspective.* This view looks to the consequences that will likely flow from the action or practice and judges it right to the degree those consequences are the best for society over the long term.

I will argue that the unprecedented action by the current administration in manipulating the bankruptcies of Chrysler and GM, and in effect nationalizing the companies, is egregiously unethical by every one of these major ethical perspectives. For this reason, I believe that this action makes it morally imperative for Americans to boycott these socialized companies.

Consider first the facts. In these two cases, rather than let the free market and the legal system (specifically, the bankruptcy court) handle the reorganization of the failing automakers in the normal way, the Obama administration spent tens of billions in taxpayers' dollars to take control of the companies and force the outcome it wanted. President Obama, who received millions in contributions from the United Auto Workers union, has forced a settlement that will give the UAW far more equity in the companies when they come out of bankruptcy than it was due compared to the secured debt holders.

In the case of GM, the bondholders likely will get 10% of the common stock in the reorganized company for the $27 billion they are owed. The UAW will get $10 billion in taxpayer cash, plus 17.5% of the new company's common stock, $2.5 billion in bonds, and $6.5 billion in new preferred stock, paying a 9% dividend, all for the $20 billion it is owed.[1] In the case of Chrysler, the bondholders will get $2 billion in cash for the $6.9 billion they are owed, with no equity. The UAW will get 55% of the new company for "forgiving" $6 billion in promised retiree health care—really, just unsecured debt that would have been in second place in a proper bankruptcy.[2]

Obama's agents used threats and intimidation (calling holdout bondholders "speculators" and "hedge funds" at one point) to get the creditors to accept being shafted.[3] The result is that the vast majority of the two companies will be almost clearly owned by the federal government and the UAW, and the UAW arguably controls the federal government.

The result is drenched in irony. The UAW was a major reason the companies hit the wall, and now the UAW will be rewarded with major control and ownership. It is as if a rape victim were forced to marry her rapist. The result makes the crony capitalism we saw in Russia look clean by comparison; it, at least, was a kind of capitalism.

This situation is ethically repugnant form every perspective. Consider the facts from the *rights perspective.* The secured creditors' rights to a just settlement have been completely violated. And these bondholders, despite the defamation of Obama and his myrmidons, are not just soulless capitalist speculators. They include regular folk, yes, and even some blue-collar workers, who held these assets as part of their retirement portfolios.[4] It also included teacher and police pension funds and state infrastructure construction funds.[5]

The rights of all the stakeholders at the competing car companies have been violated as well. Their workers, stockholders, and managers will now be compelled to pay taxes that will fund their competitors. Consumers of other car companies will wind up paying taxes to build the very cars they chose not to buy. And taxpayers with no health insurance will pay to maintain the sweet health benefits of UAW members.

From the *consistency perspective,* the nationalization of Chrysler and GM seems obviously wrong. By using his political power, Obama has forced the bankruptcy court to put aside longstanding settled principles, especially the rule that secured creditors get priority in receiving assets from a defunct entity. Worse yet, Obama abused his power to benefit his supporter and benefactor, the UAW. What if every president did this sort of thing? Would any legal system that gave citizens equal protection under the law even be possible? Hardly.

From the *virtue perspective,* again we see that the nationalization is unacceptable. It will corrupt unions and businesses alike by leading them to negotiate obviously unsustainable contracts, safe in the knowledge that by paying off the pols, the federal government will step in to save them from the consequences of their dishonesty.

Finally, from the *utilitarian perspective,* the forced nationalization of the auto industry is unethical. We are seeing just the start of the negative consequences that will flow from this act of statist hubris.

To start with the obvious, even though Obama denies that he will manage the companies, we have all learned by now that he has no problem doing the very thing he is denying. (In ordinary life, this political artfulness is called lying). He fired one CEO, forced Chrysler to accept Fiat,[6] told GM that it cannot move its headquarters out of Detroit,[7] and may have ordered that whoever buys GM's European automaker Opel must agree not to export cars to the United States.[8] These decisions were made in secret with no congressional oversight by a man with no training or experience of any kind in business, never mind the auto business.

The companies will be run by politicians, who will make decisions for the benefit of political agendas rather than on sound business principles. The result will be that the auto companies and the union will not make the deep changes required to make the companies profitable, so we can anticipate many more cash infusions.

Worse yet, we can foresee that now that the UAW and feds have control of Chrysler and GM, they won't stop there. Their natural instinct will be to achieve monopolistic control. The UAW has helped drive Chrysler and GM to the wall and is now co-owner with the government of most of the equity. They will likely next target Ford to get equity ownership of it. Then look for the UAW and the administration it controls to attempt to force the employees of foreign automakers in this country to join the UAW or use environmental and other regulatory laws to put those companies out of business.

But the negative consequences will spread well beyond the auto industry. By so conspicuously short-changing the bondholders in favor of his political supporters, Obama has made raising capital vastly more difficult. Every investor now knows that past bankruptcy law means nothing; if the president is paid enough by some special interest group, he will rip off the secured debt holders to satisfy his supporters. This will surely lower the demand for corporate bonds, leading to less capital for business expansion, hence fewer jobs.

We have, in this debacle, an ironic illustration of what the economist Frederic Bastiat warned us about in his classic essay, "The Seen and the Unseen." What President Obama hopes we will see are the thousands of UAW jobs that have been "saved." What he knows we won't see are all the jobs that will be lost or not created because of his corrupt, dictatorial conduct—not to mention the fact that had a normal bankruptcy been allowed, most of the existing jobs would have been saved anyway.

The citizenry needs to make it clear this nationalization will not be permitted to succeed. We need to boycott these companies and tell this rogue administration exactly what we are doing. The alternative is that they will do this again.

Notes

1. "Political Bankruptcy," in the *Wall Street Journal,* June 1, 2009.
2. Serena Ng and Annelena Lobb, "U.S. Tactics Spark Worries Over Lenders' Rights," in the *Wall Street Journal,* May 1, 2009.
3. Neil King and Jeffrey McCracken, "U.S. Forced Chrysler's Creditors to Blink," in the *Wall Street journal,* May 11, 2009.
4. Dennis Buchholtz, "GM Bondholders Are People Like You and Me," in the *Wall Street Journal,* May 5, 2009.
5. "About Those 'Speculators'" in the *Wall Street Journal,* May 21, 2009.
6. Neil King and Jeffrey McCracken, "U.S. Pushed Fiat Deal on Chrysler," in the *Wall Street Journal,* June 6, 2009.
7. "Busy Not Running GM," in the *Wall Street Journal,* June 3, 2009.
8. "The Obama Motor Co," in the *Wall Street Journal,* June 2, 2009.

Reprinted by permission of *The American Thinker.*

33

"The Case for Free Trade"

first appeared in Liberty on December 2010

Books discussed in this review essay:

- *An Introduction to Business Ethics*, 3rd edition, by Joseph Desjardins. New York: McGraw-Hill, 2009, 281 pages.
- *Mad About Trade: Why Main Street America Should Embrace Globalization*, by Daniel Griswold. Washington, DC: Cato Institute, 2009, 203 pages.

A common topic in business ethics courses is international trade, which is typically covered under the rubric of "globalization." Rare is the student who doesn't have deeply unfavorable opinions about free trade. And rare is the business ethics text that takes a deeply favorable view of it. I want to explore the case for free trade and why it meets continuing resistance.

To put the discussion in context, let me briefly review the way in which a standard business text treats the issue. Let's look at Joseph Desjardins' book, a widely used text authored by a respected expert in the field. I consider it a good text; indeed, it is one of the texts I routinely use in my own business ethics classes.

Desjardins begins every chapter with a "discussion case"—almost always one in which some business or group of businesses is alleged to have behaved immorally. The case-study approach is common among business ethics texts, but the cases selected almost always have to do with unethical business behavior. As such, they are invitations to a hasty generalization: the student meets just a few examples of business behavior, and these are examples of unethical behavior. No text I know of mentions the fact that there are about 27 million businesses in

America and that the vast majority of them provide valuable goods and services, meanwhile causing no harm. And no business ethics text I know of discusses cases of *governmental* malfeasance.

The case that Desjardins starts with concerns the practice, allegedly widespread among apparel retailers, of using sweatshops, mostly located abroad. (I should note that Desjardins never defines what he means by "sweatshop.") He notes[1] that in August 1995, Los Angeles police arrested the operators of a shop employing seventy illegal Asian immigrants. These workers were paid much less than minimum wage and forced to live in an apartment complex set up like a prison. In the same year, Desjardins notes, it was discovered that Kathie Lee Gifford's line of sportswear, sold at Wal-Mart stores, was manufactured by sweatshops in Honduras that employed teenagers working fourteen-hour days. And he discusses in detail the accusations that Nike has readily used foreign sweatshops to manufacture its shoes—observing, however, that by 1992 Nike had responded to bad publicity on this score by developing a code of conduct that requires its suppliers to meet high standards for wages and working conditions. So here we have three cases, all more than fifteen years old.

This is the extent of the data he gives for this case study, yet it informs all the rest of the chapter, inviting students to view all foreign trade as consisting of American industries cutting domestic production to use foreign sweatshops.

Desjardins then sketches two broad categories of ethical issues regarding international business: micro-level issues about the degree to which managers should apply their own ethical standards in foreign business dealings and macro-level issues surrounding globalization generally.

Desjardins' discussion of the first set of issues is brief.[2] He admits that different countries seem to have different ethical systems—for example when it comes to bribery. He rightly stipulates that the fact that ethical norms may vary does not imply that they are all equally valid and that none are ultimately right or wrong. He also rightly observes that customs may not vary as much as is generally supposed. For instance, he notes that when Indonesia was ruled by President Suharto, corruption was common and widely recognized. But that didn't mean the average people approved of it: Suharto was eventually overthrown and anticorruption laws enacted.

That said, of course, the issue becomes, what universal values should bind all American countries doing business abroad? Here Desjardins is not very helpful. He quotes[3] another philosopher, Tom Donaldson, who distinguishes between "minimalist" and "maximalist" answers to the question. The minimalist approach holds that a business is free to pursue its interests in another country so long as certain minimal rights are respected in the process. The maximalist approach holds that besides respecting certain basic rights, a company must actually produce benefits for the host country.

Donaldson takes a minimalist tack, listing universal rights that any company with operations abroad must respect: freedom of movement, ownership of property, freedom from torture, fair trials, nondiscriminatory treatment, physical security, freedom of speech and association, minimal education, political participation, and subsistence. But Desjardins doesn't say whether these are to be taken as positive or merely negative rights (indeed, nowhere in his text does he even discuss the distinction) or whether "respect" means "provide" or merely "not interfere with." So the moral view is unclear: if I am opening a manufacturing plant in a dictatorship, am I to try to guarantee my employees the power to vote in that society (and how could I possibly achieve that without getting all of us killed?) or merely not stop them from voting? Or is doing business in countries without political freedom always immoral?

Donaldson's account doesn't tell us to whom the catalogue of rights applies: is employing a fifteen-year-old to run a sewing machine, with her and her parents' consent, in a country where general education ends at the fourteenth year, violating her rights? Nor does it say exactly how the Donaldson list is to be reconciled with or proven superior to other lists of rights that other people may come up with. For example, nowhere on his list is a right that most Americans generally hold dearly, the right to keep and bear arms. What is his rationale for excluding it? We aren't told.

Even more vague and questionable is the maximalist account that Desjardins cites,[4] abstracted from another business ethicist, Richard DeGeorge. This requires that the company doing business in another country do no direct harm, produce more good than harm for the host country, contribute to the host country's development, and a number of other things. But how would a company know whether it is, on balance, benefiting the country, other than the authorities in that country who have agreed to the operation? And why is it the obligation of a company to contribute to the host country's development over and above the fact that it brings jobs and money to that country?

Desjardins then takes up the macro-level issues of global trade and globalization. He recognizes that the term "globalization" is unclear, though it certainly brings out the demonstrators every time the G20 meets, sometimes causing millions of dollars in damages. So he proceeds to define it, in a loaded way: "*globalization* refers to a process of international economic integration. While international trade and cooperation have existed as long as there have been nations, this process of international economic integration has become increasingly more common …" He cites the General Agreement on Tariffs and Trade (GATT), the North American Free Trade Agreement (NAFTA), and the European Union (EU).

It is true that international trade has gone on for millennia, but there may have been (and we will soon find good evidence to suppose that there has been) a recent, huge jump in its volume. However, we shouldn't conflate simple free trade associations, such as NAFTA, with more intense forms of association such as the EU. The EU was set up by its founders to be something like a United States of Europe, where the sovereign identity and powers of the member states would eventually be subsumed in political and economic union. In contrast, most free trade organizations are groups of countries that do not desire to integrate their economies, much less surrender their sovereignty and merge into one nation, but merely want to enjoy the benefits of increased trade.

Desjardins sketchily states the standard argument for free trade, the utilitarian idea that free movement of goods and capital among nations allows resources to be allocated in the most efficient manner, producing the greatest possible well-being for everyone. As corollaries, he notes (without crediting Adam Smith) that this line of thought suggests that free trade is the best way to eliminate poverty around the world and (without crediting Frédéric Bastiat) that increased economic cooperation among nations decreases the likelihood of warfare. As Bastiat put it, "When goods do not cross borders, armies will."

Desjardins gives no data to support or even flesh out these arguments. He only says,[5] "As we saw in the opening discussion case for the chapter [the one on sweatshops], a variety of public interest groups so disagree with these arguments that they have been willing to take to the streets to demonstrate against globalization." This is very feeble. To be precise, it is a howling *ad populum* fallacy. The fact that demonstrators, or even rioters, oppose globalization no more indicates that globalization is bad than the fact that riots occurred on Kristallnacht proves that Jews are bad.

Desjardins does rehearse[6] three common broad arguments against globalization: globalization hurts rather than helps the poor, globalization invites a "race to the bottom" of environmental and worker protections, globalization undermines equal rights and autonomy.

In respect to the question of whether globalization harms or helps the poor, he considers "market theory" from the "empirical," "conceptual," and "ethical" perspectives to see whether free trade actually does improve living standards. Market theory (in his view) provides that in trade involving a more developed country and a less developed country, the likely result is that jobs will be "exported" from the developed country to the developing one, because labor costs will be lower there. This, in theory, will depress wages among workers in the developed country and increase unemployment there. In time, however, economic growth in the developing country should increase demand for the more "industrialized" products of the more developed country, resulting in higher employment there.

Desjardins has doubts. He thinks it is "empirical" that specific, identifiable workers in the developed country will lose their jobs, but it is only "theoretical" that other workers will eventually get jobs elsewhere in the economy, and the ethical question is whether the benefits outweigh the costs. Framed in that way, the question would certainly be hard to answer.

His discussion here is breathtakingly tendentious. Nowhere does he mention the consumer. If prices drop in the developed country, consumers there obviously benefit. Nor does he note the Bastiat point that the domestic consumers who save money from buying cheaper foreign good will either invest or spend those saved dollars elsewhere, which in turn creates more domestic jobs.

And nowhere does he mention the existence of the host of "safety net" programs that are universal in the developed countries—unemployment insurance, universal education, health care systems, job training programs, and so on. Nor does it even occur to him to ask whether trade always or even typically involves companies in a developed country opening plants in developing countries, as opposed to other developed countries. This is hardly an empirically informed discussion.

Moreover, Desjardins has an impoverished view of what counts as "empirical." The fact that we can't always "identify" the jobs created in a developed economy when it expands trade abroad—although you sometimes can, as when foreign companies open affiliates here—hardly means that you can't empirically measure the effects. You can, for example, measure unemployment rates for a set period before trade expansion and then for an equal period after it to see if unemployment goes up or down.

Again, "market theory" suggests that workers in newly opened plants in a developing country will be better off—after all, they chose the job, so clearly they feel themselves better off. But Desjardins argues that if desperately poor people only have the choice of working in sweatshops or starving, the choice is not really free. From that dubious assumption flow a variety of dogmatic moral demands. He recommends that economic indicators be used to set a minimum wage in the host country roughly equivalent to that of the developed country and that companies not be allowed to employ contractors abroad without "taking full and direct responsibility for how those workers are treated," preferably by making them direct employees.

Other deductions proceed from the cliché "race to the bottom." Desjardins takes seriously the idea that competition induced by free trade results in countries lowering their environmental, labor, health, and safety regulations. For example, OSHA's extensive safety regulations make production more costly here, encouraging American manufacturers to move production lines to countries with less regulation. Desjardins ruefully notes[7] that the WTO will not allow tariffs designed to punish countries with lower safety standards, as well as prohibiting tariffs against other countries that fail to protect against dolphins being caught while harvesting tuna or countries that feed hormones to cattle. He admits that we don't see a lessening of regulations in the developed countries that allow free trade—indeed, quite the reverse—yet amazingly, he doesn't wonder if the developed countries may possibly have too many regulations to begin with and whether many of those regulations may be bad. Yes, many European countries prohibit using hormones in cattle and the marketing of genetically modified grains, but it is quite disputable whether those regulations are scientifically defensible.

I turn now to the argument about globalization's threat to democratic or humane political values—the argument that institutions such as the WTO, the World Bank, and the IMF are undemocratic bureaucracies in conflict with democracy and self-determination and that the reach of international corporations threatens the world with cultural homogeneity. Desjardins takes this argument seriously.[8] He feels comfortable imposing Western or American values (especially as embodied in business regulations) on other cultures, but he objects to the IMF and the WTO imposing their own values, such as free trade.

However, participation in these organizations is voluntary. It seems fair to say that if you want the benefits that membership gives you, you have to agree to the rules, annoying as they sometimes are. And while international corporations can get certain products adopted worldwide, the Coca-Cola market hardly amounts to the destruction of other cultures. If the modern consumer society is being adopted worldwide, perhaps that's because it appeals to most people in developing countries. Despite the fact that people—especially philosophy professors—in developed countries complain about shallow materialist consumerism, you seldom see them leaving developed countries to live in the developing ones.

The point here is entirely general: critics of "globalization" too often equate the diffusion of good ideas across cultures with what they deride as "cultural imperialism." When I was young, if you suggested to me that we should eat raw fish with sticky rice, held together by seaweed, I (and most of my cohort) would have regarded you as insane. But today, many Americans love going to sushi bars, and none view it as Japanese cultural imperialism.

In sum, the view of free trade offered by a typical, widely used business ethics text is very unfavorable. Free trade is presented as a way to ship jobs abroad in pursuit of lower wages. Free trade is shown to result in sweatshops. It is said to lower wages and cost identifiable jobs while any offsetting job gains are held to be theoretical. It is presented as leading to a "race to the bottom." It is claimed to involve rich nations exploiting poor ones. The suggested solution is to strongly limit trade by regulation. Support for these ideas comes not from detailed empirical data but from the moral intuitions of philosophy professors.

We are lucky to have a superb new book on the subject, written from a contrary point of view. Daniel Griswold's *Mad about Trade* is a comprehensive yet crisp and spirited consideration of the major defenses of free trade. It provides copious evidence that should surprise and interest even the most skeptical student.

Griswold, an economist at the Cato Institute who specializes in trade, starts with a brief survey of America's increasingly globalized economy. He shows, in a telling graph,[9] that imports and import income payments as a portion of GDP hovered around 5% from 1900 until the early 1970s, when they went nearly linearly upward to about 23% in 2000. Exports and export income receipts as a portion of GDP are a slightly more complicated picture, essentially bouncing between 5% and 10% from 1900 till the early 1970s (but with spikes during WWI and WWII, when America exported a lot of munitions) and then going steeply upward to about 18% in 2000.

These figures explain not only how much more globalized our economy has become over the last thirty-five years but also why it has aroused increasing concern: it is growing explosively. Griswold explores the reasons for increased foreign trade, from free trade agreements (FTAs) to falling transportation costs (sealed container ships have cut losses from theft, jet aircraft are increasingly efficient, and so on).

But does free trade, on balance, help society, from consumers to workers? Griswold stresses the important point that free trade benefits consumers enormously, in the form of lower prices. No surprise there—that was Adam Smith's argument for supporting free trade in opposition to mercantilism. But Griswold gives substantial confirming data,[10] showing, for instance, that the industries which saw the biggest price reductions from 2000 to 2007 were almost always the ones that faced foreign competition. A recent study indicates that by lowering prices, global trade has raised the real income of Americans by 3% (or about $5,000) from 1972 to 2001. (This is another point Desjardins didn't explore.)

Besides lowering prices, free trade provides greater product choice, greater product availability (e.g., fresh fruit in the middle of winter), and products of better quality. Griswold refutes the notions that our increased global trade is almost entirely with China (which accounts for only 15% of American imports) and that big-box retailers are hurting the consumer (Wal-Mart alone saves consumers about $2,300 a year per household).[11]

Less clear, of course, is whether the effect of free trade in the industries facing competition is so severe that America winds up with lower prices at the cost of higher unemployment or lower levels of worker compensation. Here Griswold argues that free trade doesn't so much significantly increase or decrease the overall level of employment (i.e., the net number of jobs) as shift people from worse (less productive) jobs to better (more productive) jobs. He denies the claim, heard from some exponents of free trade, that it dramatically increases the level of domestic employment. And he recognizes that competition from free trade puts some companies out of business and temporarily eliminates some jobs. But he argues that any such temporary specific job losses from trade don't lower the overall employment rate—for three reasons.

First, trade creates other jobs that quickly replace the ones lost. For example, lower prices for materials bought from foreign trade allow domestic producers to lower prices, thus increasing sales at home and abroad and in turn creating new jobs. Also, the lower costs brought by trade increase the profits of domestic producers, inviting foreign investment and jobs expansion. (Griswold also should have mentioned Bastiat's observation that with the money saved from trade-induced lower prices, consumers can buy more of other products made domestically, again increasing jobs).

Second—and here Griswold does mention David Ricardo—if we lose our competitive edge in one area (because of lower prices abroad or, for that matter, some change in technology at home), the other areas of our economy will likely have their competitive advantage enhanced.

Third, there are powerful economic factors, such as foreign exchange rates and government monetary policy, involved in trade. A rapid increase in imports would rapidly increase the amount of our currency in foreign banks, which would tend to weaken the dollar, thus lowering the price of American-manufactured goods, resulting in increased foreign purchases of our products.

Griswold explores these concepts conceptually but also adduces considerable empirical data to show that free trade does not increase unemployment over the long run. He also explores in detail a point often overlooked by critics of free trade—that normally the jobs lost because of foreign trade are a minor part of the general normal "job churn" the American economy experiences every year. Take a high estimate of jobs lost by trade (say, a figure put out by a think tank tied to organized labor), and it is still only about 3% of the jobs lost in any given year.[12] What "kills" the vast majority of jobs in America is technology, not trade.

And I would add that this is a good thing too: the replacement of manual switchboards by computer switches killed tens of thousands of unproductive jobs but created new more productive jobs, especially for women, who were the vast majority of those telephone operators. Women are now doctors, lawyers, professors, and scientists, rather than people who plug wires into boards. It is curious that Griswold doesn't mention Joseph Schumpeter and his theory of creative destruction, for it explains this process remarkably well.

Griswold also marshals evidence to rebut the theory that trade results in stagnating wages. Crucial to his discussion is a critique of the use of "average real hourly wage" as a measure of the well-being of workers, which is the normal practice of critics of free trade. For one thing, the real hourly wage doesn't reflect all compensation—it only looks at monetary compensation, not other forms of payment (including major ones such as health care benefits and 401k matching contributions). Yes, during the period from 1964 to 2006, real hourly *wages* remained essentially flat. But real hourly *compensation* rose by nearly 80%, with an upward spurt during the 1990s, when there was broad bipartisan support for free trade.[13] Griswold also notes that the Consumer Price Index doesn't adequately reflect the lower prices that trade brings or the increased variety and quality of goods available to Americans.

He takes on the claim made by commentator Lou Dobbs and others that we are losing our manufacturing base and, with it, our middle class. The key point is that while our manufacturing sector has lost jobs, we have gained more highly paid jobs elsewhere in the service industry. (Griswold might have noted additionally that *all* the top manufacturing countries—including China, South Korea, and Mexico—have lost manufacturing jobs over the past decade.[14]) Our level of manufacturing output has risen; we just manufacture more with fewer people. Simply put, automation is lowering manufacturing employment all around the world.

Moreover, from 1967 to 2007, median household income rose; and while the percentage of households with middle-class income went down, so did the percentage of poor households, leaving only the percentage of wealthy households going up.[15]

But don't trade deficits harm society? Griswold observes that economists distinguish between the merchandise trade balance (which measures cross-border flows of agricultural goods, commodities, and manufactured goods), the trade balance (which measures the cross-border flows of all goods and services), and the current account balance (which measures cross-border flows of all goods and services, together with income earned from all investments and all transfers of money). Now over the past several decades, we have experienced a large trade deficit. But this is not generally a problem, because the surplus money that flowed abroad flowed back in the form of investments in the United States, which created jobs here. Empirical data from 1982 to 2008 show that periods of rising trade deficits are periods in which there is faster job growth, and periods of shrinking deficits are periods in which there is slower job growth.[16]

Griswold reviews in considerable depth the range of foreign companies' operations in America. About 4.6% of America's private workforce is now employed by foreign companies and affiliates—up by a third in twenty years.[17] Workers for these foreign affiliates earn an average of $63,400 yearly, well above the average salary for American company employees ($48,200, 2006 figures). Foreign affiliates accounted for 19% of all U.S. exports, 26% of all U.S. imports, and 14% of all U.S. R & D spending (or about $34 billion annually).

Even when foreign investors don't open operations here, but just passively invest in stocks, corporate bonds, bank deposits, government bonds, and various derivatives, Americans still benefit. The $15.3 trillion in foreign passive investment, which represents an expanded pool of investment capital, has lowered the interest rates Americans have to pay on mortgages and other consumer and business loans. Lower mortgages and consumer loans mean more houses built and products made, and that means more jobs. Lower costs of borrowing for businesses and farmers mean expansion of operations and equipment, which again leads to more jobs.

Does the $20 trillion in foreign-owned American assets constitute a threat to our sovereignty? Hardly. It is less than 20% of the total $110 trillion in American assets held by businesses (profit and nonprofit) and households.[18] And only 3% of total American assets are held by foreign government agencies. If some big government holder of U.S. Treasury bills (such as China, which holds $600 billion of them) were to try to dump them in order to hurt our economy, it would be unlikely to harm us; it would be working with a small proportion of our sovereign debt and an even smaller proportion of our total asset base. Not to mention the fact that it would be wielding a double-edged sword, hurting the value of its own assets. (I would add that such an attempt to harm us would doubtless be met with an American embargo that would economically devastate the dumpers.)

More currently controversial is American investment abroad. Companies that set up operations on foreign shores are routinely demonized by leftist demagogues, such as Barack Obama and John Kerry (remember his anger at "Benedict

Arnold CEOs"?). Certainly, there are a lot of companies with foreign operations. Over 2,500 American firms own about 24,000 affiliates abroad—affiliates that in 2006 posted over $4 trillion in sales, employed 9.5 million foreign workers, and earned $644 billion in net income for the parent companies. Individual Americans owned $17 trillion in foreign assets, earning over $800 billion annually.[19] So what does all this foreign investment do to American jobs?

The case that investment abroad does not cost domestic jobs starts with the fact that earnings from abroad are generally used to purchase American products, thus producing American jobs. The evidence shows that foreign and domestic operations of multinational corporations expand together since more production and sales abroad require more home staff (managers, professionals such as accountants and lawyers, and R & D people such as engineers). If you graph U.S. parent-company employment alongside foreign-affiliate employment from 1982 to 2006, they track each other very closely.[20]

Griswold makes an interesting point about those who wax demagogic about investment in China and Mexico (to take the cases most demonized by neo-mercantilist populists). Between 2003 and 2007, U.S. manufacturing companies invested a total of $10 billion in China and $9 billion in Mexico—but they invested $110 billion in Europe[21]! You don't hear the neo-mercantilists ranting about jobs being shipped to England. Could there be some racism lurking on the Left?

Further evidence showing that manufacturing jobs are not being "shipped" to China and Mexico: between 2000 and 2006, U.S. manufacturing lost 3 million jobs, net; but employment by American corporate affiliates abroad gained a minuscule 128,000 jobs (i.e., fewer than 22,000 jobs per year).[22] Again, the jobs were not shipped abroad—they were lost to automation.

In rebutting the neo-mercantilist "race to the bottom" myth, it is important to note that in the years 2003–2007, over 70% of all American manufacturing investment abroad went to these wealthy countries: Australia, Canada, Japan, New Zealand, and the European states.[23] This seems paradoxical, but it isn't: pace Desjardins, what companies want is not cheap labor but more profit, and a company can turn a profit in a rich country as easily as it can in a poor one. Rich countries have the wealthiest consumers, best-educated workers, most open economies, and most stable and transparent legal and political systems. As Griswold nicely puts it, "All that explains why more U.S. FDI [foreign domestic investment] flows to Ireland (population 4 million) than to the entire continent of Africa (population 700 million). More U.S. FDI flows to the tiny but rich European Low Countries of Belgium, the Netherlands, and Luxembourg (population 27.5 million) than to

China, Mexico, and India combined (population 2.5 billion)".[24] None of these points is even mentioned by Desjardins' text, much less addressed.

Griswold considers in detail the history of free trade in America, arguing compellingly that the early tariff barriers didn't help the American economy on the whole, that there were more recessions per decade during the protectionist years than in the post-WWII period of globalization, that the American economy has performed better after NAFTA than before it, and that not only do FTAs not violate our sovereignty—they enhance it by giving us all the right to purchase from a greater number of places.

Griswold cites a study by Scott C. Bradford, Paul L.E. Grieco, and Gary Clyde Hufbauer, calculating the benefits of lowered trade barriers to the American economy since World War II.[25] They estimate that about $1 trillion of America's current yearly GDP (or roughly $7,100 per typical household) comes from global trade. They further estimate that achieving full global free trade would add an additional $450 billion to our annual GDP (or as much as $4,000 per typical household).

What of the effects of globalization on the developing world? Griswold refers to a study by economists Kym Anderson and L. Alan Winters showing that opening a country up to trade increases its GDP growth by several points for many years.[26] The impact of global free trade is astoundingly favorable. Over the past quarter century, during which trade as a share of world GDP went from about a third to well over a half, the percentage of the world's population living in profound poverty has been more than cut in half. Over the past fifty years, the average life span in the developing countries increased by 45%, from forty-five to sixty-five years. Global infant mortality dropped by 60%.[27] The percentage of children inoculated against measles, diphtheria, tetanus, and whooping cough has increased by 75%. The share of people in developing countries who are undernourished has been cut by more than 50%. The rate of literacy in developing countries has risen from less than half to more than two-thirds. The amount of schooling that girls receive as a percentage of what boys receive went from 56% to 73%. And (again pace Desjardins) the percentage of working children, ages 10–14, fell from 25% to less than 10%, and it continues to drop.

Griswold also makes the case that Mexico is better off after NAFTA than it was before and cites Freedom House figures showing that over the past thirty years, the number of "not free" countries declined by a third while the number of "free" countries doubled. All of this is hard to square with the neo-mercantilist rhetoric—such as that found in Desjardins' text—about globalization leading to poverty, sweatshops, and child-labor abuse in developing countries.

Griswold concludes his argument by demonstrating that America is far from the free trade Mecca that the neo-mercantilists portray. In the most recent Economic Freedom of the World report, we are twenty-seventh among 140 nations ranked in terms of economic freedom, well behind places such as Hong Kong and Singapore.[28] He shows in detail the crazy-quilt tariff system we currently have and what it costs consumers. We have a trade-weighted average tariff on clothing and footwear of over 10%. Now consider sugar. Because of our subsidies and tariffs, American consumers have, for decades, paid two to three times the world price for sugar. Indeed, our trade barriers on agricultural products cost our consumers $12 billion a year.

And barriers extend well beyond food and clothing. We put tariffs on vehicles (2.5% on cars and 25% on trucks). We keep foreign-owned carriers from flying between one U.S. airport and another. Foreigners cannot own more than 25% of any domestic airline. And our law (the Jones Act) requires all ships carrying goods between American ports to be American built, registered, owned, and manned. All this drives up the cost of shipping and distribution enormously, impoverishing us all.

Griswold's book is unabashedly one-sided. But if it is used to balance business ethics texts that are unabashedly one-sided against free trade, it will do much good. It is a compendium of relevant facts and statistics that increase the specificity of the discussion. In those respects it is tremendously useful. As full a case as Griswold presents, however, there is even more to be said in defense of free trade.

Consider a point he touches on, in his brief discussion of the Smoot-Hawley tariffs, but doesn't elaborate in detail: what happens to a country when it indulges in protectionism? Of course, the usual result is retaliation by other nations—a trade war. The present administration presents a good illustration of this.

The Obama administration is by far the most anti–free trade, protectionist regime since Hoover. Besides stalling the implementation of the three free trade agreements (with Colombia, Panama, and South Korea) that were negotiated by the Bush administration but not yet enacted when Obama took office, Obama hasn't done a thing about free trade. He hasn't negotiated one new treaty; he hasn't even shown any interest in doing so. Worse, his administration has enacted a number of protectionist measures that have drawn retaliatory measures from abroad.

For example, under the terms of NAFTA, a small number of Mexican truckers were allowed access to the U.S. market on a tightly monitored basis. Furious at the prospect of foreign truckers competing with their members, the Teamsters union, big contributors to Obama, got him to cancel the program last year. The result was predictable: Mexico put steep tariffs (as high as 45%) on a wide range of U.S. goods, from paper to grapes. The tariffs have totaled $2.4 billion. As a consequence, workers in businesses from paper mills in Wisconsin to farms in Washington State—an estimated twenty-five thousand people—have lost their jobs.

Thus, to protect a couple hundred politically well-connected truckers, hundreds of millions of consumers are paying higher prices, and tens of thousands of workers are losing their jobs.

Another example concerns Brazil. Lavish government subsidies to American cotton growers have in effect frozen Brazilian cotton growers out of our market. Not surprisingly, Brazil filed a case against us with the World Trade Organization and prevailed. Brazil now has the right to retaliate and is now warning us that it is prepared to hit over a hundred categories of American exports with tariffs of up to 100%. The Obama administration is now proposing to subsidize the *Brazilian* cotton growers to the tune of $147 million.

So to protect a relatively few American cotton growers, hundreds of millions of consumers must pay higher prices, and tens of millions of taxpayers must pay higher taxes.

If the case for free trade is so rationally and empirically compelling, why do people—including bright students and even some of their teachers—so often oppose it? I suggest that the reasons are not logical but psychological.

Start with the most obvious psychological motive for opposing free trade—greed, simple greed. The two groups most opposed to free trade are organized labor and inefficient business. Both spend enormous amounts of money running ads against free trade and trying to elect candidates who will enact laws to stop it. In the 2008 election alone, organized labor spent $450 million to elect candidates (well over 90% of the money flowing to Democrats), and as a result, we have the most protectionist regime in nearly three quarters of a century. And many if not most industries have in the past lobbied for protection, with some (such as the auto and steel industries) becoming notorious for it.

But to understand why there is resistance to free trade among the public generally, we should turn to the psychology of persuasion and behavioral economics. Robert Cialdini's approach is instructive (as, for example, in his book *Influence: the Psychology of Persuasion*[29]).

He notes that all animals (humans included) have a variety of built-in psychological mechanisms (or "fixed-action patterns"). A psychological mechanism is a pattern of behavior that occurs whenever a specific feature of the environment (the "trigger feature") is encountered. A female turkey will exhibit "mothering" behavior (such as warming, cleaning, and huddling chicks beneath it) whenever she hears a specific *cheep-cheep* noise typically emitted by turkey chicks. This is not a rational response to observing a distressed chick. If a tape recorder buried on a stuffed skunk (a natural enemy of the turkey) emits the same noise, the turkey will exhibit the mothering behavior toward the stuffed skunk.

These mechanisms are wired into animals by evolution. They usually have worked well in the animal's environment—they have survival value. But they can occasionally prove dysfunctional. Other animals may learn to mimic the triggers, as when females of one firefly species mimic the mating signals of another species, luring males of that second species in, to become their food. Or the environment may change dramatically: humans evolved in conditions where food was scarce, so we crave sugar and fat, but that craving leads to obesity when food becomes plentiful.

Humans have many wired-in psychological mechanisms—and some of them are pertinent to the issue of free trade.

One is a weakness for *social proof.* People tend to judge what is proper by looking at what other people do. TV sitcoms have laugh tracks because when you hear other people laughing, you feel as if you should laugh as well. Then there is *association:* when two things occur together, people tend to think they are connected, even if there is no real causal connection between them—as when we associate favorable traits such as honesty and kindness with physical attractiveness. In addition, there is *salience:* people tend to notice what is novel or striking in a situation. In a robbery, they focus on the gun, rather than, for instance, the clothes that the robber may be wearing. *Sympathy* is also a factor: people tend to want to help others in need. Shown a picture of someone being pursued by wolves, we innately hope that he or she escapes. It's easy to see that people also practice *entrenchment:* once committed to a course of action, they prefer to stay in it, even if the consequences are unexpectedly bad. Behavioral economist (and Nobel laureate in economics) Daniel Kahneman has shown that people are loss-averse: they will risk more to keep the $200 they have than to earn $200 more. And to complete this brief list of examples, there is the reaction to *scarcity:* people tend to value more what they perceive to be in short supply. For example, in times of gasoline shortage, people will tend to top off their gasoline tanks more quickly than in normal times.

Several of these mechanisms help explain the aversion people feel toward free trade. The mechanism of salience explains why we are so struck by the jobs that are lost when an industry fails while not being struck by the new jobs created by more productive industries. In Bastiat's terminology, we see what is salient and what is not salient remains unseen. Sympathy leads us to be concerned with salient images of workers laid off, perhaps because of foreign competition in their industry. Protectionists exploit that concern, arguing that we should protect what is salient, the workers employed by an inefficient company. The workers who could have been employed in more productive enterprises had the company been allowed to fail are unseen so do not elicit the same sympathy.

Entrenchment explains why we want to cling to manifestly less productive jobs, rather than the more productive ones we get when we open our borders to trade. And association—to cite a third example—plays a big role in the protectionist's arsenal. I see an FTA signed and plants close, so I assume the FTA caused the plant to close, when in fact the plants often close for other reasons.

If it is indeed true that people resist free trade for reasons that are more often psychological than logical or empirical, it suggests two points for those who want to see free trade flourish.

First, any politician who seeks to advance free trade had better be prepared to make the case forcefully and often to the voting public, combating the forces of entrenchment and all the rest of the mechanisms. The best illustration of what I am getting at is Obama's immediate predecessor in the White House, George Bush.

Bush's record on free trade is arguably the best of any American president. He received "fast-track authority," a power conferred by Congress to negotiate FTAs free from congressional meddling, a full two years after he was inaugurated for his first term; and he had it taken away from him early by a deeply protectionist Democratic Congress five years later. But in those five years he negotiated more FTAs than all his predecessors combined. The list is long indeed: Australia, Bahrain, Chile, Colombia, Costa Rica, the Dominican Republic, El Salvador, Guatemala, Honduras, Morocco, Oman, Panama, Peru, Singapore, and South Korea. All but three of his agreements were ratified.

Bush tried to conclude an even further-reaching agreement, proposing a Free Trade Area of the Pacific at the 2007 meeting of the Asia-Pacific Economic Cooperation Conference. The proposed free trade zone would have included the United States and most of the other Pacific countries of the Western Hemisphere, along with China, Japan, South Korea, and most other Asian nations. Given the rising protectionist sentiment in Congress and divisions among the Asian countries, this proved to be a bridge too far, but at least Bush tried to cross it.

Yet for all the effort he put into developing FTAs, he spent little time in explaining to the public just why free trade is so beneficial. He was the first president with an MBA, so he could have done this well, one supposes. But he rarely spoke on the matter. He let resistance to free trade grow (stoked by a lot of advertising money spent by organized labor, long the arch foe of free trade) without spending any time publicly and decisively refuting it. This was a failure to lead, and it should serve as an object lesson to proponents of free trade in the future.

Second, in making the case for free trade, political leaders would do well to use arguments for free trade that also tap into the psychological mechanisms I listed besides providing the sort of data that Griswold supplies to rebut the arguments of the protectionist.

Consider an argument for free trade that Griswold doesn't happen to explore—the rapid growth of FTAs around the world. Unnoticed by American protectionists is the fact that most other countries, especially those in Asia and Europe, are increasingly embracing free trade.

Looking at the FTAs the WTO has recorded since 1995, we see that both their number and the pace with which they are being signed are increasing. From 1995 to 2003, there were on average seven FTAs signed per year. From 2004 to 09, the number rose to a yearly average of fifteen. There are now 266 bilateral or regional FTAs recorded with the WTO and roughly another 100 of which the WTO hasn't yet been notified.

When you look at where these FTAs are being negotiated, it is obvious that Asia and Europe, rather than the United States, are moving furthest towards free trade. Of the sixty-four FTAs signed since 2005, America is party to only five (all signed by Bush), compared to eight to which the EU is party, and nine to which Japan is party. The EU now has a total of thirty FTAs, compared to the U.S. total of seventeen (all pre-Obama).

The EU total includes a deal signed in May of 2010 with the Central American nations, as well as the one it concluded in late 2009 with South Korea. And the EU is close to signing an FTA with India. Still more impressive is the regional FTA signed in early 2010 between China and the Association of Southeast Asia Nations (ASEAN). This FTA eliminated more than seven thousand tariffs instantly and created the world's third largest free trade zone, a zone covering one-third of the world's population, with a trading volume of $200 billion. At the same time, ASEAN signed a similar FTA with India, creating a free trade zone encompassing 1.5 billion people with a trading volume of $50 billion. Even more potentially game-changing, China and India are negotiating an FTA which, if concluded, would cover nearly half the planet's population.

The result is that while we have buried our heads in protectionist sand and go month over month with nearly 10% unemployment and anemic growth, the Asian countries have embraced free trade and continue to grow briskly at annual rates from 6% to 10%.

Now not only is such an observation empirically sound, but it touches on at least two of the mechanisms we discussed earlier: social proof and scarcity. It indicates to Americans who are skeptical about or hostile about free trade that the other nations are embracing it rapidly. So if free trade is as bad as Obama and politicians of his ilk say, then why is the rest of the world embracing it? And if we keep delaying the expansion of free trade, we may find ourselves frozen out. Better get while the getting's good.

Consider another argument for free trade, one recently given by the presidents of Uganda and Tanzania.[30] Malaria is a vicious disease that is common in Africa. Over 200 million people suffer from it, and it kills 800,000 a year, disproportionately children. During the past decade, new diagnostic tests, drugs, and mosquito-proof netting have been developed. But as Kikwete and Museveni note, a lot of African nations still have high tariff and tax barriers to protect their domestic industries. When some of them eliminated trade barriers on antimalarial products, the cost of those products dropped, and usage correspondingly increased. So did the number of local entrepreneurs who create homegrown medical businesses producing antimalarial products.

Here is a good and forceful argument for free trade, forceful because it taps into our feelings of sympathy, especially toward children, and good because in this case those feelings are entirely appropriate.

Free trade is crucial to eliminating poverty and increasing global peace and prosperity. One can only hope that popular support for free trade will be increased by compelling arguments and cogent facts, especially those aimed at the same psychological mechanisms exploited by the neo-mercantilists. Plainly, however, it will take an endless repetition of those facts and arguments to overcome not only the greed of organized interests opposed to economic freedom but also the age-old mechanisms by which hominids respond to the realities they perceive.

Notes

1. Desjardins, p. 261.
2. Desjardins, pp. 265–8
3. Desjardins, p. 268.
4. Desjardins, pp. 269–70.
5. Desjardins, p. 271.
6. Desjardins, pp. 272–274.
7. Desjardins, p. 275.

8. Desjardins, p. 277.
9. Griswold, p. 4.
10. Griswold, p. 15.
11. Griswold, p. 24.
12. Griswold, p. 32.
13. Griswold, p. 35.
14. See Walter Williams, "Disappearing Manufacturing Jobs," *Townhall.com*, May 3, 2006.
15. Griswold, p. 41.
16. Griswold, p. 81.
17. Griswold, p. 93.
18. Griswold, p. 96.
19. Griswold, pp. 98–9.
20. Griswold, p. 102.
21. Griswold, p. 102.
22. Griswold, p. 103.
23. Griswold, p. 105.
24. Griswold, p. 106.
25. Griswold, p. 124.
26. Griswold, p. 126.
27. Griswold, p. 131.
28. Griswold, p. 147.
29. Robert Cialdini, *Influence: The Psychology of Persuasion*, New York: Morrow, 1993.
30. See Yoweri Museveni and Jakaya Mrisho Kikwete, "Free Trade and the Fight Against Malaria," *The Wall Street Journal*, July 26, 2010.

Reprinted by permission of Liberty Magazine.

34

My review of: *Happiness, Economics, and Public Policy*

(by Helen Johns and Paul Ormerod, London: Institute for Economic Affairs, 2010) first appeared in The Independent Review, Vol. 14, No. 3, Winter 2010, pp. 458–460

Happiness has been a topic of philosophic discussion for thousands of years, but it has recently attracted the attention of behavioral and social scientists. During the past three decades, an explosion of research on happiness has occurred, with a concentration on how to measure it and what relationship it has to national wealth and social policy. Nearly 4,400 articles on this topic were published in the year 2000 alone.

Economists Helen Johns and Paul Ormerod have written a concise and trenchant critique of "happiness economics" as a reliable tool for making policy decisions. They note that strong policy prescriptions are being drawn from the data on happiness. The prime example has its origin in the early literature. The happiness data seem to show that during the past several decades, the level of happiness in the developed world has remained constant, whereas real income per capita has doubled. This lack of association is often referred to as "the Easterlin paradox" because economist Richard O. Easterlin was the first to provide data purportedly showing that past a certain point, increases in income are not associated with increases in happiness. A number of researchers have explained this paradox by saying that happiness depends on a person's relative, not absolute, amount of income. The conclusion all too cheerfully drawn by those of a statist inclination is that steep, progressive taxation is needed to diminish relative income differences and thereby increase people's happiness. The conclusion also helps to justify extensive state economic intervention. A number of economic studies have shown that more state controls reduce the rate of economic growth, but if economic growth does not increase happiness, the objection loses much of its force.

Johns and Ormerod explore a number of criticisms of this line of happiness research and its use in supporting redistributionist policies. First, they note that although rising gross domestic product (GDP) does not correlate with rising levels of happiness, many other relevant factors also fail to correlate. For example, they point out that in the United Kingdom, during a period when government spending increased by 50 percent, happiness remained constant, but none of the statist policy wonks concluded that big government is irrelevant to happiness.

In the United States, during a period in which violent crime nearly doubled then dropped to its earlier level, the happiness level remained constant. During the same period, life expectancy increased, and gender inequality of income decreased, but, again, happiness remained constant. It is counterintuitive, to say the least, to conclude that decreasing crime, increasing longevity, and increasing gender equality have no impact on happiness. Moreover, the authors point out, the level of income disparity in a given country and that country's happiness level is not significantly associated.

A second critique the authors explore is of the idea of replacing GDP, the standard measure of economic success, as a policymaking tool with a happiness-based metric, perhaps "gross national happiness." They review the history of alternative measures of economic health, such as the measure of economic welfare and the index of sustainable economic welfare, and show that such measures tend to be very subjective and often involve highly dubious empirical assumptions. They note that Nobel Laureate Daniel Kahneman, himself a major contributor to happiness research, has expressed doubt about its use in policymaking.[1]

A third area of critique Johns and Ormerod investigate involves the suggestion that a happiness metric would help us to measure welfare better than measures such as GDP do. The idea here starts with the obvious fact that certain goods lack market prices. Public goods, such as a healthy ecosystem, come to mind here: it is clear that green, open spaces are important to human flourishing and happiness, but the free market often does not price them. Of course, we might ask people to use money as a trade-off metric: we can assess how much a person values open space by asking how much of their income they are willing to spend, recognizing that they will thus have less to spend for other things. Many happiness policy wonks, however, want to use a "holistic" measure (one that includes the level of happiness) instead.

As the authors note, the problem of trade-offs remains. For example, in the United Kingdom, happiness-policy mavens advocate spending a great deal more money to hire therapists to treat depression. But Kahneman and others have shown that after a disabling accident, the disabled tend to return to their prior level of happiness.[2]

So are we to conclude that we should eliminate spending for prevention and treatment of disabilities and instead spend the money for therapists for the depressed on the theory that net happiness will be increased?

Here Johns and Ormerod discuss a point that they might well have pursued further. They argue that the drive for a "holistic" conception of welfare is a manifestation of the statist view that people are intellectually incapable of determining what is truly in their best interests.

This point ties in with the one made earlier: happiness research has been useful from the statist perspective. Faced with the unpleasant fact that freer economies are wealthier, the statist dismisses it; faced with the fact people do not make the same trade-offs that he does, he dismisses them.

Although Johns and Ormerod have written an excellent critique of the happiness literature, two additional points deserve notice. First, granting that the happiness data produce a crude measure of the underlying phenomena, we might note that serious problems also afflict most other data that economists and social scientists use. Second, the research is still evolving. For example, in a major work written recently, Betsey Stevenson and Justin Wolfers provide compelling evidence that the Easterlin paradox is simply false—at no point do increases in income cease increasing happiness.[3]

Notes

1. See D. Kahneman, "The Science of Well-Being," seminar at the Institute for Public Policy Research, London, September 1, 2006.
2. D. Kahneman and A. Krueger, "Developments in the Measure of Subjective Wellbeing," *Journal of Economic Perspectives* 20, 2006: 3–24.
3. *Economic Growth and Subjective Well-Being: Reassessing the Easterlin Paradox*, Working Paper no. 2394, Munich: CESIfo, September 2008.

My thanks to *The Independent Review.*

35

My review of *A Rat Is a Pig Is a Dog Is a Boy*

The Human Cost of the Animal Rights Movement (Wesley Smith, Encounter Books, 2010, 312 pp.) first appeared in Liberty, September 2010

To paraphrase George Orwell, there are some ideas so absurd that only intellectuals can believe them. Certainly one of the most absurd ideas that are widespread among today's intellectuals is the notion that animals have rights. Since the public, to the extent that it's even aware of the animal rights movement, usually misunderstands it, Wesley Smith's new book explaining this movement and its costs to society is most welcome.

Smith is a senior fellow in human rights and bioethics at the Discovery Institute. He has written several other books broadly within the realm of bioethics.

Smith starts this book by surveying and contrasting the views of the intellectuals behind the animal rights movement. They include Gary Francione, Richard Ryder, Charles Patterson, Tom Regan, and, most notably, Peter Singer, the philosopher who wrote the seminal work in this area, *Animal Liberation*, in 1975. Singer is credited with popularizing the notion of "speciesism" that equates preferring the human species to preferring one's own race. Singer is a utilitarian, so as Smith rightly notes, he doesn't base his views on natural rights as such. His call for animal liberation proceeds, instead, from the notion that animals can feel pain and pleasure so should be considered in the calculus of pleasures and pains that determine (in his view) right and wrong actions. What Smith doesn't note is that Singer's philosophical take on animals harks back to one of the earliest exponents of utilitarian ethics, Jeremy Bentham (1748–1832), and that Bentham's most acute follower rejected it. I will return to this point.

Smith also discusses the worldwide efforts to give animals legal rights. On the national scene, law professors such as Steven Wise and the Center for Expansion of Fundamental Rights come in for considerable scrutiny, as do such famous legal authorities as Cass Sunstein and Lawrence Tribe. All have sought to give legal standing to animals in the courts. But (a point Smith doesn't explore) none of these worthies has seen one of the obvious results of giving animals legal rights logically—it opens the way for animals to be arrested for victimizing other animals and for animals to sue other animals. If a mouse has legal standing to sue people in a court of law, why shouldn't it be allowed to sue any cat that attacks it or see the cat stand trial for assault?

Smith covers the actions of animal rights groups such as PETA (People for the Ethical Treatment of Animals) and HSUS (the Humane Society of the United States). They have used some unsavory and even despicable tactics to sway public opinion, including the operation of grossly misleading propaganda campaigns (such as the notorious PETA campaign equating the cooking of chickens by Kentucky Fried Chicken with the killing of millions of people in the Holocaust). They have had no scruples about pushing propaganda in the public schools. Other groups have infiltrated medical labs to destroy research and "liberate" the animals.

The book reviews in detail the animal rights terrorist groups such as ALF (the Animal Liberation Front), ELF (the Earth Liberation Front), and SHAC (Stop Huntingdon Animal Cruelty). These groups have committed grave crimes and caused great harm, but they have received a lot of direct and indirect support from members of so-called moderate groups.

Perhaps the most useful feature of the book is its explanation and defense of the use of animals in medical research. The usual specious arguments against this practice put forward by the animal rights activists (that animals aren't physiologically analogous to humans, that computer modeling can always replace experimentation, and so on) are refuted. Smith reviews in detail the evolution of our testing procedures, including the development of protections for lab animals by the medical and pharmaceutical industries. Especially useful has been a private nonprofit organization AAALAC (the Association for Assessment and Accreditation of Laboratory Animal Care International). In a supplement to the book, Smith provides a table of nearly seventy-five entries of Nobel Prizes awarded for research conducted using animals.

Working from the natural rights ethical perspective, Smith gives a compelling account of why animals don't have rights. Essentially, they don't have rights because they cannot enter into the realm of rights (i.e., the community of morally autonomous, rights-recognizing individuals). Animals cannot recognize any rights in humans or any other animals. Only humans can—which is why we don't try, say, a bear for attacking a tourist. We may kill it to prevent further attacks, but no one but a madman would blame it. The bear views us as simply part of the environment.

To the common reply by animal rights supporters that many humans (such as infants and the mentally impaired) are similarly incapable of recognizing rights, Smith rightly responds that they are still members of the rights community, because they have the potential to recognize other peoples' rights in the future or did so in the past or because even though they are diminished in mental abilities, they are still capable of recognizing rights. This moral autonomy is just part of being human. I would add that when humans—such as violent criminals—show no recognition of the rights of others, we colloquially call them animals and incarcerate or even execute them.

My only criticism of the book is that it attempts to explain why the animal rights ideology is unsound from solely the natural rights ethical framework. In truth, the ideology can be seen as morally dubious from almost any ethical perspective. Consider the utilitarian view. Even from the hedonistic utilitarian perspective, the ideology can be criticized for equating the pleasures that a pig can experience with the pleasures that a person can experience. John Stuart Mill, the protégé of Bentham, took precisely this tack. Or we can just drop hedonism entirely, which many later utilitarians did, and say that other things besides pleasure—artistic achievement, scientific knowledge, literature, and so on—are inherently desirable. From that utilitarian perspective, one can easily hold that animals are not on the same moral plane as people.

Again, an ethics that puts the focus of morality on autonomous deliberative choice would tend to view animals as being of different moral status from true persons. Similarly, virtue ethics—which views the rational, trained control of emotions as being central to ethics—would likely put animals in a different category from humans.

Smith is to be thanked for giving us a concise but comprehensive survey of the ideas, thinkers, advocacy organizations, and terrorist groups responsible for making an aberrational ideology as influential as it has been and for showing just how detrimental to human flourishing its further empowerment would be.

Reprinted by permission of Liberty Magazine.

Part Four

Miscellany

36

"Is the Soul-Making Defense Sound?"

first appeared in Metanoia Vol. XII, No. 1 (1980)

The "problem of evil" is a problem for any traditional Judeo- Christian faith, in that evil is conceded to exist, yet it is held not to be evidence for the non-existence of God. Perhaps the most common defense against the problem of evil is the "soul-making" defense, as it is called by John Hick.[1]

Those who adopt this defense argue that God's purpose for man is that he be a free agent, endowed with the opportunity for character development through the exercise of free choice. And for this purpose to be achieved, evil (both natural and moral) must exist. Natural evil is required to present us with the opportunity to exercise free will (e.g., the only way for me to have the opportunity to be charitable is for me to see the poverty of others). And moral evil is the inevitable result of man's exercise of that free will (e.g., the horror of the Holocaust was due to the immoral choices of a large number of free agents).[2]

More to the point, moral evil must be permitted for a soul to be "made", since the agent learns from seeing the unpleasant consequences of his choices. Hick puts the matter thus:

> Christianity, however, has never supposed that God's purpose in the creation of the world was to construct a paradise whose inhabitants would experience a maximum of pleasure and a minimum of pain… Following hints from St. Paul, Irenaeus taught that man has been made as a person in the image of God but

> has not yet been brought as a free and responsible agent into the finite likeness of God...Our world, with all its rough edges, is the sphere in which this second and harder stage of the creative process is taking place.[3]

The soul-making defense against the problem of evil seems implausible, at least absent any proof that soul-making requires exactly the amount of natural and moral evil that exists, and no less. (After all, if soul-making could succeed—as seems likely—with one less earthquake than has occurred, then God would be immoral to have allowed it). But I will shoulder the burden of proof, attempting to outline an alternate technique for soul-making, which would require less evil (of both kinds) for the achievement of the same purpose.

Consider a possible world in which God exists, and deceives each person occasionally into thinking (erroneously) that an earthquake has occurred, or an acquaintance is gravely ill and needs a kidney transplant, or such like. Further, suppose that God allows the person to make decisions, but when evil results are about to occur from a decision, He intervenes to stop the action, creating at the same time in the agent's mind the illusion that what would have transpired (had He not intervened) actually did. God could cease maintaining the illusion after the agent has learned whatever lesson God intended the agent to learn (or demonstrated his failure to learn it), or after the agent has risen to the occasion afforded by the (in fact illusory) natural evil (or failed to rise to it). God might erase the incident from the agent's memory. Alternatively, God could allow the illusion to continue indefinitely, if He wanted to continue to give the agent the opportunity to learn or repent. I call such a possible world one in which God practices **benign deception** ("BD" for short).

As an example of how BD might be used, consider a typical "morality play" situation in which soul-making is supposed to occur. I stand to inherit a million dollars if I kill my uncle and get away with it. I decide to do the evil deed, creep into his mansion, pull a knife and plunge it into his heart. But I am then overcome by remorse, and suddenly learn that money isn't everything. (Or alternatively, I do not feel remorse, but instead joy, thus proving my immorality.) In this case, my soul is either perfected or else shown to be irretrievably bad, but at the cost of another's life.

If, on the other hand, God had practiced BD, everything would have been the same, except that when I plunged the knife downwards, the knife would never have struck home. God would have "clouded my mind," thus making it only appear to me that I succeeded in my action. Once I had learned my lesson (or demonstrated my wickedness), God could have unclouded my mind, or unclouded my mind and erased my memory of the whole incident, or left me under the illusion.

It is clear that most, if not all, evil can be averted by the exercise of BD. Natural evil need not *actually* occur, to present people with opportunities for moral choice; creating the illusion of disasters in their minds will do. And it is not necessary for people to see the *actual* consequences of their decisions to learn or to be judged; the illusion of those consequences having come to pass, the mere appearance of what would have happened (if the action had in fact been carried out), will do.

So it appears that BD is possible, and could be used by God to achieve His soul-making purposes; and since it is not being practiced, the soul-making defense fails. Let me consider three possible replies.

First, it might be argued that if God engaged in BD, He would be a deceiver, thus immoral, which is contrary to His nature. God would never choose to be a cosmic liar.

The reply here seems clear. Certainly, lying is justifiable in certain situations, especially where it minimizes pain. (Who would condemn a man for lying to his baby daughter about her chances for surviving her leukemia?) Which is morally preferable, a Cosmic Liar, or a Cosmic Crippler?

A second objection is this: we can't verify whether or not BD is in fact being practiced. Perhaps God is practicing BD and we don't know it.

My reply is that, even if this objection is true, it may be of comfort to the Christian Scientist, but certainly not to the traditional Christian. Again quoting Hick:

> To say, for example (with contemporary Christian Science), that evil is an illusion of the human mind is impossible within a religion based upon the stark realism of the Bible. Its pages faithfully reflect the characteristic mixture of good and evil in human experience. They record every kind of sorrow and suffering, every mode of man's inhumanity to man.[4]

A third objection might be that for it to be possible for a person to learn from his actions, it must be possible for him to observe the consequences of his actions. So if God engaged in BD, He would defeat the soul-making purpose. But this is just false: one need not really (veridically) observe the results of a choice to learn from it; one need only have the illusion.

Were God to exist, with the powers and purposes imputed to him by the traditional Christian who adopts the soul-making defense, BD would occur. It doesn't. Thus the soul-making defense fails, and the problem of evil remains a problem.

Notes

1. 'The Soul Building Argument," by John Hick, in *Philosophy: Paradox and Discovery,* ed. by Arthur Minton (New York: McGraw-Hill, 1976) pp. 43–49.
2. For a refutation of this claim, see "The Irrelevance of the Free Will Defense," by Steven Boer, *Analysis* 38, 110–112, March, 1978.
3. Hick, *op. cit.,* p. 47.
4. Hick, *op. cit.,* p. 44.

My thanks to *Metanoia* and the Department of Philosophy of Loyola Marymount University.

37

“Roadblocks to Research: One Part-Timer’s View”

first appeared in the anthology Part-Time Academic Employment in the Humanities (ed. by M. E. Wallace, New York: Modern Language Association of America, 1984) pp. 66–68

Billie Holiday, a gifted artist, was also a keen observer of the human condition. She observed in a classic ballad:

> Them that’s got shall get,
> Them that’s not shall lose,
> So the Bible says
> And it still is news.
> Papa may have,
> Mama may have,
> But God bless the child
> that’s got his own.

Her point is that the social system often puts people on tracks—the winning track and the losing track—and, once on the lower track, it is virtually impossible to get on the higher one.

I believe that Holiday's law governs the academic world no less than the social system as a whole, specifically, that two tracks have developed in the college world, one holding most full-timers and one holding most part-timers, and that once on the part-time track it is nearly impossible to get off. My personal experience suggests (at least to me) this but of course doesn't prove it (especially to others). Nonetheless, my experience may give readers insight into aspects of part-time employment they may have overlooked.

On what basis are people hired for tenure-track positions? My experience, garnered at the four universities I have attended and at the dozen colleges and community colleges where I have taught, is that the primary factor in hiring is the publications list a candidate can present. If such is the case, you may wonder why part-timers don't simply publish as much as full-timers. The answer is that Holiday's law works against them: part-timers face impediments to research that full-timers rarely face, and this makes it a very unfair race.

For example, since part-timers are almost never paid pro rata, they face much lower incomes. For example, I currently teach four large classes per semester at two colleges but earn only about $1,000 per teaching month. Consequently, part-timers must either get nonacademic jobs, in addition to teaching, or else must "overload"—teach *six to nine courses* per term, and extra courses during the summer. Either way, they wind up with little time to spare for research of any kind.

Moreover, traveling time (from one job to another) further limits the time available for writing. (My own case again: I teach at two colleges eighty miles apart and spend eight hours a week commuting.) Needless to say, traveling expenses further reduce income, which reinforces the first impediment.

In addition, part-timers are usually assigned to teach lower-division classes, which have much higher enrollments and therefore require much more work per student. (Lower-division students also tend to require more "intensive care" to develop their skills.) More time for the freshmen, less time for research, hence less chance to join the blessed: Holiday's law again.

Of course, it is obvious that teaching upper-division and graduate-level courses in one's field of specialization enhances the opportunity for publication. But since part-timers teach mainly lower-division courses, few of which touch on their immediate areas of specialization, they are thus further handicapped. Moreover, since their outside work and the inordinate amount of grading they do take up so much time, they don't experience the kind of interaction with well-established colleagues that sparks research.

Failure to produce scholarly articles has another consequence. Grants usually go to academics with publications and a record of past grants. Part-timers—in my experience at least—almost never get research grants. Often those who least need the grants get them, while those who are desperate for just six months' financial support to get some ideas down on paper are denied any opportunity to do so. Again, let me make the point concrete with an example from my own career. Two years ago, I co-authored a paper with a political scientist on the impact of warfare on technology. It was accepted for publication immediately. But we have found it impossible to get even a small grant for follow-up research, because we lack the track record of prior grants. Without such a grant, the data coding (of patent statistics) cannot be done, and a novel approach to an important issue has been stopped dead.

Need I add that part-timers never get sabbaticals? Nor can they take leaves of absence with the assurance that their jobs will still be there when they return.

And is it surprising that they usually lack the wherewithal to attend lectures, seminars, and conferences in their respective fields?

Another impediment to research facing part-timers is lack of secretarial support. At many (though, thank goodness, not at all) colleges, part-timers can have neither scholarly papers nor even *class handouts* typed. Thus, it seems, the rich get richer while the poor get poorer: those with publications get full-time jobs and support for producing more articles; those without publications have impediments put in their path.

A scholar vitally needs to have his or her ideas challenged, clarified, and encouraged. But those on the lower track almost never get to the track on which such fruitful dialogue takes place. This leads to a sort of anomie or even alienation among part-timers. They often feel themselves strangers, half in the academic world and half out, uncertain where they belong.

As a philosopher I cannot resist an ethical observation. The Holiday syndrome offends, not merely because it wastes human potential. It offends because it is unjust. It is unjust to deny qualified scholars the opportunity to add their voices and their ideas to the scholarly dialog. In the long run, scholarship itself is the ultimate loser because of the roadblocks put in the way of part-timers.

My thanks to M. E. Wallace and the Modern Language Association of America.

38

My review of: *Can Modern War Be Just?*

(by James Turner Johnson, New Haven: Yale University Press, 1986, 190 pp.) first appeared in Chronicles of Culture June, 1987

There is nothing quite so fatuous as the nuclear pacifism currently fashionable among leftist theologians and their ilk. Visions of mushroom clouds (brought on by repeated viewings of *On the Beach* and *Dr. Strangelove*) cloud many minds. The result is the fuzzy-minded view that we must either accept the current MAD standoff with the Soviets, or else we must unilaterally disarm. Nuclear pacifism thus paralyzes the West, allowing the Soviets to replace pro-Western governments with proxy regimes.

Such fuzzy-mindedness and paralysis might be avoided if we relied more upon the "just war" theory, developed by philosophers and theologians since Augustine. Sketchily put, just war theory distinguishes questions about *jus ad bellum* (i.e., questions about what justifies resort to war) from questions about *jus in bello* (i.e., questions about which forms of force in war are justifiable). The consensus view has been that a war is justified if and only if there is a just cause (reason) for it, it is ordered by the right (proper) authority, with the right intent, as a last resort, with the end goal of peace, and the evil it produces is proportionate to the good. And a form of violence or weaponry is acceptable in a war if and only if it discriminates between combatants and noncombatants, and it is proportionate (i.e., not excessive) in the destruction it causes.

James T. Johnson has applied just war theory to questions about modern war. He is certainly well-versed in that tradition, having written earlier two books on the history of just war doctrines: *Ideology, Reason and the Limitation of War*, and *Just War Tradition and the Restraint of War*. These books were intended for an academic audience. In *Can Modern War Be Just?* Johnson attempts to address the lay audience as well.

Essentially, Johnson's book consists of a number of previously written essays more or less modified to constitute chapters. In each essay/chapter he applies just war theory to some feature of modern war—either particular wars (such as Israel's incursion into Lebanon) or specific weapons (such as the neutron bomb) or specific issues (such as conscientious objection). The results of his inquiries do not fall neatly into the current liberal/conservative dichotomy.

Some of his arguments are nicely drawn, and persuasive. He neatly punctures the ban-the-bomb balloon, rightly pointing out that unilateral disarmament is the real desire of people who want to ban the bomb, and that unilateral disarmament will increase—not decrease—the chances of nuclear war. He urges a move toward counter-force rather than counter-population strategy (i.e., developing weapons directed at the enemy's military power, rather than at his population centers). This latter point of view has not been popular with the professional "peace" activists, causing Johnson some puzzlement. He observes that "there is no small irony in the fact that some of the opponents of counter-population strategy on moral grounds have been vocally opposed to efforts to transform our national defense posture away from this strategy, alleging the creation of instability." He is surely right in thinking that there is a curious inconsistency in opposing nuclear holocaust yet opposing any move toward a less deadly strategy—such as President Reagan's plans to put a defensive net in space. Johnson also argues well for the acceptability of the neutron bomb and cruise missile.

However, on a number of issues his arguments are much less persuasive. Occasionally, such as in his discussion of Israel's incursion into Lebanon, his arguments fail to convince because they are hopelessly brief and superficial—a consequence of addressing far too many issues in a 190-page book, a book which has, moreover, a great amount of redundancy. In other cases, Johnson doesn't fully come to grips with the issues. For example, he seems to urge that we pursue a "decapitation" strategy—develop weapons with the goal of wiping out the Soviets' command and control structure. But he himself notes that this will violate the doctrine of avoiding noncombatants (the Soviet leaders, after all, reside in Moscow).

Though his effort is not satisfactory in every respect, Johnson does seriously attempt to balance principles and respect facts. For this he is to be praised.

My thanks to *The Chronicles of Culture.*

39

"Using Philosophical Dilemmas to Teach Composition"

first appeared in Teaching English in the Two Year College, Vol. 12, No. 3 (1985)

Philosophy is one of the oldest academic disciplines and, traditionally, one of the most influential. In recent decades, however, philosophers have become progressively more isolated, interacting very little with colleagues in other disciplines. As an academic philosopher myself, I am ashamed to say that philosophers themselves are to blame for their isolation: we have made no real effort to let others know our domain of research and methodology, nor have we particularly sought the expertise of others.

I offer this essay as a step toward an interdisciplinary exchange program. Specifically, I want to indicate how a traditional philosophical technique can be used profitably by composition teachers.

The decline in writing skills is apparent to all of us, especially to those of us who teach in two-year colleges. Combating this problem will involve requiring students to write critical essays far more often than they do now and to write essays in more classes than just their English classes. But this creates a bit of a problem: how can students in introductory courses write expository essays of any useful depth in subjects they know almost nothing about?

I suggest that the philosophic technique known as "thought experimentation" can be of use. Philosophers often want to focus on some crucial concept that interests them, such as social justice or the notion of personal identity. But real-life situations are complicated by a huge number of variables that hide underlying philosophic issues. To get around this, philosophers will often construct an imaginary "what if" situation, a scenario which is realistic enough to be imagined and reasoned about, but which allows the philosopher to scrape away irrelevant factual complications.

This technique is not reserved for philosophers alone. Scientists often employ thought experiments when ordinary experiments are not feasible—indeed, the very phrase "thought experiment" was coined by Einstein.

It seems to me that this technique can be used to allow students to write substantial essays on interesting topics (as opposed to "How I Spent My Summer Vacation" kinds of topics) with a minimum of research and with no background knowledge presupposed.

Indeed, I employ this technique in my own classes to teach the students how to write "contrast and compare" essays.

I begin by giving my students some heuristic tips about writing such essays. In a "contrast and compare" essay you are presented with a number of alternatives (or theories, or points of view), asked to critically contrast each with the others, and (often) to select the one that you find closest to the truth. Thus I advise my students to take the following steps in their essays, although the order in which the steps are taken will depend of course on style and context:

Step 1: State the issue clearly and the alternatives open to you.
Step 2: State your position early, clearly, and fairly.
Step 3: State logically good reasons for your position (avoid fallacies!).
Step 4: Discuss the bad points of the alternatives.
Step 5: (This step adds great power to your essay.) Anticipate the major problems with your position, and answer them.
Step 6: (This step adds even more power.) Mention the good points of the alternatives you are rejecting and show how your position combines all those good points.

I then read with them a thought experiment such as the following, which focuses upon the idea of social justice:

Social Justice in Liberal City

Liberal City is a small community which takes pride in living up to its name. In particular, the residents are always discussing what they call "social justice," that is, how to guarantee that each group of citizens gets its fair share of the economic pie. As you might imagine, there is considerable argument about who is entitled to what.

These discussions have gotten quite heated lately because of proposals on the upcoming ballot. You see, Liberal City's whole economy rests on woodcarving. Most families carve furniture and art objects, and take them to the local soccer field. A helicopter from Big City picks them up, and takes those carvings to auction houses where they are sold to the highest bidders. (The helicopter company takes one percent of the proceeds, leaving the rest for the woodcarving families.)

Now, unfortunately, not everybody in Liberal City has the same carving ability. Some of the residents can carve breathtakingly beautiful objects out of even the roughest block of wood, which of course bring the highest prices at the Big City auctions. Other residents can carve fairly nice furniture and such like, not magnificent but certainly nice looking, which fetch a pretty good price at auction. But some of the residents are simply untalented: their carvings almost never sell—and when they sell, they fetch a low price, indeed! And since there are no other jobs open, the untalented woodcarvers have no choice but to accept their low wages. This situation has resulted in a division of the citizens into the wealthy (talented), the middle class (not so talented), and the poor (the untalented). And that is what the upcoming election is all about: how should Liberal City react to this situation, given its commitment to "social justice"?

There are several proposals afoot. (1) Some say that since the talented have ethically earned their money themselves, they are entitled to keep it. So nothing should be done about the disparity of income, except of course by acts of charity done at the discretion of the rich/talented. (2) Others say that since the talented did not "earn" their talents—they just were lucky enough to be born with them—what they earn should be heavily taxed, and the proceeds distributed to the less talented, everybody getting an equal share. (3) Still others say that proposal number two doesn't go far enough. They argue that the talented will always rise to the top, circumventing the redistributive tax system. They thus propose that the talented be handicapped in some way, perhaps by restricting the number of days they can work or limiting their access to the woodcarving schools. (4) Some have argued that it would be best to redistribute the income, as proposal two would have it, but on the basis of effort, not equality. (5) Another proposal is to institute genetic engineering, trying to ensure that all people eventually start with the same ability—thus nobody could complain about lack of wealth.

Remember, there are essentially no other jobs in Liberal City besides woodcarving, and the people of Liberal City cannot emigrate (for political reasons we need not examine). Thus the election is very important.

Which proposal should Liberal City adopt, and why?

I then lead the class in discussion of the merits and drawbacks of each course of action. Some of the problems we touch on are:

Proposal 1: If the residents are much inclined to charity, why are there poor people at all? And if no charity is given, people may starve. Should that be allowed?

Proposal 2: Won't equal rewards eliminate the incentive to work hard? Isn't forcing a talented person to support an untalented person making the talented person a slave of the untalented?

Proposal 3: If we handicap the rich, won't that just lower everybody's standard of living?

Proposal 4: How can we measure effort? And isn't the ability to put forth an effort just a special kind of talent, just as inherited as wood-carving ability? (If so, then rewarding for effort is just as bad as rewarding for production.)

Proposal 5: Even supposing that the technical problems involved in genetic engineering can be solved, wouldn't this proposal involve forcing some people to forego having children? Is that compatible with human rights?

I then assign them the task of writing an essay on Liberal City, arguing for one of the five alternatives, and against the others.

The second essay they are assigned is a step up in difficulty, in that I do not lay out the alternatives and the problems each faces in class, but instead leave it to them to dig that out of the description of the scenario.

The Nationalist Dilemma

The year is 2180, and due to wars and subsequent national fusion there are only two countries in the world: America and Etrangia. These two nations are bitter, bitter enemies. Etrangia, for no reason at all except spite, has kidnapped fifty Americans (who were foolish enough to be yachting in the "wrong"—not illegal—area), and the dictator of Etrangia, Vlad, has announced that the hostages will be killed next week. Vlad is so confident of the "weakness" (as he calls it) of the Americans that he has made this boastful promise: if America kills some Etrangians (which Vlad feels the Americans are too weak to do), and only if they do so, will he let the Americans go.

The American government calls upon Professor Hardnose, a specialist in Etrangian history and politics at Duck University, for advice. Hardnose has recommended that Doom, an Etrangian town of one hundred people, be annihilated.

His reasoning is this. Etrangia is a highly fortified huge island uniformly covered by highly armed towns. No American raiding party could possibly succeed. Besides, the Americans have no idea where the hostages are being held, except of course that they are not being held in Doom. On the other hand, America has weapons of mass destruction while Etrangia does not, so Etrangia cannot retaliate by destroying any American cities. Nor can it possibly invade or even raid America, since America is well fortified, too.

Moreover, says Hardnose, the Etrangian culture is one that despises mercy and views concern for innocent lives as weakness. Further, the dictator Vlad is a madman, a blood monster who is unpredictable in every way save one: he always keeps his word.

Finally, reasons Hardnose, Doom is the very smallest town in Etrangia. There are no single families in outlying areas who could be killed instead. Nor do we know where the Etrangian soldiers live. So we know that we will get the Americans back if, and only if, we kill some Etrangians; and the fewest we can kill is one hundred. Maybe it would be nice if we could kill soldiers instead of innocent civilians, but we can't.

(Assume the facts Hardnose cites are correct.)

Hardnose's proposal is not without opposition. One of his colleagues, Professor Softie, stopped him in the hall today, and they had this conversation:

H: You admit, then, that in our current crisis, there are only two choices. We either kill one hundred enemy civilians, or our fifty innocent compatriots will die horribly. Clearly, we should kill the enemy.

S: I agree that we only have those two choices, but I dislike the loaded words you use. Words like "enemy" and "our innocent compatriots" disguise the obvious fact that all the people involved, the fifty you want to save and the hundred people you propose killing, are all equally innocent. What sense does it make to say that we should save fifty innocent people by killing one hundred innocent ones? No, my truculent buddy, I'm afraid that the only moral thing we can do is let the fifty Americans die.

H: I cannot fathom your stupidity. The point is that the fifty to be saved are Americans, while the others are Etrangians. Don't we owe something to our countrymen?

S: We owe something to every human being, countryman or not.

H: Well, maybe—but the point is that we owe more to our own people. Look, maybe what's bothering you is that one hundred Etrangians will have to be killed to save the Americans. Maybe you think Americans aren't worth double what Etrangians are, so to speak. Personally, I think I would rather see a million Etrangians die than one American, but then, you see, 1 really love my country. You obviously can't understand that. But suppose we could find an Etrangian town of fifty-one people: would you then agree to destroy it?

S: They should call you "Hardhead" instead of "Hardnose." I love my countrymen, just as I love all human beings. I am a man of love, not hate. And because of that, I want to minimize the killing of innocent people. For that reason, I would not choose to kill the fifty-one Etrangians.

H: I cannot understand your position. Suppose we find an Etrangian town of fifty people. Surely then you would favor having the Etrangians rather than the Americans die? After all, the same number of lives is involved!

S: Well, I guess I am enough of a nationalist to say that if a certain number of people are going to die no matter what, then I prefer that they not be American.

H: Well, then you and I basically agree on the fact that a nation is a real thing, that citizens of a country owe more to each other (all things being equal) than they do to citizens of other countries. I just feel that nationalistic bond more deeply than you do.

Quicklad, one of Softie's students, had been listening to the dialogue. He bursts in:

Q: Doesn't either of you realize that a nation is just a historical accident, a figment of your imagination? The point is, if fifty Americans or fifty Etrangians are going to die, and who dies depends upon my choice, I would flip a coin. I owe no more consideration to Americans (as you call them) than to anyone else! Moreover, you are calling upon us to go out and kill Etrangians. I say it is immoral. Let the Etrangians be immoral and do the killing.

H: Fine speech, Quicklad, but empty of ideas. Why do you deny the reality of national bonds? Would you do the same for familial bonds as well? Is your family a figment of your imagination? It surely is an accident of history! If your mother or a stranger were to die, and it were your choice that decided the matter, whom would you choose? Or would you flip a coin?

Quicklad's girlfriend, Tuffi, decided to join the argument.

T: Quicklad, he's got you there. Either you admit the validity of the family bond and explain why the national bond isn't also valid, or you deny all common sense and say that the family bond is also just a fiction. If it is, why do you want to marry me? But Mr. Hardnose overlooks an important point. Citizens of a country, because of their national bonds, are all guilty when their government (which is just a group of citizens) commits a crime. We ought to bomb them all—but of course we can't because the Americans may be anywhere. So we can only bomb Doom. But when we get the Americans back, we should retaliate by bombing the hell out of them!

Q: Tuffi, by your logic, if your brother kills my brother, I would be justified in punishing you!

At this point, the participants in the conversation stopped conversing when the bell sounded signaling that classes were resuming.

Whose view do you like the most and why? Hint: try telling me how you view a human being—bring in your religious and social views.

The third assignment is somewhat more difficult since I neither list the alternatives (and the problems each faces) in class, nor do I do so in the description of the scenario. A typical assignment would be to ask the students to make common sense assumptions where appropriate, but to tell the reader explicitly what is being assumed.

Christine's Dilemma

Christine was called to the hospital this morning, where she faces a dilemma. The doctors have told her that her mother will die soon unless Christine donates one of her kidneys. (Assume kidney dialysis machines have not been invented.) Tissue typing has been done, and Christine's kidneys are the only close match. The doctors estimate that if Christine undergoes the operation, her chance of surviving is 95 percent; her chance of living normally with one kidney is 95 percent. And her mother's chance of living normally with the transplanted kidney is 80 percent.

Christine is an only child of twenty-six. Her father, a philosophy teacher, died long ago, a victim of an assassin's bullet. Her mother is a woman of fifty years, in good health other than the acute kidney disease.

There is a complication. The doctors have also informed Christine that her second cousin, Dotty, is also dying of kidney failure. Dotty is a woman of twenty-five, single, without children, and her parents are deceased.

The doctors have also told Christine that by pure chance there is a third person dying of kidney disease. This woman, Zsa Zsa, who is thirty, is on the verge of a breakthrough in solar power research that will enable the world to end forever its dependence on fossil fuels. Moreover, she has nine wonderful children who worship the very ground she walks on, and her parents—both alive and well—love her deeply.

The doctors have said that with the kidney transplant both Dotty and Zsa Zsa would have an 80 percent chance of living normally.

Assume all the facts are true.

What should Christine do, and why?

It has been my experience that adroit use of thought experiments can not only be an effective tool in teaching philosophy, but in teaching composition skills as well. The reader is of course free to use mine, or devise his or her own.

Permission to reprint courtesy of the National Council of Teachers of English. I wish to thank the journal Teaching English in the Two Year College as well.

40

My review of: *Abusing Science: The Case against Creationism*

(by Philip Kitcher, Boston: MIT Press, 1985. 212 pp.) first appeared in California Review November, 1985

Some conservatives lately have urged that evolutionary theory is somehow antithetical to conservatism. It appears that these antievolutionist conservatives reason that a strong form of Christianity is a prerequisite for a consistent conservative outlook, and that evolutionary theory is incompatible with a strong form of Christianity.

Both premises of the argument are dubious. There are, after all, conservative Jews, Moslems, even agnostics, so a strong Christian orientation evidently is not a necessary condition for conservatism. Moreover, such an orientation seems to be not even a sufficient condition for conservatism—witness the all-too-numerous leftish Catholics and Protestants.

But of more interest here are the issues surrounding the second premise: is evolutionary theory true, and is it really incompatible with a strong form of Christianity? These are the issues which Philip Kitcher addresses in his fine little book, *Abusing Science: The Case against Creationism.*

Kitcher is extremely well qualified to examine the evolutionist/creationist debate. He is a highly respected and much published philosopher of biology. Thus it is not surprising that he shows exceptional understanding of what constitutes genuine science, and what constitutes mere pseudoscience.

Such an understanding is necessary when dealing with the issue about whether evolutionary theory is true. We must distinguish the question of whether it is true that species evolve over time, from the question how such evolution takes place. As regards to the first question, the evidence from a wide variety of sources is absolutely overwhelming that species do alter over time, or more exactly, that new species arise over time. We know the existence of gravity is a fact, even though we cannot see it. We accept it as a fact because of the huge number of other facts gravity explains: the motion of the planets; the behavior of moving bodies on Earth; the tidal movement of the oceans; and so on. Similarly, the diversity of fossil forms, the results of radio-carbon and other dating techniques, and many other data together lead virtually all biologists to accept evolution as a fact.

Of course, less clear even now is the exact explanation of evolution, Darwin's theory was that species evolve solely because the environment selects favorable variants ("survival of the fittest"), and that this struggle for survival results in a slow evolution of new species better adapted to specific environments ("niches"). Naturally, in the hundred years since Darwin wrote *The Origin of Species*, biologists have learned much more about the nature of genes and populations, and have developed more sophisticated theories about evolution. But that being so no more means that biologists doubt the fact of evolution, than the uncertainty among physicists about what causes gravity (i.e., whether or not there are gravity "particles') means that physicists doubt the existence of gravity.

Kitcher explains these and other points with great clarity. Along the way he discusses a number of interesting topics: the nature of scientific research; the basic concepts of genetics; the history of creationism; the major criticisms of evolutionary theory put forward by the creationists; and the inconsistencies and inaccuracies inherent in the creationist "theory." These discussions are invariably interesting and often witty. For example, the phenomenon of coprophagy is used to point up the difficulties of creationist theology; would an omnipotent being create animals which have no other way to fully digest their food but by eating their own droppings? Yet evolutionary theory accounts for the existence of such animals easily.

Thus as regards the issue whether evolution is true, Kitcher presents a clear and compelling presentation of the case for evolutionary theory. Most scientists, of course, are surprised to hear that many people have doubts about evolution, which is why the recent creationist critics have such an easy time of it. The scientific community rightly feels that the whole issue was settled more than a century ago.

About the issue whether evolutionary theory is incompatible with strong Christian faith, Kitcher has less to say. That is understandable, given that he is not a theologian. Of course, evolutionary theory is no theological threat whatsoever to those Christians who do not believe that the Genesis story is literal truth. Such Christians need only say that at a certain point in the evolutionary process—namely, when. Homo sapiens first appeared—God chose to reveal himself.

But there are many fundamentalist Christians who do hold the Genesis account to be literal truth. Kitcher quite rightly does not say that those fundamentalists should be forbidden to accept that view on faith. He just denies that that faith constitutes some kind of scientific theory, to be taught in schools on a par with genuine biology.

Conservatives who are tempted to side with the creationists in forcing schools to teach creationism really ought to read Kitcher's book. I, for one, would hate to see the conservative movement suffer the same loss of face in opposing evolution that the Catholic Church suffered in opposing Copernican astronomical theory. Conservatism should be about how to maintain and protect a virtuous society, and not about biology.

My thanks to *The California Review.*

41

My review of: *Profiles, Probabilities, and Stereotypes*

(Frederick Schauer, Cambridge, MA: Belknap Press, 2003. 359 pp.) first appeared in Academic Questions, Vol. 1, No. 2 Spring 2004, pp. 80–84

I often hear from my critical thinking students utter mantras such as "You shouldn't generalize!" and "Stereotyping is bad!" I typically reply that, putting aside the self-contradictory nature of these assertions ("One shouldn't generalize" being itself a generalization), common sense tells us that they are patently false. We have to generalize to survive—the trick is to do it reasonably. In this regard, Frederick Schauer has done something unusual for an Ivy League professor by defending (to some degree) common sense. Specifically, he has written a book defending the use of generalizations, albeit with limitations. For this he should be praised, albeit with limitations.

The strength of Schauer's book is his focus on actual and realistic hypothetical cases in which we use generalizations, in daily life and in more formal settings such as legal proceedings. He makes the point that many generalizations are spurious (i.e., empirically unsound) by looking at such common cases as astrology and phrenology—the reason we are reluctant to judge a person's character traits by his astrological sign is because astrological generalizations are spurious (e.g., there is no evidence that Libras are more apt to see both sides of an issue than anyone else.)

More interestingly, Schauer makes the point that generalizing and using generalizations are unavoidable by looking at the generalization, "Pit bulls are dangerous dogs." In fact, there has been considerable controversy about whether pit bulls should be allowed as pets, and certainly most insurance companies ask any applicant for home liability insurance (among other pertinent questions) whether there is a pit bull—or dog of several other breeds—present in the home. Now, pit bull owners often argue that their pets should be judged as individuals, and resist ordinances banning their favorite breed. Instead, they favor banning only dogs proven to be aggressive—laws should "deal with deeds not breeds," as the slogan goes.

But this presents two problems. First, there are the enormous costs of maintaining databases of reported bites and attacks, or testing each dog by (say) observing the dog's behavior toward childlike dolls. And if we wait until dogs severely attack people, the cost to society is high, indeed. Second, even if we suppose that the increased reliability of generalizing based upon observed individual behavior is worth the huge cost, it is still generalizing. For example, if Winston the pit bull is presented with a child-like doll and attacks it, we are generalizing when we conclude Winston is aggressive—he could, after all, just be having a bad day—and we are assuming the generalization that dogs who attack dolls are more apt to attack children than dogs who don't attack dolls. Yet this sort of squeamishness at stating and employing statistically sound generalizations about breeds of dogs led the American Kennel Club to remove from its guide to dogs (*Complete Dog Book*) breed profiles that describe certain breeds as not good with children—surely an important thing for parents to know before selecting a dog as a family pet.

In a similar fashion, Schauer argues that the use of generalization and profiling is justified in a wide variety of cases: laws limiting speeding; age restrictions on pilots (e.g., must be under 60) and auto driver's licenses (e.g., must be over 16); laws prohibiting carrying large amounts of hidden cash abroad; tax agencies targeting income-tax filers who fit a certain profile (e.g., declaring a large number of exemptions, or claiming a home-office deduction); and a variety of other cases as well. Along the way he gives some nice surveys of legal writings on presumed offenses, the concept of treating like cases alike, and sentencing guidelines.

I have two issues with the book. First, it has a repetitious, meandering style. A more tightly systematic treatment would have been clearer and may have freed space for a closer look at racial profiling, affirmative action, and other more contentious cases of the use of generalizations. This leads to my second issue: his treatment of the contentious cases is cursory and overly politically correct.

For instance, he covers the issue of profiling young Middle Eastern men at airports for security purposes (viz., reducing the risk of terrorist attacks or airplane hijacking). The current profiling system (the CAPPS system) uses various criteria to determine only which luggage (not which passengers) to search, and the Commission on Aviation Safety and Security (headed by then Vice President Al Gore) specifically excluded using ethnicity as a criterion. Schauer admits that the evidence we have indicates that using Middle Eastern ethnicity as a factor would increase significantly the effectiveness of a passenger screening algorithm. However, he opposes it because: (a) it would likely be overused by airport personnel (because of the salience of ethnicity); (b) the cost of the policy would fall disproportionately on young men of Middle Eastern appearance; and (c) the cost of not ethnically profiling to society is probably not more lost lives, but rather merely having to arrive "thirty minutes earlier" at the airport. This crucial issue is given far less exposition than the discussion of pit bulls, and his position on the matter is unpersuasive, based, as it is, upon not much more than bland assurance. Why not simply give airport personnel a list of factors with a fixed weighting so that the aggregate score determines who gets searched, and allow ethnicity as one but only one of those factors? This might result in some extra cost to young male Middle Easterners, but considering the chance of, yes, saving lives, it is at least arguable that it is worth it. And what if the cost of searching everyone, disabled blind elderly Swedish women and all, is not just 30 extra minutes but 12 extra hours—resulting in the cancellation of half the flights, with attendant job loss in the airline and tourism industries? What then?

This PC reluctance to address the real costs of failing to use statistically sound generalizations is even more striking in Schauer's treatment of gender issues. Schauer is against gender discrimination based upon gender generalizations, such as the exclusion of women from military schools, fire departments, and such like for several reasons. First, he finds many (perhaps most?) gender generalizations (i.e., claims of statistically significant differences between women and men in physical, emotional, or cognitive matters) simply false (spurious). He supports his incredibly sweeping claim that "it is well documented that gender-based generalizations are certainly historically, and to a considerable extent still, routinely exaggerated" by a footnote that cites a paltry four articles in psychology journals by a handful of writers. Second, even looking at differences between men and women that are statistically significant, many of those are more a product of discrimination than a justification for it. Schauer cites as example an Idaho law (overturned by the Supreme Court) that mandated a preference of men over women as administrators of estates. He supposes that the generalization behind that law was that men are generally more knowledgeable about business matters than women, but he rightly notes that even if that generalization were at one time true—it surely isn't now—it was because women were historically discouraged from entering fields such as accounting and investment banking. Third, Schauer holds that even in cases in which there is a statistically genuine, biological rather than sociological, gender difference (such as upper-body strength), some of these are cases in which gender is used "as a proxy," where those women who are exceptions to the norm are wrongly discriminated against. If you want baggage handlers able to lift bags (say) over 75 pounds, why not let everybody try out, and select all people—women and men—who can do the job? Schauer's view here is that even where there is a statistically significant difference between men and women as regards physical strength and aggressiveness, that difference is often used merely as a rationalization for the prior sexist decision to discriminate against women. Schauer argues boldly (154) that, "For too long too many people have assumed that because generalization is wrong then gender-based discrimination is wrong. But this reasoning is backwards. The truth is that it is because gender discrimination is wrong that gender-based generalization, even when statistically rational, is wrong as well."

I find his account here empirically antiquated and tendentious. To begin with empirical adequacy, Schauer cites a few psychologists who hold that non-spurious gender differences are rare. This was the dominant thinking in psychology and social science generally from the time of Margaret Mead's first writings in the late 1920s (latterly debunked by Derek Freeman) until perhaps the early 1980s. But over the last two decades, there has been a paradigm shift in thinking about gender. Here Schauer might have profited from a review of the recent literature documenting significant (indeed, profound) cognitive and emotional gender differences. One thinks of two recent clear treatments of the matter, Doreen Kimura's *Sex and Cognition* (MIT Press, 1999) and Deborah Blum's *Sex on the Brain: The Biological Differences between Men and Women* (Viking Press, 1997). Suffice it to say that in many areas gender generalizations have now been empirically well documented, often confirming beliefs that for millennia have been regarded as common sense.

The tendentiousness of Schauer's treatment is seen in several ways. First, he forgets his own point about the tradeoffs between costs and benefits of trying to refine generalizations by allowing individual testing. Yes, no doubt there are 12-year-olds physically and mentally capable of driving cars, but testing many millions of 12-year-olds to find the perhaps one thousand who are capable of safe driving would be inordinately expensive. Similarly, when a military school argues that their physical and emotional criteria for admission are such that very few women would qualify or even desire to attend, this may not simply be a bad faith argument being put forward by rank sexists, but may be an expression of how costly it is to accommodate the few females who will want to enter the school and can pass the physical tests. For instance, privacy does require separate facilities, which are typically costly.

Worse, Schauer poses the issues surrounding gender generalizations as being cases in which a generalization unfavorable to women is examined by the courts and typically held to be spurious, or used in bad faith (i.e., merely as excuse for sexist discrimination), or as an unnecessary proxy. But in our era of unlimited affirmative action, this manifestly is not the whole story. Instead, the egalitarian generalization is often assumed that in any profession, women should constitute at least 50 percent of the work force, and when they are less than that, the only explanation must be invidious discrimination. (Interestingly, when women constitute more than 50 percent, the converse inference—viz., that men are being discriminated against—is never drawn.)

Statistical disparities are often taken by activist judges and scholars as *ipso facto* proof of discrimination. (Curiously, Schauer doesn't consider affirmative action in any depth). But consider a specific case: the fact is that while women are statistically overrepresented in U.S. colleges in overall enrollments, they are underrepresented in math and engineering programs. Feminist organizations such as the American Association of University Women have made the argument that this shows that those programs are illegally discriminating against women, and push for affirmative action in the form of quotas or preferences to remedy the unequal enrollments. But (as fairly conclusively shown by Kimura in her work) it seems clear that as regards mathematical aptitude, men have a statistically non-spurious edge, and as regards preference for dealing with machines rather than people, there is also a statistically non-spurious difference, both of which likely explain the discrepancies in enrollments.

The point here is that, in truth, what is happening in many courts now is that the generalization that men and women are innately cognitively and emotionally identical is taken as patently obvious, despite the now overwhelming evidence that it is not only not obviously true, but indeed empirically false. Coming back to costs, Jessica Gavora has recently argued in her book *Tilting the Playing Field: Schools, Sports, Sex, and Title IX* (Encounter Books, 2002) that the rigid adherence to gender equity has resulted in the needless elimination of many men's sports programs. All reasonable people support a law that requires schools to make sure that all girls who want to participate in sports are enabled to do so. But it doesn't follow that to allow women equal access to sports will necessarily result in equal numbers of participants, unless you assume that girls and boys are identical in their desire to play sports—an assumption that is empirically dubious, to understate the matter.

Given the widespread squeamishness about generalizations and profiling, Schauer has done us all a service by rehabilitating an important topic. That he went all wobbly on a few of the more controversial aspects of the issue is easily forgivable.

Permission to reprint courtesy of Springer.
I wish to thank the journal *Academic Questions* as well.

42

My review of *Explaining Postmodernism*

Skepticism and Socialism from Rousseau to Foucault (Stephen Hicks, Tempe, AZ: Scholarly Publishing, Inc. 2004) first appeared in Liberty, June 2005, pp. 46–50

Over the last 20 years or so the philosophic orientation known as "postmodernism" (or "po-mo," to the cognoscenti) has become the dominant mindset in many humanities departments in American universities, especially in English departments. To the extent that professors in, say, science and engineering departments have heard of postmodernism, it seems mystifying. They see colleagues in humanities departments delivering papers filled with incomprehensible prose, making outrageous claims (such as that there is no correct interpretation of any text), and offering bizarre courses (such as the history of comic books). Stephen Hicks, a professor of philosophy at Rockford College, has produced a clearly written, concise book explaining just what postmodern philosophy is and how it arose, and he has done so in an admirable way.

Hicks begins by sketching out in broad terms what modernism is. Modernism is the worldview produced by the Enlightenment over the last four centuries. Roughly characterized, modernism involves naturalism in metaphysics, with the confidence that modern science is capable of, and is actually succeeding in, giving us an understanding of the physical universe. Modernism involves what he calls objectivism in epistemology, meaning the view that experience and reason are capable of gaining real knowledge, although modernist philosophers have hotly contested the specifics of this (with Rationalism, Empiricism, and Pragmatism being the most historically active epistemological schools). Modernism involves individualism in ethics, and a commitment to human rights, religious toleration, and democracy in political theory. Modernism also involves the acceptance of free-market economics and the technological revolution that it has spawned. In sum, modernism is the mindset that is common to the West, the laborious product of many great minds—Bacon, Locke, Descartes, Smith, Hobbes, Spinoza, Galileo, Newton, and Hume, among others. Most of us view this as a considerable leap forward from the Medieval period of supernaturalism, mysticism, excessive reliance on faith, and feudalist political and economic systems.

In the last 30 years or so, however, a group of thinkers have set themselves in opposition to the whole Enlightenment project. These *soi-disant* postmodernists reject the Enlightenment root and branch. Chief among the postmodern thinkers are Jacques Derrida, Michel Foucault, Jean-Francois Lyotard and (amazingly, an American) Richard Rorty. These thinkers, together with a host of smaller fry (such as Stanley Fish, Jacques Lacan, Andreas Huyssen, Frank Lentricchia and others), have developed a large following in the humanities—especially literature, less so in philosophy—and in the social sciences. They have developed virtually no following in science, math, computer science, and engineering for reasons that will become clear below.

The postmodern mindset views the whole Enlightenment project as a failure. The po-mo view is metaphysically anti-realist and anti-naturalist, holding that the physical universe is not ultimately describable in final terms. It is socially subjectivist in epistemology, holding that the "world" is what we socially construct, and each "group" (racial, gender, linguistic, ethnic, national or what have you) constructs the world according to its group identity. Postmodernists are egalitarian and collectivist in matters ethical and political. (If there are any postmodern libertarians or conservatives, I have yet to hear of them.)

Postmodernism has had a powerful impact on a number of areas of academic study. In literary theory, it has rejected the notion that literary texts have objective meanings open to better or worse interpretation, in favor of the notion that the text is simply a vehicle for the critic to exercise wordplay upon, or to deconstruct and thus expose the racial, class, or gender biases of the author. In law, postmodernists known as Critical Legal Theorists reject the notion of universally valid legal principles and objective legal reasoning, essentially viewing legal reasoning as subjective plumping for one's race, class, gender, or political preferences. In education theory, postmodernism junks the notion that education should develop a child's cognitive abilities and impart factual knowledge to enable her to function as a productive member of our free-market democracy. Instead, the postmodernist believes education should mold a student's racial, class, and gender identity. Postmodernists try to focus on the achievements of women, non-whites, and the poor, exposing the history of American democracy as a history of oppression, and denying the existence of any objective scientific method. For this reason, natural scientists and engineers find postmodernism silly—try convincing engineers who have successfully sent a robotic probe to the surface of Mars that objectively true scientific laws don't exist. Also, most modern philosophers, who since Descartes have concentrated on epistemology, have tended to view natural science as the most successful knowledge-generating human enterprise, and thus are not inclined to dismiss it lightly.

In short, postmodernism is relativism run riot, skepticism on stilts. In terms of the culture wars, it informs the arguments of those who think that American society is inferior to others and on the decline, that there are no "Great Books" of a higher order of merit than others, that science and technology are socially constructed and are not making genuine progress, and that modern free-market economics has lowered living standards. As Hicks notes, there is a contradictory tone to all this: all cultures are equal, but ours stinks; all truth is relative, except the unquestionable po-mo truth; no race, class or gender is superior, but middle class white males are clearly inferior; and no books are superior, except, of course, those by third-world authors.

Where does this farrago of resentment come from?

Hicks rightly views postmodernist philosophy as the most recent manifestation of the reaction against the Enlightenment, what we might call the Counter-Enlightenment. The Counter-Enlightenment in Hicks' view goes back at least to the work of Kant and Rousseau in the 18th century. The epistemological and metaphysical side of the Counter-Enlightenment Hicks traces back to Kant. Kant, Hicks claims, should not be considered an Enlightenment advocate of reason, for he held that we can know only the phenomenal realm, i.e., the realm of what we directly experience via the senses, while the noumenal realm—the "world-in-itself"—is beyond our knowledge. The mind has built-in organizing features (causality, temporality, and so on) which it imposes upon the raw input of the senses to construct the world of experience. Kant begot Hegel, who sought to fuse the phenomenal and the noumenal realms—viewing reality as being ultimately all mental or spiritual (metaphysical idealism). Hegel's ideas certainly informed Marx's philosophy, contributing to the rise of collectivism. But Kant also begot the strain of irrationalist philosophers, most importantly Schleiermacher, Schopenhauer, Nietzsche, and Kierkegaard. This strand of thought attempts to get around the Kantian problem of reason's inability to apprehend the noumenal world directly by thinking that intuition or other non-rational approaches (leaps of faith or super-human acts of will) will bridge the gap.

Hicks focuses upon two strands of 20th century metaphysics and epistemology as direct precursors of postmodernism. He discusses Heidegger in some detail, appropriately, given that Derrida and Foucault describe themselves as followers of Heidegger. Heidegger grounded his philosophy in phenomenology, the close examination of the given field of immediate experience. He came to the view that logic and reason are impotent in answering ultimate metaphysical questions, leaving dark emotions such as boredom, guilt, and dread as the only tools, and reaching a metaphysical nihilism in which pure Being and pure Nothing are one and the same. Heidegger thus provides the postmodernists with some of their core beliefs: that reason and logic are subjective and metaphysically sterile; that words and concepts are obstacles to be destroyed or unmasked; that feelings are a more reliable tool than logic and scientific method; and that the Western philosophic tradition (based upon the law of non-contradiction and the subject-object distinction) is something that needs to be overcome. As Hicks notes:

> The postmoderrnists will effect a compromise between Heidegger and Nietzsche. Common to Heidegger and Nietzsche epistemologically is a contemptuous rejection of reason. Metaphysically, though, the postmodernists will drop the remnants of Heidegger's metaphysical quest for Being, and put Nietzschean power struggles at the core of our being. And especially in the cases of Foucault and Derrida, most major postmodernists will abandon Nietzsche's sense of the exalted potential of man and embrace Heidegger's anti-humanism. (p. 67).

The question arises, then, how can a philosophic trend so rooted (or mired) in the Continental tradition of Kant, Hegel, Marx, Nietzsche, and Heidegger come to be so attractive to the American academy—indeed, apparently now more the stronghold of postmodernism than Europe, its birthplace—given the Anglo-American tradition of Enlightenment empiricism? Hicks rightly puts the focus on the collapse of the logical empiricist project. Hicks briefly surveys the rise of logical empiricism from its early sources in the advances in modern logic by Frege and Russell, and the work of the Vienna Circle, to its demise at the hands of Hanson, Feyerabend, Quine, and Kuhn. The logical positivists had attempted to rigorously analyze scientific method and the structure of knowledge using the tools provided by modern symbolic logic, but their program was demolished in the 1950s and 1960s. This left a vacuum which attracted skepticism. That vacuum, together with the work of Kuhn and Quine—which gave perspectivalism a rebirth in an analytic context—provided the soil for anti-Enlightenment epistemology to flourish.

Turning from metaphysics and epistemology to politics, Hicks notes that postmodernists aren't just skeptics who vary in their political beliefs. No, postmodernists are all committed leftists. The fact that postmodernists are uniformly drawn to collectivism is even more puzzling, given that socialists have traditionally, a la Marx, argued that socialism is scientific, while postmodernists view science with contempt, and worship subjectivity and irrationality. Hicks explains this in detail over several chapters by exploring an external factor, namely, the collapse of socialism in theory and practice. Postmodernism is a fusion between Leftist politics and skepticism. But the dream of socialism died in the latter half of the 20th century. Socialism was tried in a variety of forms, from Leninism to National Socialism to Maoism and so on, with the clear result that, far from being superior to capitalism, it is completely inferior. Socialism promised to free workers from capitalist bondage, but it chained them to the means of production they purportedly owned. It promised to out-produce capitalism, but the prosperity achieved by capitalist economies totally eclipsed the poverty wrought by socialism. Socialism promised to usher in an era of peace and humane values, but it delivered decades of police states and gulags. Free-market democracy, i. e., classical liberalism, won decisively in the developed world, and is rapidly transforming the rest of the planet as well.

The failure of socialism, both empirically and theoretically (once Mises demolished socialist theory with his publication of "Socialism" in 1920), brought about a crisis of faith among socialists, and postmodernism is their response. Hicks puts it well:

> Postmodernism is born of the marriage of Left politics and skeptical epistemology. As socialist political thought was reaching a crisis in the 1950s, academic epistemology had, in Europe, come to take seriously Nietzsche and Heidegger and, in the Anglo-American world, it had seen the decline of Logical Positivism into Quine and Kuhn. The dominance of subjectivist and relativist epistemologies in academic philosophy thus provided the academic Left with a new tactic. Confronted by harsh evidence and ruthless logic, the far Left had a reply: That is only logic and evidence; logic and evidence are subjective; you cannot really prove anything; feelings are deeper than logic; and our feelings say socialism… Postmodernism is a response to the crisis in faith of the academic far Left. Its

> epistemology justifies the leap of faith necessary to continue believing in socialism, and the same epistemology justifies using language not as a vehicle for seeking truth but as a rhetorical weapon in the continuing battle against capitalism. (p. 90).

I have a few slight quibbles with Hicks' book. First, he has a tendency to blur the distinction between a skeptic, accurately so called, and a failed anti-skeptic. The difference is important in historical exegesis. Descartes tried mightily to devise a theory of knowledge that would do justice to the rapidly rising scientific revolution of his time—a revolution to which he himself was a tremendous contributor. But his program—pure Rationalism, at least as it's coquettishly flaunted in the "Meditations"—clearly failed. Locke, following Bacon and Hobbes, tried to devise an Empiricist epistemology that would do justice to the scientific revolution—but it was an epistemology that ultimately failed to refute skepticism, as Hume so deftly demonstrated. Locke and Descartes failed to refute the skeptic—but not for lack of sincere effort. It is with this understanding that we need to look at Kant. Kant was no anti-objectivist crypto-skeptic. He truly was challenged by Hume's devastating skepticism (which roused him from his dogmatic slumbers, as he put it). His epistemology was a brilliant attempt to answer Humean skepticism. That later philosophers, most notoriously Nietzsche, used it to devise a perspectivalist skepticism shouldn't lead one to think that Kant would have been at all sympathetic to that skepticism.

Second, Hicks might have looked a bit more at the pragmatic tradition. This epistemology reached its apogee in the work of C. S. Peirce, who called himself a pragmaticist to distinguish his thought from people such as James and Dewey.

Pragmaticism is a very novel and reasonable stab at combating skepticism, with a more realistic approach to scientific enterprise. Unlike Rationalism, Empiricism, and even Kantian Perspectivalism, Peirce (a prolific polymath who actually did significant scientific research) gave up the idea of founding knowledge on certainty. Instead, he noted that knowledge, while real, is inherently fallible. Pragmatism of Peirce's sort is absolutely unsympathetic to the po-mo pragmatism of Rorty.

Third, Hicks leaves things hanging, epistemologically speaking. Yeah, okay, the cheap, trendy collectivist skepticism of postmodernism is silly, in the face of the continuing global advance of scientific knowledge, new technology, free-market economics, and political democracy. But does anyone yet have an adequate account of the nature of knowledge and scientific method that Hicks can recommend?

But I ought not be hyper-critical. Hicks has written a lucid and readable book explaining an influential, albeit puzzling, intellectual phenomenon. He has a balanced internalist and externalist approach, discussing the narrow evolution of ideas within philosophy and the wider influence of political and economic trends on the evolution of those ideas. His book deserves a wide audience.

Reprinted by permission of Liberty Magazine.

Index

A

AAALAC, 368
abduction, 208, 245
abductive inference, x
Abstract Data Type, x, 93
ad baculum, 47, 51, 54, 55, 58
Ad Hominem Argument, ix, 129
Ad Hominem Arguments, ix, 151
ad ignorantiam, 47
ad populum, 42, 45, 116, 122, 346
Adam Smith, 346, 349
Adolf Grunbaum, 220, 249, 252
agency shops, 331, 336, 337, 338
AI, 61, 65, 68, 71, 72, 89, 93, 94, 99, 101, 102, 126, 127, 223, 224, 226, 227, 228, 229, 233, 241, 242
ALF, 368
Anderson, Alan Ross, 92
Aquist, Lennart, 92
argument, 3, 4, 5, 6, 10, 20, 23, 24, 25, 26, 39, 44, 47, 48, 51, 52, 53, 54, 55, 104, 107, 113, 116, 122, 123, 133, 134, 138, 139, 140, 142, 143, 144, 145, 146, 147, 148, 149, 150, 177, 181, 184, 186, 187, 188, 189, 190, 191, 192, 193, 205, 206, 207, 215, 216, 217, 275, 285, 300, 307, 313, 328, 332, 333, 334, 335, 346, 348, 349, 355, 359, 360, 387, 391, 393, 401
argumentum ad baculum, 51
Argumentum ad Baculum, ix
Artificial Intelligence, x, 92, 101, 232, 241, 244, 295
assertoric logic, 180, 184

B

Bartley, W. W., 92
BD, 374, 375

begging the question, 43, 47, 49, 112, 246, 250
benign deception, 374
Betsey Stevenson and Justin Wolfers, 365
British rule, xi
Bromberger, Sylvain, 92

C

Charles Baird, 334, 338
Christopher Johnson, 129
Chrysler and GM, 339, 341
closed shops, 331, 332, 335, 336, 337, 338
Closed Shops, xi, 331, 338
Cognitive Psychology, 224
coherentist, 218
completeness-claim specification, 77
Compound questions, 71
Computer Ethics, xi, 289, 294
conversation games, 8
conversation theory, 3, 20
Conversation Theory, x, 3, 4
corrective answer, 79, 131
Craig Duncan, 297
Creationism, xii, 393

D

Daniel Griswold, 343, 349
Daniel Kahneman, 309, 357, 364
Database Queries, x, 65
David Ricardo, 350
Deborah Johnson, 294
deductive logic, 3, 4, 9, 10, 16, 18, 20, 188, 192, 196, 206, 207
deductively valid, 3, 4, 52, 145, 191, 192, 202, 204
default specification, 78
deontologism, xi, 266, 270, 308
Deontologism, xi, 265, 288
detensifiers, 104, 110, 111, 112
dialog, x, xi, 68, 93, 94, 95, 96, 98, 99, 100
dialog logic, x, xi, 94, 95, 98, 99, 100
direct answer, 69, 78, 79, 131
distinctness-claim specification, 78
divine command theory, 266, 268, 269, 271, 272
domain closure axiom, 88
Douglas Walton, 47

E

Edward Erwin, 249
egoism, 265, 308
ELF, 368
Elizabeth Loftus, 259, 260
entrenchment, 246, 357, 358
epistemic community, 11, 27
epistemology, x, 129, 130, 151, 209, 217, 225, 226, 295, 404, 406, 407, 408
Ernest Gellner, 249, 253
erotetic logic, x, 15, 20, 65, 69, 88, 89, 91, 193, 236
EU, 346, 359
evolutionary psychology, xi

F

fallacy, 30, 36, 39, 41, 45, 48, 49, 51, 52, 53, 54, 55, 103, 104, 105, 107, 111, 112, 113, 116, 117, 122, 123, 134, 139, 140, 148, 149, 246, 276, 346
fallibilism, 202, 204, 209, 213, 215, 216, 218
fee-shifting, 326

formal dialectic, x, 30, 47, 48, 49, 191, 192, 274, 275
Foundationalism, 217
fourth generation logic, 65
Frank Cioffi, 249, 251, 252
Frédéric Bastiat, 346
Frederick C. Crews, 249
Frederick Schauer, 397
Free Trade, xi, 343, 346, 358, 361
free trade agreements, 349, 355
Freudian psychoanalytic theory, x
FTA, 358, 359

G

Garth Wood, 219
GATT, 346
GDP, 320, 349, 354, 364
globalization, 343, 344, 345, 346, 348, 354

H

H.P. Grice, 7
Haack, Susan, 92, 217
Hamblin, C. L., 100
Hans Eysenck, 220, 249
happiness, xi, 147, 282, 283, 284, 286, 287, 288, 298, 363, 364, 365
hedging, 43, 103, 104, 105, 106, 111, 112
Hedging, x, 103, 111
Helen Johns and Paul Ormerod, 363
Hinman, 23, 24, 25, 26, 130, 145, 151
Hintikka, Jaakko, 100
Howard Gardner, 223
How-questions, 71
HSUS, 368
Hughes, G. E., 92
hypethetico-deductivist, 13, 15

I

ignoratio elenchi, 334
IMF, 348
inductive logic, x, 3, 4, 16, 20, 24, 180, 188, 191, 192, 204, 205, 207
inductively strong, 3, 4, 52, 145, 182, 184, 205, 207
informal fallacies, ix, x, 47, 48, 49, 94, 99
informal logic, x, 3, 112
integrity constraint, 74

J

James Turner Johnson, 381
Jessica Gavora, 401
job churn, 350
John Hick, 373, 376
John Stuart Mill, 312, 335, 369
Jorgenson, Jorgen, 92
Joseph DesJardins, 332, 338
Joseph Schumpeter, 351
jus ad bellum, 381
jus in bello, 381
just war theory, 381, 382
just-war doctrine, xii

K

Kambartel, Friedrick, 100
Kant, 141, 225, 266, 270, 271, 273, 274, 280, 302, 327, 405, 406, 408
Kantianism, 273, 294, 308
Kerry Howley, 313, 318
Kubinski, Tadeus, 92

L

ladenness, 111
Laura Meckler, 311, 318
Lawrence McQuillan, 319
Lewis Carroll, 52, 66, 92
libertarianism, 286, 297, 298, 299, 305, 306, 308, 309, 312
Libertarianism, xi
logic, ix, x, xii, 3, 4, 9, 10, 13, 15, 20, 21, 23, 29, 30, 45, 47, 51, 52, 53, 55, 61, 62, 65, 66, 67, 68, 69, 70, 72, 74, 88, 89, 90, 91, 93, 94, 95, 99, 100, 102, 107, 115, 116, 123, 126, 127, 131, 132, 155, 163, 180, 188, 189, 190, 192, 196, 203, 204, 205, 206, 207, 209, 212, 213, 216, 217, 224, 236, 242, 245, 246, 274, 281, 334, 391, 406, 407
loser pay, xi
loser-pays, 326, 327, 328, 329

M

M. J. Cresseell, 92
Mackenzie, Jim, 100
Many-valued logic, 65
Maurice Finocchiaro, 45
Mendelson, Elliot, 92
moral evil, 373, 374
Morton Schagrin, 61

N

N.R. Hanson, 166, 178
NAFTA, 346, 354, 355
National Organ Transplant Act, 311
Natural evil, 373, 375
neo-mercantilist populists, 353
Neurosis, x, 219
non-moral worth, 282, 286, 287
non-standard logics, x
NOTA, 311, 318
Nuel Belnap, 20, 92, 199

O

On Liberty, 308, 335
organ sales, 311, 312, 313, 315, 316, 317
OSHA, 348

P

Paul Feyerabend, 166
Paul Harmon and David King, 101
Peirce, x, 11, 66, 67, 122, 179, 198, 199, 203, 207, 208, 214, 216, 218, 281, 408
People for the Ethical Treatment of Animals, 368
PETA, 368
Peter Huber, 325, 329
Philip Kitcher, 393
philosophy of science, x, 72, 271
phlogiston theory, 159, 160, 214
po-mo, 403, 404, 408
pooh-poohing, 117
post hoc ergo propter hoc, 37, 121
Postmodernism, xii, 403, 404, 407
pragmaticism, xi
presupposition, 10, 72, 78, 79, 92, 117, 121
pseudoscience, x, 135, 246, 249, 252, 325, 393
pseudosciences, 245
psychoanalytic theory, 167, 169, 220, 250, 251, 254

Q

Quine, W. V, 92

R

race to the bottom, 300, 346, 348, 349, 353
Randall Dipert, 61
Raymond Turner, 125
relational language, 73, 74, 85, 87
request, 70, 74, 77, 78, 79, 80, 122, 333
Rescher, Nicholas, 92
retroduction, 180, 181, 182, 208
Richard DeGeorge, 345
Richard J. McNally, 255
Richard O. Easterlin, 363
Robert Cialdini, 149, 356, 361
Robert Todd Carroll, 245
rules of response, 9, 10, 11, 12, 13, 15, 16, 17, 18, 84

S

Scare tactics, ix, 52, 55, 56, 57, 58
Schneider, Hans Julius, 100
selection-size specification, 77
SHAC, 368
Shoenfield, Joseph, 92
Skyrms, Brian, 217
Smoot-Hawley tariffs, 355
social proof, 357, 360
soul-making, xi, 373, 374, 375
Soul-Making, xi, 373
Stephen Hicks, 403
Stop Huntingdon Animal Cruelty, 368
sweatshop, 344
Sympathy, 357

T

Taft-Hartley Act, 331, 338
the Animal Liberation Front, 368
the animal rights movement, xi, 367
the Association for Assessment and Accreditation of Laboratory Animal Care International, 368
the Center for Expansion of Fundamental Rights, 368
the Charlie W. Norwood Living Organ Donation Act, 317
the Earth Liberation Front, 368
the Easterlin paradox, 363
the English Rule, 326
the European Union, 346
the General Agreement on Tariffs and Trade, 346
the harm principle, 312
the Humane Society of the United States, 368
the interpretive principal of charity, 116
the logic of questions, x, 10, 131
the logic of scientific discovery, x
The McQuillan group, 319, 320, 321
the motivational principle of charity, 116
the problem of convergence, x, 209, 215, 216, 217
the problem of evil, xi, 290, 373, 374, 376
The Role of Error, x
the UAW, 340, 341
the United Auto Workers, 340
the video-recorder theory of memory, 260
the World Bank, 348
theodicy, xi
Thomas Kuhn, 135
Thomas Papadimos and Alexa Papadimos, 318

Thomas, Stephen, 92, 112
Tibor Machan, 297
tort reform, 323, 329
Tort Reform, xi, 319, 322
tort system, 307, 319, 320, 322, 323, 324, 327
Toulmin, 112, 173, 174, 175
trade war, 355
Turner, Raymond, 92

U

union shops, 331, 333
unique name axioms, 87, 88
utilitarianism, 265, 294, 308

V

vagueness, 111, 112, 129, 142, 144, 156
Virtue Epistemology, ix, 129

W

W.D. Ross, xi, 270, 308
Wal-Mart, 344, 350
Wesley Smith, 367
Whether-questions, 70
Which-questions, 70, 76, 77, 90
Why-questions, 92
William Rapaport, 61
WTO, 348, 359